mmm...

## General Information 1

## Entertainment & Leisure 20

## Sporting Activities 94



## Food & Drink 132



## Shopping



## Maps & Indexes 283

**Explorer Publishing**
**P.O.Box 53041, Dubai**
**United Arab Emirates**

**Tel:** (+971-4) 822 661
**Fax:** (+971-4) 822 710

**Email:** Info@The-Explorer.com
**Home:** www.The-Explorer.com

**2nd Edition - 1997/8**

Publishers: **Alistair MacKenzie**, **Laetitia Susini**, **Harald Karlos**

Group Publisher: **Ocean Wave Ltd**
Bel Royal House
Hilgrove St, St Helier
Jersey UK-JE2 4WG

Editor-in-Chief / Chief Explorer: **Alistair MacKenzie**

Editors: **Linda Benbow**, **Melanie Gill**

Chief Checker: **Helga Becker**

Graphics/Icons: **Fiona MacKenzie**
***MacKenzie Cox Assoc. (MCA)* - London**

Front Cover:
- Map Painting **MCA**
- Photograph **Paul Thuysbaert**
- Overall Design **Turning Heads**

*First Published 1996*
Printed by *Technical Printing Press*
Colour Separations by *Rainbow*

**ISBN 0 9531647 0 5**

Once again, we are indebted to the many people who offered their advice. Enormous thanks are owed to our wonderful reporters and special friends:

**Alison, Anna, Celine, David, Dianne, Doug, Elaine, Ellie, Fiona, Francis, Helga, Jackie, Janette, Linda, Louise.D, Louise, Lydia, Maha, Mark, Matt, Melanie, Micky, Mohan, Neil, Paul, Peter, Reinhard, Rene, Sandra, Simon, Steve, Stewart, Sarosh and Zaki.**

# Introduction

Welcome to the second edition of ***The Dubai Explorer***! This is Dubai's most comprehensive, authoritative and fastest selling entertainment guidebook. An awesome concoction of leisure & sporting activities, dining and shopping opportunities, together with general information on Dubai, and the essential maps!

We have written with you in mind, hoping to pre-empt any questions you may have regarding how to spend your time in Dubai. The second edition sees a complete overhaul of the guide's structure, as well as updating and incorporating new venues in town. New larger scale maps, based on the most recent photography, reflects the rapid change of growth in Dubai.

Our team of reporters have independently reviewed every food and entertainment venue, and we hope in doing so, we can give a realistic and useful view of each. No payment of any kind has secured or influenced these reviews.

Whether a tourist, a long-term resident or short-term visitor, we have produced this book for you and we welcome your comments - whether they be suggestions, criticisms or praise! At the back of the guide, you will find a *Response Form,* we want to hear from you!

Our warm thanks must go to all who helped make this new edition of ***The Dubai Explorer*** possible, from the companies who have supported us through advertising, all our reporters and to the outlets themselves. Many thanks.

***The Dubai Explorer*** unlocks the door to the wealth of secrets hidden in and around Dubai, which were only previously heard about through word of mouth, or by luck! Once again, we hope you enjoy using this guide in the spirit in which it was created. Dubai has so much more to offer when you are willing to explore...

**The Only Complete & Authoritative Entertainment & Leisure Guide to Dubai**

# Quick Reference Symbols

## General

**Opening Details.** We've given closing times, as opposed to last orders which are typically at least half an hours earlier. Timings are as at date of review, but hours and days of opening change frequently here, so it's best to check.

**Map Location.** On the left of the icon, we've indicated address and area name, and on the right, map reference details. Map page number (Maps start on page **283** ), followed by Grid reference, followed by point number if relevant.

**Recommended by *The Dubai Explorer* -** If on a short visit, or unable to decide, make sure you try at least one of these recommended outlets. The price range will give you a realistic idea of what you'll expect. More is not necessarily better! Be warned, they have been chosen for a number of different reasons - find out why!

## Food & Drink

**Outside Terrace**

**Reservations Recommended**. Normally applies for Thursday and Public Holidays.

**Live Band.** Check for their night off!

**Alcohol.** Outlet is licensed to serve alcoholic beverages.

**Happy Hour.** They operate a Happy Hour at this outlet.

**Credit Cards.** The symbol indicates whether credit cards are accepted. Typically this will always include at least one of the major cards: American Express, Mastercard or Visa.

**Offers Children's Menus/Discounts.** We've tried to reflect the degree of welcome extended to babies and children in restaurants. Many of the restaurants listed will provide smaller portions, or reduced price children's portions, provide high chairs or have a kids play area nearby. If there is no icon, this is probably a good indication that the restaurant is unsuitable.

**Serves Vegetarian Dishes.** We have highlighted only the restaurants that have one or more vegetarian main course on their menus, or where the chef is prepared to make something special.

**Dress Smartly.** As expected, most restaurateurs dislike inappropriately dressed customers. As a quick guide, most hotels prefer customers who wear "smart casuals", with some stuffier establishments requiring jacket and tie. Indicated are the outlets we feel are worth the effort to dress up and conform, but not necessarily with black tie!

**Average Price Range.** This is intended to provide an indication of what you can expect to pay in Dirhams (Dhs.3.65 ~ US$1) for a typical three-course meal, for one, with no beverages. This covers, a starter, main course, dessert and tax, unless otherwise specified. Prices given are purely for guidance purposes.

**Tipping -** You will normally be charged 15% service charge and 5% Municipality tax (Often referenced as ++). In addition if satisfied, it is customary to leave a 10% tip.

# General Information

Tropicus Cancri

# Overview

## History

Dubai, originally a small fishing settlement, was taken over in about 1830 by a branch of the Bani Yas tribe from the Liwa oasis, led by the Maktoum family who still rule the emirate today. Traditional activities included sheep and goat herding, cultivating dates, fishing and pearl diving.

The liberal attitudes of the rulers made Dubai attractive to traders from India and Persia who began to settle in the growing town, which soon developed a reputation as the leading commercial mart for the region.

An independent emirate for most of its history, on the British withdrawl in 1971 Dubai came together with Abu Dhabi, Sharjah, Ajman, Umm Al Quwain, Fujairah and (in 1972) Ras Al Khaimah to create the federation of the United Arab Emirates.

This was shortly after the discovery of oil in 1966 which was soon to dramatically transform the emirate by allowing the development of an economic and social infrastructure which is the template of today's modern society. Much of the credit for this development can be traced to the vision of the late Ruler, HH Sheikh Rashid bin Saeed Al Maktoum, who ensured that Dubai's oil revenues were deployed to maximum effect. His work has been continued by the present Ruler, HH Sheikh Maktoum bin Rashid Al Maktoum.

## Geography

The United Arab Emirates (UAE) comprises seven members: Abu Dhabi (the capital city), Dubai, Sharjah, Ajman, Umm Al Qwain, Ras Al Khaimah and Fujairah.

The total area of the country is about 83,600 square kilometres, much of it in Abu Dhabi, and with an area of 3,885 square kilometres, Dubai is the second largest emirate. Situated on the banks of the Dubai Creek, a natural inlet from the Gulf which divides the city into the Deira district to its north and Bur Dubai on its south, the city ranks as the UAE's most important port and commercial centre.

The UAE has 700 kilometres of coastline, of which 100 kilometres are on the Gulf of Oman. Along the Arabian Gulf coast there are offshore islands, coral reefs and sabkha, or salt-marshes. Stretches of gravel plain and sandy desert characterise the island region.

To the east, a range of mountains lies close to the Gulf of Oman and forms a backbone through the Mussandam Peninsula. The western interior of the country, most of it in Abu Dhabi, consists mainly of desert interspersed with oases.

---

- The map shown on page 2 was reproduced with kind permission of ***Dubai Municipality.***

- Within this section, selected information and photography assistance is provided courtesy of the ***Government of Dubai,* Department of Tourism and Commerce Marketing.**

# Dubai and Surrounding Emirates

## Government & Ruling Family

The Supreme Council of the UAE, comprising the hereditary rulers of the seven emirates, is the highest federal authority. It is responsible for general policy matters involving communications, education, defence, foreign affairs and development, and for ratifying federal laws. The President, HH Sheikh Zayed bin Sultan Al Nahyan, who is also Ruler of Abu Dhabi, and the Vice-President, HH Sheikh Maktoum bin Rashid Al Maktoum, who is also Ruler of Dubai, are elected by the Supreme Council from among its members.

The Federal Council of Ministers, responsible to the Supreme Council, has executive authority to initiate and implement laws. The Federal National Council is a consultative assembly of 40 representatives who are appointed for two years by the individual emirates. The council monitors and debates government policy but has no power of veto.

## The Dubai Ruling Family (Al Maktoum)

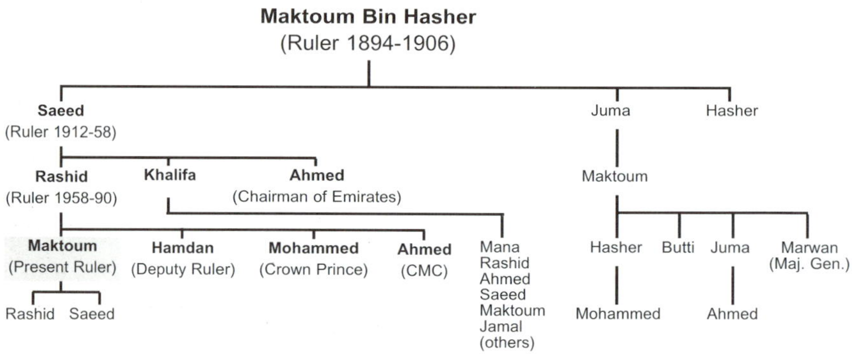


## International Relations

The UAE became a member of the Untied Nations and the Arab League in 1971. It is a member of the International Monetary Fund, the Organisation of Petroleum Exporting Countries (OPEC), World Trade Organisation and other international and Arab organisations, including the Arab Gulf Co-operation Council (AGCC), whose other members are Saudi Arabia, Oman, Qatar, Bahrain and Kuwait. In its foreign relations, the UAE's stance is one of non-alignment but it is committed to the support of Arab unity.

## Economy

While oil has been crucial to Dubai's development since the late 1960's, the non-oil sector currently contributes some 80% of total gross domestic product and is continuing to expand in importance. Manufacturing, tourism and services are all growing strongly, helping to create a well balanced and diversified economy. However, trade remains the lifeblood of Dubai's business life, as it has for generations.

This long trading tradition, which earned Dubai the reputation within the Middle East as "the city of merchants", remains an important consideration for foreign companies looking at opportunities in the region today. It is reflected not just in a regulatory environment which is open and liberal, but also in the local business community's thorough familiarity with international commercial practices and in the city's cosmopolitan lifestyle.

## Local Time

The UAE is four hours ahead of UCT (Universal Coordinated Time).

## Population

According to the *Ministry of Planning*, the population of the UAE expanded from 2,230,000 in 1994, to 2,377,453 in 1995. Dubai's population stood at 674,101 in 1995. Growth rate is estimated at 3.5% a year.

**Population By Expatriates - 1995**

| UAE | Population | % |
|---|---|---|
| Nationals | 646,000 | 27.0% |
| Arabs | 283,000 | 12.0% |
| Asians | 1,399,000 | 59.0% |
| Europeans | 32,000 | 1.3% |
| Others | 17,000 | 0.7% |
| **Total:** | **2,377,000** | |

Source: *Ministry of Planning & UAE Ministry of Interior*

**Population by Emirate ('000s) - 1997**

| Emirates | Male | Female | Total |
|---|---|---|---|
| Abu Dhabi | 690 | 310 | 1,000 |
| Dubai | 514 | 223 | 737 |
| Fujairah | 50 | 33 | 83 |
| Sharjah | 274 | 148 | 435 |
| Ras Al Khaimah | 90 | 63 | 153 |
| Umm Al Quwain | 23 | 16 | 39 |
| **Total:** | **1,720** | **860** | **2,580** |

# Entering Dubai

## Visas

All visitors except AGCC nationals (Bahrain, Kuwait, Qatar, Oman and Saudi Arabia) require a visa sponsored by a local entity such as a hotel or tour company. British citizens with the right of abode in the UK and expatriate residents of the AGCC of certain nationalities and professions, may qualify for automatic 30 day visit visas on arrival, but current regulations should be checked before travelling.

There are two types: transit visas for 14 days and visit visas for 30 days (renewable). Airlines may require confirmation that the sponsor is holding a valid visa for incoming visitors.

German and US citizens may obtain visas from the UAE Embassies in their respective countries. Visas are easily obtainable for other visitors except Israelis and travellers whose passports bear Israeli stamps.

## Health Requirements

No health certificates are required for entry to Dubai, but it is always wise to check before departure as health restrictions may vary depending upon the situation at the time.

## Customs

Duty Free allowances: Cigarettes - 2,000; cigars - 400; tobacco - 2 kg; alcohol (non-Muslim adults only) - 2 litres of spirits and 2 litres of wine; perfume - a reasonable amount.

Dubai Duty Free has a sales outlet in the Arrivals Hall (but alcohol may only be purchased on departure). It is forbidden to import drugs and pornographic items such as videos, books and magazines.

No customs duty is levied on personal effects entering Dubai.

# Climate and Clothing

## Climate

Dubai has a sub-tropical, arid climate and sunny blue skies can be expected most of the year. Rainfall is infrequent and irregular, falling mainly in winter - November to March (13 cm/yr). Temperatures range from a low of around 10 C/50 F, to a high of 48 C/118 F. The mean daily maximum is 24 C/75 F in January, rising to 41 C/106 F in July. Humidity can be a killer in summer - prepare to sweat!

## Clothing

Lightweight summer clothing is suitable for most of the year, but something slightly warmer may be needed for the winter months.

With its liberal attitude, there isn't much you can't wear. As in all countries, a healthy amount of respect for the local customs won't go a miss. Short or tight clothing may be worn, but it will attract attention...most of it unwelcome!

When it comes to evenings, pretty much anything goes, with all blends of western, Arabic and Asian styles in the restaurants and clubs. Be sure to take some sort of jacket or sweater as the air conditioning, especially in summer, can be pretty fierce! As in any place with loads of sun, good quality sunglasses, hats, and buckets of suncream are needed to avoid the lobster look.

# Culture and Lifestyle

## Culture

Dubai is tolerant, welcoming and virtually crimefree. Dubai's culture is firmly rooted in the Islamic traditions of Arabia, where courtesy and hospitality are among the most highly prized virtues, and visitors are sure to be charmed by the genuine warmth and friendliness of the people.

Foreigners are free to practice their own religion, alcohol is served in hotels and the dress code is liberal. Women face no discrimination and may drive and walk around un-escorted.

Despite rapid economic development in recent years Dubai remains close to its heritage. Local citizens dress in traditional robes (Dishdash for men/Abaya for women) and headdress.

Arab culture and folklore find expression in poetry, dancing, songs and traditional art. Weddings and other celebrations are colourful occasions of feasting and music. Traditional sports such as falconry, camel racing and dhow racing at sea continue to thrive.

# Language

The official language is Arabic, although English, Urdu and Hindi are widely spoken and, with some perseverence, understood. Arabic and English are the official business launguages.

# Religion

Islam is the official religion of the UAE, and the large number of mosques certainly make their presence felt through the regular call to prayer! Other religions are respected and Dubai has two Christian churches, St Mary's (RC) and Holy Trinity (inter-denominational).

# Holidays

The Islamic calendar starts from the year 622 AD, the year of the Prophet Mohammad's migration (Hijra) from Makkah to Al-Madinah, hence the Islamic year is called the Hijri year and dates are followed by AH - After Hijra.

The Hijri calendar is based on lunar months, there are 354 or 355 days in the Hijri year, which is divided into 12 months, and is thus 11 days shorter than the Gregorian year.

As they are based on the sighting of the moon and not fixed dates on the Hijri calendar, the dates of Islamic holidays are notoriously unprecise, with holidays frequently being announced less than 24 hours in advance. Some non-Muslim holidays are fixed according to the Gregorian calendar:

| **Fixed** | |
|---|---|
| National Day | Dec 2 |
| New Years Day | Jan 1 |
| Fridays *(Saturdays for some)* | |

| **Movable** | |
|---|---|
| Lailat Al Mi'Raj | ~ Nov 28, 1997 |
| Lailat Al Bar'a | ~ Dec 14, 1997 |

| **Movable** (cont) | |
|---|---|
| Ramadam Begins | ~ Dec 30, 1997 |
| Lailat Al Qadar | ~ Jan 25, 1998 |
| Eid Al Fitr - 3 days | ~ Jan 29, 1998 |
| Eid Al Adha - 3 days | ~ Apr 6, 1998 |
| Islamic New Year's Day | ~ Apr 28, 1998 |
| Ashoora | ~ May 7, 1998 |
| Prophet's Birthday | ~ Jul 7, 1998 |

# Ramadan

Ramadan is the holy month in which Muslims commemorate the revelation of the Holy Koran. As mentioned above, the timing of Ramadan is not fixed in terms of the western calendar, but each year it occurs 10 days earlier than the previous year. In 1998 in Ramadan will commence around December 31. It is a time of fasting, when Muslims abstain from all food, drinks and cigarettes during daylight hours from dawn to dusk.

Visitors are also required to refrain from eating or smoking in public places during this time as a sign of respect.

# Alcohol

Alcohol is served in most outlets associated with hotels - ie. clubs, hotel restaurants and bars. Restaurants outside the hotels are not permitted to serve alcohol. Permanent residents who are non-Muslims can obtain liquor supplies without difficulty under a permit system (see page 266).

## Pharmacies

Each emirate offers at least one 24 hour pharmacy. Address and telephone numbers can be found in the daily newspapers.

## Photography

Normal tourist photography is acceptable, but it is considered offensive to photograph Muslim women and it is also courteous to ask permission before photographing men. In general, photographs of government buildings, military installations, ports and airports should not be taken.

# Getting There

Dubai's location at the cross-roads of Europe, Asia and Africa makes for easy accessibility. London is seven hours away; Frankfurt six; Hong Kong eight; and Nairobi four.

Most European capitals and other major cities have direct flights to Dubai, many with a choice of operator. Over 80 airlines take advantage of Dubai's open skies policy and operate to and from Dubai International Airport to over 120 destinations. Dubai, one of the world's busiest airports is the home base of Emirates, the award-winning international airline of the UAE, which operates scheduled services to more than 38 destinations.

# Getting Around

## Taxis

Taxis are the most common way of getting around. Metered taxis from Dubai Transport Corporation, recognised by their cream colour, are efficient, with relatively well trained and courteous drivers. The fare is Dhs.2 for pickup, followed by Dhs.1 per kilometre. A fixed scale of charges is applied to trips outside the city boundaries.

The fares of non-metered taxis are negotiated between driver and passenger, starting at a minimum of around Dhs.5 for short local journeys. However, Dhs.10 - Dhs.15 is the rule of thumb if you cross the Creek. The journey to the town centre from the airport costs around Dhs.30 - 35 in specially registered airport taxis.

Most hotels operate a pick-up / drop-off service for their guests.

## Car Hire

Self-drive cars are available and the rental company will arrange temporary local driving licences for visitors. Renters must produce their passport, two photographs and either a valid international, or national licence from one of the following countries: Austria, Belgium, Canada, Denmark, Finland, France, Germany, Greece, Holland, Ireland, Italy, Japan, Norway, Spain, Sweden, Switzerland, Turkey, UK and USA.

## Roads & Highways

Over the past two decades, Dubai has built an impressive first-class network of roads. There are two bridges and a tunnel linking the two main districts of Dubai and Deira on either side of the Creek. Roads to all major towns and villages are excellent and an eight lane highway heads southwards from the city to Abu Dhabi.

Whilst the infrastructure is superb, the general standard of driving is not and it helps to have eyes in the back of your head at all times!

## Trains / Bus / Walking

There are no trains in the UAE, but a recently introduced bus service in Dubai covers most areas of interest, although be prepared to be be packed in tightly - not necessarily a pleasant experience in the heat of summer!.

Walking during the day is not a common occurance, and physically impossible during certain months! However, promenading in the evening is a popular pastime.

# Money & Shopping

## Currency

The monetary unit is the Dirham (Dhs.) which is divided into 100 fils. Notes are available in denominations of Dhs.5/-, Dhs.10/-, Dhs.50/-, Dhs.100/-, Dhs.200/- and Dhs.500/-. Coin denominations are Dhs.1/-, 50 fils and 25 fils, but be warned, there are two versions of each coin and they can look very similar. The Dirham has been fixed against the US Dollar since the end of 1980, at a mid-rate of approximately US$ 1= Dhs.3.68.

The exchange rates of all major currencies are published daily in the newspapers. Cash notes and travellers cheques can be exchanged in licensed exchange offices, banks and international hotels - as usual a passport is required for exchanging travellers cheques. There are no restictions on the import or export of any currency.

## Banks

Both local and international banks provide the usual commercial banking services. Transfers can be made without difficulty as there is no exchange control and the Dirham is freely convertible.

Banking hours are 08:00 - 13:00, Saturday - Wednesday, although some also open from 16:30 - 18:30. On Thursdays banks, like all government and official offices, only operate from 08:00 - 12:00. Exchange houses are open from 08:30 - 13:00 and 16:30 - 20:30.

Global network
Key to great service
Reliable & safe hands
THE LARGEST GLOBAL CORRESPONDENT NETWORK OF BANKS COVERING THE 5 CONTINENTS.
STATE-OF-THE-ART TECHNOLOGY IN TRANSFERS TO PROVIDE A HIGH LEVEL OF CUSTOMER SATISFACTION.
THE MOST COMPETITIVE EXCHANGE RATES, FOR BOTH RETAIL & WHOLESALE.
DEMAND DRAFTS, TELEX TRANSFERS AND THE FASTEST ELECTRONIC TRANSFERS.
FOR EXPATRIATES SENDING HARD-EARNED MONEY BACK HOME, ALFARDAN EXCHANGE OFFERS THE MOST RELIABLE & TRUSTED SERVICE.
AL FARDAN EXCHANGE
We are determined to be your First Choice Exchange House in the UAE
• DEIRA: AL MAKTOUM STREET, TEL: 280004 •
• BUR DUBAI: IMAM ALI ROAD, TEL: 531121 •
• SHARJAH: CLOCK TOWER, TEL: 373581 •
• ABU DHABI : LIWA ST, AMIN TOWER, TEL: 223222 •
• AL AIN: AL TAKHIT STREET, TEL: 656325 •

## Money Exchanges

| | | | |
|---|---|---|---|
| Al Anasari Exchange | Tel: 256 263 | Lari Money Exchange | Tel: 267 249 |
| Al Fardan Exchange | Tel: 280 004 | Orient Exchange Company | Tel: 267 154 |
| Al Ghurair Exchange | Tel: 518 895 | Thomas Cook Al Rostamani Exchange | Tel: 223 564 |
| First Gulf Exchange | Tel: 253 535 | Wall Street Exchange Centre | Tel: 800 4871 |

## Credit Cards

Most shops, hotels and restaurants accept the major credit cards (Visa, Mastercard, American Express, Diners Club). Smaller retailers may not be so keen, but wherever you are, expect an extra five percent to be added for processing (and it is no use telling them that it's a contravention of the card company rules - you have to take it or leave it!)

When negotiating your 'best price', tell the shopkeeper if you intend to pay by credit card, otherwise the bargaining will start all over again.

## Tipping

Tipping practices are similar to most parts of the world. Some restaurants include service, although it is unlikely to end up with your waiter, otherwise 10 per cent is usual.

## Business Hours

The weekend has traditionally been Thursday afternoon and Friday, but some more westernized organisations now close on Friday and Saturday. Government offices are open from 07:30 - 13:30 (07:30 - 12:00 on Thursday).

Private sector office hours vary, but are generally from 08:00 to 13:00, re-opening at either 15:00 or 16:00, and closing at 18:00 or 19:00.

Shop hours are similar in their opening times, but remain open on a Friday, apart from Prayer Times (11:30 - 13:30). Many of the larger shops only open Friday afternoons at 16:00 or 17:00.

Embassies and Consulates are generally open from 08:45 to 13:30 and are closed on Fridays, and in most cases on Saturdays, but will leave an emergency number on their answering machines.

## Bargaining

Bargaining is expected in the souks and common elsewhere, and vendors will usually drop the price - often quite substantially - particularly for a cash sale. In the case of certain electronics products, the margins are very low and therefore bartering is minimal.

There is not usually any bartering in departmental stores, although you will quite often be told that the price shown is 'before discount', and they will reduce it by a set amount. Even pharmicies have a "last price" system whereby they will come down from the price shown on the price tag.

# What to Buy?

Dubai offers some of the best shopping in the world with competitive prices in almost every aspect of shopping from inexpensive goods, to designer labels and international brands.

### Gold / Jewellery

Dubai's gold souk is famed the world over for its low prices and sheer variety on offer. The general rule of thumb is that he who bargains hardest gets "best price". Gold is priced according to the international daily gold rate, and is available in every form imaginable, from bracelets and necklaces, to ingots and gold bars. 18, 21, 22 and 24 carats are available, and in addition to the weight prices, a small charge will be added for craftmanship which varies depending on the intricacy of the design.

### Clothes

There are boutiques and designer label shops for men, women and children aplenty in Dubai. Inexpensive items can be found in Karama, Bur Dubai, Deira and in the major shopping centres. Satwa has trendy boutiques and Karama an amazing range of fashionable, almost-designer clothes from the Far East. For smart, elegant men's suits, jackets and casuals, there are a number of shops along the Creek in Deira, and each shopping mall has a mixture of expensive and cheaper clothes.

Tailors will make up an outfit direct from a drawing or photograph. Many will copy outfits purchased elsewhere if you can leave the original for a few days. The results are usually excellent and prices very reasonable.

### Fabrics

The shops in Bur Dubai's textile market are a treasure trove of textiles, colours, textures and weaves. Shimmering threads adorn thin voile and broderie anglais, velvets jostle with peach skin, and satin and silk tempt, while serge and wool worsted simply beg to be made into classy gents suits and taken to colder climes.

### Electronics

Prices for electronic goods in Dubai are generally lower than in most parts of the world. Stores stock both well-known and not so instantly recognisable brands, with guarantees and after-sales service available from local agents and dealers.

Chat with the salesman and tell him which country the item will be taken to and he will make sure you have chosen the right model for operating 'back home'.

### Watches

A multitude of timepieces waits for you to inspect and buy. Choose from classic collections, high precision, superbly designed, functional, versatile and elegant watches. Prices range anywhere from a few Dirhams upwards. In addition to the accredited agents for well-known brands (Swatch, Longines, Alfred Dunhill, Rolex, Tag, Breitling, Cartier, Philippe Chabrol, etc), the souq abounds with watch shops offering all kinds of designs, for all ages and tastes.

### Perfumes

Just about every perfume in the world is available in Dubai, somewhere. Many stores distribute various brands of perfume for both men and women, and new fragrances are introduced to the market almost as soon as they are launched in their own countries. Look out for the local perfumes which are heady mixtures of aromatic Arabian oils blended to suit your own taste - one dab can last a few days!

### Traditional Items

Popular gifts are local ethnic items such as brass coffee pots, silver and wooden dhows, khanjars (short curved knives in elaborately wrought sheaths), ancient rifles, muzzle loading guns, falconry accoutrements, minatures of camels in wood or brass, and worry beads. All these are widely available, but prices vary enormously, the souks offer by far the best buys.

### Carpets

Numerous shops specialise in carpets, with countries of origin ranging from Iran, Pakistan, China and Central Asia. Deira Tower shopping mall in Al Nasr Square has the largest number of carpet outlets under one roof, with the majority of traders from Iran. Take the salesman's advice on quality and design, as it is often hard for the unpracticed eye to detect variations, and bargain hard - be sure to visit a number of shops before deciding on a purchase.

# Communications & Services

## Newspapers

Gulf News, Khaleej Times and The Gulf Today are the daily English-language newspapers. Local Arabic newspapers include Al Bayan, Al-Ittihad and Al-Khaleej. Foreign newspapers, most prominently British and Asian, are readily available in hotel bookshops and supermarkets.

## Telephones

Telecommunications are excellent, both within the UAE and with the outside world. Telephone calls within Dubai city are free and direct dialling is available to most countries, although charges are high. Access to the Internet has recently been introduced.

## Internet

Recently introduced by, ETISALAT is the sole provider of these services within the UAE. A couple of "internet" cafes have opened up, which provide easy and relatively cheap access. Most organisations which have their own will have an eight charachter email address, with the following extension *emirates.net.ae*, e.g.: explore@emirates.net.ae

## Radio

There are two English-language radio stations available - Dubai FM broadcasts daily on 92Mhz FM, 24- hours a day, and the latest arrival Channel 4 FM broadcasts daily on 104.8Mhz FM, 24- hours a day. Daily schedules can be found in the local newspapers.

Playing the Widest
Selection Of Music
WITH EXTENSIVE COVERAGE OF MAJOR EVENTS
DUBAI 92 FM
The Gulf's No. 1
TO CAPTURE THE WIDEST AUDIENCE IN THE GULF,
ADVERTISE ON The Gulf's No. 1
CALL OUR COMMERCIAL SALES DEPARTMENT
ON 04-370599

## Electricity

There's plenty of it! The electricity supply in Dubai is 220/240 volts and 50 cycles - hence most US-made appliances will need a transformer. Socket type is identical to the British system.

## Water

More expensive than oil! Tap water is quite safe to drink, but not particularly pleasant, and visitors usually prefer locally bottled mineral water which is widely available. Bottled water is usually served in hotels and restaurants too.

## Medical Care

Dubai has many well-equipped hospitals. The Dubai Department of Health and Medical Services runs Dubai, Rashid, Maktoum and Al Wasl hospitals. Dubai Hospital is one of the best medical centres in the Middle East, with specialised clinics; Al Wasl is a specialised maternity and gynaecology hospital.

The Department also operates a number of out-patient clinics, one of which is situated in Jebel Ali.

| Hospital | Tel |
|---|---|
| Al Amal Hospital | 444 010 |
| Al Dowall Private Hospital* | 212 484 |
| Al Maktoum Hospital | 221 211 |
| Al Wasl Hospital* | 341 111 |
| American Hospital* | 367 777 |
| Belhoul Intern. Hosp. Cen. | 454 000 |
| Iranian Hospital* | 440 250 |
| Kuwait Hospital* | 731 200 |
| New Dubai Hospital* | 714 444 |
| Rashid Hospital* | 374 000 |

| Dentists | Tel |
|---|---|
| American Dental Clinic | 313 668 |
| Jumeira Beach Dental Clinic | 499 433 |
| Swedish Dental Clinic | 231 297 |

| Centres/Clinics | Tel |
|---|---|
| Al Borj Medical Centre* | 454 666 |
| Al Zahra Private Med. Cent. | 315 000 |
| Dubai London Clinic | 446 663 |
| Dr. Akel's General Medical Clinic* | 442 773 |
| Dr. M.S. Ahmadi Clinic | 445 550 |
| Dubai Physiotherapy Clinic | 496 333 |
| General Medical Centre* | 495 959 |
| Manchester Clinic | 440 300 |

** Denotes: 24-hour Emergency service*

## Television / Satellite TV

Most leading hotels now receive international news and entertainment broadcasts via satellite. The Hong Kong-based Star TV and the Rome based Orbit are among the satellite networks which transmit a wide variety of programmes, including BBC World and CNN.

Locally, there are six channels: Dubai 2, 10, 30, 38 and 41 which show Arabic programmes, and Dubai 33, which broadcasts in English. Emirates Dubai Television broadcasts by satellite throughout the world in Arabic and English.

Reception from Abu Dhabi, Sharjah, Qatar and Bahrain is usually possible and programme details are published in the local press.

The skies of the Middle East are saturated with television satellites. Considering the vast diversity in the people watching, it is but natural that programmes of all hues, flavours and taste are available. From the one that started it all - Star TV to the latest entrant in the fray - DSTV. U.A.E. viewers have never had it better. They can choose from a variety of

channels which cater to their requirement, especially English spoken programmes. The various channels available are of three types:

### 1. Pay TV Channels

Channels which require a cost for installation, equipment such as the antenna etc. and a decoder, followed by a subscription towards the channel you choose to watch, e.g. Dubai cabel vision.

### 2. Air Channels

Channels which require a cost of installation and reception equipment but no viewing subscription (correct at the time of going to print). The following below are the major focused satellites transmitting TV channels to this area. Many other regional channels are available.

### 3. Terrestrial Channels

Channel 33 - The English channel of Dubai Television transmitting a mixed fare of serials, documentaries and films. Abu Dhabi Channel 2 - The English channel of Abu Dhabi TV. Sharjah & Ajman TV have terrestrial channels which have some programmes in English.

Equipment can be bought in various locations, from second hand shops, classified ads, or directly from dealers. Majority of companies will offer installation. For apartment blocks and buildings with a large number of viewing points, a central system is recommended, making it economical as well as offering more choice. Get your landlord to install!

# Satellite TV

## Pay-TV services

| Networks. | Channels | Requirements | Cost | Dealers |
|---|---|---|---|---|
| Orbit (Digital) | Al-Oula,Al-Thania,Egypt1, Egypt2,Orbit News,Fun Channel, Music Now,Hollywood Channel, America Plus, Super Movies, Orbit-ESPN sports, CNN, The Disney Channel, Radio Orbit. | 90 cm Dish, Orbit Decoder | Dhs 2995 (Decoder) + Installation + subscription | Star Distributions, 04/826262 |
| Showtime (Digital) | The Movie Channel,MTV Europe, VH-1 Music,Nickelodeon,Paramount TV Land,Bloomberg TV, Discovery Channel, Style TV. | 90 cm Dish, Showtime Decoder | Dhs.2,750-3,100(Decoder Installation + Subscription | Gulf Satellite, 04/823941 |
| 1st net Bouquet (Digital) | Art1,Art2,Art3,Art4,Art5,Esc 2, Future Gold, LBC Plus,MCM,Nile Drama, TNT/CN,Art2 Sports,Art2 Music,LBC Plus, Future TV. | 90 cm Dish, 1st Net Decoder subscription | Dhs.2,750 (Decoder) + Installation + | MediaVision 04/345284 |
| Star Select (Digital) | Star Plus(Int'l), Star Movies,Star Sports,NBC,CNBC,Fox Kids Network,Sky News, Channel V(Int'l), Viva Cinema. | 90 cm Dish, Orbit Decoder subscription | Dhs.2,995 (Decoder) + Installation + | Star Distributions 04/826262 |
| Zee Cinema (Analog) | Zee Cinema | 6-8ft Dish Analogue IRD | Dhs 1060 (Decoder) + subscription | Star TV 04/838500 |

## Most Popular Satellites

| Satellites | Channels | Requirements | Languages | Cost |
|---|---|---|---|---|
| Asiasat-1 | Star sports, Channel V, EL TV Zee TV,Star Plus,PTV. | 6-8 ft Dish | English, Hindi,Urdu. | Dhs 800-1000 |
| Arabsat-2A (C/Ku-band) | Sharjah TV, LBC,Egypt,ART,Nile,Bahrain CNN,Future Vision,Orbit,Sudan,Saudi 1, Saudi 2,CFI,Abu Dhabi,Dubai,Syria,MBC, Oman,Kuwait,Yemen, Al-Jazeera,JRTV-Amman,Abu Dhabi,Libya,ART,MBC. | 6-8 ft Dish | Arabic, English,French. | Dhs1550-1850 |
| PAS-4 | ABN,Home TV,BBC,CNN,TNT/Cartoon Network,Sony,DD int'l,Music Asia,ATN MTV. | 6 ft Dish | English,Hindi. | Dhs1220-1520 |

STAR MOVIES
the fun
STAR WORLD
HOLLYWOOD CHANNEL
DISNEY CHANNEL
AMERICA PLUS
SKY NEWS
CNN INTERNATIONAL
Orbit ESPN
Super MOVIES
Orbit NEWS

# Entertainment & Leisure

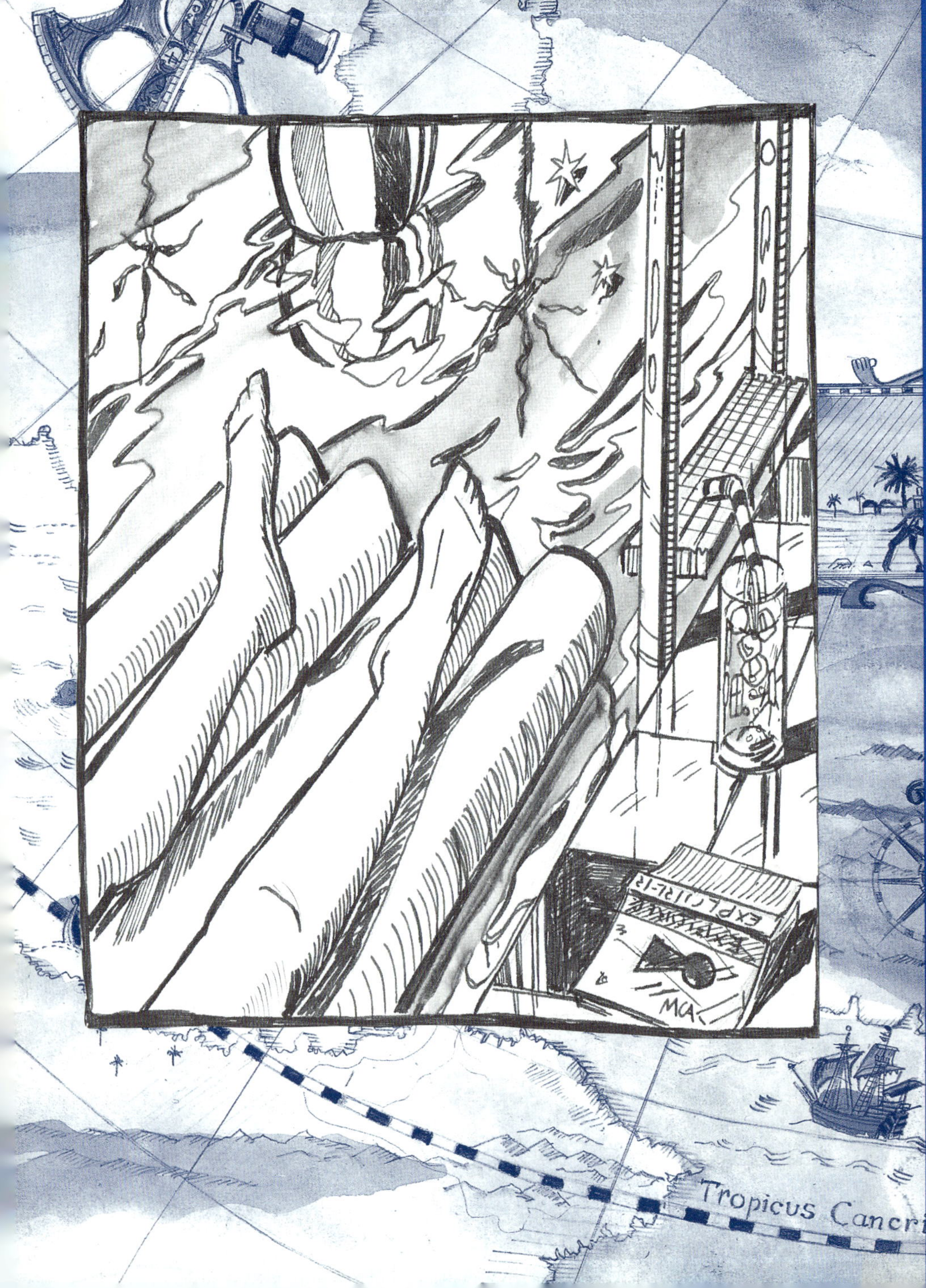

# Visitors Check List

### General

- [ ] Arabic Food*
- [ ] Smoked Shisha Pipe*
- [ ] Camel Ride/ Eat Dates !
- [ ] Beaches - Sunbathing
- [ ] Water Sports
- [ ] Museums
- [ ] Shopping
- [ ] Desert Trips
- [ ] Postcards

### Museums / Historic

- [ ] Dubai Museum*
- [ ] Sharjah Museums
- [ ] Sheikh Rashids House
- [ ] Heritage & Diving Village
- [ ] Bastakia

### Sporting

- [ ] Golf
- [ ] Diving
- [ ] Water Skiing
- [ ] Parasailing
- [ ] Jet Skiing

### Shopping

- [ ] Shopping Malls
- [ ] Al Fahid Street

### Souks / Markets

- [ ] Spice Souk*
- [ ] Gold Souk*
- [ ] Fruit & Vegetable Market
- [ ] Fish Market
- [ ] Sharjah Souk
- [ ] Karama*

### Sight Seeing Tours

- [ ] Jumeira Mosque
- [ ] Abra Ride
- [ ] Dhow Wharfage
- [ ] Visit the parks

### Out of Dubai

- [ ] Al-Ain
- [ ] Abu Dhabi
- [ ] Hatta
- [ ] Jebel Hafit
- [ ] East Coast

*** Note:**
For those on a short trip, this indicates the essential places / things to do.

# Tours & Charters

## Bird Watching

### Hobby Holidays

On Request | Various Locations | Tel: **485 277**

Colin Richardson, UAE Bird Recorder and author of 'The Birds of the United Arab Emirates' organises day and half-day tours for small groups. The UAE's varied landscape supports over 400 bird species, many not easily found anywhere in Europe or elsewhere in the Middle East.

The tours include a visit to the mudflats at Khor Dubai where thousands of Arctic shorebirds and flamingos winter, the Hajar mountains with its many species, the East Coast where the rare and threatened White-collared Kingsfisher is found and fields around Ras Al Khaimah in the north of the UAE, where Indian Rollers and Little Green Bee-Eaters are abundant. There will be times to relax too and plenty of photo opportunities. Tours are designed to suit individual bird spotting needs, and prices range from Dhs.165 for a half-day to Dhs.430 for the longer day trips when lunch and refreshments are supplied.

## Camel Racing / Rides

Camel races normally take place on Thursday and Fridays during the winter months, and can be one of the most memorable highlights of any visit to Dubai. In addition to the racing, spectators may wander around the paddocks, and buy camel "accessories" including blankets, rugs and beads form the nearby market. Check for the dates and timing of these races in the local press.

Camel racing is an exciting and extraordinary sport, with large numbers of camels, their owners and families congregating at the race track. Bred for the track and reared on a highly nutritious diet their careers, health and breeding potential is closely monitored. Races are held mainly during National Days and other public holidays. Most tour operators offer a chance to ride camels at their desert camp sites.

# Creek Tours

## Abra Crossing

06:00 - 24:00 | Both Sides Bur Dubai / Deira | Page 7 A 3 | Tel: **NA**

From the textile souk area across the Creek to the Al Seef Road part of Bur Dubai takes five minutes by water taxi. These basic wooden boats seat about 30 people and are used by the ordinary working man as a cheap method of transportation. Dhs.0.50 will get you from one side of the Creek to the other. For Dhs.30-Dhs.50, however, you can hire the boat and driver for a short river tour of about half an hour for you and your guests alone. Step carefully down the steep stone steps, so as not to lose your balance while stepping across to your negotiated boat. Than sit on the low deck to enjoy the view of Dubai by water.

## Coastline Leisure

Every 2 hrs 11:30 - 17:30 | Nr. Sheraton Hotel Deira | Page 10 C 1 | Tel: **450 867**

The only company to offer daily guided tours of Dubai tours use professionally recorded tapes (music and narratives - one even available in Russian if required!), which include a brief history of Dubai, places of interest, palace, souks, fort, basically offering a full perspective. This is probably the most informative all round way to tour Dubai, plus it provides ideal photo opporunities. Daily tours at 11:30, 13:30, 15:30 and 17:30. Cost is Dhs.35 for adults and Dhs.20 for children over eight.

As an exciting alternative aimed at both tourists and residents, is the new *Mamzar Park Cruise* (sea conditions permiting) which leaves every Saturday at 11:00 sharp and heads up the coast for one and half hours to Al Mamzar park. Drop anchor, and relax for about an hour with good music and the sun. Steps at the back of the boat allow you easy access in/out of the water. Reasonably priced at Dhs.160 (Dhs.300/couple), which includes a packed lunch. Refreshments also available for purchase.

## Creek Cruises

09:00 - 13:00 16:00 - 20:00 | Quay 2/3, Dhow Wharfage Deira | Page 10 C 2 | Tel: **533 554**

This magnificent vessel has become a potent symbol of the Gulf's rich cultural heritage and a poignant reminder of a way of life that existed virtually unchanged for centuries. The Malika Al Khor (Queen of the Creek) is the largest dhow of its kind on the Creek, and is easy to find at the new dhow wharfage, at the far end of quay 2 and 3. Plenty of parking. Fitted with the latest safety equipment, this spacious double-deck dhow has been designed with the comfort, safety and enjoyment of all passengers in mind.

Coastline Leisure

This includes an air-conditioned lower deck, an Arabic style Majlis on the upper deck, and can accommodate up to 125 guests! Fitted with a professional sound system, dance floor and two toilets. If you wish to hire the dhow and its crew privately, the cost is Dhs.1,200 per hour (min 2 hours). Catering can be provided from Dhs.85 onwards.

# Dinner Cruises

What can be better than a slow easy evening plowing the waters of the Creek on a typical wooden dhow. View the illiminated creekside bustle while tucking into traditional fare, buffet style, in truly Arabian surroundings. With Persian carpets underfoot and whilte vait unf..... wave, the upstairs Majlis is perfect for stargazing. Very romantic!

## Al Boom Tourist Village

**Daily 20:30** | **Al Boom Tourist Village, Nr. Al Garhoud Bridge** | **Page 14 A 3** | Tel: **341 000**

As part of the new Al Boom Tourist village complex, these are the biggest operators of dhows on the Creek, currently with five dhows catering to capacities of 20 - 160 passengers.

There is also a two-hour daily dinner cruise starting at 20:30, departing from the TheTourist Village. The menu consists of seafood and meat barbecue buffet, with all grilled food items are cooked on board. The cost is a very reasonable Dhs.100, including soft-drinks, mineral water and tea/coffee.

## Coastline Leisure

**Daily 20:30 But Check!** | **Nr. Sheraton Hotel Deira** | **Page 10 C 1** | Tel: **450 867**

Different menues and prices, depending on the night. For example, every Sunday and Tuesday evening the traditional Dhow "Tour Dubai" operates an Arabic Buffet style dinner cruise catered by a five-star hotel. Boarding is from 20:10, departure at 20:30, return at 23:00, cost Dhs.240 (Dhs.260 if you wish a pick-up at your hotel). Call for an exact map/location details. The dhow has an 18' x 30' function deck, Arabic Majlis and a VIP Majlis, two toilets and a professional sound system with over 200 mixed CD's to ensure that every function is a great success. There are, big plans to offer

something different. From a cheap evening out, with a cruise, snack, and live soul/rock. This boat will be out every night. Anything goes!

## Creek Cruises

On Request | Quay 2/3, Dhow Wharfage Deira | Page 10 C 2 | Tel: **533 554**

The Malika Al Khor (Queen of the Creek) is the largest dhow of its kind on the Creek. This magnificent vessel has become a potent symbol of the Gulf's rich cultural heritage and a poinant reminder of a way of life that existed virtually unchanged for centuries.

On Sunday and Wednesday evenings you can join the Malika Al Khor for a two hour "Arabic Nights" cruise for Dhs.200. Enjoy a wonderful meal with a live band playing music on a moving Creek cruiser. This floating restaurant cruises along the Creek twice a day. An open buffet style lunch and dinner catered by a five-star hotel. The cost is Dhs.150 per person and the cruise takes about 2 hours.

Fitted with the latest safety equipment, this spacious double-deck dhow has been designed with the comfort, safety and enjoyment of all passengers in mind. This includes an air-conditioned lower deck, an Arabic style Majlis on the upper deck, and can accommodate up to 125 guests! Fitted with a professional sound system, dance floor and two toilets.

## Sun Tours

20:00 - 22:20 | Creekside Park Nr. Wafi/Maktoum Bridge | Page 14 B 1 | Tel: **214 555**

The newest operator in Dubai to make a splash. They are the only company to offer dinner cruises, not in a dhow, but in a regular canal cruise boat! Daily departures from the Creekside park at 20:00. The boat can take up to 300 people, with 200 seating. Two decks, AC. Standard Arabic buffet for Dhs.170 which also includes live entertainment.

# Falconry Tours

## Santier Tours

On Request | Various | Tel: **313 300**

Santier Tours offer this exclusive tour from October to early March. Starting at 15:00, the visit begins at the Falcon Hospital to view the state-of-the-art facilities provided for the care of these precious birds. Then drive out to the desert to visit a farm and watch a falcon demonstration (provided the weather is good and they are training on that day). An optional BBQ dinner can be arranged at a nominal extra charge (Sunday, Tuesday and Thursdays only) to finish off the afternoon. Price: Dhs.275 pp (min. 4 pax; max 6). Dhs.30 extra for optional BBQ dinner.

For special interest groups, a visit to the *Falcon and Camel Hospital* can be arranged. A two and a half hour tour unravels the mystery of the 'ships of the desert' and these prized 'birds of prey'. While visiting the camel hospital, you will get an insight into how camels survive the blistering heat of the desert. How fast can they run? How long do they live? All will be revealed !. In the falcon hospital you can see how these meat eaters can be as gentle as pigeons if treated the right way. During the visits to both, the vets will show you how their day to day work is helping to control diseases particular to these animals. This tour occurs only once a week (no fixed day): time of day optional. Price per person: Dhs.150 (min. 2 pax). Santier Tours offer friendly, quality tours in small groups (max 6 pax).

# Helicopter Tours

## Aerogulf Services Company

**On Request** | **Dubai Creek Golf Club Al Garhoud** | **Page 14 C 2** | Tel: **823 157**

What better way to view the many sights of Dubai than from a helicopter? Short sightseeing tours of the city provide a truly splendid way to see and photograph Dubai city. Fare: Dhs.700 for 10-15 min. flight. Booking necessary.

Another popular option is a trip to Hatta Fort Hotel for a day trip or weekend jaunt, the journey takes just over one hour at a return cost of Dhs.3,500 for four people. Other options include desert safari flights involving skimming over the dunes, being met by a 4WD vehicle on landing, before being driven to a Bedouin tent for a sunset dinner. Flights customised to suit.

# Hot Air Ballooning

## Gulf Explorers

**On Request** | **Muscat Oman** | Tel: **+968 704 739**

Currently only operating in Oman, but with plans to try and offer flights within the UAE. Permission has been obtained by Gulf Explorers to offer balloon flights in a number of interesting new locations such as Nakhl (fort and Ghubra Bowl), Ras Al Had (turtle beach), Sohar (one of Sindbad's ports) and Sur (wooden dhow building on the beach) in addition to the original flight sites of Nizwa, Jabrin and Al Qabil. There are sites nearer to Muscat for residents who prefer their adventuring closer to home.

The company's balloons called 'Renaissance' and 'Gulf Air' are operated by Virgin Balloon Flights (UK) and are fully insured. Passengers are invited to assist in the inflation, launch and packing away of the balloon to add to their enoyment of the trip, but this is not obligatory. Tea, coffee and croissants are served prior to the early morning flight and a full Arabic style breakfast is served on landing. Take your camera and plenty of film.

# Scenic Flights

## Fujairah Aviation Centre

On Request | Fujairah International Airport, Fujairah | Tel: **09 224 747**

A stunning mixture of coastline, rugged mountains, beautiful valleys, cities, villages and date plantations - available every day for 1- 3 people at Dhs.400/hr. Flights can be for half an hour, if you just want a quick look at the surrounding area, or as long as four hours, which will enable you to see almost the entire UAE. Below are some suggested routes, however the pilots would be delighted to prepare a route especially for you, at no extra charge.

Scenic Flight 1 : Fujairah - Dibba - Masafi - Fujairah

Scenic Flight 2 : Fujairah - Hatta - Dhaid - Masafi - Fujairah

Scenic Flight 3 : Fujairah - Al Ain - Abu Dhabi - Dubai - Sharjah - Ajman - Umm Al Quwain - Ras Al Khaimah - Dibba - Fujairah.

# *The Classic Tours*

## City Tours

The list of tours given is by no means exhaustive, but covers the most popular tours provided by the main tour operators (Tour operator contact details and costing provided on page 34). Generally speaking, tours will include a lunch stop allowing time for meals to be purchased at an individual's own choice of eatery. Meals only provided when stated.

Each tour operator offers their own individual style and hence quality of tour. Decide on which criteria are important, and then choose your tour operator.

Prices varies according to seasons. You are advised to check the finer details before booking.

### Abu Dhabi Tour

The route from Dubai passes Jebel Ali Port which is the world's largest man made sea port. Abu Dhabi was founded in 1761 and stands on an island, it is the capital of the United Arab Emirates. Visit the Women's Handicraft Centre, Heritage Village and the Petroleum Exhibition with a film show guide to the history of oil in the region. A tour of the city includes both ancient and modern areas.

### Al Ain Tour

Al Ain used to be a necessary oasis stopover on the caravan trail from UAE to Oman. Many major historical attractions, from one of the first forts to be built by the Al Nahyan family over 175 years ago, to prehistoric tombs at Hilli said to be over 5000 years old, can be seen. The museum is housed in an old fort, or visit the camel market, see an ancient irrigation system still in use and browse in a quaint souk.

## Dubai City Tour

Slightly different depending on the agency you book with, most of them give you an overview of the old and the new part of Dubai. Fish and fruit market, mosques, abra (local water taxi), old wind towered houses (earliest form of air conditioning), commercial centre and modern buildings are usual inclusions. A lot of fascinating places which will surprise you.

## Dubai By Night

Drive around the palaces, mosques and souks while enjoying the early evening lights of Dubai. See the multitude of shoppers in their different national costumes, fountains coloured with lights and streets ablaze with character. Afterwards enjoy dinner in one of many different places depending which agency you book with.

## Ras Al Khaimah Tour

Drive up country along the so-called Pirate Coast through Ajman, Umm Al Quwain and small villages. Explore ancient sites dating back centuries and discover the old town of Ras Al Khaimah and its museum. The return voyage passes natural hot springs, date groves at Khatt and along the starkly beautiful Hajar mountains. Most trips include a visit to a small historic fort.

## Sharjah & Ajman Emirate Tour

Watch local craftsmen skillfully drilling with only the help of string powered wooden tools. Ajman is the place to visit if you want to see wooden dhows being built today just as they were hundreds of years ago. Take in the museum before driving to the neighbouring emirate of Sharjah, where a multitude of old and new souks await discovery. Souk Al Majarrah has a unique golden dome with the 12 zodiac signs depicted in intricate mosaic. The bird and fish markets can be visited on the way to Souk Al Markazi which is a splendid example of Islamic architecture. Walk around the restored Al Naboodah house to see how the locals used to live.

## Shopping Tour

Dubai is a shopper's paradise when it comes to a wide and diverse range of goods and prices. Discover the shops of Al Karama where almost-designer clothes can be bought at incredibly low prices. Al Fahidi Street is the place to go for electronics and watches, while the Textile Souk pulsates with colours and bolts of cloth from India and the Far East.

Then there are the malls... Ultra modern, air-conditioned enclosed malls selling perfumes, clothing, art and a multitude of items you didn't know you wanted. Bargain your way through the day. See the first section of the book for what to buy!

# 'Safari' Tours

## East Coast

Journey northwards to Dhaid, a small oasis town known for its fruit and vegetable plantations. Catch glimpses of dramatic mountain gorges while journeying to Dibba and Khorfakkan on the East Coast, with the Indian Ocean lapping their shores. Take time for a refreshing swim, discover places to eat and visit the oldest mosque in the UAE, nestling below ruins of a coastal fort, and a favourite scene with local artists.

## Overnight Safari

A 24-hour tour starting approx.15:00 with a drive through the desert dunes to a campsite which has been set up Bedouin style. Dine under the stars, sleep in the fresh air and awake to the smell of coffee brewing in the clear air. Visit an impromptu camel race, if available. If not, the guides will take you to a racing camel camp to see animals in training. Drive along wadis (dried river beds), and enjoy a buffet lunch before crossing the big sand dunes and returning back to town.

## Mountain Safari

Turn right at Ras Al Khaimah, the oldest sea port in the region, and drive into the spectacular Hajar mountains. Rumble through canyons, steep rugged winding tracks, deep gorges and terraced mountain sides following Wadi Bih. Old houses made of mountain stones are still inhabited by villagers who grow crops such as tobacco for subsistence 1,200 metres above sea level, before the pass leads to Dibba where a highway will quickly return you to Dubai before 18:00. Some tours operate in reverse, starting from Dibba.

## Safari Tour

This day-long tour differs from company to company. Usually it will include visiting a traditional Bedouin village, crossing sand dunes of varying colours and heights, and may include a visit to Fossil Rock, - a smaller version of Australia's famous Ayres Rock. A cold buffet lunch in the shade of a friendly thorn tree is generally welcomed by all, prior to a desert drive home on graded track or tarmac road.

## Wadi Hatta

Modern highways, soft undulating sand dunes and a kaleidoscope of colours in both sand and mountain rocks leads the way to Hatta valley at the foothills of the Al Hajar mountain range. Dip your toes, or whole body, into the pools of spring water and see the hidden waterfall inside a gorge. The journey usually includes a stop at Hatta Fort Hotel which lies nestled at the foot of the mountains in landscaped gardens, a nine hole golf course, archery lawn and clay pigeon shooting area. Take time to rest and enjoy a swim in the hotel's swimming pool.

# Special Dinner Tours

## Arabian Night

Sundown brings a light show to Dubai town with subtle shading on mosques and old buildings. A drive through it's glittering streets is arranged to show visitors famous landmarks on many of the roundabouts, the Sheikh's Palace, various souks, the famous illuminated Creek, and of course, the fruit and vegetable markets. Then a pleasant evening walk through the dazzling gold souk will work up an appetite for dinner, which is provided, with Arabic music and a belly dancer to liven up the evening.

## Dune Dinner

The cooler, late afternoon hours are ideal for enjoying the thrill of driving up and down golden sand dunes in a 4-wheel drive vehicle. Departure around 16:00. The route to the dunes passes the camel race track and villages which pose ideal photo opportunities. An Arabic campsite has already been set up where a sumptuous dinner awaits you. Enjoy the sunset, calm and starlit desert night. Return around 22:00.

## See Also:

**Tours - Dinner Cruises** (p25)

# Tour Operators & Pricing Details

| Tours | Al Boom Tourist Village Tel: 341 000 | Arabian Adventures Tel: 317 373 | Arabian Link Tours Tel: 06 726 666 | Creek Cruises Tel: 533 554 | Coastline Leisure Tel: 450 867 | Desert Rangers Tel: 460 808 | Europcar Tel: 515 153 | Gulf Dunes Tel: 714 506 | Gulf Ventures Tel: 305 102 | Net Tours Tel: 668 661 | Orient Tours Tel: 06 668 661 | Santier Tours Tel: 313 300 | SNTTA Tel: 06 548 296 | Sun Tours Tel: 214 555 | Thomas Cook Al R. Tel: 236 060 |
|---|---|---|---|---|---|---|---|---|---|---|---|---|---|---|---|
| **City Tours** | | | | | | | | | | | | | | | |
| Abu Dhabi | - | 160 | 175 | - | - | - | 250 | 350 | 120 | 185 | 150 | 200 | 175 | 250 | 150 |
| Al Ain | - | 160 | 175 | - | - | 175 | 250 | 350 | 120 | 185 | 150 | 200 | 175 | 240 | 110 |
| Dubai City | - | 100 | 110 | - | - | 175 | 100 | 355 | 90 | 90 | 95 | 120 | 110 | 100 | 100 |
| Dhow Cruise | - | 260 | 233 | - | 35 | - | - | - | 200 | 200 | 240 | 55 | 260 | 170 | 275 |
| Dubai by Night | - | 100 | 110 | - | - | 200 | - | 250 | - | - | - | 80 | - | 100 | - |
| Ras Al Khaimah | - | - | 175 | - | - | 350 | - | 350 | - | - | 150 | 200 | - | - | 110 |
| Sharjah & Ajman | - | 100 | 110 | - | - | 350 | 150 | 350 | 100 | 90 | 95 | 150 | 110 | 140 | 110 |
| Shopping Tour | - | 100 | 110 | - | - | 275 | - | 350 | 100 | - | 100 | 100 | 110 | - | 100 |
| **Safari Tours** | | | | | | | | | | | | | | | |
| East Coast | - | 160 | 175 | - | - | 175 | 250 | 350 | 230 | 185 | 150 | 200 | 175 | 250 | 200 |
| Mountain Safari | - | 235 | 340 | - | - | 350 | 200 | - | 250 | - | 225 | 250 | 340 | 250 | - |
| Overnight Safari | - | 490 | 490 | - | - | 450 | 300 | 425 | 350 | 335 | 475 | 410 | 495 | 300 | 475 |
| Safari Tour | - | 240 | 182 | - | - | 200 | 250 | 456 | 200 | 235 | 200 | 220 | 295 | 200 | - |
| Wadi Hatta | | 235 | 245 | | | 200 | 250 | - | 250 | 285 | 225 | - | 245 | 250 | 225 |
| **Special Dinner Tours** | - | | | - | - | | | | | | | | | | |
| Arabian Night | - | - | 200 | - | - | 255 | - | - | 295 | - | 275 | - | 300 | 200 | 260 |
| Dune Dinner | - | 245 | 182 | - | - | 255 | - | 220 | 200 | - | - | 220 | 260 | 200 | 260 |
| Dinner Cruise | 100 | - | - | 150 | 240 | - | - | - | - | - | - | - | - | - | - |

# Museums / Historical Sites

Museums and Heritage Sites are generally open during normal trading hours of 08:00 - 13:00 and 16:00 -18:00. If in doubt, phone before you go to check holiday and weekend times which change with some seasons. Entrance fee is either free or Dhs.2 per person. The museums are listed by city.

## Dubai

### Dubai Museum

**08:30 - 19:30**
**Closed Fri am**

**Old Al Fahidi Fort**
**Bur Dubai - Bastakia**

**Page 7**
**B 3**

Tel: **531 862**

Built last century as a fort for sea defences, the Al Fahidi Fort was renovated in 1970 to house a museum showing everyday artifacts and archaeological finds from the area, some dating back 4,000 years. Pearl merchants, fishermen, housewives, and wedding finery are all represented.

Recent expansion has significantly expanded the site and it now includes modern hands-on displays and information cases. Enter the Souk of the 1950's and walk through an amazing labyrinth of shops and craftsmen's dwellings. Life-size static displays and hologram-like movies show a pottery, spice store, carpenter at work, fabric seller, tailor, food shop, and date seller ... you can even peek into an Islamic school, get a glimpse into the social life, games and costumes of the day.

Then enter a new world of life at an oasis, complete with camel, goats and a falaj running with water. Other displays include the Desert at Night, surrounded by stars and crackling camp fire; Bedouin Crafts; Archeology; Natural Habitation and a tribute to the Sea. Note: no cameras allowed

### Heritage & Diving Village

**16:30 - 22:00**

**Nr. Al Shindagha Tunnel**
**Al Shindagha**

**Page 7**
**B 1**

Tel: **NA**

Situated in the Shindagha area near the Creek mouth, the Heritage and Diving Villages provide a glimpse of Dubai's traditional culture and lifestyle. Focusing on the Emirate's maritime past, pearl diving traditions and architecture, the villages offer storybook displays as well as a tented Bedouin village, ancient armoury wooden chests and cooking utensils. Several shops also sell handicrafts. Ideal for family visits, the village is close to the site of Sheikh Saeed Al Maktoum's house.

Thomas Cook
Al Rostamani
TRAVEL & HOLIDAYS
To ensure the perfect holiday, you need the right connections.
COSMOS
The Apartment Service
EURAIL
FLAG INTERNATIONAL
British Rail International
We have them all.
One of the things that distinguishes Thomas Cook Al Rostamani Travel & Holidays is its connections with the very best travel-related companies. As the exclusive General Sales Agent of Cosmos Tours, BritRail, Eurail, The Apartment Service and Flag International, it makes sure you enjoy the very best holidays. So if you're planning a holiday, make a vital connection... call Thomas Cook Al Rostamani Travel & Holidays.
TELEPHONE
Call us today!
Abu Dhabi - 727500 Deira - 236060 Jebel Ali - 818169 Jumeirah - 490408
A member of Al Rostamani group

## Juma Al Majid Cultural & Heritage Centre

08:00 - 13:00
16:00 - 19:30 Closed Fri am

Off Salah Al Din Rd
Deira

Page 9
C9-99

Tel: **624 999**

Established in 1991, this is a non-profit library and research institute. The library's collections include 350,000 Arab-language titles, with a concentration on Arab and Islamic heritage plus 17,000 titles in English, French, German, Russian and other languages. There is a separate national heritage collection in different languages, with books and materials relating only to the Arabian Gulf.

## Majlis Al Ghoraifa

NA

Al Jumeira Rd
Jumeira / Umm Sequim

Page 9
C9-99

Tel: **NA**

Originally constructed in 1955 the Majlis Al Ghoraifa was used by the late Sheikh Rashid Bin Saeed Al Maktoum as a summer resort. Situated on the boundaries of Jumeira and Umm Suqueim this tiny park is a pretty museum of how life used to be.

The Majlis is a simple two storey building made from coral stone and gypsum. The ground floor is an open veranda called (Leewan) or (Rewaaq) with a small storeroom near the stairs, on the second floor, the Majlis is decorated with carpets, pillows, lanterns, rifles and a firebox of Arabic coffee pots. The doors and windows are made from solid teak wood (Saaj).

Dubai Municipality has planned an Arabic garden including a traditional channel irrigation system (Falaj), palm trees, and a pond, and a barasti palms cafe will occupy the corner of the property. Look for the brown Municipality Historical Places sign posts along Beach Rd. past the Jumeira Beach Park, near No.1 Supermarket.

## Sheikh Saeed Al Maktoum House

08:00 - 13:00

Nr. Al Shindagha Tunnel
Al Shindagha

Page 7
A 1

Tel: **531 723**

The modest sandstone home of Dubai's much-loved former ruler, this is the original site from which Dubai grew. Originally strategically situated at the mouth of Dubai's lifeline, the Creek, this carefully restored house-turned-museum now lies close to the Bur Dubai side of Shindagha Tunnel and next to the recently completed Heritage and Diving Village.

# Fujairah

## Fujairah Museum

08:00 - 13:00
16:00 - 18:00 Closed Sat

Nr. Fujairah Fort
Fujairah

Tel: **09 229 085**

Situated near Fujairah Fort and the old mud-brick village, the Fujarah Museum has displays of the old traditional way of life and of archaeological artefacts found in excavations throughout the emirate. Work by local and foreign archaeologists has yielded items dating back to over 4,500 years ago including Bronze and Iron Age weapons, finely painted pottery, delicately carved soapstone vessels and pre-Islamic

The museum is shortly to be enlarged to permit more finds to be displayed. Charges Dhs.2 adults/ Dhs.1 children.

## Fujairah Heritage Village

**07:30 - 13:30**
**Closed Fri**

**Nr. Fujairah Fort**
**Fujairah**

Tel: **09 227 000**

Fujairah's Heritage Village is close to Ain Madhab Gardens. These gardens are situated in a valley in the foothills of the Hajar Mountains just outside Fujairah City, and are fed by mineral springs. This warm sulphur-laden water is also used in two swimming pools available for ladies and for men. Ain Al Madhab has chalets for private use as well as large wooded gardens. On public holidays, an outdoor theatre is used for festivals which include traditional singing and folklore dances.

The Heritage Village exhibits include traditional houses, cooking utensils, farming tools and other items, well as the Al Yayarah system used for irrigating fields which uses a working bull. The village is open in the mornings, except Friday's and entry is free. Entrance fee to the park is Dhs.2 adults/ Dhs.1 child and the pool is Dhs.5 per person.

# Sharjah

## Sharjah Archaelogical Museum

**09:00 - 13:00**
**17:00 - 20:00**

**Sharjah**

Tel: **06 366 466**

A modern and hi-tech museum, the Sharjah Archaeological Museum, situated on Sharjah's Cultural Square, offers a lively and interesting display of artefacts and antiquities from this part of the world. Linked to a conference centre and used as an educational venue for local schoolchildren, the museum has installed computers in each display hall to provide in-depth information on the archaeological pieces displayed.

Segregated into separate interconnecting halls by subject matter and chronology (ie. Hall 1 gives a detailed explanation of the science of archaeology, while others contain artefacts dating back to 5,000 - 3,000 BC, 3,000 - 1,300 BC and 1,300 - 300 BC respectively), you are guided by a series of films explaining what is on display. A special area is also designated for seasonal display of all the latest discoveries from the various excavation sites in the emirate.

## Sharjah Islamic Museum

**09:00 - 13:00**
**17:00 - 20:00**

**Nr. Culture R/A**
**Sharjah**

Tel: **06 353 334**

Housed in a renovated 200 year-old structure, the Sharjah Islamic Museum displays an univalled collection of rare Islamic masterpieces and manuscripts, representing the cultural lifestyle of Muslims over a period of 1,400 years. Examples of Islamic arts and crafts such as crockery, ceramics, glass, metal work, and weapons are on show, in addition to gold and silver jewellery and textiles. There is also an impressive collection of scientific instruments.

## Sharjah Natural History Museum & Desert Park

09:00 - 20:00
Closed Sun

Junct-8
Sharjah - Daid Highway

Tel: **06 311 411**

Combining entertainment and learning in the most dynamic of atmospheres, the Sharjah Natural History Museum is located near Intersection 8, 25km outside Sharjah on the Dhaid highway.

Five main halls contain exhibits such as a 35 meter diorama of the UAE's natural habitats and wildlife; a stunning geological display with samples from all over the world - including the oldest rocks on the earth's surface; a hall showing the interactions between man and his environment - including the museum's best-known exhibit... a mechanical camel; a botanical hall with continuous video instruction on the flora of the Emirates, as well as descriptive picture windows onto the Wildflower Garden outside; and the marine hall where exact replicas of Gulf and Indian Ocean sea creatures can be seen as if from the bottom of the sea. Now also incorporating a Breeding Centre for endangered species - most famously, the Arabian Leopard, and a children's Petting Zoo, this museum is very much an interactive, hands-on experience. Great fun for all ages, a place you will want to visit time and time again.

Entry fee - Dhs.5 (children under 12 free) School classes by appointment.

## Sharjah Science Museum

09:00 - 14:00
16:30 - 20:30 Closed Fri am

Nr. Culture R/A
Sharjah

Tel: **06 514 777**

The Science Museum offers visitors hands-on exhibits and demonstration. 47 exhibits dealing with scientific subjects such as aerodynamics, light, colour and physiology, include demonstrations on electricity (which uses an 500,000 volts electrostatic generator), cryogenics (the study of super cold) and a planetarium. There's also contains a children's area where under five's and their parents can learn together. Trained staff available.

Those who become inspired to learn more about science can pursue their interest by booking a seat in the Learning Centre. This offers more in-depth programming on many of the topics presented in the museum, and includes a science lab, computer, technology lab, multi-media production centre, discovery area and a reference library. School groups welcome.

Admission: under 12 free, over 12 - Dhs.5, families - Dhs.15.

# Places to Visit



## Bastakiya

NA | Nr. Diwan - Bastakia, Bur Dubai | Page 7 B 3 | Tel: **NA**

This older part of the town has been restored in many parts so that all can view an early form of air conditioning in the shape of windtowers, built to catch breezes and funnel them down into the courtyard houses still found here. Amble down alleyways, step into two converted houses which now house art galleries, picture yourself living in a bygone era.

## Dubai Creek Front Wharfage

NA | Nr. Inter-Continental Hotel, Deira | Page 7 C 4 | Tel: **NA**

To get a real feel of old and new Dubai side by side, take a stroll along the Creek to experience the hustle and bustle of a myriad of traditional wooden dhows unloading their cargoes. Marvel at the trust which is evident from the piles of goods on the wharfage, and take in the incongruous sight of fruit, vegetables, electronics and even cars being offloaded from the same vessel. A real visual treat!.

## Dubai Zoo

10:00 - 19:00 | Al Jumeira Rd, Jumeira | Page 5 A 2 | Tel: **440 462**

It used to be a private collection of animals in a large garden but is now owned by the Municipality who charge Dhs.3 per person for admittance. An old fashioned type of zoo with caged lions, tigers, giraffe, monkeys, deer, snakes, bears, flamingoes, giant tortoise and other animals which are well looked after by Dr Rezi Khan, a dedicated Manager, and his well trained staff. Giant aviary with vultures, cranes, etc.

## Jumeira Mosque

NA | Opp Dubai Marine Beach Club, Al Jumeira Rd, Jumeira | Page 7 A 3 | Tel: **NA**

Turn on your television sets most evenings and this will be the well lit up mosque shown on your screen during the late evening prayer time. A beautiful, creative piece of architecture full of arches, sculptured details and points of interest. Situated two minutes walking distance from Spinneys supermarket on the Beach Road, definitely worth taking a photograph.

## Dubai World Trade Centre

NA | Sh Zayed Rd Za'beel | Page 9 A 2 | Tel: **NA**

This 39-storey tower, one of the tallest buildings in Dubai, hosts conferences and exhibitions, and houses the regional offices of many multinational companies.

Guided tours to the observation deck at the top are arranged twice a day. Charge for tours Dhs.5.

# Souks

## Deira Covered Souk

**08:00 - 13:00**
**16:00 - 21:00 Closed Fri am** | **Deira** | **Page 7 C 3** | Tel: **NA**

Walk from the gold souk to the spice souk and gaze into the small stone-built shops of Deira selling antiques and curios of the region. Cobblestone paths mix with mud and paving stones to give a traditional feel. Take any of the alleyways to stroll through specialised regions of trade i.e. pots and pans in one area, suitcases in another. The textile alleys are full of bright and inexpensive materials from India and the Far East.

## Deira Old Souk (Spice Souk)

**08:00 - 13:00**
**16:00 - 21:00 Closed Fri am** | **Deira** | **Page 7 B 2** | Tel: **NA**

A trader's paradise with shops selling goods in bulk for shipment or transportation to other Gulf countries. Many of the shops in this area look half closed with just a few items in the window, or on a table inside. That's all a trader needs to see for him to order dozens, hundreds or tonnes of the goods on offer. Commodities are grouped in areas, with rice and pulses being bought and sold in one area, stationery in another, textiles and clothing in a lane not far away. Between Al Nasr Square and the Creek area at the Gold Souk, i.e. most of Deira.

## Gold Souk

**08:00 - 13:00**
**16:00 - 21:00 Closed Fri am** | **Nr. Hyatt Regency Deira** | **Page 7 C 2** | Tel: **NA**

Dubai is famed for its gold shopping. Prices fluctuate with the daily international gold rate, with a little added for workmanship. Be sure to haggle to get the dealer's 'best price' as you are dazzled by the mind-boggling displays - none of which are less than 18 carat gold. Individual designs and pieces can be made within a week.

Take time to look up at the wooden covered walkway, erected to make shopping more bearable in the hot morning and afternoon sun, and wander through the mall and alleyways discovering antiques amongst the silver and gold on offer.

## Fish Market

**07:00 - 23:00** | **Nr. Hyatt Regency Hotel, Deira** | **Page 7, C 2** | Tel: **NA**

There are a few fish markets to visit with the biggest one being near the Shindagha Tunnel, opposite the Hyatt Regency hotel. Plenty of parking spaces. Don't wear your best shoes as there is a lot of water on the floor. Locally caught fish are a treat to view, a bit like going to a marine zoo. Baby sharks, blue lobsters from Fujairah, brown prawns from Iran, parrot fish, red snapper, pomfret and 5 ft long kingfish are the usual fare. Others such as cigalli and clams are available in season. Ask a wheelbarrow man to follow you round while you buy and he carries your shopping. Sild and sardines are sold by the 2 kilo weight.

Other markets are held at Deira, near Fort Museum, Karama, Hamriya and the newly built Deira indoor market near the Shindagha Tunnel.

## Fruit & Vegetable Market

**07:00 - 23:00** | **Nr. Hyatt Regency Hotel, Deira** | **Page 11, A 2** | Tel: **NA**

Where there's a fish souk there is also a fruit and vegetable souk, to help with planning a meal. Fresh produce sold by the kilo or more, you will often come across hoteliers and restaurateurs shopping for their evening customers. Everything is on view for inspection and the sellers will bargain with you for one kilo or ten kilos - a sale is a sale.

See produce from many countries - white headed cauliflower flown from Europe or a slightly yellower and cheaper version from local growers; imported bananas or small, extra sweet Omani ones; dates of varying tastes and colours; bitter gourd, prickly pear, aubergines, fresh peas in their pods, King Edward potatoes, watermelons... and much more. Also worth a visit is the wholesale market further down the coast towards Port Hamriya.

## Sharjah New Souk

**08:00 - 14:00**
**16:00 - 21:00 Closed Fri am** | **Nr. Corniche, Sharjah** | Tel: **NA**

Take your wide angle lens camera to get a photo of the outside of this beautiful traditional, but new looking building. Or buy a postcard of the view, it will be a dirham well spent. Consisting of two long buildings running parallel to each other and connected by a footbridge, Sharjah New Souk is a haven for bargain hunters. Upstairs is for antique furniture, traditional household items of a bygone era, rugs and carpets from surrounding countries, while downstairs you will find more modern items such as clothing, small electrical goods, gold jewellery and toys.

## Sharjah Old Souk

08:00 - 13:00
16:00 - 21:00 Closed Fri am

Nr. Bank St
Sharjah

Tel: **NA**

A whole area of restored shops and the former residence of the Al Naboodah family, has been restored using materials from the period such as corals, shells, African wood and palm leaves. The shops sell souvenirs, craftwork, spices, fabric, bundles of firewood, coffee pots and wedding chests.

## Textile Souk

08:00 - 13:00
16:00 - 21:00 Closed Fri am

Bur Dubai
Page 7
A 2

Tel: **NA**

Textiles galore. From printed and plain silk and linen, to cotton fabrics everywhere. Buy your material and then visit any of the nearby tailors with a photograph or sketch of the style you want - an option for both men and women.

Create your own, or have a favourite article copied "Same, same". Allow 3-5 days depending on whether the date is near to a seasonal holiday. Eid, Diwali and Christmas are popular and busy times for tailoring establishments.

# *Parks*

# Beach Parks

Parks and Gardens have been provided for all to enjoy, so please treat them with respect and leave them as you would wish to find them. Don't damage the plants, no pets or bikes are permitted and ball games can be played in the specified areas only. Many parks provide barbecue pits for cooking your meal but you must take your own wood or charcoal with you. All parks open at 08:00 and close over 12 hours later. Times vary.

Entrance to small parks are free, while larger ones charge Dhs.5 per person except for Jumeira Beach Park which costs Dhs.2 pp and Safa Park costs Dhs.3 pp.

## Al Mamzar Beach Park

08:00 - 22:00

Al Mamzar
Nr. Sharjah
Page 11
E 2

Tel: **682 527**

A very large park with barbecue sites, food kiosks, sheltered beaches and safe lagoons for swimming. Lots of children's play areas. Chalets can be privately hired for family convenience for Dhs.150 -200 depending on size. Wednesdays are for women and children only. Entrance fee is Dhs.5 per person; Dhs.30 per car, including all occupants. There is a swimming pool, plus lifeguards

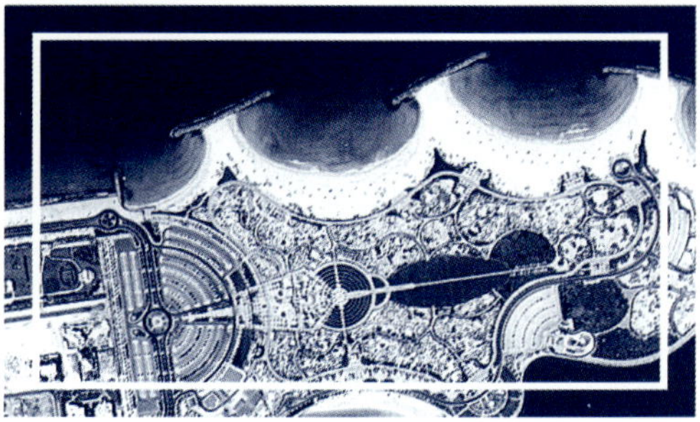

who patrol the beaches and pool area. Pool fees are Dhs.10 per adult and Dhs.5 per child, under 12's must be accompanied by an adult.

## Creekside Park

08:00 - 23:00 | Between Al Maktoum Al Garhoud Bridges | Page 14 A 1 | Tel: **369 082**

For only Dhs.5 entrance fee you can enjoy a day in the country with acres of lawn and botanic gardens as well as fishing piers, jogging tracks, barbecue sites, children's play parks, restaurants and kiosks. Situated between Al Maktoum and Al Garhoud Bridges, Bur Dubai side, with over two and a half kilometres of Creek frontage. Wednesday is for women and children only.

## Jumeira Beach Corniche

NA | Al Jumeira Rd Jumeira | Page 4 D 1 | Tel: **NA**

It is a bit like television's Baywatch programme with tourists soaking up the sun on this free beach, with its shaded picnic tables, showers and sheltered swimming area. A stroll along the promenade takes you to a paved jetty where fishermen like to try their luck with rod and line amongst the waves crashing on the breakwater.

## Jumeira Beach Park

08:00 - 22:00 | Al Jumeira Rd Jumeira | Page 4 D 1 | Tel: **443 245**

A well used park with established trees, gardens and lawns. Barbecue pits are available for public use, there are plenty hills to run up and down, and a volleyball area for ball games. Lifeguards are on duty along the beach frontage between 08:00 - 18:00. No swimming allowed after 18:00 and Saturdays and Sunday for women and children only. Entrance fee is Dhs.5 per person, Dhs.20 per car.

# Other Parks

## Mushrif Park

Sat-Wed 08:00 - 22:00
Thu-Fri 08:00 - 23:30 | Past Dubai Airport Direc. Al Khawaneej | Tel: **892 624**

A little out of town, but popular with families owing to its extensive grounds and unusual features including miniature houses from different countries which visitors can enter at will. Ask for times of the miniature train which tours the park regularly. Visit the camel and pony -ride area, swing or slide in the children's play areas. It costs Dhs.10 per adult to swim in the separate pools for men and women, Dhs.5 per child. Entrance fee to Mushrif Park is Dhs.2 per person, Dhs.10 per car.

## Safa Park

**Sat-Thu 08:00 - 22:30**
**Fri 07:30 - 23:30**
**Al Wasl Rd/Sh Zayed Rd**
**Jumeira**
**Page 4**
**C 3**
Tel: **445 428**

Drive down Al Wasl Road and look for the giant ferris wheel situated in a park opposite Jumeira Library - that's Safa Park. This big rectangular park has been artistically divided into sections and play areas to suit the nearby Jumeira residents. There is an electronic games parlour for teenagers, along with bumper cars, and the Big Wheel ride which operates at the weekend. It also has three tennis courts, volleyball, basketball and football pitches, a lake and waterfall, over 20 barbecue sites and lots of lawned grass to enjoy. And excellent obstacle course, is located near the tennis courts.

Although there is a jogging track within the grounds, lots of people also like to jog/walk around the outside perimeter of the park during the cooler hours of early morning and evening. Entrance fee is Dhs.3 per person, children under 3 year free.

# Libraries

## Archies Library

**10:00 - 14:00**
**17:00 - 22:00**
**Bottom Pyramid Building**
**Opp. Bur Juman, Al Karama**
**Page 9**
**E 1**
Tel: **365 402**

Twenty-seven thousand books! Yes, 27,000 all in English, and you don't have to buy a single one. Located in the Pyramid building opposite Bur Juman centre, this is a library with a difference. An annual membership fee of Dhs.75, and Dhs.100 deposit, entitles you to take any four books for 10 days. Depending on the book, reading charge varies between Dhs.1 - 4. Fiction, non-fiction, classics, cookery, health and fitness, management, and a vast selection of books and comics for children. Archies also caters to the magazine buffs, offering a wide selection of the latest issues.

With their ingenious and unique "Dial-a-book" service, books are delivered anywhere in the UAE for a mere Dhs.3 per delivery! This is an incredible place, and worth a visit.

## British Council

**Sat-Wed 10:00 - 13:00**
**Sat-Thu 16:00 - 18:00 Closed Fri**
**Nr. Maktoum**
**Bridge**
**Page 10**
**A 3**
Tel: **371 540**

The British Council is well known for its tutorial classes in English and exam subjects, as well as adult courses for businessmen and company employees. The library within the building is mainly used by the many students who attend these classes and courses, although others are welcome to join as library members only. The library service includes a general lending libary with particular emphasis on management and accountancy, a video library containing over 400 videos; a self access centre for students of English and CD ROM access for learning, as well as a substantial fiction section of both classics and modern literature. An annual membership fee of Dhs.175, entitles you to take any two books for two weeks.

## Dubai Lending Library

**10:00 - 13:00**
**16:00 - 18:00 Closed Fri**
**Dubai Arts Centre, Jumeira**
**Page 5, C 2**
Tel: **446 480**

The Dubai Lending Library is located in the grounds of the Dubai Arts Centre. Run by volunteers as a non-profit making service, they are always in need of new librarians especially during the summer months, so please volunteer if you would like to help. Members are issued tickets which they exchange for books. Any ticket not used must be retained by the member and not left in the library (particularly during vacations).

Annual Subscriptions : Family (may borrow five books at a time) Dhs.80. Single (may borrow two books at a time) Dhs.40. Children (may borrow two paperbacks) Dhs.20. Paperback (may borrow two paperbacks) Dhs.20. Half price for Arts Centre members.

## Public Library

**07:30 - 14:00**
**15:00 - 21:00 Closed Fri**
**Nr. St George Hotel, Deira**
**Page 7, B 2**
Tel: **262 788**

This Library was established in 1963 and is one of the oldest in the Gulf. It has an English and Arabic lending section, reading room for magazines and newspapers, plus a children's section. Books can be borrowed for two weeks at a time and there is a limit of two books per person.

Fees: Deposit Dhs.75 Children, Dhs.150 Adults (refundable), no lending fee.

# Beach Clubs

## Club Joumana

**08:30 - 22:00** | **Jebel Ali Hotel, Jebel Ali** | Tel: **836 000**

Drive slowly past the camels, reindeer, lama and, oh yes, horses in the stables on your way to this health club-with-a-few-distinct advantages. In addition to a gymnasium and sporting facilities, its situation in the spacious gardens of the Jebel Ali Hotel gives access to private beaches and jogging / cycling tracks, as well as to discounts offered at many of the food and beverage outlets. Full membership also allows reduced rates at the hotel's Shooting Club. Mooring fees in the club's private marina allows use of all facilities. Single day membership of Dhs.160 (peak) includes barbecue lunch. Entrance only is Dhs.80. Situated about half an hour's drive outside Dubai.

## Dubai International Marine Club

**08:00 - 21:00** | **Dubai International Marine Club, Al Mina Al Siyahi** | **Page 2 A 2** | Tel: **846 111**

DIMC is a rapidly growing beach club, with one of the biggest marinas in Dubai, together with a gymnasium and health spa equipped to the highest standards. Well used, but not crowded, the pool is nicely shaped and unusually paved.

Situated right next door is a small Barasti bar overlooking the length of the beach, which is approached by a boardwalk path. On weekends, a snack bar selling great pizzas and sandwiches is also open. A quiet terrace restaurant overlooking the marina in the main clubhouse area, serves buffets and a la carte menus. The club is actively involved in promoting sailing and fishing events, and hires out Hobie Catamarans (Dhs.100/hr), Ocean Kayaks (Dhs.30/half hr), Lasers (Dhs.75/hr), Boat charters (include skipper & water) for up to six people (Dhs.350/2 hr), Fishing charter (Dhs.700/half day) and a traditional Dhow.

DIMC hosts international championships such as Powerboat Racing. These occasions are usually family fun days out and include entertainment such as bouncy castle, exhibitions and music concerts, which are often televised. Entrance fee is Dhs.130 per person.

## Dubai Marine Beach Resort

**08:00 - 21:00** | **Dubai Marine Hotel, Bur Dubai** | **Page 7 A 3** | Tel: **441 221**

Open to the public after 18:00, most people see the club in the evenings due to its popular food outlets.

However, during the day it takes on a completely different atmosphere, with lounge chairs and sun worshippers dotted all around the cosy club. Green lawns, palm trees and a private beach. With a temperature-controlled outdoor swimming pool, paddling pool, small playground, floodlit tennis courts, squash courts plus billiard and table tennis room, the club also has a fully equipped gymnasium, sauna and massage room. Regular aerobic, circuit training, and aqua aerobic classes are conducted. See the schedule on the board.

Water-sport facilities (for members only) at a cost; Jet skiing (Dhs.75/30 mins), Aqua bikes, Banana rides (Dhs.15/ride), Water-skiing (Dhs.95/30 mins), Windsurfer (Dhs.70/30 min, Dhs.95 /1hr).

1998 will see the opening of both male and female Health Spas offering sauna, steam room, spa bath,plunge pool, relaxation room, and treatment rooms. The treatments will include a combination of skin, body, and lifestyle treatments including aromatheraphy, pressure point massage, holistic aromatherapy, full body massage, skin rejuvenation for all skin types, detoxifying algae wraps, as well as the more popular beauty treatments.

## Forte Grand - Jumeira Beach

**08:00 - 21:30** | **Forte Grand - Jumeira Beach, Al Mina Al Siyahi** | **Page 1 E 2** | Tel: **845 555**

Club membership entitles members to unrestricted use of the outdoor facilities which includes swimming pool, beach and mini golf course. Large undulating swimming pool has swim up bar at one end. Fun pool. Palm trees, waiter service and generous Friday barbeque makes this a luxury holiday- type club. Members are mainly hotel guests and long term residents of the city. Entrance fee Dhs.60 non-peak, Dhs.75 peak.

## Hilton Beach Club

**07:00 - 22:00** | **Al Jumeira Rd, Jumeira** | **Page 4 D 1** | Tel: **445 333**

An oasis of relaxation for business and leisure travellers, private members and Hilton hotel guests, this luxury resort consists of 48 uniquly decorated junior suites and two 2-bedroom suites. There are jacuzzis in all suites, which also feature private balconies and patios and are surrounded by landscaped gardens and streams.

Extensive leisure facilities with seven tennis courts, three squash courts, steam room, sauna, waterslides, gymnasium and two swimming pools. There is a choice of Prasino's restaurant for Mediterranean dishes and Sails restaurant offering international cuisine all day. Meeting facilities are available for up to 40 and the club is often used for private and corporate parties, with international entertainers flown in for the occasion. Water-sports include Jet skiing (Dhs.200/hr), Windsurfing (Dhs.60/hr), Water-skiing (Dhs.100/20 mins), sailing, snorkelling, aqua bikes. Entrance fee is Dhs.80 (non-members), fees for aerobic-classes are Dhs.25 (Dhs.30).

## Jazira Beach Resort

**09:00 - 23:00** | **Jazira Beach Resort & Hotel, Direction Abu Dhabi** | Tel: **02 562 9100**

If you are prepared to travel just that little bit further (65km), or just want to get out of Dubai for some peace and quiet, then this could be the ideal club to join. Good health club facilities which include tennis courts, squash courts, nine holes of crazy golf and a gymnasium with well maintained equipment. There is a small private beach bordering a man-made canal that is ideal for all water-sports such as jet skiing, windsurfing, sailing etc. as there's no problem with tides and surf. For those wishing to venture out to sea, speed-boat trips are available to take you the 6 km distance to the sea itself. Fishing trips are also possible.

Windsurfing (Dhs.50/hour), Laser or Hobie Cat sailing (Dhs.50/hr), Water-skiing (Dhs.25/hr for 10 minutes). Entrance fee Dhs.30 (Dhs.50 non-members).

## Jumeira Health & Beach Club, The

07:00 - 22:00 | Radisson SAS Jumeira, Al Mina Al Siyahi | Page 1 D 2 | Tel: **845 533**

The Jumeira Health & Beach Club is located 26km south of Dubai at the Radisson SAS Hotel. It is open to Hotel guests and an outside membership limited to 100 persons. The gymnasium is equipped with treadmills, bicycles, rowing machines, mountain climbers and a fair selection of Cybex training equipment. There is a great view over the sea during the day, but it lacks a little atmosphere, reflecting the fact it is part of a hotel, rather than a private club. Club members also have complimentary use of two squash courts, two floodlit tennis courts, a state-of-the-art golf simulator, and the pool and beach area.

The on-site Al Boom sports shop offers a good selection of water-sport equipment for hire at an additional reasonable cost. Entrance fee Dhs.50.

## Metropolitan Beach Club

08:00 - 20:00 | Metropolitan R. & Beach Club, Al Mina Al Siyah | Page 1 E 2 | Tel: **845 000**

Sun, sand and sea. The Metropolitan Beach Hotel exudes a holiday feeling that is relaxed to an almost languid and sleepy extreme and is reflected in its facilities. The sports amenities of gym and tennis courts are basic additions to the main attractions of pool and beach!

The huge mushroom-shaped swimming pool with swim up-to bar complements the pretty stretch of beach for sunbathing. Water-sports such as jet ski, water skiing, windsurfing, and charter fishing, which are available at additional cost. This family/holiday-maker beach club offers a refreshingly mellow and "laid back" environment in which to wind down and relax. Entrance is restriced to members only.

## Umm Al Quwain Tourist Club

08:00 - 24:00 | On the Coast, Umm Al Quwain | Tel: **06 651 185**

Under new management with big plans! This is one of the most laid back clubs in the UAE. A very unspoilt, unpretentious club during the week, there is a small beach, grassy area, new swimming pool and even a place to play boules. A small, busy bar offers excellent and cheap food. Situated near the lagoons of UAQ, this club offers some of the best and most interesting sailing within the Northern Emirates. Pink flamingos, jumping fish, mangrove swamps, deserted islands (unfortunately littered with blue plastic bags and suchlike).

The club offers water-skiing at Dhs.80 per half hour, with an ex Tuk-Tuk driver from Bangkok behind the boat wheel, lethal but fun. An excellent barbecue on Friday for Dhs.35, and the best Fish and Chips in the Emirates. Plenty of equipment to rent, from catamarans, to jet ski, water-skiing, glass bottom boat and windsurfers. Dhs.20 entrance.

# Health Clubs

## Athena

08:00 - 23:00 | Sheraton Deira, Deira | Page 11, A 3 | Tel: **688 888**

Located on the 5th floor of the newly opened Sheraton Deira this cosy health club caters mainly for adults, offering only single and couple membership rates. The intimate atmosphere is perfect for "getting on with getting fit".

Facilities include a gymnasium complete with the latest Nautilus equipment, a masseur is on hand at all times to help you loosen up after your work-out, he also doubles as an instructor in the gym if you require any guidance. Sauna, steam room and plunge pool are shared by men and women, however if Ladies would like a little more privacy, its Ladies only from 10:00 to 13:00 on weekdays. To top off an all over relaxing experience dive into the kidney-shaped roof top swimming pool and jacuzzi to cool off, or sit back and enjoy a healthy snack and a cold beverage from the room service menu.

Non-members are also welcomed at any time. Membership fees are a little steep for the facilities offered but you will none the less enjoy a work-out here, with the help of some very friendly staff and all the latest equipment.

## Aviation Club, The

08:00 - 23:00 | Aviation Club, The, Al Garhoud | Page 14, C 3 | Tel: **824 122**

The health club here has a sense of exclusivity and luxury. The changing room area has a variety of facilities including sauna and plunge bath, massage, steam room and a relaxing sun lounger area. Large screen TV's are everywhere, including the sauna and the locker rooms!

The state-of-the-art glass fronted gymnasium overlooks a swimming pool and landscaped gardens. An elegant snooker room is furnished with traditional leather couches and low lighting. There are squash courts and a par three golf course, but the most popular sports facilities are provided by the five international standard, floodlit, deco-turf tennis courts.

## Body Lines Leisure & Fitness Club

07:00 - 22:00 | Al Bustan Rotana Hotel, Al Garhoud | Page 14, E 3 | Tel: **828 100**

Here we have a health club that caters to your every need in both fitness and relaxation. Located in the newly opened Al Bustan Hotel, it offers a glass fronted gymnasium complete with the latest Nautilus equipment, aerobics studio with classes available throughout the day and evening, sauna, Turkish steam room, massage rooms, plunge pool, squash courts, flood-lit tennis courts, outdoor jacuzzi, temperature controlled swimming pool and children's pool, as well as child minding facilities and a grassed play area.

A full time qualified instructor is on hand to offer guidance and instruction when needed. Enjoy the after-fitness by relaxing in the lounge or around the pool, and enjoy a healthy treat at the snack bar which has been fitted out with knick-knacks from the local souks, giving a friendly atmosphere.

Reasonable membership fees for the facilities available and surroundings are designed to provide you with a totally enjoyable health experience. Underground parking and a separate entrance to the club, are an added bonus.

## Club Olympus

07:00 - 22:00 | **Hyatt Regency Hotel Deira** | **Page 7 D 2** | Tel: **706 4841**

You'll have to take a lift to get to this second floor sport and health club. Outside is a refreshing swimming pool surrounded by Roman style pillars, terracotta pots and flagstones on a patio courtyard overlooking the sea. There is also a bar and three floodlit tennis courts. Tightly squeezed in around the courts is a fitness training circuit. On the other side of the hotel are two backed squash courts and a sun deck.

Inside, the modern gymnasium is packed with weight lifting equipment, running machines, exercise bikes, etc. and staff that can advise you on a personal regime. Sauna, jacuzzi and steam bath for men and women, and an exercise room provides evening aerobic sessions.

## Griffins Health Club

06:30 - 23:00 | **JW Marriott Hotel Deira** | **Page 11 A 3** | Tel: **624 444**

Located at the top of the J.W. Marriott Hotel, Griffins offers the full range of activities and facilities expected from a five-star hotel, including Planet Cardio, the latest in exercise entertainment, a separate weight resistance gym, two squash courts, separate male and female sauna, steam and jacuzzi, and a picturesque roof- top swimming pool.

Besides the aerobic classes, swimming lessons and squash coaching, you can opt for an incredibly relaxing Chinese massage provided by the two highly qualified Chinese masseurs Jing Jing and Dong Dong. Relying solely on thumbs, hands and feet to control 364 acupressure points on the body, the experts claim the effects are amazing.

## Gym 2000

08:00 - 22:00 | **Dubai Creek Golf & Yacht Club Al Garhoud** | **Page 14 C 2** | Tel: **821 000**

As you would expect given its location, this gym is equipped with all the latest hi-tech cardiovascular machines, which are complemented with modular weight stations and free

weights. Large, luxurious changing rooms shared with the golfers, all with personalised wooden lockers, and complimentary toiletries provided.

The gym itself is fairly small but includes some unique equipment such as a Skywalker and Treadwall - a rotating climbing wall, with varying speeds and slope angles. Professional supervision is encouraged with personalised three, six and nine month fitness programs. All programs include one free fitness consultation and a six week exercise program.

Entrance fees for classes are Dhs.20 (members), Dhs.25 (non-members).

## Hiltonia Fitness Centre

07:00 - 22:00 | Hilton Hotel, Sh Zayed Rd/Trade Centre | Page 9, A 2 | Tel: **306 1139**

This well-equipped club is situated within a single storey outpost of the hotel. Park the car and walk straight through to the reception area, where staff are friendly and informative - no need to enter the main hotel at all. A busy club with many serious fitness enthusiasts, mostly Europeans. Classes are varied, popular and usually full, led by professional instructors. Exercise is the name of the game. A nearby hairdresser is a plus.

## Inter-Fitness

07:00 - 22:00 | Inter-Continental Hotel, Deira | Page 7, C 4 | Tel: **227 171**

Located on the first floor of the hotel, the club encompasses a sun lounging area overlooking the Creek, a swimming pool, a snack bar/cafe terrace decked out in wooden veranda style, and a flood-lit tennis court. In the actual health club itself are two squash courts, a gymnasium, which is open 24-hrs a day, and spa centre. The gymnasium has Universal equipment and there are regular aerobic sessions (check notice board). Completely separated and quite novel in its furnishing is the relaxation room, with comfortable chairs and couches, newspapers, magazines and a TV. The small changing room leads into the spa centre which is divided by timings and days for men and women. It also has a steam room, sauna with unusual windows, and plunge pool.

## Le Mirage

06:30 - 21:30 | Forte Grand Dubai, Al Garhoud | Page 14, E 3 | Tel: **824 040**

A large club with many facilities, the reception is very friendly and the club seems to have a large staff. The modern, state-of-the-art gym attracts customers and the nearby pool is refreshing and an interesting shape. Choose your own exercise routine and devise your own aerobic movements.

## Nautilus Fitness Centre

08:30 - 21:30 | Holiday Inn Crowne Plaza, Trade Centre / SH Zayed Rd | Page 8, D 2 | Tel: **314 055**

Nautilus Fitness Centre is located in the hotel on the floor above the Lobby, next to the coffee and fruit juice outlet. The centre has two squash courts, a medium-sized, mirrored exercise class area, a gym and a sauna in the changing rooms. Re-bounder, Aeroblast,

Super Circuit, Step Pump, Step & Tone and Total Body Work Out classes are held for both men and women. The modern, well-maintained gym is full of weight and cardio vascular equipment. There is always someone available to demonstrate the equipment to newcomers and it is best to make an appointment to be guided through the most suitable workout for you. Very reasonable membership fees. For office workers along the Abu Dhabi highway this offers a healthy way to spend your lunch time. Although not very big, the range of exercise options available is extensive.

## Nautilus Health Centre

`Dec 1997 | Metropolitan Palace, Deira | Page 10, D 2 | Tel: **270 000**

Located in the new Metropolitan Palace Hotel, this will include state-of- the-art Nautilus fitness equipment for the best work out for health conscious executives! A roof-top pool to enjoy Dubai's climate, jacuzzis and saunas for five star relaxing.

## Peak, The

07:00 - 21:00 | Princeton Hotel, Al Garhoud | Page 14, D 2 | Tel: **827 777**

A small and quiet club providing a fully equipped gym and swimming pool. The club attracts UAE nationals and businessmen which form its small membership, but it caters in the main, to hotel guests. Outsiders can enjoy the facilities for Dhs.50 per day. Thirteen pieces of exercise equipment does not leave much floor space in this triangular shaped gym, with plenty of mirrors to ensure you can't cheat. Exercise bikes, weights, treadmill, etc. Most of the usual equipment that keep-fit enthusiasts like. Sauna room next door. Nearby roof-top swimming pool and jacuzzi.

## Profiles

07:00 - 22:00 | Imperial Residence, Bur Dubai | Page 9, E 1 | Tel: **553 555**

Profiles is a well equipped center where all fitness needs are looked after. The gym is equipped with a full range of cardiovascular machines with computer displays and resistance training equipment. Includes three treadmills, two cycles, two step climbers, one rowing machine and 12 other fixed stations. The indoor swimming pool is temperature controlled and initial assessment, supervision of work-outs and guidance is available from the fitness consultant, who is also a doctor in Naturopathy, yoga and physical culture. Classes are available on Mondays, Wednesdays, Saturdays. Sauna and shower rooms.

## Pyramid Health Spa, The

`Jan 1988 | Wafi Shopping Mall, Creekside Park | Page 13, D 2 | Tel: **354 757**

A new health club opening shortly, will also include a luxurious health spa similar to those found in the Far East! Watch out for this exciting development.

# Sport Clubs

## Dubai Country Club

08:00 - 24:00 | Nr. Country Club R/A, Nadd Al Shiba | Page 12, B 3 | Tel: **331 155**

If you are looking for a club that caters for all your family's needs, join the Country Club. Sports facilities are excellent with plenty of tennis, squash courts and a fully fitted gym. The notice boards are full of clubs to interest all age groups and all levels of fitness, from circuit training to aqua aerobics. The golf club boasts the best sand course in the Emirates. There is a large pool area with plenty of sun loungers, shaded children's play areas and ball parks for toddlers.

The club has two fine restuarants, The Wind Tower, and the Oasis. Entrance fees for members and non-members depend on the activity required.

## Sharjah Wanderers Sports Club

08:00 - 23:00 | Sharjah | Tel: **06 357 505**

This is an extremely popular club, with lots of acitivity and a lot on offer. The club has a typical university sports club atmosphere, slightly run down, but well used. It has two floodlit tennis courts, two squash courts, floodlit football, rugby and hockey pitch swimming pool, gymnasium and snooker room. The pool is also used for their sub-aqua diving courses, which come complete with their own lecture factilities and compressor room.

It has two restaurants, a coffee shop and a poolside kitchen offering a wide section of food and refreshments.

It also has an 18-hole grassed golf course with food and beverage facilities and a resident golf pro for individual or group lessons.

## See Also:


Al Nasr Leisureland
Darjeeling Cricket Club
Dubai Offshore Sailing Club
Dubai Water Sports Association
Jebel Ali Sailing Club
Jebel Ali Shooting Club
Sandy Beach Diving Centre
UAQ Marine Club & Riding Centre

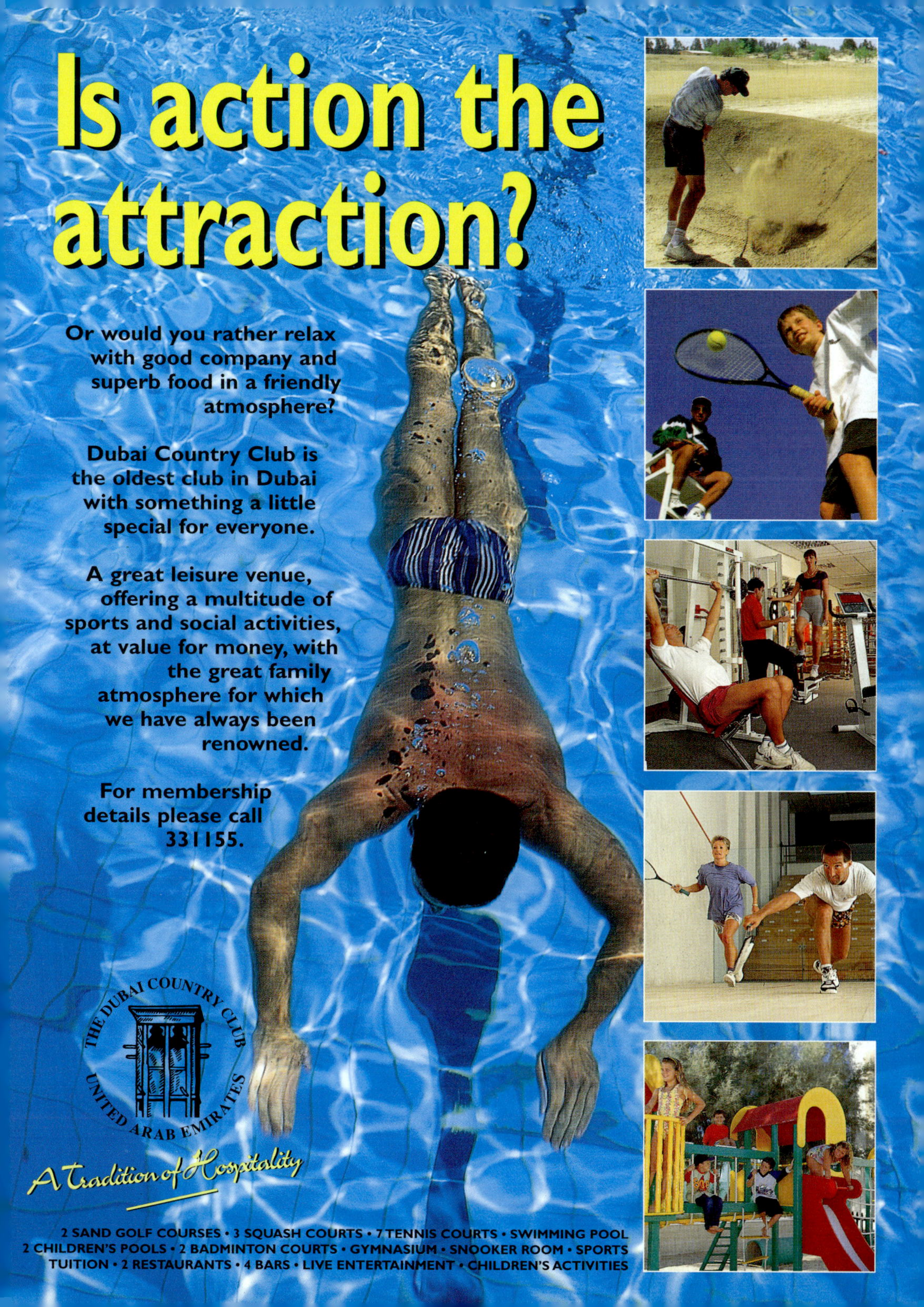
Is action the attraction?
Or would you rather relax with good company and superb food in a friendly atmosphere?
Dubai Country Club is the oldest club in Dubai with something a little special for everyone.
A great leisure venue, offering a multitude of sports and social activities, at value for money, with the great family atmosphere for which we have always been renowned.
For membership details please call 331155.
THE DUBAI COUNTRY CLUB
UNITED ARAB EMIRATES
A Tradition of Hospitality
2 SAND GOLF COURSES • 3 SQUASH COURTS • 7 TENNIS COURTS • SWIMMING POOL
2 CHILDREN'S POOLS • 2 BADMINTON COURTS • GYMNASIUM • SNOOKER ROOM • SPORTS
TUITION • 2 RESTAURANTS • 4 BARS • LIVE ENTERTAINMENT • CHILDREN'S ACTIVITIES

# Membership Details

| | Joining Fees | | | | Annual Fees | | | |
|---|---|---|---|---|---|---|---|---|
| **Beach Clubs** | Male | Female | Couple | Family | Male | Female | Couple | Family |
| **Club Joumana** | | | | | | | | |
| Full Membership | 800 | 500 | 1,300 | 1,300 | 2,200 | 1,500 | 3,700 | 3,700 |
| **Dubai Int. Marine Club** | | | | | | | | |
| Full Membership | 1,500 | 1,500 | 1,500 | 1,500 | 3,500 | 3,200 | 4,500 | 4,500 |
| **Dubai Marine Resort** | | | | | | | | |
| Full Membership | 1,700 | 1,200 | NA | 1,950 | 3,000 | 2,500 | NA | 4,250 |
| **Forte Grand - Jumeira** | | | | | | | | |
| Full Membership | NA | NA | NA | NA | 4,500 | 4,500 | 6,000 | NA |
| Sports & Leisure Club | NA | NA | NA | NA | 4,500 | 4,500 | 6,000 | NA |
| **Hilton Beach Club** | | | | | | | | |
| Full Membership | 3,000 | 3,000 | 3,250 | 3,750 | 6,000 | 6,000 | 8,000 | 9,500 |
| **Jazira Beach Resort** | | | | | | | | |
| Full Membership | NA | NA | NA | NA | 1,300 | 1,300 | 1,800 | 2,250 |
| Membership (6 months) | NA | NA | NA | NA | 850 | 850 | 1,000 | 1,275 |
| **Jumeira Beach Club** | | | | | | | | |
| Full Membership | 1,000 | 1,000 | 1,500 | 1,500 | 3,500 | 3,500 | 4,600 | 5,300 |
| **Metropolitan Resort** | | | | | | | | |
| Full Membership | NA | NA | NA | NA | 5,500 | 4,400 | NA | 7,500 |
| **UAQ Tourist Club** | | | | | | | | |
| Full Membership | NA | NA | NA | NA | 600 | 600 | 1,000 | 1,000 |
| **Golf Clubs** | | | | | | | | |
| **Dubai Creek Golf & Yacht Club** | | | | | | | | |
| Golf Membership | 4,000 | 4,000 | NA | NA | 5,000 | 13,500 | 13,500 | 16,500 |
| Social Membership | 4,000 | 4,000 | NA | NA | 5,000 | 6,000 | 6,000 | 9,000 |
| **Dubai Golf & Racing Club** | | | | | | | | |
| Golf Membership | 3,000 | 3,000 | NA | 4,000 | 8,500 | 8,500 | NA | 11,500 |
| Social Membership | 500 | 500 | NA | 500 | 1,000 | 1,000 | NA | 3,000 |
| **Emirates Golf Club** | | | | | | | | |
| Golf Membership | 5,500 | 5,500 | NA | 5500 | 12,000 | 9,000 | NA | 16,500 |
| Sports Membership | NA | NA | NA | NA | 4,500 | 3,750 | NA | 6,000 |
| **Sharjah Wanderers Golf Club** | | | | | | | | |
| Full Membership | NA | NA | NA | NA | 1,800 | 1,200 | 2,200 | NA |

| | Joining Fees | | | | Annual Fees | | | |
|---|---|---|---|---|---|---|---|---|
| **Health Clubs** | Male | Female | Couple | Family | Male | Female | Couple | Family |
| **Athena** | | | | | | | | |
| Full Membership | 500 | 500 | 500 | NA | 2,000 | 2,000 | 3,000 | NA |
| **Aviation Club, The** | | | | | | | | |
| Full Membership | 5,000 | 3,750 | 5,000 | 5,000 | 5,000 | 3,750 | 7,500 | 7,500 |
| **Body Lines** | | | | | | | | |
| Full Membership | NA | NA | NA | NA | 3,000 | 2,500 | 4,000 | 4,500 |
| **Club Olympus** | | | | | | | | |
| Full Membership | 1,000 | 1,000 | 1,000 | NA | 3,500 | 2,200 | 5,000 | NA |
| **Griffins Health Club** | | | | | | | | |
| Full Membership - Peak | 750 | 750 | 1,000 | NA | 3,000 | 2,250 | 4,500 | NA |
| Full Membership - Off Peak | 750 | 750 | 1,000 | NA | 1,800 | 1,350 | 2,700 | NA |
| **Gym 2000** | | | | | | | | |
| Full Membership (9 month) | NA | NA | NA | NA | 3,240 | 3,240 | 6,480 | NA |
| **Hiltonia Fitness Centre** | | | | | | | | |
| Full Membership | NA | NA | NA | NA | 2,670 | 2,670 | 4,200 | NA |
| Swimming Pool Membership | NA | NA | NA | NA | 1,735 | 1,735 | NA | NA |
| **Inter-Fitness** | | | | | | | | |
| Full Membership | NA | NA | NA | NA | 3,700 | 3,000 | 5,000 | 5,000 |
| **Le Mirage** | | | | | | | | |
| Gold Card Membership | NA | NA | NA | NA | 2,900 | 2,000 | 3,900 | NA |
| Silver Card Membership | NA | NA | NA | NA | 1,800 | 1,300 | 2,500 | NA |
| **Nautilus Fitness Centre** | | | | | | | | |
| Health & Squash | NA | NA | NA | NA | 2,100 | 2,100 | 3,550 | NA |
| Full Membership | NA | NA | NA | NA | 2,950 | 2,950 | 4,300 | NA |
| **Peak, The** | NA | NA | NA | NA | 2,000 | 1,500 | 3,000 | NA |
| **Profile Fitness Centre** | NA | NA | NA | NA | 1,900 | 1,900 | 2,900 | NA |
| **Sport Clubs** | | | | | | | | |
| **Al Nasr Leisureland** | | | | | | | | |
| Tennis Membership | NA | NA | NA | NA | 1,000 | 1,000 | NA | NA |
| Bowling/Squash.. Membership | NA | NA | NA | NA | 1,000 | 800 | 1,600 | NA |
| **Dubai Country Club** | | | | | | | | |
| Annual Membership | NA | NA | NA | NA | 3,150 | 2,100 | NA | 5,250 |
| Ordinary Membership | 2,000 | 500 | NA | 2,500 | 2,200 | 1,750 | NA | 3,800 |
| Country Membership | 1,000 | 500 | NA | 1,500 | 1,300 | 1,200 | NA | 2,100 |
| **Sharjah Wanders Club** | | | | | | | | |
| Full Membership | 500 | 500 | NA | 800 | 740 | 740 | NA | 1,300 |

# Facility Summary

## Beach Clubs

| Beach Clubs | Tennis | Squash | Pools | Sauna | Jacuzzi | Steam | Plunge | Aerobic | Massage |
|---|---|---|---|---|---|---|---|---|---|
| Club Joumana | 4 | 2 | 1 | • | - | - | - | - | - |
| Dubai Int. Marine Club | - | - | 1 | • | — | • | — | • | - |
| Dubai Marine Beach Resort | 2 | 2 | 1 | — | - | — | - | - | - |
| Forte Grand - Jumeira Beach | 2 | 2 | 2 | • | • | • | - | - | • |
| Hilton Beach Club | 7 | 3 | 2 | • | • | • | - | • | • |
| Jazira Beach Resort & Hotel | 2 | 1 | 1 | • | • | • | • | - | - |
| Jumeira Health & Beach Club, The | 2 | 2 | 1 | • | — | • | - | • | • |
| Metropolitan Resort & Beach Club | 3 | 2 | 1 | • | • | • | - | • | • |
| Umm Al Qwain Tourist Club | - | - | - | - | - | - | - | - | - |

## Golf Clubs

| Golf Clubs | Tennis | Squash | Pools | Sauna | Jacuzzi | Steam | Plunge | Aerobic | Massage |
|---|---|---|---|---|---|---|---|---|---|
| Dubai Creek Golf & Yacht Club | 4 | - | 1 | • | - | • | • | • | - |
| Dubai Golf & Racing Club | - | - | - | - | - | - | - | - | - |
| Emirates Golf Club | 6 | 2 | 1 | • | - | - | - | • | • |
| Sharjah Wanderers Golf Club | - | - | 1 | - | - | - | - | - | - |

## Health Clubs

| Health Clubs | Tennis | Squash | Pools | Sauna | Jacuzzi | Steam | Plunge | Aerobic | Massage |
|---|---|---|---|---|---|---|---|---|---|
| Athena | - | - | 1 | • | • | • | • | - | • |
| Aviation Club, The | 6 | 2 | 1 | • | • | • | • | • | • |
| Body Lines Leisure & Fitness Club | 3 | 2 | 1 | • | - | • | - | • | • |
| Club Olympus | 3 | 2 | 1 | • | • | • | • | • | • |
| Griffins Health Club | - | 2 | 1 | • | • | • | • | • | • |
| Gym 2000 | 4 | - | 1 | - | - | - | - | • | - |
| Hiltonia Fitness Centre | - | 1 | 1 | • | - | - | - | • | • |
| Inter-Fitness | 1 | 2 | 1 | • | • | • | • | • | • |
| Le Mirage | 6 | 2 | 1 | • | • | • | • | • | • |
| Nautilus Fitness Centre | 2 | 2 | 1 | • | • | • | - | • | • |
| Nautilus Health Centre | | | | | | | | | |
| Peak, The | - | - | 1 | • | • | - | - | - | - |
| Profile Fitness Centre | - | - | 1 | • | - | - | - | - | - |
| Pyramid Healthspa, The | - | - | 1 | • | • | • | - | - | - |

## Sport Clubs

| Sport Clubs | Tennis | Squash | Pools | Sauna | Jacuzzi | Steam | Plunge | Aerobic | Massage |
|---|---|---|---|---|---|---|---|---|---|
| Al Nasr Leisureland | 4 | 5 | 1 | • | - | - | - | - | - |
| Dubai Country Club | 6 | 3 | 3 | - | - | - | - | • | - |
| Sharjah Wanderers Sports Club | 2 | 2 | 1 | — | — | — | - | - | - |

# Beauty Salons

## Clarins Studio

07:00 - 23:00
Closed Fri

Hyatt Regency Hotel
Deira

Page 7
D 2

Tel: **706 4844**

The Clarins Studio emulates the standards and professionalism of Clarins Studios in Paris and London. All staff are Clarins trained and the studio provides clients with a full range of consultancy, products and treatments, while an intimate atmosphere reassures clients of complete privacy at all times. Full body treatments, the Clarins Paris Method Facial, bridal grooming and make-up tuition are all available. The studio is a fully operational beauty salon and offers manicure, pedicure and waxing treatments.

## Golden Salon

09:00 - 19:30
Sat - Thu

Al Karama

Page 9
C 3

Tel: **359 475**

This British run salon is set on two floors packed with every conceivable treatment for hair, face and body. All UK staff, each a specialist in her field, offer treatments that include cutting edge hair design from London, a hair extension technician with nine years experience and the latest micro current non surgical facelift. For those wishing to trim or tone the body, non-surgical body lifts and anti-cellulite treatment are available, and the newly arrived, high powered sunbed from the UK make this salon the one stop beauty shop in Dubai. A truly relaxing experience at a price that will pleasantly surprise you. Detailed free consultations available on all treatments. Situated between Zabeel and Karama, near Karama Fish Market and close to Lamcy Plaza. Plenty of car parking.

## Hair Corridor

08:30 - 18:30 Sat-Tue, Thu
08:30 - 20:00 Wed

Al Wasl Rd
Jumeira

Page 4
B 3

Tel: **385 622**

A full complement of British staff, Redken hair products and a hygienic professional approach to beauty treatments, set the Hair Corridor apart from the rest. Redkens "probe" computerised hair analysis system analyses hair structure, giving a complete picture of strengths, weaknesses and perming potential when required. Experience the full range of luxurious body treatments from pedicure to head massage, ensuring you always look and feel your best. Call for an appointment!

## Jolie Beauty Salon

08:30 - 18:30 Sat-Tue
08:30 - 19:00 Wed-Thu

Al Dhiyafah Rd
Al Satwa

Page 6
A 3

Tel: **459 666**

Manned by highly trained and well experienced Vidal Sasson, Toni and Guy of London trained stylists and UK qualified beauty therapist. Call or visit for the most updated styles and beauty treatments, at affordable prices. Quality products such as Tigi, Joico, L'Oreal, Schwarzkopf, Decleor and Sothys used.

Salon's ambience is comfortable, soothing and totally assuring.

## L'Esprit Beaute

09:00 - 22:00
Closed Fri

Al Dhiyafah Centre
Deira

Page 6
A 4

Tel: **456 369**

A highly trained team of experienced beauty therapists provide personal consultations in all aspects of body and skin care. First class treatments on offer include: Surogenic Therapy for facial lifting and toning; Soft laser treatment of scar tissue, wrinkles etc.; Cathiodermie and Colagen Therapy; AHA treatments; and selective slimming and anti-cellulite treatments, unmatched in the region. Other services include hair removal by needle-free, Transdermal electrolysis. Call for an appointment.

## Lobelia

08:00 - 19:00

Jumeira Plaza
Jumeira

Page 5
C 2

Tel: **492 600**

Lobelia is the "King of natural" - one of the only places which combines beauty salon and health club in Dubai. Very quiet and relaxing atmosphere as soon as you pass the doors. Everything you need in terms of health treatment is available - body and facial cares, gymnastics for everyone, personal diet... This is a place for you as long as you " Love the natural". Quiet a selective place in terms of prices (a little expensive).

## Marie France

08:30 - 18:30
Closed Fri

Magrudy Shopping Mall
Jumeira

Page 5
C 2

Tel: **448 739**

Whether you want to trim the fat, or have it trimmed for you, this salon with its toning tables and 12 cubicles will have a treatment suitable for the occasion. It also has specific treatments available for anti-ageing; with AHA creams and deeplift treatments using French products.

The pretty pink salon has 12 cabins covering all aspects of facial & body treatments, manicure, pedicure, waxing, eyelash, anti-ageing facials, specific facials for trouble skins, make up, body massage, body scrub, G5, heat therapy, passive stimulation etc. Troubled by unwanted hair? They have recently introduced the 'Dermal Pen' electrolysis system, which replaces the needle with a cotton tip. A permanent pain-free electrolysis. The products used are French, Sothys, which have proved over the years to perform beautifully in the harsh Gulf climate. Prices are very competitive and the salon has a peaceful ambience of professionalism and definite French charm.

Established in 1977 this was the first professional salon to open in Dubai. Staff are qualified beauticians from Europe and India.

## Reflection Beauty Care

09:00 - 18:00
Closed Fri am

Al Wasl Rd
Jumeira

Page 3
E 3

Tel: 487 272

Relax and enjoy the latest in quality hair and beauty treatments, by placing yourself in the hands of highly qualified British professionals, who will ensure you receive the very best personal services. Treatments include CACI non-surgical face lifts, advanced face and body treatments, Jessica's unique manicures and pedicures, aromatherapy, JOICO's advanced colours, perms and treatments and much more. Experience the difference!

## Regis Hair & Beauty

10:00 - 22:00

Lamcy Plaza
Al Karama

Page 9
D 4

Tel: 351 101

We all love to be pampered and one-to-one attention is exactly what Regis aims to offer for both men and women, but with the convenience of being located in a department store. With over 3,000 salons Regis is the largest hair and beauty group in the world. Customer care and the highest quality of services at affordable prices are paramount.

In the new Beauty Centre, treatments are given in private cabins with ensuite shower room for privacy. Relax with a facial treatment, aromatherapy body massages, or a luxury manicure and pedicure. Also offers hair cutting, colouring and perming. In our Barber Shop, men can also experience luxurious hair and grooming services which include scalp and body massages, facials, manicures and pedicures.

## Sasha Beauty Salon

10:00 - 20:00

Nr. Holiday Inn Crowne Plaza
Sh Zayed Rd/Trade Centre

Page 8
C 2

Tel: 444 131

A hair and Beauty Salon with highly trained therapist and hairdressers offering quality services from top to toe. Hairdresse,r Melanie, has worked in USA where she practised modern techniques in colouring, perming and hair cutting. She is backed by Katie who has experience in the local market. A ninety minute program is available with a trained professional, for a Matis facial to sort out skin problems. The therapist will advise you on day to day skin care and product use. Or try the one hour massage which helps in reducing tension and cellulite and improving circulation. Recongnize the 'Art of Natural Healing' with aromatherapy and reflexology. Range of beauty treatments also includes waxing, head oil massage, eyelash /eyebrow tint, threading, hair straightening and Acrylic Nail tips. Open daily for appointments.

## Science & Beaute Centre

09:30 - 18:30
Sat - Thu

Opp. Holiday Inn Crowne Plaza
Sh Zayed Rd/Trade Centre

Page 8
C 2

Tel: 322 655

The centre offers a new concept in hair treatment and skin care in luxurious surroundings. Specialists diagnose your skin and hair problems, using state-of-the-art computerised analysis machines, and prescribe appropriate treatments and products from Galenic and Rene Furterer ranges. All hair, skin and electrolysis consultations are confidential and completely free.

Common hair problems like dandruff and hair loss can be treated, and trained staff will cut and colour hair too. They also offer manicures, pedicures, facials, bleaching and lash tinting. For hair removal try waxing or the pain free Electrolysis system, which does not involve the use of needles.

## Touch of Class, A

**09:30 - 18:30**
**Sat - Thu**

**Wafi Shopping Mall**
**Wafi/Al Nasr**

**Page 13**
**D 2**

**Tel: 347 352**

A Touch Of Class has been operating for 10 years. All staff are European and highly trained. There are two hairdressers carrying out all aspects of hair care, including extensions with human hair. There is also a nail technician who can make short chubby hands look long and elegant, with gel or acrylic technique. They also offer beauty treatments such as facials and waxing. A friendly salon, which is open at lunchtimes, a boon for the working woman.

# Weekend Breaks - UAE

## Abu Dhabi

### Abu Dhabi Hilton

**Drive 2 Hours**
**180 Km**

**On the main Corniche**
**Abu Dhabi**

Tel: **02 661 900**

The panoramic view of the extensive Corniche as you ascend in the glass elevator, puts you in the mood for an indulgently relaxed weekend. This is the largest and oldest hotel in Abu Dhabi, located at the quiet, far end of the Corniche. It offers all the usual five star comforts and amenities, but of special note is Hemingways "the Party House of the Gulf" comprising a traditional pub with games room; the discotheque complete with a separate karaoke area; and an atmospheric jazz club. These are all located in the same compact and soundproofed area, and attract a varied and interesting crowd.

The main attraction for those seeking a weekend break is the Hiltonia Resort Club stretching across 750 metres of golden sands. This provides watersports as diverse as banana boat rides and diving - but of special interest is the possibility of chartering a boat for fishing, or snorkelling trips out to the islands. The delicious and plentiful Dhs.30 Mongolian barbecue available from 18:00 and best enjoyed with a sundowner, is almost reason enough in itself to visit the resort.

### Abu Dhabi Sheraton

**Drive 2 Hours**
**180 Km**

**On the main Corniche**
**Abu Dhabi**

Tel: **02 773 333**

Situated on Abu Dhabi's picturesque Corniche, the Sheraton offers a wealth of activities and leisure facilities including a full range of sports, such as squash and tennis, to more adventurous deep sea fishing, sailing and diving. The pool is designed for relaxing in and is well used by families. Between the pool and the beach is a garden of palm trees and sunbeds were one can relax in the shade or sun. The spicy outdoor King Creole serves food for the hungry and a pool bar ensures that your thirst will be quenched.

From a jetty The Blue Dolphin Dive Centre caters for both beginners and seasoned divers alike, with daily speciality dives and a wide range of instruction courses. Water- skiing is also on offer, but for the those who wish to relax there is a set of three jacuzzis situated on their own jetty, providing warm bubbles plus views along the Corniche and out to sea.

There are a variety of restaurants ranging from Mexican, Italian and Chinese to Iranian at Hojreh - Abu Dhabi's only five star Iranian restaurant. The Tavern also claims to be the capital's only truly genuine English style watering hole.

## Inter-Continental Hotel

**Drive 2 Hours**
**180 Km**

**On the main Corniche**
**Abu Dhabi**

Tel: **02 666 888**

Located on a beautiful beach front with private marina, The Abu Dhabi Inter-Con Hotel is located at the farthest end of the Corniche. The hotel is adjacent to the parliament building and diplomatic centre, which is also very close to the commercial centre. It is away from the immediate bustle of the city but at the same time is within easy access making it handy to get to some of the shops which are not available in Dubai.

An ideal location for a weekend getaway from Dubai, where you can enjoy the green surrounds, the beach and an excellent fitness centre within the hotel. With a plethora of excellent restaurants to choose from : Mexican, French, seafood, cocktail lounge and a more casual poolside bar, you may not want to leave the hotel surrounds. If you enjoy the healthier activities in life, then the choice may also be too much to cope with - choose from a swimming pool, beach, tennis, squash, gym, sauna, steam room, plunge pool, massage, yacht club, scuba diving, water- skiing, windsurfing and sailing. Tempted yet? You may need more than one weekend to fit everything in!

The hotel recently received three prestigious awards including the award for Best Hotel, Middle East and Africa by the Inter-Continental group, and Best hotel in Abu Dhabi by the magazine, Euromoney.

## Le Meridien Hotel & Health Spa

**Drive 2 Hours**
**180 Km**

**Near main Corniche**
**Abu Dhabi**

Tel: **02 776 666**

For the ultimate in stress relief, personal pampering and relaxation, a weekend stay at one of the capital's longest established hotels, with a course of treatments at its renowned Health Spa cannot be beaten. Comfortable rooms and five-star service act as a comforting and luxurious backdrop to the UAE's only fully-fledged spa.

Entering the spa is like being transported to another world. Treatments range from a session in the aquamedic pool, with it's carefully positioned and incredibly powerful water jets to soothe away aches and pains, to a soothing massage, and if you're brave, an incredibly stimulating seaweed wrap, before plunging into the temperature controlled pools of the Turkish bath. Other more medicinal treatments such as "pressotherapy" for lymphatic drainage, are also available, as are facials and other cosmetic applications

The sumptuous seafood extravaganza, held every Thursday night at the poolside, acts as a delicious and healthy start to your "feel good" weekend. Wake up next morning to a light, healthy breakfast, before descending to the Spa and three hours of bliss, with perhaps a session in the hotel's well equipped gym to start. Once you awaken from your treatment enhanced daze, venture out to the Meridien's popular landscaped beach and gardens for a spot of gentle sunbathing, or a snack from the extensive poolside bar menu. All in all, a real treat for both body and mind, and well worth a visit.

# Al-Ain

## Inter-Continental Hotel

Drive 1 1/2 Hours
130 Km

Al Ain

Tel: **03 686 686**

Situated on the edge of the UAE's oasis city, the hotel fits into its surroundings with it's green gardens and yellow terraced structure. The hotel has recently been fully renovated. It has four restaurants, a great sports club, a pub and two nightclubs to keep you awake to the small hours. Tennis courts, a swimming pool and horse riding are all on offer.

Wake up in the morning look out the window at the view, stretch and go 'Yes, this is the life'. Have breakfast in bed and if inclined, go for a game of tennis. Still got energy? Then swim a number lengths of the Olympic size pool or try the other gym activities. Alternatively, soak up the sun next to the paddling pool.

Don't leave Al Ain without a drive up Jebal Hafit for a spectacular mountain view or a visit to the Hilli Archeological dig. On the way back to Dubai notice that the deserts of the UAE are not as flat as you probably image them to be. A great weekend.

# Fujairah

## Fujairah Hilton

Drive 1 1/2 Hours
130 Km

On the East Coast
Fujairah

Tel: **09 222 411**

This hotel is an ideal retreat for a relaxing weekend. Located in the centre of town, set back from road and surrounded by trees, it has top quality rooms and facilities. For dining there's a Mediterranean restaurant called Neptunia which overlooks the pool, and two bars - Octavia Bistro, adjacent to the restaurant, and Tropicana, which has live entertainment on six nights of the week.

There's a covered beach-front dining area which is an ideal place to sit and have lunch, shaded from the hot sun. Alternatively, it's a nice place for sundowners overlooking the beach. The beach itself, although private, is disappointingly small and the sand is greyish in colour. There's a resident band playing popular tunes from lunch time onwards.

The Friday 'Fish Market' brunch has an excellent reputation and is definitely worth trying. After the salad or soup starter, you are invited to take a basket and select your choice of fish from twenty different varieties - lobster, oysters, mussels, tiger prawns etc. A perfect way to spend a Friday, sitting in the sun eating freshly grilled seafood.

There are many other attractions to a weekend in Fujairah including sport fishing expeditions, diving trips, water-skiing, jetskiing and leisure boat rides. The hotel can also organise excursions to local attractions which include the Old Fujairah Fort, Fujairah Museum, the oldest mosque in UAE and Kalba Lagoon.

## Sandy Beach Motel

**Drive 2 Hours**
**150 Km**

**On the Coast**
**Nr. Khor Fafkan**

Tel: **09 445 354**

Situated on the East Coast, the Sandy Beach Motel has one and two bedroom self-catering chalets with kitchenette and lounge, which are scattered around the grounds, most with a sea view. Each chalet has a terrace and BBQ facilities, ideal during the cooler winter months.

An additional wing of forty hotel rooms boast magnificent views across the Gulf of Oman. Ground floor rooms open onto a small porch, a real suntrap for mid-morning brunch. All rooms are basic, yet comfortable and clean. While self catering seems the norm, the restaurant offers a varied menu including Arabic and continental cuisine, although portions are not over generous!

Snoopy Island sits 200 metres offshore providing a rewarding snorkeller's paradise. The shallows are teaming with life, and if you want to explore further the Dive Centre is right next door. This popular PADI centre, under German management, operates regular trips along the coast, as well as day trips to Musandam. Scubapro hire equipment is reasonably priced and all abilities of divers are accepted. It's best to dive with friends rather than risk being paired with a total stranger.

The motel's location provides a base for ramblers to explore the surrounding mountains and is a popular stopping point for tour companies. The long beach provides ample breathing space for everyone and shades are provided, or you may prefer the pool or kiddies play area.

# Hatta

## Hatta Fort Hotel

**Drive 1 1/2 Hours**
**110 Km**

**Hatta**

Tel: **085 23211**

Just over an hour's drive from Dubai, the Hatta Fort Hotel lies as an oasis of tranquillity amidst the rugged beauty of the Hajar mountains. Enter one of the fifty luxurious, chalet-style rooms and you feel as though you could be the only one around - so cleverly is the site planned. Generously proportioned, thoughtfully equipped, and decorated with a comforting mix of stone and wood, each of the rooms has its own private terrace - the setting for many a romantic breakfast or dinner.

The hotel's swimming pool and sun terrace is beautifully situated, with all-round views of the majestic mountains which change colours chameleon-like throughout the day. Be warned though that during Friday afteernoon, the pool area gets very crowded. A superb poolside snacks and drinks service is run from the adjacent Coffee Shop, which is a frequent watering-hole for the many desert safari's which pass this way. Food in the Jeema Restaurant is excellent with the cuisine far exceeding its surroundings - although the ambience is certainly one of relaxation and enjoyment.

If it's activity you're looking for, Hatta Fort can oblige there too, with sports ranging from archery to clay-pigeon shooting, tennis and mini-golf, as well as walking and jogging tracks heading up into the foothills. There is also an ingenious, partly grassed cross-country golf course. Day trips through the wadis, into the desert, and to the famous Hatta pools can be arranged from the hotel, as can an exhilarating helicopter airlift to and from Dubai for those who really want to make it an occasion to remember.

Special rates for the helicopter transfers (starting from October) which are available the first Thursday of each month.

# Jebel Ali

## Jebel Ali Hotel

Drive 1/2 Hour
40 Km

Past Jebel Ali Port
Jebel Ali

Tel: **04 836 000**

Situated in luxurious tropical gardens, the Jebel Ali Hotel could be a million miles away from the hustle and bustle of Dubai, but in reality, it's a mere 30 minutes drive. Wake up to the sound of bird song and enjoy a sumptuous breakfast in your room, before venturing out into the hotel's 110 acres of ground.

A truly self-contained resort, Jebel Ali Hotel offers leisure and sporting activities to suit all tastes. The active can choose from horse riding, sailing, cycling and tennis. Those more inclined to spend their weekends relaxing can recuperate on the hotel's unrivalled beach, surrounded by swaying palm trees and constantly refreshed by the roving "Grasshoppers" serving sandwiches and ice cold drinks.

Other activities include Club Marbella with fitness facilities, and the Jebel Ali Shooting Club offering both clay-pigeon and pistol ranges, while for those of a more gentle disposition there is an immaculate croquet lawn and numerous woodland walks.

Dining options range from the formal 'Mushref' with immaculate French cuisine, to the relaxed and cheerful "Traviata's" Italian restaurant. For a little spice try the Mexican "Shooter" in the shooting club, while outside dining is offered at the Arabic "Ibn Magid". Prices reflect that it's a 5-star hotel. However, keep your eyes open for the regular holiday and weekend special deals.

# Weekend Breaks - Oman

Visas are normally required for most people wishing to enter Oman (air or road). It is a straight forward procedure to apply at the Consulate in Dubai, or let your sponsor (Hotel, Tour Operator or Omani company) apply for the visas for you (less paperwork). Typical costs are Dhs.75 for all nationalites, bar British which are Dhs.150.

If driving into Oman, your vehicle will be searched so it is advisable not to take alcohol with you. Flying takes about 1 hour to Muscat and costs Dhs.250-500 return from Dubai (depending on season/timings).

# Khasab

Khasab is the *capital* of Musandam, the separated northern area of Oman near the Straits of Hormuz, which has only relatively recently opened to tourism. It is often described as the "Norway of the Middle East", with its natural fjord-like inlets offering amazing scenic beauty.

From Dubai, follow the coast road north through Ras Al Khaimah, and at the roundabout for Shaam take the exit right and drive until you reach the UAE exit post. A nominal fee of Dhs.20 is charged per person. A word of advice for females is to dress very modestly and where possible, allow a male member of your group to deal with the form filling formalities. From here it is 2 km of graded road to Tibat, the Omani entry point. Your vehicle will be searched so it is advisable not to take alcohol with you. Travel on past Bukha where the scenery is spectacular with sheer rock cliffs dropping right down below sea level. You will pass back through generations of time, driving through small villages and finally reaching Khasab where the main road ends.

## Khasab Hotel

**Drive 3 Hours**
**150 Km**

**Khasab, Musandam**
**Oman**

Tel: **+968 830 271**

Khasab Hotel is a very simple hotel and the only one in the area ! It has 15 guest rooms, a small restaurant, lounge room and swimming pool. Although the furnishings are dated and worn, the rooms are clean and have ensuite bathrooms.

Visit Khasab Fort, built by the Portuguese for defence from enemy attacks from the sea (the fort was renovated in 1989-1992). From the coastline you can see smugglers in their powerboats waiting for nightfall to make the sea journey to Iran to drop off cigarettes and other illegal goods.

A short drive out of Khasab is the village of Tawl where you can see pre-historical cave paintings, said to be more than 2,000 years old. The highest mountain in Musandam is Jebel Harim (2,087 metres), which is a 2.5 hour drive from Khasab. To get to Jebel Harim you will pass through many small villages inhabited by Bedouin people who earn their living by goat herding.

Boat trips on traditional dhows can be organised to view the breathtaking scenery of the fjords and visit small stone-house fishing villages, only accessibleby boat whose only source of income is fishing and goat herding. The average depth of the fjords is only 30 metres therefore the water stays relatively warm all year round. The clear warm waters and the abundance of sealife and coral reefs make this an excellent location for snorkeling and swimming. Khasab Travel & Tours is the only tour operator in the area and can organise dhow trips, visas etc. However, it's a lot cheaper to just ask at the port whether anyone will take you out on their dhow- count on spending Dhs.100/hour for the dhow, not per person!

## See Also:

Khasab Diving Centre - Diving

Khasab Travel & Tours - Dhow Charter

# Muscat

## Al Bustan Palace Hotel

**Drive 4fi Hours, Fly 1 Hour**
**450 Km**

**Nr. Muttrah, Muscat**
**Oman**

Tel: **+968 740 200**

Voted the best hotel in the Middle East six times, the Al Bustan Palace Hotel's first guests were originally visiting sheikhs, presidents and rulers of the GCC countries. From the second you set foot in its magnificent mosaic covered atrium, you know you have entered somewhere special. A smiling welcome is immediately forthcoming from the Omani receptionists, before you are escorted to your room.

Choose either a 'Continental' or 'Arabic' room both of which are exquisite, tastefully decorated and eminently comfortable. The feeling of complete retreat and luxury is continued through to the hotel's grounds and beach, which stretch for a good 2km down the coast, before being abruptly halted by the jagged mountains which completely isolate the hotel from the surrounding country.

A choice of restaurants run by the Inter-Continental Hotels company offer a variety of cuisines, with what has to be one of the best weekend brunches in the region, every Friday. Well worth a visit: perfect for that special occasion or when a spot of pampering is called for.

Keep an eye open for special summer weekend packages.

## Inter-Continental Hotel

**Drive 4 1/2 Hours, Fly 1 Hour**
**430 Km**

**On Coast**
**Muscat**

Tel: **+968 600 500**

This beach hotel is perfectly situated close to town and just 15 minutes from Seeb International airport, set in the midst of the prime residential, government and diplomatic quarters. Stunning views of the Gulf of Oman and Hajar mountains, and combined with a refreshingly relaxing, well-maintained palm garden with its undulating lawn. If the deckchairs, 25m pool, 12km of beach and water-sports (windsurfing; sailing, diving school nearby) are too energetic for you, try one of the six floodlit tennis courts, two glass backed squash courts, or even the fitness centre! The hotel outlets offer a good range from an English pub, gourmet restaurant, Mediterranean grill and anNight club.

A trip into town, and especially Muttrah, is essential. Set between the mountains and a quaint port, all looks relatively quiet until you visit the back street souk that runs parallel to the coastal road. Tightly packed into its narrow winding streets are a wealth of small vendors selling their handicrafts and treasures. A real hive of activity and a truly memorable experience on all your senses!

# Weekend Break - Summary

| Hotels | Tel | Fax | No of Rooms | Price (Dhs.) | Dist. from Dubai (Km) |
|---|---|---|---|---|---|
| ***UAE*** | | | | | |
| **Abu Dhabi (+971-2)** | | | | | |
| Abu Dhabi Hilton | 661 190 | 669 696 | 350 | 638 | 180 |
| Abu Dhabi Sheraton | 773 333 | 725 149 | 256 | 986 | 180 |
| Inter-Continental Hotel | 666 888 | 669 153 | 330 | 406 | 180 |
| Le Meridien | 776 666 | 729 315 | 227 | 406 | 180 |
| **Al-Ain (+971-3)** | | | | | |
| Inter-Continental Hotel | 686 686 | 686 766 | 194 | 319 | 130 |
| **Fujairah (+971-9)** | | | | | |
| Fujairah Hilton | 222 411 | 226 541 | 192 | 520 | 130 |
| Sandy Beach Motel | 445 354 | 445 207 | 67 | 490 | 150 |
| **Hatta (+971-85)** | | | | | |
| Hatta Forte Hotel | 23211 | 23561 | 50 | 540 | 110 |

| Hotels | Tel | Fax | No of Rooms | Price (Dhs.) | Dist. from Dubai (Km) |
|---|---|---|---|---|---|
| ***Oman*** | | | | | |
| **Khasab (+968)** | | | | | |
| Khasab Hotel | 830 271 | 830 989 | 15 | 320 | 150 |
| **Muscat (+968)** | | | | | |
| Al Bustan Palace Hotel | 740 200 | 799 600 | 240 | 850 | 450 |

# Passive Activities / Trival Pursuits

## Amusement Arcades

### Fantasy Kingdom

11:30 - 24:00
Closed Fri am

Al Bustan Centre
Al Qusais

Tel: **630 000**

Fantasy Kingdom at Al Bustan Centre is one-of-a-kind having been designed along the lines of a medieval castle, creating a fairy tale atmosphere of adventure and excitement. Children enjoy the fun attractions in the comfort of an indoor play area covering over 20,000 sq.ft., which is divided into clear sections catering to children of differing ages.

While smaller children can enjoy up to 20 different rides, including five rides of the merry-go-round variety (Tea Cup Rides, Horse Rides, Musical Instrument Rides, Plane Rides and Bumper Cars), the older ones can enjoy over 50 video games, play on pinball machines and even indulge in basketball net practice. What's more, they can win coupons on scoring high points which can be redeemed for toys and gifts at a counter within the arcade itself.

### Magic Planet

10:00 - 24:00
Closed Fri am

Deira City Centre Mall
Deira

Page 14
D 1

Tel: **284 333**

Magic Planet sprawls over 70,000 sq.ft and is filled with the latest technology rides, video games and simulators, as well as a train ride, challenge miniature golf, bumper cars, a carousel and mini-bowling. It is an entertainment area for children of all ages. A system of tokens is operated, which are sold centrally and are used for all rides and amusements. The tokens are valid indefinitely, so unused tokens can be saved for another day. Also recently introduced is an unlimited Ride Pass offer at Dhs.40 for the day which includes all rides all day, plus six tokens, along with reserved seating and a meal in the Magic Planet Food court.

### Q-Zar

10:00 - 22:00

Metroplex
Sh Zayed Rd

Page 4
C 4

Tel: **494 828**

The Q-Zar way. Lights, smoke and pumping music make this the most exciting game in town. The venue is at Bur Juman Centre, your gear includes state-of-the-art chestpacks and backpacks, and a weapon that goes by the name of a laser gun. There are moving targets, otherwise called friends and colleagues, and players are divided into two teams. Score by destroying "enemy headquarters", and of course by "shooting" your opposing team members.

Either way it's a winner. When it's all over, and the adrenaline tank is running on empty, the whistle blows and it's time to check your scores... Or settle them. For teenagers and adults.

# Amusement Park

## Wonderland

Splash 12:00 - 20:00
Theme 16:00 - 22:00

Nr. Al Garhoud Bridge
Al Garhoud/Za'beel

Page 14
A 3

Tel: **341 222**

If you have driven by the Creek and noticed bright coloured roofs popping up amidst a landscaped park, then you have seen Wonderland, the most unique amusement and water attractions park in the Middle East. The Coca-Cola family centre is located on Main Street, which divides the park into two areas. Splashland is packed with water-attractions such as Speed Slides, Surf Hill and Twister. Visitors can travel down giant slides at exhilarating speeds while sitting on an inner-tube, or slide down the Wave Runner's 35ft ramp while sitting on a sled. Other rides include Bumper Cars, Log Flume and an old-fashioned Carousel.

A roller coaster promises to take visitors to new heights as it rushes up and down the tracks at thrilling speeds. Try the Wave Swinger, or race Maxi Taxis around a challenging track. Smaller children can discover their own specially made attractions including Miniature 4x4 trucks, Fort Fun and children's activity pool. One of the highlights of the park is a water mist show. This is a spectacular "Water Cinema" with films projected on a thin film of water. The Park has Indian, Arabic and Fast Food restaurants, an ice cream parlour and cafeteria. Wednesdays are for ladies only, Fridays for families.

## See Also:

**Water Parks - Sporting Activities**

## Creative Art Centre

07:30 - 13:30
18:30 - 20:30 Closed Fri/Sat am

Al Wasl Rd
Jumeria

Page 4
E1

Tel: **444 394**

Think of arty crafty things and it's probably being carried out at this homely centre which holds activity courses for all ages. Generally speaking, mornings are given over to small children at their Busy Bees nursery units, afternoons are for 4-12 year olds and evenings are for adults. Evening classes include photography, silk painting, pottery, calligraphy and dress making.

Lynda Shepherd, Managing Partner, is a well known local artist with examples of her eye catching designs on show at many major hotels in UAE and Oman. She runs a thriving framing business, with framers who will produce anything you require at competitive rates. The centre also publishes limited prints, suitable for corporate or individual gifts.

## Dubai International Arts Centre

08:30 - 16:30
Closed Thu pm and Fri

Al Jumeira Rd
Jumeira

Page 5
C 2

Tel: **444 398**

Fondly known as the 'Arts Centre' this hub of arty-crafty types is actually a small haven of tranquillity. The arty ones are busy learning, teaching, or doing whatever the muse dictates. Other visitors are gazing at original pieces of work, looking for gifts to buy, borrowing a book from the Library, or just sitting in the small garden enjoying a cup of tea with a friend.

Annual membership fee of Dhs.200 allows members and children to sign up for some of the many classes on offer each term. Dhs.300 family membership includes two adults and children. Children can have student membership for Dhs.50.

A course of classes lasts for six or eight weeks and vary in price according to the materials required during each lesson. Learn or improve your skills over 30 topics including Arabic, bridge, doll making, drawing, embroidery, French, guitar, Islamic art history, Japanese brush, painting, various other kinds of painting, patchwork and quilting, pottery, photography, sculpture, etc.

DIAC aims to encourage the development of arts and crafts by offering classes and workshops in a wide variety of traditional and contemporary subjects. It mounts major exhibitions of members work twice a year and provides a meeting point, presenting lectures and demonstrations, many of which are free of charge or have a nominal entrance fee.

# Boat Charters

See Charters - Boat/Dhow/Yacht charters

# Bull Fighting

One major attraction in Fujairah is the chance to see the Emirate's own unique form of bullfighting - not a struggle to the death of man against beast but a contest of strength between two great animals. They can be seen on occasion working on Fujairah's farms and the bulls are often pampered family pets. The fight itself is bloodless, as the bulls lock horns and wrestle until the weaker of the two gives up and turns away. A form of entertainment much loved by the local population. Bullfights take place every Friday afternoon at about 16:30 (except for the summer months) near the Fujairah - Kalba bridge area. The fight lasts just a few minutes and the bulls suffer little or no injury, except for a few scratches and a bruised ego on the part of both the losing bull, and its owner.

# Cinemas

At present, there are four cinemas in Dubai showing English language films. Many plans are underway for additional large multi-screen cinema complexes. Timings and details are printed in the daily newspapers. New movies are generally three months behind UK and USA and are usually released on Thursdays.

The cinemas tend to be cold, so make sure you take a sweater! During the weekends, extra shows are at 24:00 and 01:00. Check press for more details.

Tickets may be reserved, but have to be picked up one hour prior to show. Cash sales only. Expect the seats to be sold out for the first couple of days when a new movie hits town.

Listed below are the cinemas in Dubai and Sharjah. Under language we have indicated the language of the films shown at these cinemas. Once again, check press, or call the cinema for their screenings.

| | | | No. of Seats | | | Entrance | | | |
|---|---|---|---|---|---|---|---|---|---|
| **Dubai** | Telephone No. | Film Languages | 1 | 2 | 3 | Regular | Special | Reserve | Credit Card |
| Al Nasr Cinema | 374 353 | **E** | 750 | - | - | 20 | 20 | Yes | No |
| Almassa Cinema | 443 244 | **E** | 582 | 355 | 235 | 25 | 50 | Yes | Yes |
| Deira Cinema | 223 551 | T, M | 700 | - | - | 15 | 20 | No | No |
| Dubai Cinema | 665 009 | H, M | 380 | 900 | - | 20 | 15 | Yes | No |
| Galleria Cinema | 706 4095 | **E** | 475 | 175 | - | 23 | 23 | Yes | No |
| Lamcy Cinema | 368 808 | **E**, H | 166 | 196 | - | 20 | | Yes | No |
| Plaza Cinema | 532 683 | H | 700 | 900 | - | 20 | 15 | Yes | No |
| Rex Drive-In | 886 447 | H | 350 | - | - | 15 | | No | No |
| Strand Cinema | 370 304 | H | 926 | 500 | - | 20 | 15 | Yes | No |
| **Sharjah** | | | | | | | | | |
| Al Hamra | 06 523 953 | **E** | 250 | 700 | - | 15 | 10 | Yes | No |
| Concorde | 06 523 956 | M, T | 400 | 750 | - | 20 | 15 | Yes | No |
| Metro | 06 285 583 | **E** | 900 | - | - | 25 | 20 | Yes | No |
| Sharjah | 06 522 241 | H | 400 | 700 | - | 20 | 15 | Yes | No |

**Key:**

Arabic (A), **English (E)**, Hindi (H), Malayalam (M), Tamil (T)

# Comedy Club

## Laughter Factory, The

**Starts 20:30** **Premiere Nightclub** **Page 7**
**Check Press** **Hyatt Regency Hotel, Deira** **D 2** Tel: **731 234**

The Laughter Factory, is based on a concept which already has tremendous success in the UK, America and Hong Kong. Comedy clubs similar to this are becoming increasingly popular, providing established and up and coming comedians as acts. "Alternative comedy" (meaning an alternative to sexist and racist jokes) is definitely the comedy of the 90's.

The Laughter Factory draws on a wealth of talent from the UK, and each artist is carefully selected to suit the Middle East expatriate market. The unique feature of this concept is that it offers three different styles of comedy in one show, providing a broad spectrum of humour appealing to a wider audience. Shows will be held monthly at the Premiere Nightclub, Hyatt Regency Hotel Dubai, The Club Abu Dhabi (02-731 111) and Al Ain Inter-Continental Hotel (03-686 686) . Tickets priced at Dhs.60. Show starts 20:30.

# Desert Driving Course

Several training courses are conducted by expert safari drivers. For those who are adventurous and would like to master the art of manoeuvring a 4WD vehicle over rolling sand dunes, the following organisations offer a full-day course accompanied by their professional drivers. Both individual and group tuition per vehicle is available. Picnic lunch and soft drinks are included. Participants are expected to bring along their own 4WD vehicle to take this course. Alternatively, they can arrange a vehicle at an additional cost. Courses available on request. Expect to pay around Dhs.250 for the day.

## Al-Futtaim Training Centre

**Various** **Al Rashidiya** Tel: **850 455**

Explore the wonderful wild side of the Emirates in your 4x4 in safety and confidence. The “Desert Campus” training course will give off-road driving enthusiasts knowledge and experience of venturing into the desert. It starts with a three-hour classroom session covering the basics of our 4WD vehicle, tips on protectint it from breakdown, overheating, changing tires in sand, negotiating sand-dunes and other driving techniques. This is followed by five hours of supervised off-road driving where you take your personal 4WD up and down sand dunes! Fee for the course is Dhs.300 per person, include off-road driving manual and light snacks. The course leader is Siegfried Steur, who has 15 years of off-road driving experience.

## *See Also:*

| | | |
|---|---|---|
| **Tour Operators** | Arabian Adventures | SNTTA |
| | Europecar | Orient Tours |

# Environmental Groups

## Arabian Leopard Trust, The

Check press | Check press | Tel: **443 218**

ALT is a volunteer run, non-government organisation. With the endangered Arabian Leopard as its flagship species, ALT aims to promote the preservation of all Arabian wildlife, both predators and prey animals. In order to achieve this activities are concentrated on: education of the general public about the existence of wildlife and the dangers that it faces; research into the habits and habitats of indigenous wildlife so that its needs can be better understood; bringing together those animals that are already in captivity so that they can breed in optimal conditions; creation of nature reserves wherever possible and re-introducing wildlife whenever possible. ALT activities are funded by: membership, donations, adoptions of animals and sponsorships of special events; collection and sale of scrap steel and aluminium; production, distribution and sale of ALT promotional, and educational items.

## Dubai Natural History Group

Check press | Jumeira English School, Jumeira | Tel: **494 816**

The Dubai Natural History Group was formed in 1986 to promote interest in and further knowledge about the flora, fauna, geology, archaeology and natural environment of the Emirates. Monthly meetings are held on the first Sunday of each month at 19:30 at the Jumeira English Speaking School, free of charge. These usually take the form of lectures by both local and visiting speakers on a range of natural history topics. Most of the talks involve the UAE, e.g. illustrated lectures on resident and migrant birds, plants of the mountains, desert and gravel plains, marine life, insects, hydrology, astronomy, and Bedouin culture and findings from fossil sites in the Emirates. DNHG also arranges field trips an a regular basis to mountain wadis, coastal mangroves, archaeological sites and research institutions in the UAE.

In addition, DNHG maintains a modest library of natural history publications which is readily available to members. Annual membership fee is Dhs.50 per family and members receive a monthly newsletter, "The Gazelle", which details future activities and those of related groups in Abu Dhabi and Al Ain, together with various news and items. Tel. Valerie Chalmers, Vice Chairman and Secretary, 494 816, and Gary Feulner, Chairman, 313 320.

## Emirates Environmental Group

Check press | Check press | Fax: **529 600**

E.E.G. is a voluntary, non-profit making organisation which aims to increase public awareness of environmental issues and promote action to protect and preserve the environment. Activities include regular free meetings with speakers on environmental topics, and special events such as recycling collections and beach clean-ups. Members receive a monthly newsletter.

The group also produces an occasional publication called "The Wastepaper" which is distributed free. There are three project groups focusing on recycling, education and publications, which are always in need of volunteers. Annual Membership: Dhs.50, students

Dhs.10, open to all nationalities. Contact: Habiba Marashi, Chairperson, PO Box 7013 Dubai.

## Sharjah Environmental Group

Check press | Check press | Tel: **06 549 333**

Founded on 23rd June 1997, Sharjah Environmental Group is a non-profit making group open to men and women of all nationalities, which aims to help safeguard the future of the Emirates. Registered as a non-Governmental organisation, but recognised by the Sharjah Government, all group meetings are held in English, with committee meetings once a month. Group Chairman is Sheikh Faisal bin Khaled Al Qasimi, Chairman of Orient Tours, founding members of the Group.

Activities include encouraging participation in specific projects such as clean-up campaigns for schools and individuals, providing general public with information regarding recycling facilities, recruiting cooperation from the Municipality, Traffic Police etc. and generally increasing public awareness of local and global environmental issues. Membership is free. Toll free contact number 800 6789.

# Fashion Shows

## Fashion Cafe

11:00 - 02:00 | Deira City Centre Mall, Deira | Page 14, D 1 | Tel: **828 595**

Owned by super models Claudia Schiffer, Naomi Campbell and Elle MacPherson, Fashion Café is a festival of style. This is also the venue for a series of fashion shows, ranging from the top names of haute couture to speciality fashion houses of the Gulf. Call, fax, or e-mail in advance for a schedule of shows and ticket information. (Fax: 821 887, E-Mail: mytable@fc-dubai.com). See Fashion Cafe; Restaurants - American.

# Fishing

Fishing rods and bait available in various clubs for beach/rock fishing. Average rate of Dhs.10/1 hr, Dhs.35/half day plus Dhs.5 for a packet of bait.

### *See Also:*

Deep Sea Fishing

# Gardening

## Dubai Gardening Group

15:30
Last Wed Month | International Arts Centre
Al Jumeira Rd | Page 5
C 2 | Tel: **445 999**

The Gardening Group was established 17 years ago under the umbrella of The Dubai International Arts Centre. Members aim to share their love and knowledge of gardening in a friendly and informal atmosphere. Meetings are generally held on the last Wednesday of every month, commencing at 15:30 at DIAC. During cooler months trips to greenhouses, nurseries, farms and parks are arranged. Speakers, who are experts in various fields, address the meetings and where necessary give practical demonstrations.

Annual Flower Show: The highlight of the season, the Annual Flower Show is held at the Dubai Country Club, usually in March. This is a spectacular showing by members and their children, of flowers, vegetables and fruit. Annual membership is Dhs.100 and this includes an informative booklet. Dhs.75 for renewal. Call for more information.

# Horse Racing

## Dubai Racing Club

See Calendar Below
Most Thu/Sun | Dubai Racing Club
Nadd Al Shiba | Tel: **313 311**

The Dubai Racing Club at Nadd Al Shiba is one of the leading racing facilities of it's kind, with top champion jockeys from Europe, USA and Australia regularly taking part in races throughout the season of November to April.

Nadd Al Sheba is 5 kms south east of Dubai and is signposted from Sheikh Zayed Road at the Metropolitan Hotel junction, and from the roundabout close to the Dubai Polo Club and Country Club. Car parking is free, with a reserved area for badge holders and members.

General admission is free and the public have access to most areas. The Club House Restaurant charges Dhs.70 for day membership, which allows access to the Members Box located on the second level of the grandstand. Racing takes place at night under flood lights. There are usually six-seven races per night held at 30 minute intervals, with the first race taking place at 19:00, except during Ramadan when the first race takes place at 21:00. See the race schedule on the next page for exact dates.

Dress code in the public enclosures is casual, while racegoers are encouraged to dress smart casual in the Club House and in the private viewing boxes. Racegoers are invited to take part in various free competitions to select the winning horses with the ultimate aim of taking home cash or substantial prizes. Other competitions are on the reserve side of the Pick 6 form.

Fourteen hospitality suites provide companies and/or private individuals with an excellent opportunity to entertain clients and guests, although availability is limited due to high demand. Catering is organised upon request. Suites are also available in the Club House on a nightly basis.

# Horse Racing Calendar

## Nad Al Sheba Season 1997/8

**November 1997**

| | |
|---|---|
| Thursday | 6, 13, 27 |

**December 1997**

| | |
|---|---|
| Sunday | 7, 28 |
| Thursday | 11, 18 |

**January 1998 *(Ramadan)***

| | |
|---|---|
| Thursday | 1, 8, 15, 22, 29 |
| Sunday | 4, 11, 18 |

**February 1998**

| | |
|---|---|
| Sunday | 1, 8, 15, 22 |
| Thursday | 5, 12, 19 |

**March 1998**

| | |
|---|---|
| Sunday | 1 |
| Thursday | 5, 12 |
| Friday | 27 |
| Saturday | 28 |

**April 1998**

| | |
|---|---|
| Thursday | 2, 9, 16 |

**Important Races** during the season include the Dubai World Cup (March 28, 1998), Dubai Duty Free race, Sheikh Maktoum bin Rashid Al Maktoum Challenge, Nad Al Sheba Sprint, Nad Al Sheba Mile, and Arabian Classic.

# Language Schools

## Alliance Française

**09:00 - 13:00**
**16:00 - 19:30 Closed Thu pm**

**Nr. American Hospital** — **Page 13 E 1**

Tel: **358 712**

The Aliance Française is a non-profit organisation, supported by the French Government, founded in Paris in 1883 with the goal of promoting French language and culture. The Alliance Française is known in Dubai as the best place to learn French. Since its establishment in Dubai in 1982, the number of students at present reaches over 200 of all ages and nationalities.

The centre proposes special morning classesfor ladies, afternoon classes for children and evening classes for everybody. For adults the academic year is composed of five terms. Each term represents one educational level and last for seven weeks (Dhs.1,000). For children they offer a long session of 12 weeks from Sep - Dec and three sessions of seven weeks from Jan - Jun. The lessons take place three times a week, on Saturdays, Mondays and Wednesdays. Teaching remains dynamic thanks to the combined use of various methods such as video, authentic written material, audio tapes and role playing. An emphasis is placed on communication to facilitate your comprehension and enrich your written and oral expression.

Also has a library with 5,000 titles and daily, weekly and monthly French press (24 titles) as well as more than 300 videos. Library membership is Dhs.250/year. Library and Video membership Dhs.500/year. The students have free access to the library.

# Arabic Language Centre

Various
Closed Fri

Dubai World Trade Centre
Sh Zayed Rd

Page 9
A 2

Tel: **308 6036**

The Arabic Language Centre, a division of the Dubai World Trade Centre, was established in 1980 as a centre to teach Arabic as a foreign language. It's programmes offer an opportunity to take Arabic Studies from a Beginners course through to Advanced standard.

Courses are run five time a year with each course being of 30 hours duration. Sessions are held 09:00 - 11:00, 13:30 - 15:30 and 16:15 - 20:15. All materials are provided by the Centre and are included in the course fees of Dhs.1,500.

Specialist courses are designed to meet the requirements of the Hotel, Banking, Hospital, Motor and Electronic industries. Private courses offer individual tuition and flexible timings. Conveniently located next to Hall 4 of the D.W.T.C. Exhibition Complex.

# British Council

09:00 - 13:00
16:00 - 21:00 Closed Fri

International Arts Centre
Al Jumeira Rd

Page 10
A 3

Tel: **370 109**

The teaching centre offers English language courses for adults, young learners aged 4-15 years, ladies, and company groups at all levels, from beginners to advanced. Arabic courses are also offered, along with an MBA in partnership with Strathclyde University, the Competent Manager Program from the Institute of Management and, from October, Computer courses including Internet.

Fees: English courses (36 hours), Dhs.1,400 - New Students, including course material; Arabic courses (24 hours) Dhs.900, three evenings a week, not during summer; Computer courses (24 hours) Dhs.1,000, three mornings a week , not during summer.

Discount for re-registering students, morning programmes are for ladies only. For those wishing to study in Britain there are facilities to access information on higher education CD ROM databases, or find relevant information in university prospectii or brochures. The Information Officer is available for interviews by appointment. Can also make the arrangements for students to be registered at English language schools in Britain. Acts as a centre for examinations leading to British qualifications with more than 50 exam boards.

# Polyglot Language Institute, The

09:00 - 13:00
16:00 - 21:00 Closed Fri

International Arts Centre
Al Jumeira Rd

Page 5
C 2

Tel: **223 429**

The institute is situated on the 4th floor of Al Masaeed Builing in Maktoum Street, above the Iran Insurance Company, and directly behind the Hotel Intercontinental Plaza. Centrally located in the heart of Deira, the Polyglot Language Institute offers year-round courses in modern languages, secretarial and computer skills. Opened in 1969, it has an ever-growing list of company clients requiring in-service training for their staff.

Courses offered include: general English, Business English, TOEFL preparation, Arabic, French, German, Typing, Computer, Office Skills and Secretarial. There is also a high quality translation service in four languages. Bright, spacious classrooms and modern facilities, it is open six days a week, Saturday - Thursday 09:00 - 13:00 and 16:00 - 21:00. Each course lasts 10 weeks and consists of classes three times a week, in the evenings at 17:00 - 19:00 or 19:00 - 21:00. All books and materials are provided. Costs: Arabic course Dhs.1,500, other courses Dhs.1,350.

# Music / Singing

## Dubai Harmony Chorus

**Weekly Rehearsals** — Tel: **482 431**

Imagine creating exciting choral music and being part of a harmonious blending of voices - Barbershop Style...and then do it. Tel. Phyllis Holmqvist on 482 431 or Kathy Young on 489 395 for details.

Barbershop harmonising is different from any other kind of group singing. Finding the right part for your voice is the initial step, but this won't be difficult as any woman of average singing ability, with or without music or vocal training, will find a part that fits her range.

The Dubai Harmony Chorus boasts a membership of thirty singers from many different countries with a shared love of singing. Weekly rehearsals.

## Dubai Wind Band

**Tue 19:15** — **Jumeira English School, Jumeira** — Tel: **440 824**

This is a group of woodwind and brass musicians who meet on a Tuesday evening between 19:15 and 20:30 at Jumeira English Speaking School. The band consists of 50 members, both students and adults. New members of all abilities are welcome. Ranging from beginners to Grade 8 plus. The band is in popular demand during December for seasonal singing and music engagements at clubs, malls and hotels. Contact Mark Needs for more information.

### *See Also:*

**Dancing** **Theatre**

# Theatre

## British Airways Playhouse

**Check Press** — **Dubai Inter-Continental Hotel, Deira** — **Page 7 C 4** — Tel: **227 171**

Renowned for providing regular theatre and comedy evenings for nearly two decades, the British Airways Playhouse is one of the enduring events that theatre lovers in Dubai look forward to, and was the first dinner theatre to be staged in Dubai. Under the artful direction of Derek Nimmo, the Playhouse stages four seasons every year. These shows are rehearsed, produced and cast in London, and have in the past starred such names as Leslie Phillips, Patrick McNee, Alfred Marks, Dora Bryan and John Inman, to name but a few.

The Inter-Continental hotel is also the venue for the Indian Playhouse organised by Burjor Patel Productions and features satires throughout the year with a well known cast of actors.

## Cut Throat Theatre

On Request | Various Location | Pager: **939 47419**

Cut Throat Theatre specialises in murder! Directed by Suzanne Radford, writers and actors create theatrical "happenings" for entertainment, or as training vehicles. Cut Throat provides original plots for hotels, corporate events and private parties in true murder mystery style. No audience is too small or too large, as audiences are introduced to characters from 1920's England, or see adventures from Arabia. From the 1990's dating game, to the glamour of Hollywood, a variety of themes are on offer.

The murders take place over dinner with hilarious consequences. Surprise is the main ingredient, as the guests get to interrogate the suspects. What gives Cut Throat the edge, is the company's ability to be versatile both in form and content. Events can be tailor-made to requirements, so any setting or plot can be designed upon demand. Cost of Dhs.100 p.p. includes dinner. They perform in the hotels and clubs once a month. To have your own theatre performed for you costs Dhs.500 - Dhs.2,500 depending on requests. Contact Suzanne Radford on Pager: 939-47419, Fax 386 097.

## Dubai Drama Group

Check Press | British Council<br>Nr. Maktoum Bridge/Al Karama | Page 10<br>A 3 | Tel: **846 155**

To entertain is the 'raison d'etre' for the many residents who willingly take to the stage, help behind the scenes, paint backdrops, sing, dance, switch on lights and sew costumes for the Dubai Drama Group. Annual membership costs Dhs.50, which entitles you to a monthly newsletter and a lot of hard work and fun. This amateur dramatic society has been in existence for approximately 12 years. They put on four productions each year, a pantomime at Christmas, and the other three can be anything brought to the Committee for approval. They have tried farce, comedy, thrillers, modern theatre and One-Act plays.

Everyone is welcome to go along to the British Council, where rehearsals are held on Saturday, Sunday and Tuesday at 20:00. They always need help and expertise in all areas of stagecraft, from make-up to set building. For more details, contact Philippe Duquenoy.

## Front Row Theatre

On Request | Various Locations | Pager: **939 47419**

Front Row was created by Suzanne Radford who has ten years experience both in performance and as a trainer/teacher providing workshops for both children and adults. This is a children's theatre, which ignites the mind with original and familiar stories shown through stage performances, street theatre or through participatory workshops. With tales like 'The Legend of Croc Island' and 'Merry Hood and His Robin Men', audiences are delighted to meet characters such as pirates, princesses, heroes and baddies. Using mime and movement, music and dialogue, and other techniques, children are guaranteed an enchanting experience.

Storytelling, script, improvisation and an educational approach makes this colourful company an ideal choice for children's parties, hotel events, promotions and theatre productions. Contact Suzanne Radford on Pager: 939-47419, Fax 386 097.

## Youth Theatre

**Check** | **Ballet Centre, The, Jumeira** | **Page 6, C 3** | Tel: **459 771**

These days a theatre company has to be able to sing, dance and act. Within the Youth Theatre Group children are taught how to do all three for both theatre and studio. They are educated in stage make-up, as well as costume and set design skills to further their appreciation of the theatre.

# Charters

# Boat/Yacht Charters

## Coastline Leisure

**On Request** | **Nr. Sheraton Hotel, Deira** | **Page 10, C 1** | Tel: **450 867**

One of the most professional operators with fully certified safety equipement, and much more. They can arrange anything from a traditional Arabic Dhow, to a 70' luxury yacht for charter during the day or night. All their rates include captain and crew.

## Ocean Wave Ltd

**On Request** | **Summer - Meditterean, Winter - Caribbean/S.E Asia** | Tel: **822 661**

The sole representative for in the Middle East, of four of the worlds most prestigious privately owned charter yachts, working directly with the yachts' owners operating through *Mediterranean Yachts S.A* of Greece. These represent

- *Princess Tanya* (57m / 189ft) 18 guests
- *Princess Lauren* (54m / 175ft) 14-16 guests
- *Rosenkavalier* (67m / 218ft) 12 - 14 guests
- *Princess Sophia* (30m / 100ft) 10 guests

These magnificent yachts are available for private charter in the Mediterranean for the summer, and in the Caribbean and South East Asia over the Winter period. At present the yachts are based in the French Riviera and the Greek Islands and surpass the quality and standards displayed by many others. A personal on-board visit can be arragned for the serious charter. Call for more information, and speak to Alistair.

# Dhow Charters

## Al Boom Tourist Village

**On Request** | **Al Boom Tourist Village, Nr. Al Garhoud Bridge** | **Page 14, A 3** | Tel: **341 000**

As part of their new Al Boom Tourist village complex, they are the biggest operators of

# Four of the world's most prestigious privately owned charter yachts.

These magnificent yachts are available for private charter in the Mediterranean for the summer and in the Carribbean and South East Asia in the winter period.

66m/218' sleep 14 Rosenkavalier

53m/175' sleep 14-16 Princess Lauren

58m/189' sleep 18 Princess Tanya

30m/100' sleep 10 Princess Sophia

For further details please contact:

**Ocean Wave Ltd.**
P.O.Box 53041, Dubai, United Arab Emirates
Tel: 822 661, Fax: 822 710

dhow boats on the creek. Currently have five dhows ranging from a capacity of 20 - 160 passengers. The prices range from Dhs.400 per hour for the Al Taweel single decker, with a capacity of 20 passengers, to Dhs.2,500 for the Kahti double decker with a capacity of 160 passengers. Along with each private charter, they offer a range of menues, with self-explanatroy names as follows: Sea paradise, International Delicacies, Local delights, Far East Feast and finally Indian Cuisine.

## Coastline Leisure

**On Request** | **Nr. Sheraton Hotel, Deira** | **Page 10, C 1** | Tel: **450 867**

One of the most professional operators with fully certified safety equipement, and much more. They are well known in Dubai for their repeat business, and as the organisation who will offer the complete service. Ideal for corporate entertainment or parties. Tour Dubai dhow is available for private charter for business or pleasure. It has an 18' x 30' function deck, Arabic Majlis and a VIP Majlis, two conventional toilets and a professional sound system with over 200 mixed CD's to ensure that every function is a great success.

The cheapest dhow in town. Costs Dhs.850 per hour (min 2 hours), with a maximum of 50 passengers. As part of their service, live bands, entertainers, belly dancers and DJ's can be arranged at extra cost. Optional choice if you wish to organise your food and beverage. Can also tailor make decorations, ballons and even banners.

## Creek Cruises

**On Request** | **Quay 2/3, Dhow Wharfage, Deira** | **Page 10, C 2** | Tel: **533 554**

The Malika Al Khor (Queen of the Creek) is the largest dhow of its kind on the creek. This magnificent vessel has become a potent symbol of the gulf's rich cultural heritage and a poignant reminder of a way of life that existed virtually unchanged for centuries. Easy to find at the new dhow wharfage, at the far end of quay 2 and 3. Plenty of parking. Fitted with the latest safety equipment, this spacious double-deck dhow has been designed with the comfort, safety and enjoyment of all passengers in mind. This includes an air-conditioned lower deck, an Arabic style Majlis on the upper deck, and can accommodate up to 125 guests! Fitted with a professional sound system, dance floor and two toilets. If you wish to hire the dhow and its crew privately, the cost is Dhs.1,200 per hour (min 2 hours). Once again catering can be provided from Dhs.85 onwards by a 5-star hotel.

## Khasab Travel & Tours

**On Request** | **Khasab, Oman** | Tel: **+968 830 464**

Charter a dhow for the day, or cruise on a dhow and experience Arabian seamanship with Arabian refreshments, Omani coffee and dates being served in a traditional manner. Cruises range from Dhs.80 to Dhs.200, charters are from Dhs.1,000 - 3,000. Snorkelling gear can be hired for Dhs.10.

DISTRIBUTOR
SUN & SAND SPORTS L.L.C. P.O. Box 894 Dubai - UAE
Head office phone : (04) 443085 Sales office phone : (04) 529666

# Sporting Activities

# Sporting Activities

## Abseiling

### Adventure Unlimited

**On Request** | **Al Ain** | Tel: **03 687 458**

Brian Goggin, a former sergeant with an elite British armed forces unit, and his son Kyle run the company. Brian also served in the Sultan of Oman's Special Forces and the Royal Oman Police Task Force, all of which starts to give you an idea of exactly how adventurous you should be. These are activities to get the adrenaline going and the blood rushing through the veins. Based roughly on the Outward Bound schools situated all over UK, this is your chance to learn new skills and stretch yourself with the help of trained and skilled instructors.

If you want to go caving you have to find a convenient mountain with a cave in it first. Perhaps that is why this company is based in Al Ain near the jebels, wadis and desert. Very handy for abseiling or rappelling, parascending or hang gliding, potholing or caving, and the hire of dune buggies - which are the other activities on offer at a price of Dhs.275 for a single activity, Dhs.325 for a day with two choices, and Dhs.425 for a weekend/two days. More adventurous options will be available soon including an overnight mountain-biking trek, two-day basic course in survival and another in navigation. Also planned is an overnight buggy trekking adventure.

### Desert Rangers

**On Request** | **Dune Centre Al Satwa** | **Page 5 E 3** | Tel: **460 808**

Control your own roped descent down a rock face of approximately 50 - 100ft in height. You will be under the watchful guidance of a fully qualified Ranger at all times. Test your nerve to the limit. Only two people will be on the rock face at one time. The rest will watch until their time comes. Location Wadi Asma, Hatta. Cost Dhs.275 per person.

## Aerobics

Most beach, health and sport clubs offer some form of aerobics on a regular basis. For a complete list of classes, timings and instructors, either call the clubs, or refer to the *Connector* or *Aquarius* magazines.

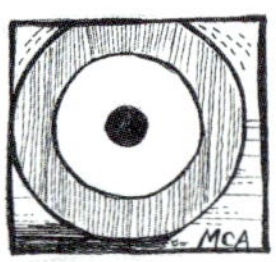

## Archery

### Dubai Archery Club

**Tuesdays 20:00 - 22:00** | **Check as changing** | **Page 12 B 3** | Tel: **331 746**

Used to be held at the Darjeeling Cricket Club, it costs Dhs.200 to become a member and Dhs.10 per night, which goes towards replacing the targets annually. A small and friendly gathering. Membership includes use of clubhouse. Currently the club may not exist as they are looking for suitable premises. Telephone for more updated information.

# Boules

## Le Boules Brothers

20:30 Tue
Fri DIMC

Darjeeling Cricket Club &
The DIMC

Page 12
B 3

Tel: **846 111**

Boules Brothers (BB) meet every Tuesday evening at the Darjeeling Cricket Club 20:30 for informal practice in the 'pentanque'. 'Pentanque' also play at the DIMC on Fridays and selected days of the week. Le BB was responsible for the 1st major tournoi in Dubai in 1995 and the subsequent tounoi in 1996 attracting in excess of 90 boulistes from as far a field as Abu Dhabi and Al Ain.

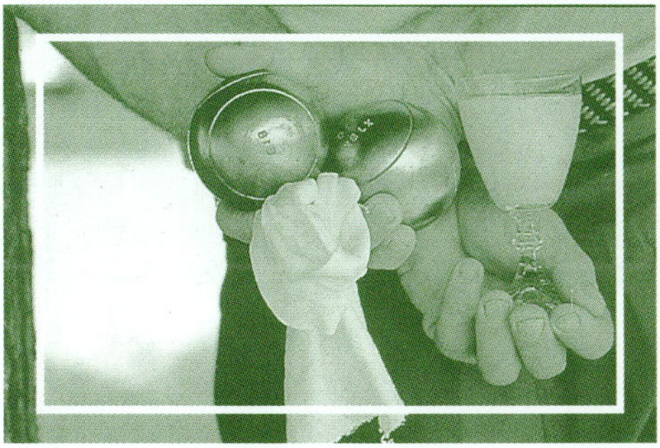

Le comite are at present organising the '3rd Dubai Boules Open' to be held this autumn at the DIMC on custom boulodrome over lookin la mer. Boulistes from all corners of the emirates will attend including the French Navy. More details may be obtained from the fineset boulist in Dubai, Jacky Gerault (846 111) or Ken Hassall (050 654 8625). A bientot boulistes!

# Bowling

## Al Nasr Leisureland

07:00 - 23:00

Al Nasr Leisureland
Nr. Lodge/American Hospital

Page 9
E 4

Tel: **371 234**

One of Dubai's original leisure venues, Al Nasr Leisureland is popular with all. The recently renovated 8-lane bowling alley is synthetic, and thus smarter looking and faster! Shoes etc can be hired as usual, and sustenance provided by the fast food outlets. Alcohol is also served at the bar. Booking is most definitely recommended. Dhs.10 entrance, Dhs.7 per game and free shoe rental.

## Dubai Bowling Centre

15:00 - 01:00

Airport Rd/Nr. Deira City Centre
Al Garhoud

Page 14
E 1

Tel: **283 819**

The first bowling centre to arrive in Dubai, this is not the newest of clubs or equipment, but great for a night out. Ten lanes, with each game costing Dhs.8, and shoes Dhs. 2. Make sure you bring along some socks! Open non-stop, seven days a week. Loads of tournaments scheduled, so the centre is booked out on Saturday, Monday and Wednesday. Booking is advisable for the remaining days. Popular place with the talented Filipino bowlers. The Centre also has a couple of arcade type games, five snooker tables and two billiards tables. Small bar serving soft and alcoholic drinks and snacks (club sandwiches, hamburgers, chips & salad for Dhs. 15).

# Canoeing

## Desert Rangers

On Request | **Dune Centre Al Satwa** | **Page 5 E 3** | Tel: **460 808**

Two/four-person "Red Indian" canoes with single bladed paddles. Initial instruction is given, followed by brief hands-on manoeuvres to develop skills & confidence. Then you paddle through the mangrove lagoon and experience its unique scenery and wildlife, found only in the UAE. There are eight, 2-4 seater canoes and one instructor's Kayak. Location: Kalba, Umm All Quwain. Cost Dhs.300 per person.

## For Rental See:

| | | |
|---|---|---|
| **Beach Clubs** | Dubai International Marine Club | Le Mirage |
| | Metropolitan Beach Club | |

# Caving

See Abseiling - Adventure Unlimited

# Cricket

## Darjeeling Cricket Club

**09:00 - 22:00** | **Darjeeling Cricket Club Nr. Country Club R/A** | **Page 12 B 3** | Tel: **331 746**

Formed in 1969 by a group of expatriates, the name comes from the Darjeeling Sports Shop in Bahrain which kindly provided the first playing kit.

Cricket is the main sport played here and matches of 25 overs start at 09:00 and 13:30 every Friday, with net practice taking place under floodlights every Tuesday evening. Early March sees a six-a-side Gulf tournament and the rest of the year sees matches against visiting Test sides when they are competing at Sharjah.

Hockey is played on Wednesday, with Youth teams at 18:00 - 19:00, and both men and women's teams at 19:30. Archery and Boules, on different parts of the grounds, every Tuesday at 20:00. Clubhouse, with bar, open Tuesday - Sunday. Membership costs Dhs.500 per playing member and Dhs.200 per social member. There are no match fees.

# Croquet

A classic croquet lawn is setup in Club Joumna, Jebel Ali hotel. See under Beach Clubs and Weekend Breaks.

# Cycling

A great way to see Dubai's parks, four wheel, five-seater bicycles can be hired in both Safa and Creekside Park.

## See Also:

**Mountain Biking**

# Dancing

## Al Naadi

| | | |
|---|---|---|
| **Mon 15:15 - 19:45** | **Al Ghurair Centre Deira** — **Page 10 D 1** | Tel: **276 476** |

This Club offers ballet classes on Mondays 15:15 - 19:45 at the studio. Sally Bigland, a ballet teacher from the U.K., has a wide range of experience when it comes to dancing. She is a fully qualified teacher taking students up to Royal Academy of Dancing examination standard. Certificates presented to those who pass. Cost is Dhs.400 per term consisting of 11 sessions for children aged 4 to 10.

## American Square Dancing Club

| | | |
|---|---|---|
| **Sat 20:00 -** | **Check Location Jumeira** — **Page Z** | Tel: **487 580** |

Grab your partner by the hand, get on the dance floor and get ready to heel-toe, heel-toe all evening. A lively evening of old fashioned barn dancing, country dancing and square dancing in the old Wild West style. No need to wear check shirts or flouncy dresses, but do wear comfortable shoes as you will be energetically twirling and moving over every inch of space on the floor.

All standards of dancers welcome, whether beginners, "I've forgotten my schooltime steps" or experts. Couples welcome, singles too. Held every Saturday in Jumeira at 20:00. Tel.487 580 Liz/442 591 Lena, for more details.

## Arabesque

08:00 - 19:00
Closed Fri

Al Jumeira Rd
Jumeira

Page 4
D 2

Tel: **447 638**

Arabesque is primarily a ballet school for children but also offers an extensive range of classes including jazz and tap dancing, music movement, gymnastics and karate.

Adult exercise classes are offered Sunday and Wednesday at 09:00, ranging from a low impact workout, to step classes and a high impact class using weights. It also offers yoga and specialises in pregnancy yoga. Children's classes range from Dhs.20 to Dhs.30 per class and all adult classes are Dhs.25 each. There is a delightful coffee shop situated in the central courtyard of this old style Arabic villa on the Beach Road in Jumeira.

## Ballet Centre, The

Check

Behind Pizza Hut
Al Dhiyafah St - Al Satwa

Page 5
E 3

Tel: **459 771**

Who better to run a dance school than an ex-professional dancer of stage and television? Terri Dean is the busy lady who, together with a staff of professional teachers, offers Royal Academy of Dancing syllabi and examinations to children from the age of three upwards. The school has a 100% pass rate, with many of the children passing with distinction. Older children can also learn jazz dancing, the martial of art of Taekwondo and join a Youth Theatre.

Evenings see adults using the two studios for various fitness workouts including Step & Tone and Cardio Combo, which is a fun class to tone the boltom, abdomen and thighs. There's even a belly dancing course and ballroom dancing classes.

## Ballroom Dancing

Tues

Forte Grand Airport
Al Garhoud

Page 14
E 3

Tel: **702 2475**

Having won her first ballroom dancing competition just three months after beginning classes it is no wonder that Mika Simkunoite kept on with the classes and kept on with the winning. She has danced her way through numerous countries and has now settled in Dubai with the aim of helping others learn the joy and fun of dancing.

Classes are held every Tuesday at Le Mirage Health Club, Forte Grand where up to a dozen people of varying nationalities waltz, cha cha cha, samba, quickstep, lambada and foxtrot around the spacious room. Dhs.25 for members, Dhs.35 for non-members of the Club.

## Indian Classical Dance

On Request

Tel: **354 311**

Indian classical dances have a unique style of their own, with fast rhythmic footwork and facial expressions. They are not only soothing to the mind, but also act as yoga excersises for the people who learn this art form.

Mrs. Geetha Krishnan, a reputed Bharatnatyam and Kuchipudi teacher in Dubai, holds classes for those who are interested in learning these dance forms, aged six years and upwards. After completion of the course, which takes around four years, the pupil performs her Arangetram, a performance in front of reputed maestro's and critics. Two of

Mrs. Geetha Krishnan's students have successfully performed their Arangetrams in Dubai to a live orchestra.

Mrs. Krishnan also choreographs classical and folk dances, plus fashion shows, when her students get a chance to show-off their talents. Recent achievements have included the Dubai Shopping Festival where she presented "India in the Past" and Indian folklore displays.

## Vanessa Chapman

**Check** | **Various Locations** | Tel: **390 362**

Vanessa Chapman a fully qualified professional dancer, teacher and choreograher offers a broad range of classes to all age groups, (Hilton Beach Club, Lobelia Health Retreat and Dubai Country Club).

Join a "Stepping Out Class" to learn the wonderous art of tap dancing, or "Dance Workout" to strenghten, strech, flex & dance. "Body & Soul" is a unique collection of exersices to help you achieve and maintain flexibility, strength and leanness. Private lessons available to ladies only. Also teaches children aged 2 - 13 years. Fees Dhs.20-30.

# Deep Sea Fishing

## Creek Cruises

**On Request** | **Quay 2/3, Dhow Wharfage Deira** | **Page 10 C 2** | Tel: **533 554**

*The Discovery* is a 42 foot yacht which is available for luxury cruising and sports fishing. The yacht has an air-conditioned cabin, a large sun deck, a rest room, music system, safety kit and can accomodate a maximum of 10 guests. For its fishing trips, the Discovery is equipped with professional fishing kit, fish finder and bottom riggers.

## Dubai Creek Golf & Yacht Club

**On Request** | **Dubai Creek Marina Opp. Deira City Centre, Deira** | **Page 14 C 2** | Tel: **821 000**

Imagine reclining on the deck of the Halleras 32 Sport Fisherman, plying the Gulf's sun-splashed waters. From atop the skyscraping tower, your spotter calls down the location of a fast-moving school. You jump into action, matching wits with Sailfish, King Fish, Cobia, Queen Fish, Barracuda, Tuna, Dorado or Jacks. Comfortable accommodation for up to six passengers. The rates (4 Hrs - Dhs .1,500, 8 Hrs - Dhs.2,200, Add. Hr Dhs.200) include everything: boat, tackle, bait, fuel, insurance and a friendly crew that knows how to find great fishing. Hey, sometimes it gets a little sticky out there. Not a problem! The spacious lavatory includes a stand-up shower for even the tallest adventurer.

When your appetite demands attention there is a galley stocked full of your choice of beverages (alcoholic and non-alcoholic) and hearty boxed lunches. What a day!

## DIMC

**On Request** | **DIMC Al Mina Al Siyah** | **Page 2 A 2** | Tel: **846 111**

Enjoy a full or half-day fishing trip in one of the best game fishing grounds in the Arabian Gulf. The experienced skippers will guide you to what could be the most exciting catch of a lifetime! Half day: Dhs.750, Full day: Dhs.1,400. To book a trip, call.

## Samharam Deep Sea Fishing - *Salalah*

**On Request** | **Salalah Oman** | Fax: **050 644 2432**

Salalah and the banks that lie offshore are virgin fishing territory! There are Blue, Black and Striped Marlin in the waters, in what is a "Jurassic park" for deep sea fishing. Sailfish are abundant too, along with Wahoo, Dorado (Dolphinfish), huge Yellowfin Tuna and more!

You will get a skipper and mate, and the boat is fully equipped with quality tackle (you are welcome to bring your own if you want to). Trolling deadbait or lures is the norm, but livebaiting is practised too. "Kismet" is a 33 foot Aquabell Sportfisherman powered by twin diesels for a cruise speed of 24 knots. She is a rugged sea-boat that has all the necessary comforts, including toilet, required for a day or night at sea. A full complement of safety equipment is provided: lifejacket's, marine radio, E.P.I.R.B., and sea anchor (drogue).

Trip options range from half day trips (4 hours) up to a long day (9 hours). Fruit and soft drinks are provided gratis. Special seasonal and midweek rates are available on request. Please note: The tag and release of Billfish is encouraged and International Game Fishing Association rules and regulations are adhered to. For further information contact: Simon and Ruth Bracey, Mobile 050-644 2432.

## Seahorse Fishing Company

**On Request** | **Various Locations UAE East/West Coast** | Tel: **06 377 828**

Fully dedicated to Game Fishing in the UAE Seahorse Fishing Co. provides fishing trips from two to 10 hours, depending on which kind of fishing customers prefer. Two options on where to fish: 'coastline fishing' from the coast up to 10 miles form the shore, and 'deep-sea fishing' from 10 to 40 miles from shore. Once again, two options on how to fish: 'Bottom fishing', where the boat is stopped over reefs or wrecks, mainly for small and medium size fish. Day and night trips available. Then there is 'Trawling', where the boat moves slowly and baits are trawled behind the boat. Mainly for medium and big size fish.

Prices range from Dhs.600 for two hours (4 people) up to Dhs.2,400 for eight hours, including all necessary equipment for fishing, technical advice, soft drinks and food. It operates from DIMC (Dubai Marine International Club) for the Arabian Gulf and from Khorfakhan for the Gulf of Oman.

The best fishing period is October - April, although fishing is still possible in summer for fish such as Barracuda and Queen Fish in Dubai.

Going fishing in Khorfakhan in summer is much better and fish such as Sailfish can still be caught during the hot season. Two day trips to Oman will be available at prices ranging from Dhs.1,300 to Dhs.1,900 per person, which includes the cost of all visas, equipment, camping food, drinks, etc. Khasab is near the Straits of Hormuz and takes five hours to reach by boat from Dubai.

## Sun Tours

**On Request** | **Check Location** | Tel: **214 555**

Enjoy your day with an exciting fishing trip in one of the best fishing grounds of the Arabian Gulf. Trips from three to ten hours. The boat takes up to six passengers from Al Jazira Resort and is well equipped with all sorts of fishing equipment, baits and soft drinks. Cost is Dhs.300 pp for 1 - 3 hours, and Dhs.100 for each additional hour.

# Diving

## Al Boom Marine-Diving Unlimited

**Sat-Thur 09:00 - 21:00**
**Fri 15:00 - 21:00**

**Nr. EPPCO Station**
**Al Jumeira Rd - Jumeira 3**

**Page 4**
**B 2**

Tel: **389 710**

Experience life from a different perspective...Al Boom offers a full range of P.A.D.I. diving courses - ranging from 'Discover Scuba', to' Assistant Instructor'. Available seven days a week between the hours of 09:00 to 21:00, and 15:00 to 21:00 on Friday. Full time P.A.D.I. instructors can advise you the courses which best suit your requirements and can adapt course schedule's to fit in with your own.

'Dive into adventure' qualifying courses start with the Open Water Course at Dhs.1,200, the Advanced Open Water Dhs.800, Specialities start at Dhs.250. They offer daily dive trips from the Dubai Coast, as well as day and weekend trips from the East Coast from Dhs.120 for a two tank dive. This is the ideal time to give yourself a break, even for the kids. Courses for kids aged eight years upwards, are available upon request.

The retail store offers a full range of U.S Divers equipment to suit any tastes and the staff are more than willing to assist with any questions or requirements you may have. Give them a call, they are never to busy to help you ....

## Dubai Sports Divers Club

**Tue 20:00**

**Club House**
**Al Quoz Industrial Area**

Tel: **441 693**

Operative word being club. The only dive club in Dubai, founded in 1982, now has over 100 members, of which 22 are instructors. This strong club is a branch of the British

Sub Aqua Club (BSAC), which allows them to certify their training. Open to all qualified divers who are certified by a recognised agency. The club has three boats and two compressors. Lively club night every Monday, with refreshments. Membership (Dhs.850 Male, Dhs.550 Female) includes free use of the compressor and all dive trips offshore! Diving takes place most Fridays, weather permitting. Variety of BSAC courses on offer: rescue management, boat navigation and handling (RYA standards) and first aid (for diving). What else? Well, your best bet is to go along to their club night and see whether you like who you meet, or contact their chairperson, Bob MacGregor. Simple!

## Inner Space Diving Centre

**10:00 - 13:00**
**16:00 - 21:00**

**City Tower, Shop 1**
**Sh Zayed Rd/Trade Centre**

**Page 8**
**C 2**

Tel: **310 203**

This is a bona fide PADI 5-star establishment which is doing a roaring trade in renting equipment and organising weekend trips to the East Coast. Full range of PADI courses from beginner to instructor level on offer, as well as teaching handicapped people under the HSA scheme. All the above courses are taught in Arabic, English, Persian, Hindi and Dutch.

PADI Open water course (Dhs.1,400), PADI Advanced (Dhs.900), Complete dive set rental (Dhs.60), Dive computer rental (Dhs.50), Diving Trips on the West coast, Port Rashid wrecks (Dhs.60/dive), Sharraf III - Car barge (Dhs.75/dive), Off Dubai (Dhs.100/dive). Trips on the East coast; Rat Island (Dhs.275/two dives), Dibba Rock (Dhs.125), Night Dive - Musandam (Dhs.100/dive), plus many more...

## Khasab Diving Centre

**On Request**

**Khasab, Musandam**
**Oman**

Tel: **420 553**

Often described as the "Norway of the Middle East", with its natural fjord-like inlets offering a multitude of diving sites, with regular sightings of dolphins, the scenic beauty both above and below the water here is amazing.

This new dive centre, run by *Scuba International*, offers diving packages including transfers where needed, entry/exit visas, and accommodation. It is run by Bas Van Den Brandeler who speaks Dutch, English, French, Italian, German, Portuguese, Spanish and Arabic.

Diving is from a traditional Arabian dhow on a tank and weights basis. Whilst the centre has a few sets of full equipment, these are primarily for replacement only, should a customer have an equipment problem. Diving in the Musandam area is certainly more adventurous than in other local areas and you are advised to consider your experience level before booking on these trips. All the dives are guided, but it is not an area that is suited to novice divers.

Accommodation is either at the Khasab Motel, or sharing villa/apartments on a bed and breakfast basis. The Khasab Motel has a bar and a restaurant which is open to non-residents. Bookings can be made through the Dubai office 420 553. Summer Package: two nights accommodation (Hotel or Villa), four dives - tank and weights, visa fee, breakfast and daily lunch Dhs.1,150 per person (US and UK Citizens add Dhs.100 - Additional Visa Fees)

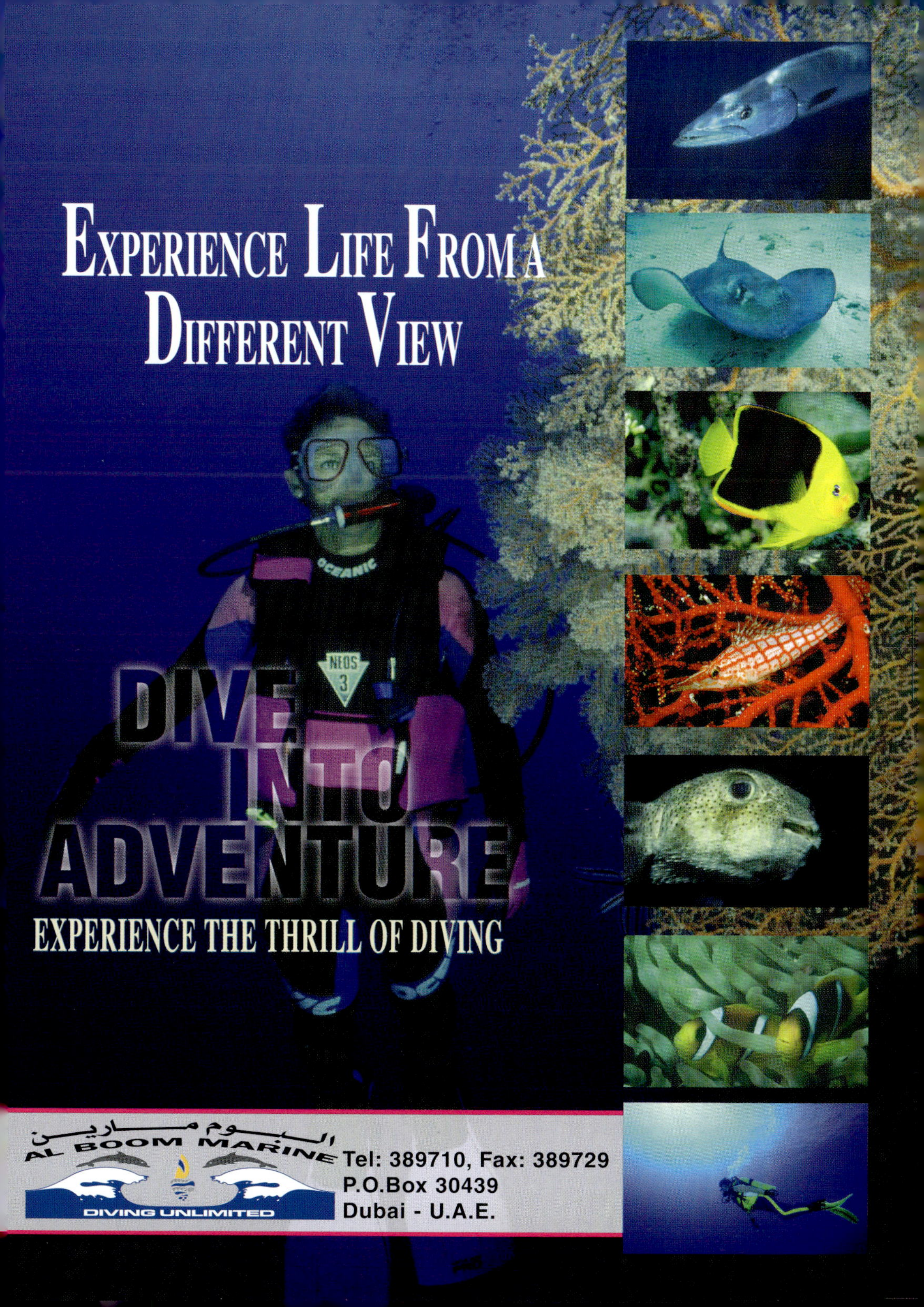
EXPERIENCE LIFE FROM A DIFFERENT VIEW
DIVE INTO ADVENTURE
EXPERIENCE THE THRILL OF DIVING
البوم مارين
AL BOOM MARINE
DIVING UNLIMITED
Tel: 389710, Fax: 389729
P.O.Box 30439
Dubai - U.A.E.

## Lukhma Diver's Service

On Request | Al Kawab Build, Sh Zayed Rd | Page 8, A 2 | Tel: **446 944**

Lukhama is Arabic for Sting ray! Lukhma Divers is a PADI 5-star Dive Centre having diving facilities to the local wrecks in Dubai, as well as coral beds off the East Coast. Provides the full range of PADI courses, from Open Water to Assistant Instructor. Speciality courses from Dhs.300. Daylight dives with two dives for Dhs.100-200. Equipment needs are fulfilled with the latest Sherwood and Genesis Scuba items available from the shop, which is open Saturday - Thursday. Also offers special rates at the Holiday Beach Motel.

## Ocean Divers' Centre

On Request | Oceanic Hotel, Khorfakkan - East Coast | Tel: **09 382 971**

Located on the UAE's East Coast, this PADI 5-star Diving Centre is managed by Scuba International. Diving excursions for qualified divers, courses for beginners and 'Discover Scuba' experiences for those who haven't decided yet on whether they want to learn. Nearby rocky islands in the Indian Ocean offer beautiful pictures of hard and soft coral, turtles, barracuda and tropical reef fish. PADI open water course, PADI Advanced, Dive Trips, Night Dive. Air fills Dhs.20. Mask, fins, snorkel, boots Dhs.20.

## Sandy Beach Diving Centre

On Request | Sandy Beach Motel, East Coast | Tel: **09 445 050**

Open all year round, the German managed UTS Diving Centre is located at Sandy Beach Motel. Its own 27 ft. boat, equipped with two 200 HP outboard motors, can take divers to a multitude of sites within 20 minutes. Local dive sites between Khorfakkan and Dibba have a depth range of 6-27 metres. Sample the pleasures of underwater scenery from a beginners first dive, up to certification stage. See colourful coral and rock formations, creatures of the deep like groupers, turkey fish, angel and surgeonfish, puffers and morays. The lucky ones are rewarded with rare sightings of turtles, sting-rays and sandsharks.

Wetsuits are available for hire as are tanks, scubapro jackets with regulators, underwater lighting and snorkel equipment, along with U.W. photo and video camera. To maintain their high standard of performance all equipment is serviced every six months. Dry and clean air in the diving tanks are taken care of by BAUER and Posiedon compressors.

## Scuba Dubai

09:00 - 13:00, 16:00 - 20:30 Closed Fri | Block C, Trade Centre App., Sh Zayed Rd | Page 8, D 2 | Tel: **317 433**

One of the leading scuba diving retailers in Dubai, providing totally professional and personalised service. Their well used motto is "If we can't help you, then we will find someone who can!" The only full time scuba equipment repair workshop in the Gulf, employing two full time diving technicians qualified to repair all major brands of diving equipment.

This is an Aladdin's cave of all those little acessories that you have read about in international magazines, but didn't know you could buy locally. As well as a retail outlet offering a wide range of equipment, air can be filled (up to 300 bar) and diving equipment rented, as long as you are certified. Open Thursday from 09:00 - 19:00, plus free sweets!

## Scuba International

10:00 - 1900
Closed Fri

500m from Iranian Hospital
Al Wasl Rd

Page 5
C 3

Tel: **420 553**

If the question is diving, the answer is Scuba International who are waiting to introduce you to an underwater world. Offers the full range of PADI diving courses from beginner to instructor. People who know how to schedule a course to fit into your busy lifestyle, whilst still enabling you to learn at your own pace. Experienced instructors make your transition from above, to below the sea line a safe and enjoyable one. Go on, take the plunge and see what diving is all about!

Extensive menu of courses; Open water Dhs.1,400. Advanced open water Dhs.700. Specialities from Dhs.300. Daily dive trips from the East Coast Centre in Fujairah with prices starting from Dhs.150 for a two-tank trip.

## Scubatec

09:00 - 21:00
Closed Fri

Sana Building
Al Karama

Page 9
C 1

Tel: **348 988**

Professional PADI instructors who are available for hire either to teach diving or take groups of qualified divers to interesting sites. Dive trips, including hire of full gear costs Dhs.125 to a local wreck site, Dhs.250 for two dives at a wreck site 10 km offshore from Dubai, and Dhs.225 for two dives at a man made reef near Khorfakkan.

Friendly instruction in various languages, i.e. German, English, Arabic, Persian and Urdu. Open Water diver course provides students with elemental knowledge and skills needed to safely dive independently. The course consists of five class room sessions, five pool sessions and four open water sessions. Duration: 31 hours (five days) Dhs.1,400. The PADI Advance Open Water course may be taken by certified open water divers. Five dives. Duration: 15 hours (two days) Dhs.1,000.

Rescue Diver course is designed to develop necessary knowledge and skills for individuals to effectively perform diver rescues, manage accident situations and render proper first aid. Duration: 25 hours (4 days)-Dhs.1,500. PADI Night Diver course is an introduction to night diving and helps develop skills, knowledge and techniques necessary to safely participate in night-diving activities. Duration: 12 hours (two nights) Dhs.600.

## Sun Tours

On Request

Various Locations

Tel: **214 555**

Full range of PADI, SSI, CMAS and discovery courses for beginners, as well as diving excursions for qualified divers. Diving courses: PADI and SSI Open Water Dive Dhs.1,580, CMAS basic course Dhs.1,050, Discovery course Dhs.320. Rate for self-equipped dives: Dhs.125 per dive, Dhs.335 for three dives, Dhs.635 for six dives. Base equipped: Dhs.160 for one dive, Dhs.430 for three dives, Dhs.815 for six dives. Rental rates of equipment: Mask, Fins, Snorkel, Suit and Computer at Dhs.25. Regulator & Octopus, Jacket and Torch at Dhs.35.

# Dune Buggys

## Desert Rangers

**On Request** | **Dune Centre Al Satwa** | **Page 5 E 3** | Tel: **460 808**

Explore the wonders of the desert in dune buggies designed and built in the UK. They are safe, lots of fun and environmentally friendly. Having been given a full-face helmet and protective overalls, plus a brief talk on safety, you are led onto the course for familiarisation with the buggy. After that, you're on your own. All activities are closely monitored by experienced Rangers.

There are two-seater and single seater buggies, allowing 13 people to be on course at a time. It is possible to run relay of participants at intervals of 10 -15 minutes.

Location Khanwaneej Rally track. Cost Dhs.375 per person

## See Also:

Adventure Unlimited - **Abseiling**

# Fishing

Fishing rods and bait available in various clubs for beach/rock fishing. Average rate of Dhs.10/one hr, Dhs.35/half day plus Dhs.5 for a packet of bait.

For the really adventurous, and those with spare cash, check out the *Deep Sea Fishing* section.

# Flying

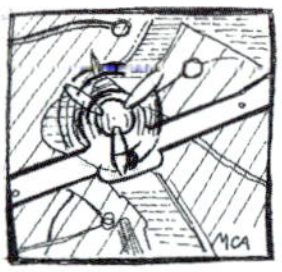


## Dubai Model Flying

**Most Fridays** | **Nr. Emirates Golf Club Sh Zayed Rd/Al Mina Al Siyahi** | **Page 1 E 3** | Tel: **381 210**

All great pilots start this way! Group of 20 or so model flying enthusiasts who meet regularly near the Emirates Golf Course. They have their own wind sock, white board with the different radio frequencies being used, and most importantly, insurance... just in case their planes hit something! They are looking at possibly making their own paved runway. A great show of acrobatic aircraft. Best place to go if you want to meet the experts!

## Emirates Flying School

**On Request** | **Nr. Cargo Village Dubai International Airprt** | **Page 14 E 2** | Tel: **244 684**

As expected, EFS is located at the airport, to the East of the main terminal building at Dubai International Airport, adjacent to the staff car park. Dhs.160 will buy you a trial 20 minutes up in the air, for hands-on experience of whether you really want to go ahead and learn to fly. But it's not all high flying, there are 35 hours of lectures on ground subjects, as well as manuals, charts and navigation equipment to master, plus a minimum of 40 flying hours before gaining your internationally recognised UAE Private Pilot License. Great fun. Pay as you fly price of Dhs.500 per hour.

## Fujairah Aviation Centre

**On Request** | **Fujairah International Airport, Fujairah** | Tel: **09 224 747**

This is a company that grew from a hobby into a business. The Fujairah National Group's Chairman, is a keen aviator who set up the Centre ten years ago, more for self-fulfilment than with profits in mind. As a result of the high calibre of instructors involved, FAC received accreditation as a flying school from the Civil Authorities in UAE and UK, as soon as the Centre was established.

Twin and single engine training aircraft, plus special training equipment including an instrument flight simulator are available. Qualified to train students for private pilot's license and advanced ratings. Own workshop for repairs to own and other aircraft. English is the international language of civil aviation and so pupils must be conversant in written and oral English. All ages welcome, but students must be 17 or over to fly solo, and 18 when a licence is issued. Trial flying lesson available for Dhs.200/half hr and Dhs.400/hr. Gift vouchers available.

Ground training costs Dhs.50/hr, flight training Dhs.400/hr, and FAC membership is Dhs.300/year.

## See Also:


Hang Gliding
Hot Air Ballooning
Microlights
Paragliding
Parasailing
Scenic Flights - **Tours**


# Football

## Creek Football Club

**Check** | **Nr Country Club, Nadd Al Sheba** | **Page 12 B 3** | Tel: **331 291**

In 1975, eight teams formed an expat league with Creek F.C. dominating the soccer scene for the first decade. CFC is considered the unofficial headquarters of the Dubai-Sharjah league and hosts several other expatriate football and social competitions throughout the year. Opened in 1980 by ex-England and Leeds Manager, the late Don Revie, the club has hosted many of football's top stars, even the (infamous) George Best visited and played (drank) at the club. The clubhouse consists of a licensed bar, c/w satellite TV, changing rooms and shower facilities.

Oct-May sees the UAE expatriate league and cup football competitions being played between teams from Dubai, Sharjah, Abu Dhabi and Al Ain. July-Oct is when CFC hosts a 12 team, seven-a-side summer football league competition played on Wednesday evenings.

The club is also the organiser of the annual Dubai Raft Race which celebrated its 25th anniversary at DIMC in 1996. The clubhouse and floodlit pitch are available an a rental basis, but if you just want a game of football, or require further information on the local soccer scene, please Tel. 331 291 and ask for the Chairman (Gary Foote).

# Golf

Dubai is quite rightly becoming known as the golf destination of the Gulf with its three fully grassed courses and two brown (sand). The top quality grass of Emirates Golf Club is the setting for the Dubai Desert Classic each winter, part of the PGA European tour, while Dubai Creek Golf & Yacht Club, home of the Asian PGA Tour event 'Dubai Creek Open', combines a magnificent 18-hole course with a marina, complete with workshop and chandlery. Nad Al Sheba is a Golf & Racing Club with a 9-hole links course sited within a top grade horse racing track and a further 9-hole course outside.

Brown courses are available to members and guests of the Dubai Country Club and Sharjah Wanderers Golf Club.

## Dubai Creek Golf & Yacht Club

**07:00 - 22:00** **Dubai Creek Golf & Yacht Club, Al Garhoud** **Page 14, C 2** Tel: **821 000**

This course is open to all on a pay-as-you-play basis. June-September is when this tournament quality, 18-hole golf course is available to play at a special rate of Dhs.140 from 16:00 until dark. Known as 'Twilight Golf', this is a good way to enjoy as much golf as possible in the fading light and heat of this part of the world. Normal rates on this 18-hole championship course are Dhs.235 (Sunday to Wednesday), and Dhs.265 on Thursday, Friday, Saturday and Public holidays. Cart hire at Dhs.35 per person. Visitors can hire clubs (Dhs. 80), etc.

The beautiful landscaped par 72 is very challenging - deceptively snaking between six man made lakes, rolling green dunes and clusters of palm trees. Try a short game on the Par 3, 9-hole, floodlit course which takes approximately one hour to go round, for Dhs.25. Variety of shots playable. Good practice for putting, pitching and placing. Practice balls are Dhs.20 per bucket.

## Dubai Golf & Racing Club

**07:30 - 24:00** **Dubai Golf & Racing Club, Nadd Al Sheba** **Page 12, A 3** Tel: **363 666**

Day or night play is available on this fully floodlit 18 hole links style course. The back nine is built inside the perimeter of Dubai's main race course at Nad Al Sheba, home of the $4 million Dubai World Cup Horserace, while the front nine, opened in 1996, runs alongside the 'home straight'. Don't expect to get a game on Thursdays or Sundays when this dual purpose club is taken over by horse flesh.

With the last tee-time for 9-hole being at 22:00 this is a popular choice for businessmen who have spent a hard day at the office. They, and their wives, come here to spend a hard evening on the golf course, and a sociable get together at the clubhouse bar afterwards. Floodlit driving range until 22:00.

Fees for members are Dhs.200 (non-members Dhs.220) for 18-holes, Dhs.100 (Dhs.110) for a 9-hole game. Carts available for hire (9-hole Dhs.20, 18-hole, Dhs.35). Dhs.20 for a bucket of approx. 50 balls to use on the driving range independent of whether or not you will be playing a round of golf.

## Emirates Golf Club

06:00 - 21:30 | Emirates Golf Club, Sh Zayed Rd/Al Mina Al Siyahi | Page 2, A 3 | Tel: **480 222**

The unique clubhouse and buildings are immediately recognisable by their Beduin tent design which disguises plush, modern, air conditioned interiors. Membership is highly

sought after for this club and standards throughout are high. Boasting 36 championship holes in total, split between the Majlis and Wadi courses. Fully grassed, the Club hosts the annual Dubai Desert Classic tournament, which is part of the ATP European tour. The large swimming pool and patio area is often the site of concerts and shows. Luxury changing rooms, cordon bleu cuisine and attentive service, are the expected norm by the members of this establishment... and they get it. Fees: Majlis Course- Dhs330, Wadi Course - Dhs.265. All guests must produce a valid handicap certificate (<28 men/<36 women). Driving range: Dhs.20 for 50 balls. Cart hire (compulsory) - Dhs.40.

## See Also:

Dubai Country Club - **Sports Club**
Sharjah Wanders - **Sports Club**
**Mini Golf**

# Golf Academys

## Dubai Creek Golf Academy

On Request | Dubai Creek Golf & Yacht Club, Al Garhoud | Page 14, C 2 | Tel: **822 789**

Learn to play golf with professional coaches. Hi-tech video swing analysis room, on-course instruction on adjoining Par 3 course. Driving range open 07:00 - 22:00. One-month course for Dhs.695, Intermediate's three-month course for Dhs.1,700 and a 12-month Players Programme costs Dhs.5,000. Junior lessons available for Dhs.2,000/12-months or five Group lessons (min. 4 children) for Dhs.200 each child.

## Emirates Golf Academy

On Request | Emirates Golf Club, Sh Zayed Rd/Al Mina Al Siyahi | Page 2, A 3 | Tel: **480 222**

Golf tuition is available for members and their families by professional instructors. Group or individual sessions, single or course of lessons. Many of the players from this club go on to win local championships. Junior sessions on Saturdays to fit in with school timetables.

# Hang Gliding

## See:

**Flying** **Paragliding** Adventure Unlimited - **Abseiling**

# Hashing

## Creek Hash House Harriers

**Tues pm**
**Check Press**
**Various Locations**
Tel: **446 773**

CH3 is a men-only social running club that meets on Tuesday evenings thoughout the year. Different locations each week. Start times are normally 30 minutes before sunset, with runs usually lasting 40 to 50 minutes.

The concept of hashing is not to race but to follow pre-marked trails, and false trails, with the keen runners covering much more ground than the social members who jog and walk their way round at the rear of the pack. Cost is Dhs.50 per run, which includes as much beverage as can be consumed during the social circle around a bonfire following the run.

Special runs approximately once a month also include food and T-Shirt. Location and details may be obtained from On Sec Heinz "Snoopy" Zuccelli on 823 171 (off)/ 234 579 (res) or G.M. Norman "FK Buck" Warren on 406 2277 (off)/ 446 773 (res).

## Desert Hash House Harriers

**Check**
**Various Locations**
**Dubai**
Tel: **352 532**

DH3 is the longest established hash in Dubai. Initially started in 1979, it has weekly runs every Sunday at various locations. Weekly attendance is between 60-80 men and women. Runs commence one hour before sunset, lasting 50 minutes on average. The cost per run is Dhs.35, inclusive of food and beverage. New runners and visitors are always welcome. Details of the run location is published each Sunday in the personal announcements column of the local newspapers.

In addition DH3 holds many novelty runs, together with a monthly Curry Club, camping weekends and varied social evenings. More details can be obtained from the On Sec Rob Hughes.

## Falcon Hash

**Mondays**
**Various Locations**
**Sharjah/Ajman**
Tel: **06 334 540**

Falcon Hash is fondly known throughout the Emirates as the "Budgie" hash. FH3 is a family event and welcomes children. It is the only Hash covering Sharjah and Ajman.

Run/jog/walk/talk at different locations each week, on Monday evenings an hour before sunset. Runs cover various terrain and distances lasting between 35 to 55 minutes, with a halfway short-cut alternative for walkers and wimps. Cost, which covers social events at certain times of the year, is Dhs.10 for adults, no charge for children.

Maps are placed at Sahrjah Wanderers Sports Club each week or call On Sec Anne Gibbs on 06 334 540 for information and location.

# Hiking

## Desert Rangers

On Request | Dune Centre, Al Satwa | Page 5, E 3 | Tel: **460 808**

Walk among the majestic mountains of the United Arab Emirates accompanied by experienced and qualified Rangers. Ascend several summits to enjoy the freedom of rough mountain country and see its dramatic sun baked features at close quarters. Notes: They can easily handle groups of 100 pax, but will divide them into smaller groups and take different routes to the summits. We can take various tracks in order to suit the age and fitness level of the individuals.

Locations: Fujairah, Dibba Kalba, Masafi, Hatta. Cost Dhs.200 per person.

## See Also:

**Mountaineering**

# Horse Riding

## Club Joumana

Check | Jebel Ali Hotel, Nr. Jebel Ali | Tel: **836 000**

Situated about half an hour's drive outside Dubai, the riding centre is located within the beautiful grounds of the Jebel Ali hotel. Relatively small paddock area, surrounded by trees (rare!). Keith Brown is the riding instructor and manger of the centre.

Rates are very competive with tuition at Dhs.50 for 30 minutes, and beach rides at Dhs.100 per hour.

## Dubai Equestrian Centre

See Text | Nr. Camel Race Track, Nadd Al Shiba | Tel: **361 394**

D.E.C. is located near the Dubai Racing Club, Nad Al Sheba. It was formed in 1983 under the patronage of H.H Sheikh Maktoum Bin Rashid Al Maktoum. The Centre has 147 horses and facilities such as a big international-sized floodlit arena, riding school arenas, dressage arenas, lunging ring, trail rides and hacks. Weekly ridership of both adults and children is 600 per week, includes the local Defence Force Cadets and National Team members. It holds at least two competitions and three school shows per month, as well as weekly gymkhanas from October to early May. Registered with the British Pony Club.

DEC's 10 instructors (qualified by the British Horse Society) offer training in show jumping, dressage, musical dressage, side saddle, vaulting and cross country. The centre also holds regular clinics and stable management courses.

Lesson Timings: Summer 06:30 -08:30 and 17:00-19:00, Winter 07:00-10:00 and 16:00-18:00.

## Jebel Ali Equestrian Club

Check | Jebel Ali Village, Sh Zayed Rd | Tel: 845 566

"Just like the stables back home" describes the comfortable atmosphere here. The horsey smell, tossing of hay, local residents of Jebel Ali Village where the stables are situated, a buzz of equine activities. Both children and adults learn to ride here and for the more experienced, dressage, jumping and hacking are options. Children can also join stable management courses as JAEC is an approved branch of UK's Pony Club.

Livery service and air conditioned stables available for those who own their own horse.

## Sharjah Equestrian Centre

Check | Sharjah | Tel: 06 311 155

S.E.C. is situated about 20 minutes drive from the centre of Sharjah and was originally built in 1984, under the supervision of H.H Sheikh Abdullah Bin Majid Al Qasimi. It held its first competition a year later.

The Centre keeps 95 horses for riding. Facilities include a big floodlit sand arena, a floodlit paddock, sand show jumping arena and hack trails into the desert. Regular ridership numbers about 80 (plus other occasional riders) for dressage, show jumping and hacks. Three full-time instructors, as well as part-time instructors offer training up to national champion level.

## Umm Al Quwain Marine Club & Riding Centre

Check | On the Beach, Umm Al Quwain | Tel: 06 666 644

UAQ RC was established in 1979 with the donation of six horses by H.H Sheikh Rashid Bin Ahmed Al Moalla, and is now a thriving riding centre, with more than 40 horses and a team of qualified British Horse Society instructors.

Facilities include a show jumping arena, dressage arenas, paddocks and swimming area. Private and group lessons are offered, from beginner to advanced levels in dressage, show jumping, carriage driving and side saddle, right up to the British Horse Society qualification level. The Club also provides hacks along the beaches, into the desert and overnight rides to Ras Al Khaimah.

## See Also:

**Polo**

# Ice Hockey

## Dubai Junior Ice Hockey

**Check** | **Hyatt Regency Hotel** | **Page 7**
**Practice Sat/Sun** | **Deira** | **D 2** | Tel: **440 861**

DJIH was started four years ago and now boasts a standing membership of 94 children between the ages of six to 17.

The 1996/7 season was very successful with it's highlight being a mini hockey camp. 66 of the players participating in the camp received ten hours of training from two professional coaches from Canada. With the backing of many volunteers, dedicated coaches and regular sponsors Toyota, Concept, Music Master and Philips, the club is able to run practice sessions from September through to April.

Practice sessions are at Galleria Ice Rink on Saturday and Sunday nights. Fees are Dh.450.

## Dubai Mighty Camels Ice Hockey Club

**Check** | **Al Nasr Leisureland** | **Page 9**
**Nr. Lodge/American Hospital** | **E 4** | Tel: **289 234**

This club has grown dramatically over the last two years as the profile of the sport has been raised in the public eye through such successful events as international tournaments. The current club numbers in excess of 40 players consisting of more than a dozen nationalities, making the club one of the most multinational sports groups in Dubai. If you have your own equipment, do go along and try out for the two to three teams there. No age limit! Ice hockey has been a fixture on the local sport scene since Al Nasr Leisureland opened in 1979. Social get togethers and barbecues. For more information, contact: Chris Reynolds.

# Ice Skating

## Al Nasr Leisureland

**2hr sessions** | **Al Nasr Leisureland** | **Page 9**
**10:00 - 22:00** | **Nr. Lodge/American Hospital** | **E 4** | Tel: **371 234**

Well, if it's large enough to hold an ice hockey tournament then it's large enough for energetic youngster's birthday party, or to just skate around to your heart's content. Open to the general public except when rented by clubs. Skating costs Dhs.10 for two hours, and includes boot hire. Two hour sessions start at 10:00, 13:00, 16:00 and 19:30. Closes at 22:00. Part of the Leisureland complex which also contains a bowling alley, fast food outlets, arcade amusements and small shops.

Occasionally the rink is drained, dried and used in the evening as a concert venue.

## Galleria Ice Rink

**10:00 - 13:30** | **Hyatt Regency Hotel** | **Page 7**
**14:00 - 21:30** | **Deira** | **D 2** | Tel: **706 4880**

All welcome to skate! The use of socks is mandatory in rental boots you may use your own or purchase them at Dhs.5 per pair. Membership Rates: Dhs.1,000 for one year. Dhs.625/up to 10 people for one year. Lessons are not included in the membership fees

(provide 2 passport size photos when joining). Private Lessons Rate (per block of five lessons): Dhs.250 member, Dhs.300 non-member. Each lesson is for 30 minutes. Individual lessons are also available at Dhs.50 members, Dhs.60 non-members.

# Jet Skiing

Every afternoon sees trailer loads of jet skies parked near the Al Garhoud Bridge, downstream of the Dubai Creek Golf & Yacht Club, or at the Al Mamzar beach park. Most are available for hire at approx. Dhs.100/half hour. In addition most beach clubs offer them for rental, see below.

## See Also:

| Tour-Operators | Beach Clubs | |
|---|---|---|
| Creek Cruises | Hilton Beach Club | Metropolitan Beach Club |
| Sun Tours | Jazira Resort | Umm Al Qwain Tourist Club |

# Judo / Karate

See *Martial Arts* section

# Karting

## Desert Rangers

**On Request** | **Dune Centre Al Satwa** | **Page 5 E 3** | Tel: **460 808**

You are given a briefing on the safety requirements and track regulations before you get to practice on the full, international size track here. Then the heats begin on the reduced size track, which is more exciting and requires greater skill & timing. Location Jebel Ali Racing Circuit. Cost Dhs.275 per person.

## Dubai Kart Club

**Most Fridays Check** | **Nr. Jebel Ali Hotel Jebel Ali** | Tel: **846 442**

Founded 20 years ago, the Dubai Kart Club is well known on the international karting scene, hosting the 12-round UAE championship on its purpose-built circuit, next to the Jebel Ali Hotel. Once on the 1km track it becomes as competitive as any other high speed motor sport, and the race days, held every Friday (September-April) are thoroughly entertaining for competitors and spectators alike.

Membership is Dhs.650 per year and there are always karts for sale at reasonable

prices. Facilities include grandstands, ample parking and catering provided by Jebel Ali Hotel.

For further details call Dion Koojiman (846 442) or Jean Louis Hissette (050 646 3411).

## Formula One

09:00 - 21:30 | Sh Zayed Rd, Al Quoz | Page 4, A 3 | Tel: **388 828**

Formula One's indoor go-karting allows you to experience the rush of adrenaline in purpose designed race karts, just two centimeters off the tarmac, racing at speeds of up to 75km/h. Provides the ideal introduction to the thrill of competitive motorsport. Open seven days a week from 10:30 to 20:00. Corporate entertainment, individual practice sessions or lessons for older children. Membership is available but not essential. You will be given a full safety briefing, race suits, helmets, gloves and the Kart, of course.

Rates: "Endurance Race" (one hr) for minimum of eight drivers: Dhs.180 each member, Dhs.220 each non-member. "Grand Prix", for a minimum of 16 Drivers: Dhs.180/each morning, Dhs.200/each afternoon, Dhs.220 each evening. No experience necessary, extremely exhilirating and entertaining! New Chicanes Diner catering for all types of fast food.

## Wonderland

New Track ~ Oct 1997 | Nr . Al Garhoud Bridge, Al Garhoud/Al Wasl | Page 14, A 3 | Tel: **341 222**

Scheduled for opening in October 1997, the new 800m outdoor track is called the Chevrolait Grand Prix and will be operated by Formula One. Check press for more details on pricing and timings.

# Martial Arts

## Dubai Karate Centre

16:00 - 19:00 | Al Karama | Page 5, A 4 | Tel: **447 797**

This club is a member of the Japanese Karate Association (JKA), and has been established in Dubai since 1985. High grade tuition from beginner to Black Belt, for everyone aged six years and above. A team of professional, black belt, JKA qualified, instructors teach a style of karate called Shotokan, the oldest and most popular form of karate. Very little chance of being injured, as it is a non contact sport! Courses are taught most evenings 16:30 - 19:00 depending on experience. Monthly membership fees, which include tuition, are Dhs.150 for children /students and Dhs.200 for adults. This includes three, one hour sessions a week. Uniforms are available from the club in different sizes, from Dhs.70.

## Taekwondo

**Check** | **Ballet Centre Al Jumeira Rd** | **Page 6 C3** | Tel: **459 771**

The Ballet Centre is fortunate to have Mr. Mounir Ghawi (5th Dan Black Belt) teaching Taekwondo. This form of martial art teaches children mental calmness, courage, strength and humility, courtesy, integrity, perseverance, self-control and indomitable spirit!

## See Also:

Al Nasr Club
Deira Karate Club
Desert Rangers
Dubai Country Club
Golden Falcon Karate Centre

# Microlights

## UAQ Microlights

**Most Fridays** | **16 Km from UAQ Roundabout direction RAK** | Tel: **NA**

This is a group of flying enthusiasts who meet most Thursday afternoons or Fridays to experience the cheapest way to fly. Located 16 km along the road from UAQ roundabout

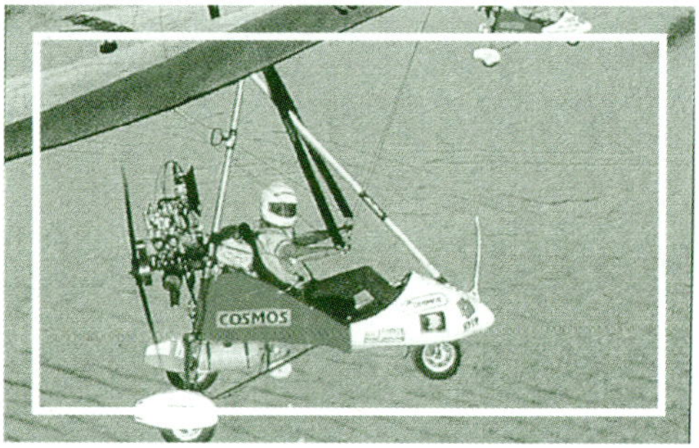


heading in the direction of Ras Al Khaimah, just before *Dreamland* you will see a big hangar on the left hand side of the road. The club is equipped with a wind sock and two sand runways. There are currently approx. 20 privately owned Microlights. Hangar rental fee per micro. is Dhs.375 per month. Some are for sale with new ones costing from Dhs.80,000+. Much friendly advice from experienced pilots, most of whom have their professional pilot's licence. Perfect area to fly over: beautiful lagoons and deserted beaches of UAQ, away from the main international airports. Stop by on a Friday and say "hello".

## See Also:

**Flying** **Hang Gliding** **Paragliding**

# Mini Golf

## Hyatt Golf Park

**07:00 - 23:00** | **Hyatt Regency Hotel Deira** | **Page 7 D 2** | Tel: **706 4894**

Surrounded by lush greenery with a beautiful pond and waterfall, the Golf Park is the hotel's green oasis. Adjacent to the side car cark, a 9-hole pitch and putt grass golf course awaits the avid golfer to improve his short game. For family enjoyment there is an 18-hole crazy golf course. Prices are: 9-hole pitch & putt : one round Dhs.15, two rounds Dhs.25. Clubs provided free of charge and golf balls can be purchased for Dhs.8 per ball. 18-hole crazy golf - Dhs.10 per person (ball and club provided free of charge). The entire park is floodlit in the evenings and is open daily from 07:00 to 23:00. A Club House in the centre of the park overlooks a small lagoon. Golf, or simply enjoy a drink at the 19th Hole.

### See Also:

**Golf** Aviation Club Jazira Beach Resort Hatta Forte Hotel

# Motor Cross

## Dubai Dirt Donks

**Most Fridays**
**Check**

**Nr. Wimpey R/A**
**Al Awir Ind. Area**

Tel: **484 478**

There are bikes for pedalling and bikes for posing. You won't find either at this club. What you will find are rugged bikes for those who love nothing better than to ride across lumpy, bumpy country, with as many twists and turns as they can: Motocross bikes. Dubai Dirt Donks is affiliated to Al Nasr Motor Sports Club and has been established in a low-key sort of way for almost 20 years. Mid January is when an International Championship is held, with champion riders coming from various parts of the globe to compete against local champions. Located 100 metres or so past the "Wimpey" roundabout on the road to Al-Awir (Hatta). For more info contact Hamad Summers.

# Mountain Biking

## Biking Frontiers

**Most Fridays/Saturdays**
**Check**

**Various Locations**

Tel: **443 942**

So you're here in the Emirates and you want to mountain bike. If you don't mind thrashing yourself over rough and gnarly trails up twisted and steep mountains, or through soggy, mushy wadis and have a learning towards getting lost, or hoisting your bike over your shoulder for a mountain climb... then this is the club for you! Helmets and proper riding gear highly essential. This is a fairly serious group of cyclists who all have their own bikes, but all serious riders welcome. Give them a call for advice, or new info on routes etc, as they have a lot of good local terrain knowledge.

For Friday and Saturday rides in the dead of summer, or anytime, call Barry.

## Desert Rangers

**On Request** | **Dune Centre, Al Satwa** | **Page 5, E 3** | Tel: **460 808**

One of the latest outward-bound and leisure companies to specialise in more interesting activities. Whether you are a fanatical biker craving challenging terrain, or a complete beginner preferring a gentler introduction to the delights of off-road biking, they will determine a suitable route, depending on your group size and requirements. Dhs.275 per person is inclusive of pick-up and drop-off, bike, helmet, guiding and soft drinks.

Alternatively, you may rent the mountain bikes for Dhs.75 per day, with a Dhs.500 deposit per bike required.

# Mountaineering

Whilst the area immediately surrounding Dubai is mostly flat with sandy desert, the Western Hajar Mountains to the East, form the border between the UAE and Oman. These mountains stretch from the Musandam peninsula, North of Ras Al Kaimah, and continue for several hundred kilometres into the Empty Quarter of Saudi Arabia. They provide a number of excellent mountain trips, ranging from short, easy walks to spectacular viewpoints; through long, all day treks to higher peaks, over difficult terrain; to mountaineering routes on faces of alpine proportions. The region is a paradise for the adventurous mountain walker.

## Desert Rangers

**On Request** | **Dune Centre, Al Satwa** | **Page 5, E 3** | Tel: **460 808**

Under expert guidance, you are taken to the foot of cliffs which offer exciting rock climbs of approximately 50ft. Each route is graded to suit a range of abilities and you are shown basic techniques and closely monitored up the ascent. Only two people allowed on the rock face at one time, the rest will until it is their turn. Location Ajman, Hatta, Umm Al Quwain. Cost Dhs.275 per person.

## Mountaineering Club

**Check** | **Various Locations** | Tel: **06 351 459**

Some 'Extremely Severe' (E2 British grade) routes have been climbed, with the majority of routes being classified as Severe' (US grade 5.5) or harder. Due to the nature of the rock, some of the routes are much more serious than their technical grade would suggest. The majority of routes, even in the easier grades are difficult propositions with loose rock, poor belays and difficult descents - often by abseil, and therefore not for total novices.

No modern "sport" routes with bolt protection, exist. However, some extremely difficult lines exist where bolts may offer the only feasible method of protection. The placing of bolts on existing routes will not be tolerated. No formal climbing or mountaineering club exists, but an effective telephone "grapevine" means that visiting climbers can generally be pointed in the right direction. Climbing is a hazardous sport, and whilst new climbers are welcomed, the group does not run, or wish to run, courses for beginners who have no equipment or experience. As there are no mountain rescue services available, it is expected that anyone venturing out into the mountains is basically competent, even if they do not climb to a high standard of difficulty. For more information please contact: Alan Stark 06 351 459, Bill Wheeler 04 557 407, Pete Wilson 02 789 662.

## See Also:

**Abseiling** **Caving**

# Netball

## Dubai Netball League

**Wed**
**19:00 - 22:00**

**Nr. Dubai Country Club** **Page 12**
**Nadd Al Sheba** **B 3**

Tel: **382 268**

The Dubai Netball League was originally established in the mid '70s with six teams vying for the League title. Today, it is sponsored by 'The WAFI Centre', with 13 teams being divided into two divisions. Players range from teenagers to grandmothers, beginners to experts, a cosmopolitan league with players from various countries. Games are played on Wednesday evenings 19:00 - 22:00, September to April, on the two courts at the Dubai Exiles Rugby Football Club. During the season, players are selected for the Gulf Netball Championships a competition which brings together representative teams from Abu Dhabi, Bahrain, Dubai, Fujairah, Kuwait and Oman. New players are always welcome, telephone for more information.

# Paintballing

## Pursuit Games

**Check**

**Sh Zayed Rd** **Page 4**
**Al Quoz** **A 3**

Tel: **494 223**

The first Paintball site in the Middle East is here in Dubai. A fun, commando style fighting game for teenagers and adults where the bullets ...are balls of paint. Get a crowd together and they will soon be divided into two teams by the experts, who go through a very thorough safety demonstration before equipping you with thick, padded overalls, Darth Vader type face masks and special guns equipped with balls of ammunition.

This is a strategy game played by shooting balls of paint onto your opponent thus marking and eliminating them. Usually involves two teams with a specific aim e.g. capturing the opponent's flag. Stalk your enemies, duck behind whatever hiding place you can find, and get them before they get you. If you are hit by a bullet of paint, you're dead - until the next game. A typical two hour game with 125 paint balls, gun and gas, will cost Dhs.120 (If you run out, an extra 100 paintballs will cost you Dhs.60).

# Paragliding

## Dubai Paramotor Club

**Most Fridays - Check Wind Permitting!** | **Various Locations** | Tel: **822 661**

Paramotors are paragliders with motors strapped to the pilot's back. Originated in France, these devices enable you to fly to heights of 5,000 ft, and then switch the engine off, and glide down. Luc is the main driving force behind this club, also promoting the leading *DK Whisper* product.which currently offers the smallest and most powerful motors, setting you back around Dhs.25,000 including the canopy.

The club was set up over a year ago by a couple of enthusiasts. Flying primarily in the desert on Fridays, or at their practice ground opposite the Dubai Police headquarters, all with the prior permission of the Department of Civil Aviation. Training takes about 10 hours of ground lessons, with theory. If you want to fly, are reasonably fit, then this is the cheapest form of flying with the equipement fitting nicely into your car! No rentals available for safety purposes. Hence only for the seriously interested. Call Luc or Alistair for info.

## See Also:

**Flying** **Hang Gliding**

# Parasailing

## Sun Tours

**On Request** | **Various Locations** | Tel: **214 555**

Currently the only company in Dubai that offers this exciting activity. Sun Tours provides specially designed craft that allow you to take off and land on the boat. (In other words you don't get wet if you don't want to!) Cost of each flight is Dhs.100 per person, for an exhilarating 10 minute flight. A boatload of up to six people venutre into the warm Gulf waters and each person has a turn at parasailing. Just turn up at Jumeira Open Beach, or at Al Mamzar Park, and have the most exciting day of your life. Other water sports also on offer at Mamzar Park beach.

# Polo

## Dubai Polo Club

**Check** | **Al Awir Rd Nr. Nadd Al Sheba** | **Page 12 B 3** | Tel: **331 188**

Before you can play Polo you have to be able to ride a horse which is why this club also gives riding lessons. May-September are the hot months so lessons in both riding and polo are given during the cooler hours of the day, 16:00 - 17:30 and 18:00 - 21:00. October sees the start of the playing season when games are played four days a week on Sunday, Tuesday, Thursday and Friday. Junior and adult riders welcome. There are three instructors for riding, and one for polo.

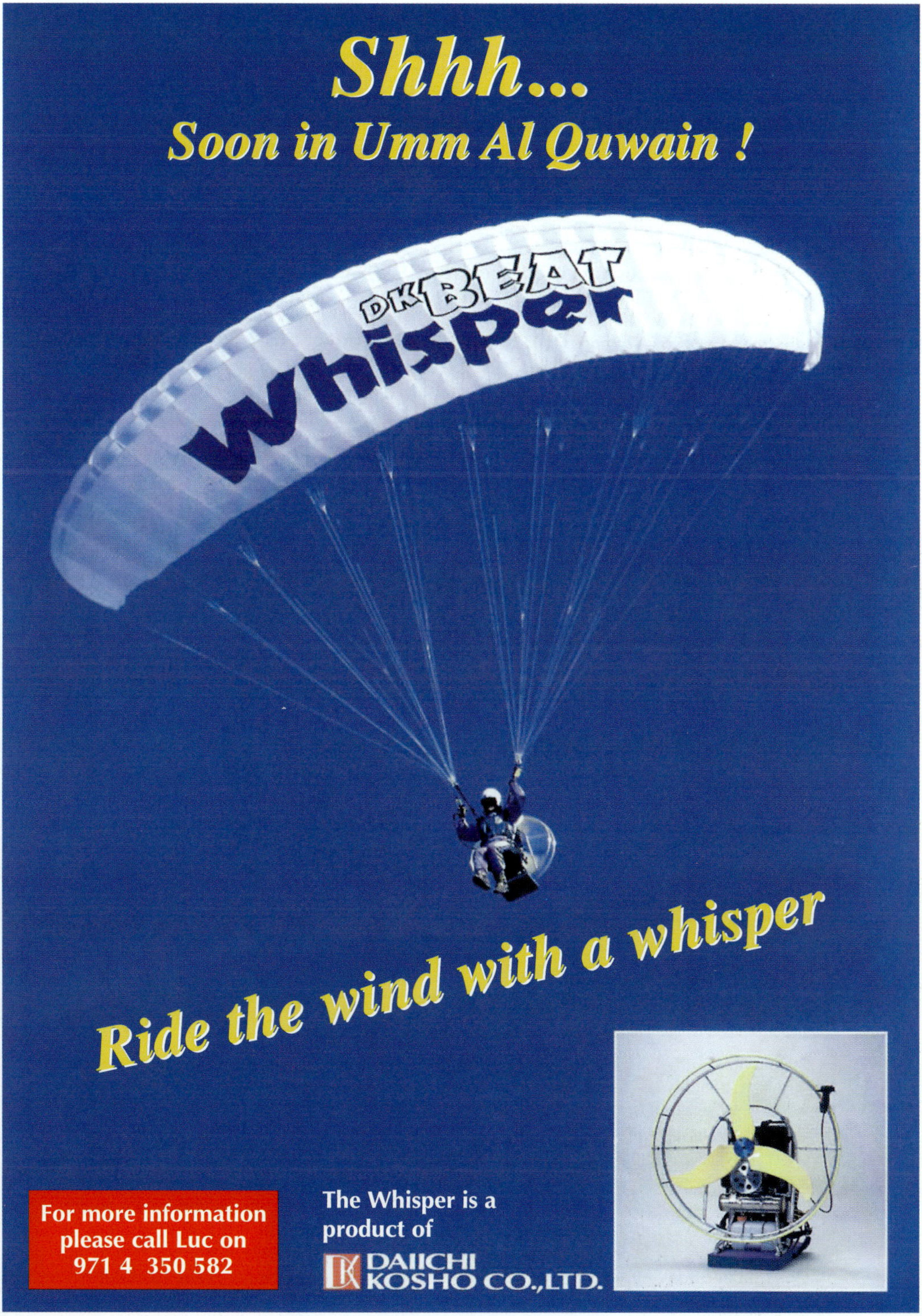
Shhh...
Soon in Umm Al Quwain !
DK BEAT
Whisper
Ride the wind with a whisper
For more information please call Luc on 971 4 350 582
The Whisper is a product of
DAIICHI KOSHO CO.,LTD.

## Ghantoot

Check | Nr. Jazira Resort, Sh Zayed Rd | Tel: **02 562 9050**

The facilities at Ghantoot are first class, with the only floodlit grass polo field in the world and a turf race track, with it's magnificent 2,000 seater Grandstand. It is located off the Abu Dhabi Highway, next to Jazira and close to Jebel Ali Free Zone, some 30 minutes from Dubai.

The Club - Sit on the veranda overlooking the polo field, sipping a drink and enjoying a light snack, or at the poolside, in the bar or the Club's restaurant. With a "state-of-the-art" gym and sauna, business centre, boutique, children's playroom/creche, tennis and archery already planned, the Club will cater for more than just polo players - all the family will be able to enjoy the relaxed and friendly ambience. The Club will offer a broad range of memberships - Social, Racing, Corporate, as well as Polo!

**Polo Season:** Starts in mid October and continues through until the end of April. The calendar is full with regular chukkas, tournaments and high profile international invitations. The quality of horses is high and spectators are always welcomed and encouraged.

**Polo School:** A new and exiting concept designed to introduce Polo to a broader base. A special Polo School Field and top instructional facilities, are managed by an International team of professional polo players. The school offers a wide range of tutorial schemes, from individual to group clinics, instructional chukkas and children's polo from 12 years upwards. Specialised training for the more experienced player is also available. Lessons from Dhs.150 per hour.

# Rock Climbing

See **Mountaineering**

# Roller Blading

An exciting sport, great fun and great exercise, Dubai's many parks provide some excellent locations for roller blading. Try Creek Park and Safa Park for smooth, wide pathways, with few people and enough slopes and turns to make it interesting, or along the promenade at Jumeria beach front, where taking in the views is an added bonus.

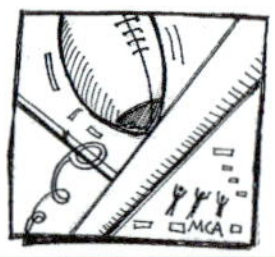

# Rugby

## Dubai Exiles Rugby Club

Friday pm, Some Wed | Nr. Dubai Country Club, Nadd Al Sheba | Page 12 B 3 | Tel: **331 198**

Definitely Dubai's 'serious' rugby club, the Exiles is the emirate's oldest and best-established bastion of the sport. With five categories of membership from Full Playing Member to Women's, Social and Veteran's memberships, training sessions are scheduled throughout the week with the 1st and 2nd XV's on Sundays and Wednesdays. The 1st XV play in the Arabian Gulf First Division, with the 2nd's in Division Two, so there's plenty of regional travel and competition. The Exiles also play host to the annual Dubai International Rugby Sevens tournament which attracts international teams from all the major rugby-playing nations. Other International 15's teams often stop off at the Exiles' ground for 'friendlies' on their way to somewhere else, as do many visiting Navy teams. There are matches most Friday afternoons, and some Wednesdays. Check local press for details.

# Running

## Dubai Road Runners

**Sat 18:30** | **Safa Park** | **Page 4 C 3** | Tel: **526 863**

Come rain or shine, 100% humidity or 50° C temperatures, the road runners meet every Saturday at 18:30 at Safa Park, in the car park by Gate Number 1. All standards, all ages and all nationalities welcome. The objective of this meeting is to run a 7 km track around the park. A Dhs.5 entrance fee is charged, and most people try to run this standard course against the clock. Contact John Nolan for more information.

## See Also:

**Hashing**

# Sailing

## Dubai Offshore Sailing Club

**08:00 - 20:00** | **Al Jumeira Rd Umm Sequim** | **Page 3 E 2** | Tel: **381 669**

Put on your co-ordinating casuals to go down to DOSC, where yachts of varying sizes from 20 ft - 40 ft are moored at a cost of Dhs.100 per foot per annum. Many of these cruisers take part in the races held twice a month. There is also an active Laser fleet which races every weekend and a Saturday Cadet Club to help children find their sea legs. A number of dinghies for hire.

The Club provides boat mooring, storage, launching facilities, sail training and a full yachting and social calendar. Membership is open to any person who is actively interested in yachting. There is a modern clubhouse with full catering facilities. DOSC is a non-profit making organisation and depends for its success on the active support of its members. It is run by a committee of volunteers. Costs Dhs.2,000 for family membership, with a joining fee of Dhs.1,500. Entrance only with members Dhs.10, Friday Dhs.20.

## Jebel Ali Sailing Club

**Sat-Wed 10:00 - 20:00**
**Fri 09:00 - 22:00** | **Nr. DIMC Al Mina Al Siyahi** | **Page 1 E 2** | Tel: **846 444**

This is a 'doing' club, where members are often asked to do a job, help out on the Rescue Boats, hoist a flag and suchlike. Of course, you can just lie on the sunloungers placed strategically on the lawn or dotted about the beach, if you want to. Or play a neighbourly game of volleyball with energetic teenagers between sailing races.

JASC is situated at Mina Seyahi harbour. Members are encouraged to be sailors/prospective sailors and own or intend to own a boat. Some boats available for private hire. Races held every weekend for Toppers, Lasers, Catamarans, Cruisers, etc. Volunteers man the rescue boats, for which NYA training is given. Social evenings. Clubhouse with bar and kitchen. Family membership costs Dhs.1,950 plus Dhs.1,200 joining fee. Entrance only with members Dhs.10.

## For boat rental, see:

Club Joumana
Dubai Creek Golf & Yacht Club
Dubai International Marine Club
Dubai Offshore Sailing Club
Jazira Beach Resort
Le Mirage
Oceanic Hotel
Sun Tours
Umm Al Qwain Marine Riding Club

# Sand Skiing

Head towards Hatta, and surf the big dunes on the way.Various tour companies will arrange your pickup and transport you out to the dunes in comfort. Most people require some sort of instruction on how to sand surf. So, if required, you will start out with a demonstration on how to stay up, and most importantly, how to fall properly! Once at the bottom, you will either run up the dune, or be driven back up again. This half day activity will cost you around Dhs.175.

## See Also:

Arabian Adventures
Desert Rangers
Net Tours
Orient

# Shooting

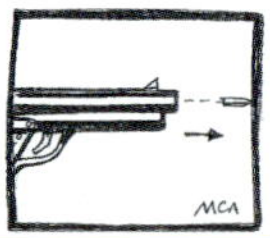

## Hatta Fort Hotel

**On request**

**Hatta Fort Hotel**
**Hatta**

Tel: **085 23211**

Clay pigeon shooting is among the many activities offered at Hatta Fort hotel, less than one hour's drive from Dubai. Other attractions include Olympic and field archery, tennis, golf, scenic walking and jogging routes, and a free-form swimming pool. More frequently visited as a retreat from the hustle and bustle of Dubai, Hatta Fort can be quite a sportsman's playground, with the added attraction of superb food and beverage facilities. Daily entrance fee of Dhs.30 is deducted from you food or drinks bill.

## Jebel Ali Shooting Club

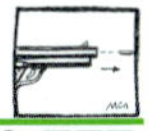

13:00 - 23:00
Closed Tue

Nr. Jebel Ali Hotel
Jebel Ali

Tel: **836 555**

Open to members and non-members, and situated near Jebel Ali Hotel, this impressive club's design was inspired by traditional Arab forts and watch towers. Greeted at the entrance by a sign asking all gun holders to kindly place them in the reception for inspection by the gunsmith, safety is a priority. According to the Senior Shooting Instructor "The club ranks amongst the best shooting facilities in the world". Quite so!

Try clay shooting on one of five floodlight shooting ranges, or practice on the 10 lane, 25m indoor pistol range. Just in case this isn't enough, try the laser gun shooting in a simulation room where the latest in technology, used by American police for training, is combined with real video scenes to help create incredible practice targets. For non-members (members), one round of trap shooting starts at Dhs.110 (Dhs.90), one round on the pistol range Dhs.85 (Dhs.65), with each round consisting of 50 bullets. As expected, the club provides coaching. Clubhouse includes a western style Mexican restaurant, VIP lounge and a pro-shop. Thursday morning is Ladies day.

## See Also:

**Amusement Arcade** - Q Zar

**Paintballing**

# Snorkelling

If you want to see what lies under the sea just hire a mask and snorkel, wade out from the beach and put your eyes under the water in safety. Available from most beach hotels. Especially good on the East Coast.

Hire of mask and snorkel typically (Dhs.20/hr), extra Dhs.5/half hr for the fins.

# Softball

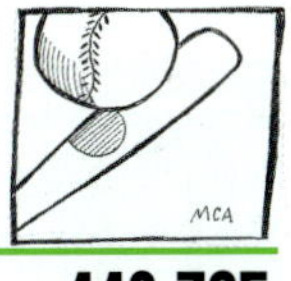

## Dubai Softball League

Check

Nr. Metropolitan Hotel
Sh Zayed Rd/Safa Park

Page 4
C 4

Tel: **443 785**

Softball first started in Dubai in the early 70's, at that time it was mostly played by American and European expatriates. Things have changed considerably since those early years and the league now boasts a truly multi-racial mix.

The grounds are located adjacent to the Metropolitan Hotel on the Dubai-Abu Dhabi highway. The League runs on Saturdays and Wednesdays, from mid-September until the beginning of December, and again from mid-January, to the end of April. After this, there is a "Sauna" league which continues once a week throughout the summer, and which encourages new players to come out and experience the fun softball has to offer. The only real criteria is that players must be over 16 years to participate - no other experience is necessary and apart from buying your own glove eventually, there is no charge.

Dubai is also host to the twice-yearly, Middle East Softball Championships. Generally held in November and April, these events attract over 500 players from around the Gulf. Softball is a true a spectator sport and everyone is welcome to come and watch. Entrance is free and food and beverages are available. If you require further info please call Carol.

# Squash / Swimming / Tennis

See: **Beach, Health & Sport Clubs**

# Wadi Bashing

Wadi bashing is an interesting form of entertainment. Bouncing over rocks and boulders in an air conditioned car, while following dried up river beds in mountainous regions, crossing streams, sometimes getting stuck in difficult terrain, and having to ask your passengers to get out and push, is all part of it. And this type of fun is what all nationalities in the Gulf countries like to do in their leisure time.

Technically an Arabian wadi is a dry river bed, but this general definition does not begin to describe the wonderful surrounding scenery in rocky mountain ranges, streams trickling over boulders (watch out for snakes and frogs), ribbons of silt that become raging torrents during the rainy season and vistas of cracked earth at dry estuaries. Try it and see for yourself, but always travel in parties of two, or more vehicles, and check the weather forecast. Rainfall, no matter how little, is dangerous!

# Water Parks

## Dreamland

**12:00 - 20:00 Sat-Wed**
**10:00 - 20:00 Thu-Fri**

**17Km North UAQ R/A**
**Direction RAK**

Tel: **06 681 888**

Recently completed, this is the biggest water park in the world! A wide range of water sport activities and entertainment in the Emirate of Umm Al Qwain, a leisurely forty minute drive from Dubai. Spread over 200,000 square metres of beach front property, with beautiful landscaping, this water park includes different types of villas and bungalows. Dreamland features over 20 water slides - most of them were exclusively designed for this park - ranging from giant to multi-slides, a crazy river, a lazy river, black holes, kamikazes and even a twin-twister, and children's pools. The kamikazes are high speed slides, where the rider experiences a free weightless fall sensation and reaches speeds up to 50 km/h. The black hole is an opaque tube where riders cannot see the course. Optic fiber lighting special effects are installed inside. You can not miss their 70 metre wave pool, which is the biggest in the world! It has 10 types of waves. Dreamland also offers a diverse range of restaurants (Arabic, Spanish, French, Russian, Italian, etc.) and snack bars, and over 21 shops. Excellent value entrance fee which includes all rides (Dhs.30 Adults/Dhs.20 Children/Family Dhs.100).

# Water Skiing

## Dubai Water Sports Association

09:00 - 18:30
Closed Mon/Wed

Nr. JADAF
Al Wasl

Tel: **342 031**

Set along Dubai's Creek, this organisation is devoted to the promotion of water sports, primarily water-skiing. Professional ski coaches often come to Dubai to instruct both members and guests. DWSA has two tournament ski boats, a slalom course, a full sized jump ramp and various items of water skiing and windsurfing equipment which are available for hire during the week for corporate entertaining. Skiing tow's cost Dhs.45 for 10-15 minutes. The club has been home to the annual Gulf Water-ski Championships for the last 17 years, with one of the highlights of the two-day event being the world famous Ski Show Team from USA which includes water ballet on ski's, paragliding, jump demonstrations and other feats.

A grass lawn with loungers, a swimming pool, jacuzzi, children's playground and BBQ area on the clubhouse site. Daily entrance fees for non-members are Dhs.15 on weekdays and Dhs.30 on Fridays and Public Holidays with a maximum of four visits per month.

## See Also:

**Beach Clubs** **Weekend Breaks**

# Windsurfing

## For rental, see:

**Beach Clubs** **Sailling** **Sun Tours - Tours**

# Yoga

## Jan Maddern Yoga

Various
Check

Various Locations
Hyatt Regency/Hilton Beach Club

Tel: **481 363**

Jan Maddern, an Australian trained yoga teacher has been teaching in Dubai for seven years. Jan was trained at the Gita International Yoga School, Melbourne (the first yoga school in Australia). Beginners Hatha Yoga Classes are for those who have done no, or very little yoga before. This class includes a series of vigorous stretches to improve flexibility, followed by breathing techniques to improve the depth and rhythm of your breath. Students are then ready to attempt ten of the classic basic yoga postures, designed to energise the body by clearing out energy blockages via the glandular system. An introduction to relaxation/visualisation/meditation techniques completes each class. Handouts on yoga philosophy and mini workouts are given in all classes .

Average Hatha Classes build on all of the above, with stronger limbering, and more advanced and varied posture work. The various relaxation/meditation exercises are designed to improve concentration and induce a deeper state of relaxation. Students are encouraged to attempt the more challenging postures such as lotus and headstand. Handouts on yoga practices and theory are given in all classes.

# Spectator Sport calendar 1997/8

## Camel Racing

| | |
|---|---|
| Oct-May | Regular Race Meetings on Thu/Fri |
| Jan/Feb | Eid Races |
| Dec 2 | National Day Races |

## Chess

| | |
|---|---|
| Jun 18 | Asian Cities Team Chess Championship |

## Dhow racing

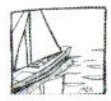

| | |
|---|---|
| May | Dhow Championship 60 ft. |
| May | Dhow Sailing Race 60 ft. |

## Four-Wheel Driving

| | |
|---|---|
| Dec 11-12 | Gulf News Fun Drive |

## Golf

| | |
|---|---|
| Feb 26 - Mar 1 | Dubai Dessert Classic 1998 |
| Jul 5 | Duty Free Dubai Golf Cup |
| Oct 15-18 | Omega Asian PGA Tour |
| Nov 15-17 | Dubai Classic Skins Tournament |
| Dec 1-2 | Dubai Duty Free Golf World Cup |

## Horse Racing

| | |
|---|---|
| Oct - Apr | Race Meetings |
| Nov 6, 13, 27 | Race Meetings |
| Dec 7, 11,18, 28 | Race Meetings |
| Jan 1, 4, 8,11,15,18, 22, 29 | Race Meetings |
| Feb 1, 5, 8, 12, 15, 19, 22 | Race Meetings |
| Mar 1, 5, 12, 27, 28 | Race Meetings |
| **Mar 28** | **Dubai World Cup** |
| Apr 2, 9, 16 | Race Meetings |

## Jet Ski

| | |
|---|---|
| Nov/Dec | Jet Ski Championship |

## Karting

| | |
|---|---|
| Nov 27-28 | 24 h Pro-kart race |

## Power Boat Racing

| | |
|---|---|
| Feb & May | Formula 4 Powerboat Race |
| Oct 31 | World Offshore Championship |
| Nov 7 | World Offshore Championship |
| Nov 7 | Emirates Grand Prix |
| Nov | DDF Powerboat Grand Prix |

## Rallying

| | |
|---|---|
| Nov 5-8 | U.A.E. Desert Challenge |
| Nov 4-9 | Pirates Raid |
| Dec 4-5 | Dubai International Rally |

## Rugby

| | |
|---|---|
| Dec 4-6 | Dubai International Rugby 7's |

## Sailing

| | |
|---|---|
| Mar 4-13 | ISAF 98 World Sailing Championships |

## Tennis

| | |
|---|---|
| Feb | Dubai Tennis Open |
| Nov | Dubai Aviation Cup |

## Wooden Boat Races

Regularly throughout the season

Advertisers want to know they are on target - reaching the right people at the right time. TV is able to deliver those audiences, but with increased competition - how do you select a particular station?

For the first time, the Arab world across five continents is now served by a station that broadcasts around the clock.

**IS YOUR CHOICE OF MEDIUM ...**

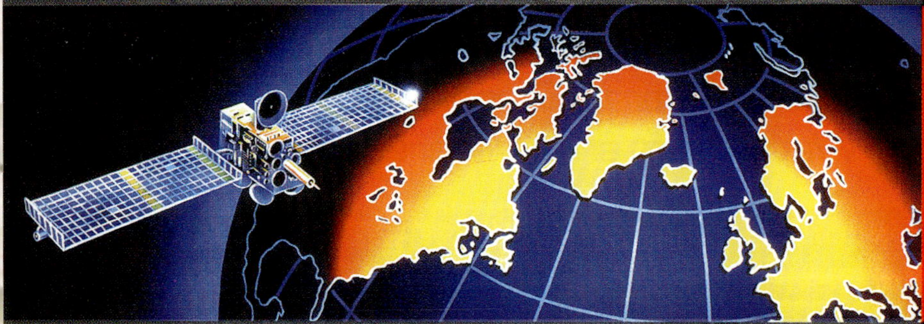

**COST EFFECTIVE?**
Emirates Dubai TV's satellite expansion into Europe and North and South America gives advertisers a highly cost-effective medium through which to reach the lucrative Arab market around the world.

**TARGETED?**
Today, millions of Arabs rely on EDTV for their entertainment and news. And for non-Arabic speaking businessmen dealing with the Middle East, there is no better source of up-to-the-minute information on what is happening in this vitally important part of the world.

**INTERNATIONAL?**
The addition of 35 million Arabs on both sides of the Atlantic to EDTV's existing coverage gives it by far the widest spread among Arabic broadcasters.
The international audience is an advertiser's dream - cosmopolitan, well-educated and affluent.

**24 HOURS A DAY?**
The EDTV viewer is a discerning one who wants a consistently high standard of programming. Only EDTV can meet these exacting demands 24 hours a day.

**REACHING MEN, WOMEN AND CHILDREN?**
EDTV's transmissions feature top class drama, variety, children's programmes and the best from film libraries and studios around the world. The language mix is predominantly Arabic with a significant English component. Each day, four hours of news are broadcast in both languages.

Sports enjoy a high priority, with all the important international events of interest to an Arab audience being covered extensively and often live.

**THE ANSWER, OF COURSE, IS.... EDTV... THE GLOBAL ARABIC SERVICE**

**For bookings and further enquiries please contact:**
**TV & Radio Services,** P.O. Box 2765, Dubai, United Arab Emirates
Telephone: 9714 370599/ 3033218 Facsimile: 9714 373480

**ARABSAT 2A**
C BAND COVERAGE FROM 31 DEGREES EAST

**GLOBAL ARABIC SERVICE**

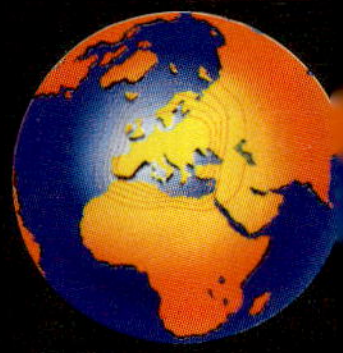

**HOTBIRD 11**
COVERAGE FROM 13 DEGREES EA

**GALAXY V11**
TRANSPONDER 17 COVERAGE FRO 91 DEGREES WEST ON C BAND

**INTELSAT K-H**
COVERAGE FROM 338.5 DEGREES E

**DUBAI**

# Food & Drink

# Africa

## African

### Out of Africa

100-150

12:00 - 16:00
18:00 - 03:00

Avari Dubai International
Deira

Page 10
D 3

Tel: **276 999**

After a difficult start and various planned changes, this restaurant is still trying to find its niche in this market. Capturing the true African spirit with it's authentic decor, the restaurant still tries to deliver a cosmopolitan atmosphere with friendly, courteous staff and an international menu to complement the African game meat on offer. The Band performs music from the 50's to the latest Chart Busters. Whether you're in the mood for a romantic dinner, or just a night out with a difference, "Out of Africa" might just be the place to try.

There are Happy Hours on Fridays and Ladies' night on Saturdays. Coming soon: unique theme nights with exciting door prizes and surprises!

### Stars Studio

100-150

12:00 - 15:00
18:00 - 02:00

Sheraton Deira
Deira

Page 11
A 3

Tel: **688 888**

An Afro/American theme fun restaurant, where guests can enjoy the best music of the 90's with a live band. A wild menu with crocodile, ostrich served with honey bees, buffalo and fried banana chips. Tasty salads, juicy marinated hamburgers, cool margaritas and first class disco. For more information, see the review under Nightclubs.

# Americas, The

## American

### Billy Blues

50-100

12:00 - 15:00
18:00 - 24:00 Closed Fri am

Plaza Hotel
Al Satwa

Page 6
A 4

Tel: **451 272**

Billy Blues is a honky tonk bar exuding a rich atmosphere of blues and '70's R&B. Pictures of some of the greatest names in music's history adorn the walls, from Elvis to John Lee Hooker. If you can negotiate your way over the peanut shells to the bar, you'll be greeted by friendly faces and a relaxed atmosphere.

Highly recommended is the home cooked Blues Platter, the Cajun seafood and rack of BBQ ribs, uniquely flavoured with Mesquite wood smoke. Or, grab a banquet and sample a selection of Cajun and BBQ food. This is Southern "feel-good" food and even the management lend a hand in the kitchen! And with the hottest chilli sauce in town, all you chilliheads should prepare to be blown away by 'Dave's "Insanity" Sauce'!

Try out Monday night's '2 for 1 ribs', Tuesday's Ladies Night and Friday evening's "Dirty Dozen". Good food, good music and a great atmosphere!

## Bourbon Street

100-150

12:00 - 15:30
19:00 - 00:30

Arif Castle
Bur Dubai

Page 6
E 2

Tel: **557 123**

Drive to the Arif Castle and all the hassles of parking in Bur Dubai will vanish as your car is instantly valet parked for you. Bourbon Street Jazz and Blues Bar transports you immediately to the heart of Old New Orleans, with it's shuttered windows, red brick walls, burning street gas lamps and wooden floors.

There are two separate bar areas: one with seating around the bar and a large TV screen at the end showing all the main sporting events, and the other, a Band Room, where live jazz plays from Monday to Saturday nights from 21:30 to 01:00, and Sunday night specialises in Soul and Reggae. A simple Cajun menu is available in both rooms with emphasis on seafood. The food is extremely expensive for the portion size and quality, but the drinks are reasonably priced with malt beverages costing Dhs.11-13 and cocktails starting at Dhs.15. Tuesday night is "Ladies Night" with two free drinks for all ladies.

## BW3 - Buffalo Wild West Wings

50-100

12:00 - 03:00

Plaza Hotel
Al Satwa

Page 6
A 4

Tel: **451 665**

BW3 is currently one of the fastest growing food chains in the US. The Buffalo Wings, which are obviously a hot item here, were voted "Best Wings" in at least eight US cities. The speciality sauce in which the chicken wings are marinaded has ten different degrees ranging from Blazin' to Mild and you can order from six to 250 wings! Traditionally the folks in Buffalo, dip the "Blazin" wings in Blue cheese and celery to soothe the palate.

The dance floor is big enough to Line dance and have a good hoe-down. BW3 also offers a wide screen TV for those who prefer watching the big games out in a pub, sipping a beer with friends. Ladies are entitled to two free drinks every Wednesday and Airline crew are offered a 15% discount throughout the week.

## Champions

50-100

12:00 - 16:00
18:00 - 02:00

JW Marriott Hotel
Deira

Page 11
A 3

Tel: **624 444**

Well, if they can have their own TV channel, I suppose it's only right that sports fans can have their own restaurant too. This American style sports bar / restaurant, the first of its name to be found outside USA, has a lively atmosphere and serves big portions of snack meals while diners watch top sporting events on overhead screens. Crowds gather on Tuesday and Thursday nights, as well as sport championship nights. Fridays are more family orientated.

Decor includes sports memorabilia, e.g. boxing gloves signed by Mohammed Ali and golf clubs used by Nick Faldo, and newspaper clippings at the dining tables to read and comment on. Other entertainments include a pool table, pin ball, hoop shot and table football game, or ask one of the bar staff for an annoying, but fun, metal chain puzzle.

Not to be missed, every two weeks is Champions "100-Club". For Dhs.100 you may eat and drink as much as you want. For obvious reasons this is an extremely popular night, with the bar being packed out by 21:00. Great music, great atmosphere, a wicked night out!

## Chilis

50-100

11:00 - 01:00 | Nr. Princeton Hotel, Al Garhoud | Page 14, D 2 | Tel: **828 484**

Chillis are definitely the name of the game here and their philosophy is - "the more the better". As the newest edition to a world-wide chain of restaurants they are expected to keep up to international standards, and they do just that. The menu is fun, offering an extensive range of Tex-Mex cuisine including a number of house specialities. Choose either regular or low-fat salsa's, sauces and dressings unique to Chilis. There is even a "Counters menu" for the health conscious so you know exactly how many grams of fat are in each portion.

The decor is mildly mexican with a lot of terracotta donkeys, bulls etc. and the country and western/rock music gives a final touch. They work on a first come, first served basis and even at busy times, it doesn't feel too crowded. The food is served at a leisurely pace, and Chilis is frequented by business people in the local area, and also families, as they offer novelties and a seperate menu for children. Takeaway menu is available. Although Chilis isn't licensed, it is definitely worth a visit.

## Fashion Cafe

100-150

11:00 - 02:00 ~ March 1998 | Deira City Centre Mall, Deira | Page 14, D 1 | Tel: **828 595**

Owned by super-models Claudia Schiffer, Naomi Campbell and Elle MacPherson, Fashion Café is a festival of style. With eye-popping computer graphics, theatrical presentations, and stunning displays of fashion memorabilia, guests are treated to an incredible perspective on the glamorous world of fashion. Features live bands and superb audio video entertainment, a place to see and to be seen.

The menu offers a refreshing mix of light, health conscious meals suitable for aspiring models, balanced by more indulgent fare for the rest of us. This is also the venue for a series of fashion shows, ranging from the top names of haute couture to speciality fashion houses of the Gulf. Call, fax, or e-mail in advance for a schedule of shows and ticket information. Watch for the grand opening in March 1998. You never know when you will casually run into a fashion celebrity at the Fashion Café Dubai! (Fax: 821 887, Email: mytable@fc-dubai.com, www.fc-dubai.com).

## Flying Tigers Diner

50-100

10:00 - 23:30 | Deira City Centre Mall, Deira | Page 14, D 1 | Tel: **227 648**

Your typical 50's diner-style American restaurant, complete with the standard memorabilia including an individual juke-box on each table, and one large counter with bar stools. Great shakes and the normal array of burgers and trimmings are on offer - you can even order a foot-long hot-dog! The service is good and fast, offering meals at average prices. If you want a quieter place to eat while visiting the City Centre mall, and want to avoid the active hype surrounding the Magic planet, this is the place to go.

FASHION CAFE
Dubai

## Hard Rock Cafe

50-100

Check Press ~ Dec 1997 | Dubai Park Hotel, Al Mina Al Siyahi | Page 2 A 3 | Tel: **487 111**

The face of the music scene in Dubai is set to change with the introduction of Hard Rock Cafe in November, in the grounds of the Dubai Park Hotel. Throughout the world Hard Rock Cafe's concentrate on their involvement with global and local community projects. With their pioneering mission being to "give something back", the chain began working with concerns such as "Save The Planet" and "Conservation International" etc. before most of them became widely supported causes.

The memorablia-decorated restaurant also places emphasis on the high quality of its moderately priced American-style food and beverages. The menu features such broadly appealing items as hamburgers, barbecued ribs, sandwiches, chicken, salads and desserts, all of which are freshly prepared daily according to special recipes and conservation practices.

## Johnny Rockets

50-100

12:00 - 24:00 | Opp. Magrudys Centre, Al Jumeira Rd | Page 5 C 2 | Tel: **447 859**

For the 'upper-class' burger lover, this joint offers a rather more superior type of freshly-made burger than the usual plastic variety sold at most fast food outlets. Select one of the 50's and 60's songs on the table-bar jukeboxes whilst your order is prepared before your very eyes. Pick a particular song, and all the chefs throw down their tools to perform the infamous Johnny Rockets song-and-dance routine. This venue is best suited for a quick bite to eat at the table-bar due to the few proper seats and tables. Great malt shakes, infact, the best shakes in the entire universe! Very healthy portions and a lively, friendly atmosphere most afternoons and nights, this is a great contender to the standard burger joints in town. A mean home-made 'apple pie to go' as well.

## Planet Hollywood

50-100

Check Press ~ May 1998 | Nr Wafi Shopping Mall, Al Wasl | Page 13 D 2 | Tel: **344 666**

Planet Hollywood was the first dining experience to be inspired by the worlds of film and television. Currently open in London, New York, Hong Kong, Paris and over forty other locations world-wide.

The merchandise shop is already open at the Wafi Shopping Mall with the restaurant earmarked to be opened in May 1998 just beside the Mall. The restaurant will be built in a format of a globe, seating over 300 guests for lunch, dinner, private functions or just drinks at the bar.

Planet Hollywood houses some of the best movie memorabilia in the world. Handprint plasters, currently on display at the merchandise shop, feature the palms of the word's most famous film and television stars, with autographed prints of Arnold Schwarzenegger, Sylvester Stalone, Demi Moore, Sharon Stone and Bruce Willis among many others. Watch this space...

## Rattle Snake

50-100

12:30 - 14:45
19:00 - 23:30

**Metropolitan Hotel**
**Sh Zayed Rd/Safa**

**Page 4**
**C 4**

Tel: **440 000**

Walk past the county jail and enter into the Western Country town of Rattle Snakes. This American themed restaurant with separate bar and dance area is designed around your good ol' Western movie town, with each corner of the restaurant offering a different scene; Courthouse, jail, railway station etc. The split-level restaurant is spacious with ample privacy for all occasions and a mellow, and relaxing atmosphere. Large wooden terrace outside, and nice almost cubicle like sections inside. One of the few Dubai American restaurants with a leisurely feel to the place.

The band offers a good selection of lively tunes, while the menu offers American-style cuisine with a small section for vegetarians and fish lovers. Decent house wine. If you're a carnivore don't miss out on the best ribs in Dubai, we mean the best, Cajun or Barbecue flavour. The enormous full rack will guarantee that you will not leave this restaurant hungry. Regular side trimmings.

## Rock Bottom Cafe

50-100

12:00 - 15:00
18:00 - 03:00

**Regent Palace Hotel**
**Al Karama**

**Page 10**
**A 1**

Tel: **353 888**

This is what you call a "Cafe with Attitude" - its just oozing with atmosphere! Sit and eat surrounded by American and Harley Davidson memorabilia and let yourself be blown away by the live band. The limited menu, with a few house specials and choice steaks of generous size, is to be expanded in near future to offer larger choices and vegetarian food. The large dance floor allows the energetic to let loose after dinner, whilst the secondary bar area allows the "ageing few" to retire and enjoy the ambience. Attracts a large crowd every night, although the action really steams on Tuesdays (Ladies Night) and Thursdays. See you there!! (Over 21's only). Door policy selection.

## Sizzlers

50-100

19:00 - 03:00

**Howard Johnson**
**Deira**

**Page 10**
**D 1**

Tel: **221 111**

As the name suggests, Sizzlers prides itself on the steaks that they serve. However the assortment of other Tex-Mex items on the menu are just as appetising. Sizzlers has re-invented itself over the past year and is now a place to enjoy a good drink, a leisurely meal and the maverick Lithuanian band, the Baltic Trio, who have a wide repertoire, from pleasant jazz and pop to groovy Russian ballads. The music is generally soft and doesn't compete with conversation.

The customers are well known by the staff and regular visitors are often surprised with complimentary starters or drinks. An extremely relaxed setting for both week nights and weekends. One leaves Sizzlers with a deeply contented feeling.

## TGI Friday's

50-100

11:00 - 24:00 | Holiday Inn Crowne Plaza, Sh Zayed Rd/Trade Centre | Page 8, D 2 | Tel: **318 010**

The original TGI Friday certainly lives up to its international reputation, particularly with its large portions! The atmosphere is relaxed and the restaurant decorated with standard Hollywood-type memorabilia. There's a great menu selection with speciality salads, appetisers and choices of pasta, fajitas, ribs and burgers. The Cajun Angels (shrimps wrapped in beef bacon and coated in bread crumbs) are a delicious appetiser. TGI's has menu promotions operating world-wide which rotate every six weeks. This restaurant chain appeals to a wide age group and is a great venue for lunch and dinner with friends, or place to treat the kids. There's even a weekend brunch on both Fridays and Saturdays. A tempting selection of non-alcoholic cocktails, malts and shakes on offer.

## TGI Thursday's

50-100

12:00 - 16:00, 18:00 - 00:30 | Astoria Hotel, Bur Dubai | Page 7, A 2 | Tel: **534 300**

"Thank God It's Thursday" is in the style of, but not related to, the well known TGI Friday chain. The food is inexpensive with favourite choices being steak sandwiches and big burgers. Bar prices are good. Atmosphere is young, noisy and lively - not a place to take Grandma! The good point is its proximity to the electrical souk and favourite nightspots such as Pancho's and The George.

The food is nothing fancy, great burgers, good value for money - a place to have a quick bite before partying, not a place to sit and linger. The adjoining bar room is frequented by visiting French sailors who often watch the bartender in fascination while he displays skillful pub games and tricks.

## Winners

50-100

15:00 - 01:00 | Sea Shell Inn, Bur Dubai | Page 6, E 2 | Tel: **551 000**

Winners is one of the newer additions to the sports theme pubs in town. Opened last year, the main attraction of Winners bar is that they regularly screen live sporting events. The bar also features fruit machines and a dart board, and the overall ambience is sporty, with various games paraphernalia dotted around the place, right down to the mountain bike on top of the bar!

Winners boasts an extensive cocktail list, all named after famous sports personalities, and a good selection of beverages. Food is also available, ranging from burgers to pies and the house speciality, open grilled sandwiches. Reasonable prices. Becomes a busy night-spot, especially on a live event screening night.

## See Also:

Jazz Bars: **Key West - Entertainment Centre**

# Californian

## Malibu

50-100

12:00 - 15:00
19:00 - 23:30

**Princeton Hotel**
**Al Garhoud**

**Page 14**
**D 2**

Tel: **827 777**

The food here is defined as a "fusion" of Mexican, Italian, Chinese and Arabic cuisine with plenty of intriguing names on the menu. For starters, try Popcorn shrimps or the freshly made Mexican Spring Rolls. Crab Stuffed Hammour or New Orleans Blackened Salmon make a tasty main. A number of large, but healthy, salad meals are available. Look out for the CalItalian section of the menu that will include stirfried noodles.

This restaurant has a light and open design with a relaxed atmosphere and friendly service. A place for good-value tasty food. The music from the band is good and quiet enough to have a conversation while enjoying the food. A place to go for business dinners or a quiet meal for two.

# Jamaican

## Island Delight

0-50

09:00 - 22:00

**Al Hana Centre**
**Al Satwa**

**Page 6**
**A 4**

Tel: **450 417**

Not really a restaurant and hidden away in the corner of the new food court of the new Al Hana Centre in Satwa, Island Delight serves delicious Jamaican dishes such as Jerk chicken, Escoveitch fish, rice and peas, Johnny cakes, and others. Great muffins and creamy cheesecakes. The pimento spice traditionally used in most of the dishes is only grown in Jamaica and is imported from the owners' sister's farm.

They also serve their own, top quality frozen yogurt imported from the States which is a healthy alternative to ice cream. This refreshing and delicious, creamy frozen yogurt is completely non-fat and only 60 calories per serving.

# Mexican

## Shooters

50-100

13:00 - 15:30
19:00 - 23:00 Closed Tue

**Jebel Ali Shooting Club**
**Jebel Ali**

Tel: **836 555**

Although Shooters is a long way from town, its location in the Jebel Ali Shooting Club makes this restaurant and bar a unique experience. A wall of bullet proof glass windows allows spectacular views across the Shooting Ranges, as well as providing riveting entertainment while you sample the delicious and hearty Western-style Mexican cuisine. Try the salad bar which is served from a traditional market vegetable barrow and decorated with daily fresh vegetables, that look so inviting they could be mistaken for part of the menu. With an excellent beverage list available it would be a shame to come here and not combine your meal with a shot.

## Sombrero

50-100

**12:00 - 15:00**
**19:00 - 01:00**

**Royal Abjar**
**Deira**
**Page 11**
**A 3**

Tel: **625 555**

Aptly named as it is the home of the worlds largest Sombrero with a circumference of 14m, diameter 4.5m and height of 1.7m. This restaurant boasts large hand-carved wooden chairs, beautiful round tables of varying sizes, including one for twelve people, with cute colourful cactii on each, aztec headdresses on the walls, and staff in traditional Latin dress, all contained under two gigantic Sombreros. Now part of the Spice Island restaurant complex.

The seafood quesadilla is excellent, as are the Camerones Rancheros, sauteed prawns in an onion sauce. Strawberry margaritas come highly recommended, as does the exquisite banana flambe with rum and raisin ice cream, along with Mexican coffee which includes Tia Maria, cream, and a cinnamon stick. Spanish band and singer are accompanied by flamenco dancers with castanets, fans, guitars and stomping feet.

## Tijuana

50-100

**13:00 - 15:30**
**19:30 - 24:00**

**Met Club, The**
**Jebel Ali**

Tel: **817 100**

If you find yourself at Jebel Ali Port then stop in at Tijuana which offers a selection of Tex-Mex treats such as fajitas and enchiladas. A live band plays on certain nights to add atmosphere to your evening meal or drink. Tijuana is ideal for a casual lunchtime meeting or after-work drinks.

# Steak-House

## 49 'ers The Gold Rush

50-100

**18:00 - 03:00**

**Sea Shell Inn**
**Bur Dubai**
**Page 6**
**E 2**

Tel: **551 000**

49'ers promotes itself not as a restaurant but as a Wild West club. There is certainly a lively, vibrant atmosphere due to the fact that it is also a bar with a dance floor. This is a noisy, blustery, fun restaurant with a rip-roaring resident band throughout the year, adding to the overall party feeling.

Although it would be fair to describe 49'ers principally as a steakhouse it does have an excellent selection of Tex-Mex choices and seafood. You will not have a great problem in choosing your meal as there is a limited selection of both starters and desserts, and all meals come with an array of vegetables. Excellent for office and 20-something birthday parties.

## Horse Shoe

50-100

12:00 - 15:00
19:00 - 03:00

Quality Inn Horizon
Deira

Page 10
E 2

Tel: **271 919**

Dubai's only 'American, non-beef steakhouse', the Horse Shoe is a relaxing alternative to 49'ers for a good value meal, in a warm atmosphere with live music. The seafood house specialities are recommended and the Louisiana Chowder is not to be missed. Choose which seafood you would like to eat and it is weighed and cooked to your liking, which is not always explained at first. Try a little muscle toning by lifting the 3Kg menu! There's a selection of Italian, French and of course, American vintages. Good value. Underground parking will be in full operation by the end of 1997.

## JW's Steakhouse

100-150

12:30 - 15:00
19:30 - 23:00

JW Marriott Hotel
Deira

Page 11
A 3

Tel: **607 7765**

A quiet and serious restaurant. Relaxed, though somehow strangely formal. The dark wooden panels and leather seats add a masculine club-type atmosphere. A stylish place for the over 30's, a business date or serious carnivore. Not for a wild night out.

Don't miss the home-made bread individually baked in its own flowerpot. Try the innovative flame grilled meat and fish, American salads and huge desserts. Excellent meat flown straight from America, remains fresh and is not frozen. A huge selection of wines available by the glass.

## Links Steakhouse, The

100-150

12:00 - 15:00
20:00 - 23:30 Closed Fri

Dubai Golf & Racing Club
Nadd Al Shiba

Page 12
A 3

Tel: **363 666**

The Links Steak House is becoming increasingly popular as more people discover its great value-for-money fare. Now there's more reason than ever for families to give it a try with the introduction of earlier opening hours, from 19:00 onwards, plus half-price reductions for children. Beverages too are sensibly priced, allow approx. Dhs.120 per person for meal plus drinks.

Excellent cuisine is another reason for eating here, with sumptuous steaks cooked order. One of the only places to have fondues, from cheese, meat, even the 'to die for'; chocolate fruit fondue. Get your woolly hats, and ski on down! Music for dancing on the small dance floor is provided by an excellent band, and of course there's added excitement on race nights. Extremely comfortable dining chairs. Make this place a great change from the other restaurants in town, offering a relaxed, but refined environment.

## Rodeo Grill

100-150

12:00 - 15:00
19:00 - 24:00

Al Bustan Rotana Hotel
Al Garhoud

Page 14
E 3

Tel: **820 000**

The Rodeo Grill bills itself as an "informal fine-dine" restaurant which offers a dining experience 'with a difference'. An American theme is evident and is supported by a range of Bourbon-based cocktails which guarantee a good stir of the gastric juices. Highly recommended is the "Dry Aged Black Angus Beef", which is held in a moisture free cold room for 21 days to allow the meat the ripen and thereby develop flavour and tenderness. However, the Grill's signature steak is definitely 'Colorado Bison', which is bred and matured for 10 years, and the Prime Rib that is supposedly low in cholesterol and fat, but rich in minerals. The cellar is well stocked with a wide selection of Spanish, S. African, Californian, Chilean, Australian, French and Italian vintages. There is a plan to open up a Cigar Bar for those who enjoy a good puff after a satisfying and enjoyable meal. Reservations are recommended and a sit down at the Bar while they prepare your table is not a bad idea at all!

## Western Steak House, The

100-150

11:30 - 15:00
19:30 - 23:30

Holiday Inn Crowne Plaza
Sh Zayed Rd/Trade Centre

Page 8
D 2

Tel: **311 111**

If you are looking for a wild steak, the kind they used to serve in the Far West, this is the place to go as the meat has been specially flown in from the U.S, accentuating the original taste. A great menu full of tasty ideas, from delicious steaks and fillets to lobsters tails, all with a variety of accompaniments. They don't just serve the finest imported Kobe steaks at their businessmen's lunch, they also serve them fast, along with a whole selection of side dishes you can pick from in a hurry.

The relaxing atmosphere makes this a good place to visit after a stressful day in the office.

# Tex-Mex

## Alamo, The

50-100

12:00 - 15:00
19:00 - 01:00

Dubai Marine Beach Resort
Jumeira

Page 5
D 2

Tel: **441 221**

The Alamo derives its name from a historical battle that took place in the mid nineteenth century during the Texan struggle for independence from Mexico. This is explained on the various posters and table mats in the airy Tex-Mex restaurant, just one step away from an unusually long, curved bar which provides lots of elbow room for the crowds that gather on weekend evenings. Large portions of well cooked Tex-Mex food at reasonable prices mean

# Ever wished there were nine days in a Week !

*Marco Polo* – The very best of Thai, Chinese and Indian Cuisine all under one roof.

*Al Qasr* – Exquisite Lebanese food, service and entertainment.

*La Capanna* – A firm favourite with everyone with its wonderful ocean view and superb Italian fare.

*Thai Bistro* – Thai food at its very best in a fabulous poolside location.

*Taverna* – A Mediterranean style beach Restaurant offering sumptuous Continental cuisine.

*Thatcher's* – A traditional English Freehouse with a relaxing atmosphere and good old English food.

*Tropicana* – Dance the night away in one of Dubai's favourite night spots.

*The Alamo* – The very best Tex-Mex in Town, once visited never forgotten.

*Ayam Zaman* – 'The good old days' Experience the atmosphere of traditional Lebanon.

DUBAI MARINE HOTEL & BEACH RESORT

Tel: 520900 / 441221

that booking is advisable for meals. A plate of spare ribs means just that you need another plate for the baked potato and salad! The chef is prepared to adapt many of the dishes to suit vegetarians if requested. Lunch times are quiet and peaceful, but the evenings can get pretty hectic at this bar/restaurant which has a dance floor and lively music. Tuesday night is Ladies Night with a free drink or two for ladies who either start their evening here before going into town, or end up here before returning home.

## Border Town

50-100

12:00 - 15:00
19:00 - 24:00

Imperial Suites Hotel, The
Bur Dubai

Page 6
E 3

Tel: **515 100**

Small Cantina-style Mexican restaurant-cum-bar / disco with seating for 50. The decoration is simple with a bar in the middle, four television sets showing sports channels and a tiny dance floor / DJ area at the end of the restaurant. There is a nightclub atmosphere after 23:00 when the place becomes packed with European, Indian and Syrian clientele.

Food is quickly served, tasty, hearty and plentiful. The usual tacos, ribs, chimichinga, etc. We recommend the tasty fajitas, pronounced FA-HEE-TARS. Excellent margaritas with different flavours.

## Cactus Cantina

50-100

12:00 - 23:30
Closed Fri Lunch

Plaza Hotel
Al Satwa

Page 6
A 4

Tel: **455 274**

Unlike other Tex-Mex's in town, the Cactus Cantina does not have a live band, so it attracts a clientele who enjoy conversation with their friends as much as their food! At the same time, it retains a lively and convivial atmosphere, particularly on Ladies night (Sunday) and Fat Friday's (two mains for the price of one, on Fridays). The menu is standard Tex-Mex fare and includes lavish complimentary portions of corn chips and salsa, freshly made each day. Starters are the size of a main, so order a half portion if you are having a main course as well. There is a good vegetarian range and quesadillas are to be recommended. Children are more than welcome, with a special menu just for them. And, of course, it is next to Billy Blues!

## El Gringo

50-100

18:00 - 03:00

Dubai Park Hotel
Sh Zayed Rd/Emirates Golf Club

Page 2
A 3

Tel: **489 934**

Whilst El Gringo may be a little off the beaten track, do not despair because the restaurant will arrange for a minibus back to town, free of charge, for parties of six or more. A lively atmosphere is augmented by a two-piece band whose cover versions are far easier on the ear than is usual. Added to this, the quality of the food is an improvement on the majority of Tex-Mex's and things may improve further judging by the manager's plans to include a wider variety of U.S. dishes.

## El Rancho

50-100

20:00 - 02:30 | Novotel Deira | Page 7 E 4 | Tel: **720 000**

Another Tex-Mex in Dubai town, and just as lively as all the others. The ceiling is worth a visit alone as cutsey little lights change colour trying to depict an open court yard. Decorated in true Western style with crazy paving floors, wooden windows and stone walls covered with lassoos, rugs, sombreros, lanterns and even a buffalo head. Live band plays catchy songs at the dance floor every day except Sunday.

Mexican cooking as well as Tex-Mex food. Fresh tomato based sauces, lightly grilled meats, fish and spicy large prawns, as well as nachos and tacos. Well made, strong margaritas are sold by the glass or jug.

## Pancho Villa's

50-100

12:00 - 16:00
19:00 - 01:00 | Astoria Hotel Bur Dubai | Page 7 A 2 | Tel: **532 146**

Don't get too comfortable, this place gets packed. Here's where it's all happening. It's the oldest Tex-Mex restaurant in the Gulf and probably still the most popular. Limbo dancing, shell fish eating, mardi gras, this place has everybody joining in. A favourite, even if you hate it! Has even appeared in Newsweek! As good a Tex-Mex as any, but with added entertainment and atmosphere.

A comprehensive menu, great margaritas and tequilas (poured down the throat on request by the Tex) and an explosive band which starts at 21:00. Try the PVQ, enormous cheese burgers or the standard Mexican fajitas. If you want to chat, avoid a table by the dance floor, and avoid Tuesdays and Thursdays. Any night and every night, this is the place to find some good solid action. The cost of a meal is slightly more than average but the portions are large enough to fill a sombrero. Definately a place for the younger crowd who enjoy a hearty meal and partying.

# Asian

## Baluchistani

### Baluchi

50-100

19:30 - 02:30

**Gulf Inn Hotel**
**Deira**

**Page 10**
**D 2**

Tel: **243 433**

Baluchi is named after the people from Baluchistan, an area of rugged terrain in Northern Pakistan. Though the name suggests a Pakistani influence, there is a strong Indian flavour to the restaurant with entertainment of Indian classical music, alternated by a Ghazal (ballad) singing duo who are accompanied by a pretty Kathak dancer. The restaurant itself is dimly lit lulling one into relaxation mode. "Saji", the house speciality, is a whole leg of baby lamb which is marinated in vinegar and pomegranate juice for 24 hours before it is cooked in the tandoor oven. Try the lentil dish of Dal Baluchi with unleavened bread called Lachha Parantha. The Kebabs are excellent and served hot from the pan. Valet parking is a welcome facility that is offered to visitors.

## Chinese

### Cascade

50-100

12:30 - 15:00
19:30 - 11:30

**Opp. India House**
**Bur Dubai**

**Page 7**
**A 3**

Tel: **522 020**

An unimposing venue with a varied bakery downstairs, Cascade must possess one of the most extensive Thai/Chinese menus in the city. In the heart of Bur Dubai's material souk this restaurant would make a convenient stop for shoppers wanting some spice. Outside catering and home delivery also make it worth picking up their card!

### China Express

50-100

12:00 - 15:00
18:00 - 01:00

**Nr. Dubai Marine Hotel**
**Bur Dubai**

**Page 6**
**E 2**

Tel: **510 001**

Forget the canned music and enjoy the bright, cheerful and clean decor with friendly service, at this upmarket fast food restaurant. Mainly western clientele. A straightforward, no-nonsense, 70-seater fast-food Chinese restaurant, which serves dishes far exceeding the normal standard of fast food fare, and at reasonable prices.

Refreshingly short menu which maintains an ample variety, with only a half dozen or so identically priced dishes under each familiar category - all adding to the convenience of the customer. Try the honeyed duck and/or chillied pepper lamb for a delicious treat. Pleasantly flavoured food which is neither overpowering or stodgy.

## China Garden

50-100

12:00 - 15:00
18:00 - 24:00

Next to Spinneys, Jumeira — Page 5, C 2

Tel: **440 253**

Although it prides itself on its take away and delivery service, the China Garden also has two very pleasant little restaurant outlets next to Spinney's, Beach Road and Park and Shop supermarket on Iranian Hospital road. The dishes are mainly Cantonese and Sechzuan, with a house speciality of BBQ duck accompanied by pancakes and a delicious plum sauce.

Decor is clean and fresh and all very green - a calming environment after a hectic shopping session around the supermarket. The atmosphere is comfortable and relaxed and it is easy to sit and gossip over a steaming cup of Jasmine tea, until the lights go out and the tables are re-laid for tomorrow's lunch.

## China Times

50-100

12:00 - 15:00
19:00 - 24:00 Closed Fri am

Jumeira Plaza, Jumeira — Page 5, C 2

Tel: **442 930**

A high quality restaurant with a relaxed atmosphere and individual style decor, combining both modern and traditional designs. The standard and choice of both food and service is excellent and Chef will alter the level of spiciness to suit your taste. Chinese-style seafood is the speciality offered. This is one Chinese restaurant which will not leave you feeling hungry a few hours later. Conveniently located for the Jumeira shops and beach.

## Chinese Diwan

50-100

11:30 - 15:00
18:30 - 24:00 Closed Fri am

Bottom of Arbift Tower, Deira — Page 10, C 1

Tel: **229 886**

Situated in the Arab Investment Bank building this is a great place for business people to pop down and tuck into a bowl of steaming noodles or crispy wontons, and sup a pot of Chinese tea. Don't be put off by the dark entrance in the corner where daytime snacks and rolls are constantly delivered throughout the building. Inside, the sunlit restaurant is adorned with attractive Chinese fans and umbrellas, simple tables and plenty of bamboo.

The restaurant does a great Lunch Pack for Dhs.15 filled with oriental goodies, delivered straight to your office.

## Chinese Kitchen

50-100

12:00 - 15:00
17:00 - 24:00

Al Wasl Rd, Jumeira — Page 4, B 2

Tel: **381 864**

Sited on Al Wasl Road, perfectly located for Jumeira residents, Mr. Chen and his staff are well known for their delicious Chinese dishes at affordable prices. Even though the majority of business is of the take away type, the high quality of food is of excellent restaurant standard.

Limited seating is available upstairs and the service is fast and efficient. The restaurant is not licensed, so try the variety of teas on offer to refresh between courses. Mr. Chen prides himself on his home-made sauces and individually made spring rolls and wontons, plus a menu that specialises in only Chinese food. Favourites include lemon chicken, garlic prawns and Shanghai rice. Outside catering and free delivery is another good reason to try this restaurant.

## Chinese Palace

50-100

12:00 - 15:30
19:00 - 23:30

Al Ghurair Centre
Deira

Page 10
D 1

Tel: **281 043**

You'd expect that a restaurant that seats up to 300 people and frequently hosts Arabic and Chinese wedding parties, would be hard to hide, but the Chinese Palace on the third floor of the Al Ghurair Centre does a pretty good job. Tucked away directly above Lal's supermarket, this restaurant serves authentic Chinese food at reasonable prices.

It is populated with Chinese customers, always a good sign, as well as a mixed clientele. Traditional dragons and lamp adornments accompany strategically placed screens to divide the restaurant into less intimidating sections. This is the only restaurant in town to boast an eat-as-much-you-can Mongolian BBQ - ideal for a Friday brunch with a difference. Also try the fast-food versions in Bur Juman and Deira City Centre.

## Chinese Pavillon

50-100

13:30 - 15:00
19:00 - 23:30

Beach Centre, The
Jumeira

Page 5
B 2

Tel: **444 432**

This small, friendly restaurant is tucked away in the far corner of the Beach Centre Shopping Mall.

Tastefully and simply decorated, with wicker furniture and dim lighting. The menu offers a good selection with specialities ranging from Singapore chicken to chilli dishes with crispy vegetables. The restaurant is not licensed to sell alcohol, so try the hot jasmine tea instead which compliments the food. Chinese Pavilion has a family lunch on Fridays with some special offers.

## Chopsticks

0-50

12:00 - 15:00
19:00 - 24:00

Sh Hamdan Coloney
Al Karama

Page 9
E 2

Tel: **372 962**

Chopsticks is a cosy little Chinese restaurant in a quiet corner of Karama which is frequented by the few who know about this place. However membership to the Chopsticks Club (Privilege Card), which qualifies the member to a 10% discount, is growing at a fast pace. The menu is extensive and focuses on the Schezuan style. Duck and Prawn dishes are particularly recommended especially as the prices are so reasonable. Take-aways, home deliveries and party orders make up for a major percentage of the restaurant's revenue and they will willingly deliver as far away as Jumeira. Chopsticks presents excellent value.

## Dynasty

50-100

12:30 - 15:00
19:30 - 24:00

Ramada Hotel
Bur Dubai

Page 6
E 3

Tel: **521 010**

Ask any businessmen who has been coming to Dubai for many years where he goes for a Chinese meal and the answer will invariably be "Dynasty". Décor consists of red lanterns, and dark wood panelling with heavy chinese tapestry on the walls. Quality service, food and surroundings make it a peaceful restaurant to do what the Chinese like to do:

eat, chat and enjoy. Clearly presented menu. The kitchen is Cantonese and Szechuan, using old traditions and modern techniques. Stylish black chopsticks are offered to all customers, as is a handy spoon for emergencies. Groups of diners may like to sit at the round table with revolving central section which makes it easy to "Pass the soy sauce, please". Food is excellent and fairly quickly served, with a wide variety of dishes. Specialities on offer include abalone and lobsters prepared oriental style. One of the rather more cosy, but not necessarily intimate, Chinese restaurants in town.

## Flying Dragons

50-100

12:30 - 15:00
19:00 - 01:00

Royal Abjar
Deira

Page 11
A 3

Tel: **625 555**

A Chinese restaurant full of Chinese patrons and waiting staff - what better recommendation? The menu at the Flying Dragons, whilst including many familiar dishes, offers several novel and creative choices. Specialising in both Szechuan and Cantonese style cooking, there is something for those whose tastes are at opposing ends of the culinary thermometer. Whether spicy or mild, your meal will be served with a rare degree of gentility. A touch of luxury at affordable prices.

## Golden Dragon

50-100

12:00 - 15:00
19:00 - 23:45

Opp. Palm Beach Hotel
Bur Dubai

Page 6
E 2

Tel: **525 617**

Touch the bell outside the Golden Dragon and it will bring you luck, goes the old saying. Two large marble lions stand proud outside the heavy entrance door and if you can manage to heave it back sufficiently to squeeze through, you will find yourself amid a 70's style decor of deep red furnishings and mirrored ceilings. The food is well prepared and nicely presented. Try a selection plate for appetisers; the dumplings are excellent, soft and perfectly insipid! There is a well balanced selection of main dishes and the prawns are very tasty, wonderfully cooked and served with a delicious sauce. Portions are satisfying. When Confucius laid down the principles of Chinese cooking around 500 BC he said eat nothing that is over-cooked, untidily cut or deficient in seasoning-.the Golden Dragon has certainly upheld his words of wisdom.

## Golden Dragon

50-100

12:00 - 15:00
19:00 - 23:45

Trade Centre Rd
Al Karama

Page 9
D 1

Tel: **366 122**

One of the oldest traditional Chinese restaurants in Dubai has relocated and is still continuing to delight patrons of every nationality with its freshly prepared food served in a welcoming environment. Now located on the Trade Centre Road, near to the Thai Terrace, it is a much more accessible location to get to, park and enjoy a menu which has been improved - hard to believe, but true! Two dragons stand guard to welcome you in at the

A tastefully decorated, clean restaurant with one private room which seats 14 people, and other areas which can be screened off. Families welcome. Highchairs available in the same material as the dining chairs!

The Peking Duck is not to be missed and is available without having to phone in 24hrs beforehand! Try the Hot and Sour Soup and the seafood dishes - you won't be disappointed. Some of the staff have been there for 20 years (John and Patrick) and all are from Chinese descent. 80% of the clientele are regulars. Excellent Chinese cuisine probably the best outside a five-star hotel. Once visited - never forgotten.

## Hai Bing

50-100

11:30 - 15:30
18:00 - 24:00

Carlton Tower, The
Deira

Page 7
C 4

Tel: **227 111**

A very loud red carpet leads into this boardroom of a restaurant. When booking, ask for a window table to get a view of the Creek. Try to eat before 23:00 as the adjoining Arabic nightclub is very loud and makes it difficult to have a conversation. Service is slow, even for drinks, so allow lots of time.

The staff are all Chinese, which is unusual, and Meng Xian Fu the mainland Chinese Chef, has devised a small but adventurous sounding menu with Glutinous Dumplings and Deep Fried Toffee Potato being but a few of the dishes on offer. Prices are quite high.

## Long Yin

50-100

12:30 - 15:00
20:00 - 24:00

Forte Grand Dubai
Al Garhoud

Page 14
E 3

Tel: **824 040**

A cosy restaurant where the black wood floor and decor, plus traditionally dressed waitresses give an authentic, relaxed atmosphere. It's a great time to perfect those chopstick techniques as no alternative is given! Choose from the Promotional Menu which changes every 2-3 weeks and offers dishes from various regions of China, or the extensive main menu where there is a choice of at least 10 different dishes for each of the various meats and seafood. If you wish to sample a little bit of everything the Mixed Dimsum Platter comes highly recommended. Try the Chef's specialities which vary from Honey Tiger Prawns to traditional fare.

Give a day's notice if you want to have an oriental fondue known as a Steam Boat meal, a hands-on and entertaining way to dine. Set menus for two to four people are reduced by Dhs.20 per person on Fridays. A private dining room is also available.

## Mini Chinese

50-100

12:00 - 14:30
18:00 - 23:00

Al Dhiyafah St
Al Satwa

Page 5
E 3

Tel: **459 976**

Situated along the busy Satwa High Street, Mini Chinese is really a fast food outlet. The decor is basic bright yellow with plastic booths, chairs, cups and easy-wipe menus - but it's clean and the service is extremely quick. The menu is good with a few specialties. Portions are big and the food tastes delicious. A place to stop off for a quick bite to eat, perhaps after a spot of shopping, or just to pick up a take away. Unfortunately, there's no delivery service, but the food is good and worth the hassle to stop and collect it!

## Mr. Chow

50-100

12:00 - 15:00
18:00 - 02:30

Imperial Suites Rd
Bur Dubai

Page 6
E 3

Tel: **510 099**

With almost 200 different choices on the menu it may take a while to decide what to order. Never fear, help is on hand with attentive waiters who will explain some of the differences between similar sounding dishes. Try the Manchurian Beef or Szechuan Duck for spice, and Kond Chen Lobster or Mongolian Lamb for pure enjoyment of the meat flavour which surmounts the mild cooking ingredients. Portions of everything are generous.

Casual ambience in typical restaurant surroundings. Good food at good prices.

## Ningxia Chinese

50-100

11:00 - 15:00
18:00 - 24:00

, Nr. Defence RA Sh Zayed
Rd/Trade Centre

Page 8
A 2

. Tel: **446 171**

Reserving a table at the Ningxia shouldn't be too much of a problem most nights of the week, which is fortunate because, given a choice, you should choose the chairs rather than the sofa seats if you want to be close enough to your food to be able to eat it! Choosing your meal will be easy, as you won't be surprised by most of the dishes on offer. Excellent value lunch box. For Dhs.18 choose a starter, main dish and either rice or noodles. Large portions, which can be delivered, provide well-loved meals for a mixed expat clientele. Convenient describes the restaurant as a whole, from easy to clean table tops to easy listening radio in the background. Plenty of parking and easy access from Sheikh Zayed Road.

## Noble House

50-100

12:30 - 15:00
19:30 - 24:00

Imperial Suites Hotel, The
Bur Dubai

Page 6
E 3

Tel: **515 100**

Chef David from Hong Kong delights in coming out of his kitchen and into the restaurant to discuss the menu with diners. His speciality is Szechuan cuisine which is more spicy than the usual take-away fare. Inexpensive dishes are respectfully served by trained staff. The food can be made to custom order, from mild to spicy, beef only or lots of sea food.

A dozen Dim Sum starters to choose from. Save room for desserts and try the speciality of Crispy Fried Milk. Monosodium Glutamate is not used in this restaurant.

## Peacock, The

50-100

19:00 - 23:30 | Radisson SAS Jumeira, Al Mina Al Siyahi | Page 1, D 2 | Tel: 845 533

A modern, spacious, restaurant situated on the mezzanine floor overlooking the hotel foyer - which can allow for some interesting people watching! The service is fluid, but allow a comfortable two hours to complete a five-course meal. Appetizers are excellent. Highly recommend the crispy duck pancakes which are accompanied by thin pancakes.

Good sized main courses, and very tasty. Desserts are presented on a trolley and a suprising selection for the sweet toothed. Good selection of reasonably priced vintages (from Dhs.65 to over Dhs.300). The trip out of town to the Radisson SAS Hotel, Jumeria Beach is well worth making if you want to enjoy good food and drink within a friendly atmosphere.

## Pumpy's

0-50

12:00 - 14:45
18:00 - 23:15 Closed Fri am | Bur Dubai | Page 7, A 3 | Tel: 528 484

A casual restaurant situated in the heart of downtown Bur Dubai above a confectionery gift shop. Located upstairs the restaurant area is small and modestly decorated with a relaxed atmosphere. Cuisine on offer is predominantly Chinese, but Pumpy's also serves steaks and speciality sizzlers.

The staff are keen to recommend their yoko style sizzlers which consist of skewered chicken and capsicum with rice and vegetables served on a hot plate cast iron platter. The food certainly arrives sizzling and there is plenty of it. Overall prices are cheap and the food is filling, a good choice if on a restricted budget.

## Shanghai Kitchen

50-100

12:00 - 15:00
18:00 - 24:00 | Nr. Dubai Plaza, Al Satwa | Page 5, E 4 | ATel: 456

Don't be judgmental about the plastic place mats and rather poor decor, for once you have ordered you will not be disappointed. This is mainly a take- away restaurant so should not be judged on the basis of its decor.

The food is excellent and well prepared. Generous portions. An Indian chef produces a delicious wonton soup, while the chicken with bamboo shoots and mushrooms is tender and rich in flavour. Service is polite and brisk should you decide to eat in the restaurant. Menu is extensive. If you want an early night sitting in front of the television watching your favourite soap then ring the Shanghai Kitchen for a take-away meal. Highly recommended.

## Summer Palace, The

100-150

13:00 - 15:00
19:00 - 24:00

Metropolitan Hotel
Sh Zayed Rd/Safa

Page 4
C 4

Tel: **440 000**

This is one of the classy Chinese restaurants in town where the table service is meticulously professional and attentive, whilst appearing unobtrusive - and the food isn't bad either. Fascinating Chinese dishes can be devoured with relish, while enjoying the classic beauty of Guan Yin, the Chinese deity. The Peking Dinner or Special Banquet set menus both include a wide variety of hors d'oeuvres, with small sized Spare Ribs being particularly delicious, and the Aromatic Duck is a house speciality! For a different dessert, try fruits coated in toffee - definitely for those with a sweet tooth!

The restaurant is particularly popular with large groups, for whom special set-menu rates are negotiable, which adds to the busy and convivial atmosphere. This contrasts delightfully with the romantic, soft, dainty pinks and whites of the decor and low intimate lighting. A great venue for a social night out as well as a private environment for those wanting a quiet lunch or dinner for two.

## Summer Plaza, The

50-100

12:30 - 14:30
19:30 - 23:30 Closed Mon

Plaza Hotel
Al Satwa

Page 6
A 4

Tel: **454 545**

Sitting on the top floor of the Plaza Hotel this restaurant offers a magnificent view of Dubai town. However, to enjoy the evening, you don't even have to consider looking out of the windows. The atmosphere is welcoming, somewhat formal, yet peaceful. There is a well stocked bar to enjoy while waiting for your fellow diners. The menu is extensive and offers Peking specialities - including the divine Peking Duck, an absolute must, which should be ordered in advance.

Silver service allows a feeling of extravagance to creep into the atmosphere. Make sure that you bring an adequate appetite with you as this chef serves large portions. And as word of caution to motorists - don't park on the pavements as you'll get a ticket - extra parking is available on the sand to the side of the hotel's car park. Oh yes, and don't give up on the lifts, they will eventually arrive!

## Taipan

50-100

12:00 - 15:00
18:00 - 24:00

Trade Centre Rd
Al Karama

Page 9
D 1

Tel: **348 835**

A friendly restaurant which is surprisingly busy even on week days. This a sure indication that the food is popular and in demand. A spacious restaurant with no close seating, allowing one to chat and talk in confidence. Decor consists of white floors, green table clothes, black wooden seats, flowery cloth wall paper and small Chinese lanterns hanging from the ceiling.

Taipan offers everyday specials. The Hot & Sour soup is delicious, while other recommended dishes include Chicken Cashew nut, Vegetarian Balls, Stir Fried Sea Food, and Prawn Fried Rice. A large portion of Taipan's business consists of outside catering.

# Indian

## '10' The Restaurant

50-100

12:00 - 15:30
18:30 - 24:00

Nr. GPO
Al Karama

Page 9
E 2

Tel: **364 547**

10 implies '10 out of 10', that is, full marks. This restaurant certainly works towards this ideal and has a spacious and well kept interior. The buffet is very tasty and allows one to sample several dishes without compromising on choice. You must try the Corn Tomato Soup and Chicken Chilli Wings.

The key to a good restaurant can quite often be gauged by its clientele. Here the clientele is predominantly Asian families, and to cater for such customers the food most certainly must be authentic and tasty. Prices are very competitive and reasonable.

## Al Tandoor

50-100

11:30 - 15:00
19:00 - 24:00

Opp. Dubai Marine Hotel
Bur Dubai

Page 6
E 2

Tel: **526 098**

In the heart of Indian restaurant-land, Al Tandoor attracts a mixed crowd of happy eaters. The menu, offering no pork or beef, is extensive and the food unusually subtle and delicate, without losing its spice. If you're also looking for Indian furniture and wall coverings, Samuel will happily take you down to his shop to continue your patronage!

## Ashiana

100-150

12:30 - 15:00
19:30 - 24:00 Closed Fri am

Sheraton Hotel
Deira

Page 10
C 1

Tel: **281 111**

Ashiana means "A Dream House", the centre of affection, where a drink of lassi, made of churned yogurt, awaits you along with poppadums and assorted dips while you discuss with the waiter how spicy or mild you want your choices to be. Flat breads are freshly baked in the clay oven at one end of the restaurant, while the glassed kitchen at the other end provides a talking point.

High prices for high quality food. This Indian restaurant is frequented by Indian families later in the evening, after 22:00. You couldn't ask for a better recommendation. Europeans and other hotel visitors prefer earlier meals. Simple, traditional decor with a central stage where the band plays surrounded by diners. Melodious live music. Dimmed lighting.

## Bombay Brasserie

50-100

12:30 - 15:00
20:00 - 01:00

Novotel Deira — Page 7 E 4

Tel: **720 000**

One of the best Indian restaurants in town. A very good menu is elaborated by a fantastic Indian cook with more than 25 years of experience.

The dishes will be spicy according to your choice, just mention your taste to the waiter. Many varieties of meat and vegetables are cooked in a multitude of spices and flavours. Indian cordon-bleu fare. Tastes and textures to delight the palate. Entertainment by a live Indian band. You won't be disappointed!

## Caesar`s

50-100

12:00 - 14:45
19:00 - 23:45

Falcon R/A Bur Dubai — Page 6 E 1

Tel: **527 300**

Over 260 items to choose from on the mainly Indian menu, which also includes Chinese and continental dishes. There's an ethnic theme throughout, with an old wooden interior and large oil paintings covering all parts of the walls. Ten exclusive wooden cabins are available on the ground floor where you can enjoy a romantic meal for two or a quiet dinner for four. Reservations required.

## Casa Goa

50-100

12:00 - 15:00
19:00 - 24:00

Palm Beach Hotel Bur Dubai — Page 6 E 2

Tel: **525 550**

There's a little corner of Goa at the top of Palm Beach Hotel where one can enjoy authentic Goan cuisine while sitting under palm thatch fringes, beside wooden lattice work. Holiday destination pictures are tantalisingly displayed on the walls, along with fishing nets and luminous orange lobsters.

As soon as you sit down, munchies are delivered to the table to assist your beverage consumption. The menu is compact, but there is a speciality every week to complement whatever is in season. The house speciality is Vindaloo - rich in spices with a lingering tangy taste of a touch of vinegar!

## Coconut Grove

50-100

12:30 - 15:30
19:30 - 24:00

Plaza Hotel Al Satwa — Page 6 A 4

Tel: **452 800**

Colour and vibrant tastes combine to form a wonderful and surprising cuisine in Coconut Crove. The innovative chef prepares a unique cuisine using spices and a mixture of Indian and Sri Lankan tasteswhich combine the best from Kerala, Tamil Nadu, Goa and old Ceylon. Palm trees and huge wooden artefacts create an exotic room. Ensure you taste the cocktails, and home-made chutneys, and also try the pineapple halwa and saffron flavoured rice. A guitarist plays each night. There is a huge buffet on Fridays.

## Daawat Restaurant, The

50-100

12:00 - 15:00
20:00 - 24:30

Sea Shell Inn
Bur Dubai

Page 6
E 2

Tel: **551 000**

Good Indian cooking, although not a huge choice, and it is wise to ask about any specialties of the house. Traditional Indian ghazal singing cheers up this rather gloomy, formal room which doubles up as the hotel's coffee shop. Service is friendly and there are often parties held here. A tasty, very quiet, and non-distracting meal.

## Darshan

50-100

19:00 - 24:00

Radisson SAS Jumeira
Al Mina Al Siyahi

Page 1
D 2

Tel: **845 533**

Situated at the far end of the lobby of the newly opened SAS Radisson, the Darshan Indian restaurant offers a modern and relaxed atmosphere however, the decor is more typical of a modern mediterranian, serving traditional Indian dishes suited towards a European palate. A friendly welcome from the colourfully dressed staff sets the scene for an enjoyable evening where guests can watch the chef preparing tandoori delicaces served in metal dishes with moderate proportions.

## Diwan-e-Moghul

50-100

13:00 - 15:00
20:00 - 23:30

Inter-Continental Hotel
Deira

Page 7
C 4

Tel: **227 171**

Diwan-e-Moghul roughly translates as 'The grand dining place of the Moghuls'. The decor and ambiance attempts to take one on a trip back in time to the days of palaces and princes. Plenty of things to look at and admire this restaurant is rich in artefacts.

The restaurant specialises in North West Frontier cuisine and Tandoor, an Indian clay oven, items, with a Chef who has over 25 years experience in the business and can be counted on to provide authentic fare. For those who are unsure if they can cope with hot food the chef will willingly temper a particular dish to cater to the palate.

## Down Town Restaurant

0-50

11:00 - 24:00
Closed Fri am

Bur Dubai

Page 6
E 2

Tel: **525 219**

Down Town is not merely a multi-cuisine restaurant, but more a close fraternity of those who have warmed to the innovative style and personality of Peter Souriraj and the excellent food that he serves. Primarily continental dishes although there is also a limited choice of other cuisines. The chefs are good at what they make.

The place is spotless and neat, friendly service and a comfortable atmosphere. Peter himself knows most of his customers well and maintains contact through a monthly newsletter. While at Down Town you can now surf the net, or as in the old days simply browse through one of the many magazines off the reading rack. Highly recommended.

## Dubai Mughal

50-100

12:00 - 15:30
19:00 - 24:00

Nr. Dubai Marine/Ramada
Bur Dubai
Page 7
A 3

Tel: **518 833**

With a name like this you would expect bhajee and poppadoms...wrong! Despite its name, the Dubai Mughal offers both Indian and Chinese cuisine, although it is fair to say that by the name, decoration and general ambiance it is primarily an Indian restaurant. Opened five years ago it has already been refurbished taking it on level above the ordinary diners.

A comprehensive menu with specialties of kebabs, and curries with rich gravies. Service is polite and attentive although you may need to wait a little while between courses. Value for money with a pleasant environment.

## Falaknuma

50-100

12:30 - 15:00
19:00 - 24:00

Arif Castle
Bur Dubai
Page 6
E 2

Tel: **557 123**

The Nawabs of Lucknow would be thrilled to visit this unique Indian restaurant and find that their recipes have been prepared by a Chef, especially brought to Dubai in order to share the secrets that have been past down from generation to generation.

The menu offers a selection of Indian cuisine combined with a number of Lucknow delicacies including the famous "Kakari Kebab". The decor is not what you'd call typically Indian, but the entertainment is, as it consists of a trio of musicians flown in directly from Lucknow who sit on a carpeted stage and turn out sedate Indian melodies.

Located in a newly opened hotel it attracts predominantly Indian families, as well as with hotel guests and the usual array of nationalities looking for a quiet, but enjoyable evening, with just a touch of tradition.

## Five Rivers

0-50

12:00 - 15:00
18:30 - 24:00

Opp. Deira Taxi Stand
Deira
Page 10
D 1

Tel: **273 484**

Named after an area in Pakistan where rivers from five countries meet and join forces, this small restaurant specialises in Pakistani and spicy Chinese cuisine. The atmosphere is a little smokey as barbecue cooking is carried out in the kitchen at the rear of the room but the delicate yet pungent tastes are worth it. Share a whole chicken or small leg of mutton which has been steam roasted, an uncommon way of cooking here in Dubai.

## Frontier

50-100

19:30 - 03:00

Howard Johnson
Deira
Page 10
D 1

Tel: **221 111**

Already attracting an Indian clientele of nearby residents, Europeans should take note as this is not a typical hot and spicy Indian curry place, but has much simpler fare as most of the food is either barbecued, or cooked in the Tandoor oven and then flavoured with traditional Himalayan spices.

This small, cosy restaurant has a low painted ceiling and dim lighting that draws its inspiration from the North West Frontier region of old India. You'll find the band tucked into a corner playing typical Indian music and a singing duo which welcomes requests.

Murg Daraanpur and Kabab -E-Bannu, are a special treat and the saffron flavoured ice cream is recommended. If you are feeling adventurous try the various range of flavoured drinks of which Jal Jeera, cumin and fresh mint, and a sour carrot drink called Kanji, are acquired tastes, but the Cream Frontier mixture of creamed almonds and pistachio is delicious.

## Gulzar

50-100

12:30 - 15:30
19:30 - 02:30

Maredias Hotel
Deira

Page 10
E 1

Tel: **289 393**

No expense has been spared in the decor of this excellent Indian restaurant; the antique carved door at the entrance originated from a royal palace in Lucknow, while the interior abounds with exquisite wood carvings, clay work and paintings, created by craftsmen and specially flown in from Lucknow and Jaipur. Add to this the statues, rugs and antiques tastefully arranged throughout the restaurant, and the result is a unique ethnic style.

Ghazal singers provide traditional entertainment and the atmosphere is enhanced by candlelit tables laid with elegant cutlery. The menu offers a tantalising selection of over 70 dishes. The Tandoor is the source of several of Gulzar's specialties, while a variety of curries include aromatic creations such as Handiwala Ghost (chunks of lamb in a spiced spinach and tomato sauce).

Vegetarians are catered for with delicious offerings such as stuffed peppers cooked on charcoal, black lentils in a buttery cream sauce and rice garnished with fruit and nuts. Dishes vary from the very spicy for the connoisseur to mild and aromatic for the beginner.

## Gungroo

50-100

21:00 - 03:00

Penninsula Hotel
Bur Dubai

Page 7
A 2

Tel: **533 000**

This Indian restaurant / nightclub is named after the silver ankle chains worn by traditional Indian dancers. The resident band play live Hindi music whilst the girls, dressed in elaborate costumes, perform dances to the beat of the tabla drums. Modest Indian decor, with a central stage for the band to sit and play, it offers a good selection of tasty dishes at average prices. Friendly atmosphere and entertainment make it a good place to visit.

## Haveli

100-150

12:30 - 15:00
19:30 - 24:00

Imperial Suites Hotel, The
Bur Dubai

Page 6 E 3

Tel: **515 100**

Amongst the best Indian restaurants in town specialising in North Indian Frontier food, the atmosphere is cozy and quite smart, without being too expensive. Specialities include 16 different types of Paratha and Masala Parers which make delicious snacks.

The traditional Indian band 'Sargam' starts playing around 21:00 and the place is normally buzzing by about 22:30. Bookings are essential.

## Kitchen

50-100

12:00 - 15:00
18:00 - 02:30

**Behind Hardey's, Al Satwa** — Page 6, A 3

Tel: **453 043**

Cheap and cheerful in the nicest possible way, the Kitchen is the perfect destination for a party with divergent tastes as it offers an extensive menu of both Indian and Chinese

dishes, including many interesting vegetarian choices. Very popular with both local and European residents for both dining in and take-away service. Twelve different types of lunch boxes available for less than Dhs.15 each with free delivery nearby.

A visit to the lavatory is a must ! You will find yourself in the illustrious company of Hudson, the butler from "Upstairs Downstairs" UK television programme (poster size only !).

## Kundan

50-100

12:00 - 15:00
19:00 - 02:00

**Quality Inn Horizon, Deira** — Page 10, E 2

Tel: **271 919**

Kundan is a brightly decorated restaurant with a flush of colour all around. It takes a while to recover from what may mildly be termed as an odd colour scheme. A few smiles later however, one is already in good humour and eagerly awaiting the next offering.

The band playing Disco-pop Hindi music, is ably assisted by the almost believable tones and beats of the Synthesizer. Though Kundan does not possess a drinks list they claim that they can provide any brew that you may desire. Finally the food was tasty though served a touch cold. The cook positioned behind a glass enclosure is possibly the most redeeming element, along with the service which is very keen, and it is truly a pleasure to watch him twirling the dough high up in the air while making his romali rotis (fine Indian bread).

## Kwality

50-100

13:00 - 14:45
20:00 - 23:45

**Opp Dubai Marine Hotel, Bur Dubai** — Page 6, E 2

Tel: **526 563**

Open the carved wooden door and climb the stairs to enjoy excellent quality food for which this restaurant has been famous for many years. Downstairs is for bachelor diners and take-away clients who collect and run, but the upstairs family customers sit and savour.

Reasonably priced Indian and simple Chinese food for all palates in big portions. Try a fish dish for starters. The restaurant is busiest from 21:30 onwards and it is advisable to book on Thursday, Friday and Public Holidays. Attracts a fairly European clientele due to somewhat westernized flavours.

## Maharajah

100-150

12:30 - 15:00
19:30 - 24:00

Sheraton Deira
Deira

Page 11
A 3

Tel: **688 888**

Beautiful presentation from the food to the interior decor and menus. This Indian restaurant specialises in dishes from the north west Indian regions of Rajasthan and Jaipur. The epitome of Indian fine-dining with dumpukt service (everything silver-served and presented on silver base plates), this restaurant is perfect for special occasions, with a traditional four-piece ghazal band serenading you as you feast on delicacies enjoyed by the ancient Maharajas.

Traditional colours of cream and dark green, intermingled with an abundance of authentic wood carvings create a serene and relaxing atmosphere in the main restaurant, while two additional dining rooms, for parties of eight or ten, allow for privacy if desired.

Ongoing promotions include a selected vintage of the month, while the businessman's "Jaldi Jaldi" lunch promises a complete meal, plus bill, in under 60 minutes. Hidden away on the top floor and through the bar, The Maharajah is perhaps a little hard to find, but definitely worth the hunt.

## Mehfil

50-100

12:00 - 15:00
19:00 - 03:00

Palm Beach Hotel
Bur Dubai

Page 6
E 2

Tel: **528 319**

This is a lively venue for those wishing to enjoy an Indian Band playing Bombay produced film music. The atmosphere is enhanced with large screen projectors showing Zee TV and Hindi film songs. It is certainly not just a place to eat and leave. Instead, one can eat slowly and enjoy the entertainment the band starts at 22:00 every evening.

Every Thursday and Friday the Mehfil hosts a variety of activities consisting of games and gifts for families. (Bachelors are not encouraged to attend on these days. The restaurant's specialities include Chutney Kebabs, Lasuni Jinga, Mixed Grills, Prawn Goan Style, Dal Dhaba Ghost and many more. The Chicken lollipop - Shezwan style is also delicious. Desserts include Rasagula and Gulab Jaman. Definitely worth a visit.

## Midnight Cafeteria

0-50

11:00 - 15:00
19:00 - 24:00

Al Karama

Page 9
E 2

Tel: **368 899**

If you must dine here, be prepared to sit outside at the pavement tables and chairs, on the busy road which leads into Karama. This is really an excellent take-away/free delivery place which caters to shoppers, local residents and office staff alike. Snacks include Punjabi samosas and Hot Dogs, but other more substantial orders can include pizzas or submarine sandwiches in mini french bread sticks.

# Mughal Mahal

50-100

12:30 - 15:30
19:30 - 23:30

Trade Centre Rd
Al Karama

Page 9
E 1

Tel: **347 600**

Formerly known as *Indian Chappan Bhog*, Mughal Mahal specialises in North Indian and Rajistani food. With over 56 outlets in India, this is the first restaurant in Dubai. Roughly translated the Hindu name means fifty six offerings - Sweet and sour. Hence the restaurant is split between the sweet counter and large dining area which is bright, exceptionally clean with large tables, and has a collection of unusual pictures depicting traditional Rajistani characters.

An extensive menu. Kabeb-e-Lazeez is recommended as a starter, consisting of an appealing assortment of Paneer, Haryali, Gobi and Alu mildly spiced, marinated and barbecued, all for Dhs.16. Also try Padpi Chat which is an unusual and refreshing mixture of gram, sweet chutney and green chutney, served on small crisp pancakes. Home-made sweets for dessert. There is an Evaluation Form for customers to fill in, proving that the management is not frightened of customers comments.

# Samarakand

50-100

11:00 - 03:00

St George Hotel
Deira

Page 7
B 2

Tel: **251 122**

Samarkand invites you to enter the world of authentic Indian and Pakistani cuisine - Burkara food (dry/BBQ). Here, traditional recipes handed down through generations come to life under the magical touch of the master chef. Succulent kebabs, clay baked tandoori delicacies are all delights from the North West Frontier to tempt you. To serenade you while the food delights your taste buds, is a four piece live band from India - with instruments such as the ghazal, tabbla, harmonica, keyboard player and singer. Shard Davadi, the Head Waiter is ready to answer any questions and assist with choosing from the menu, should you require it.

The food is very good, but the dishes mentioned on the menu are not the traditional Indian dishes you might expect and so some will need explanation. Very helpful staff. Check when reserving for a Thursday that another function hasn't been booked for the restaurant.

# Shahjahan

50-100

12:30 - 14:30
19:00 - 24:00

Metropolitan Hotel
Sh Zayed Rd/Safa

Page 4
C 4

Tel: **440 000**

The advantage of going to an Indian restaurant in a hotel is that you can have a foaming beverage with your meal. In this restaurant you can get India's finest: Kingfisher. With an airy and tranquil environment which lends itself to intimacy, Shahjahan specialises in North Indian cuisine and a range of interesting and sophisticated dishes.

Live Indian music is best appreciated in the evenings over an exotic dish of Adhraki Jhinga (tandoori prawns seasoned with ginger), Machli Zaikedar (Hammour fillet in rich curry sauce), or the Murgh Makhani (traditional butter chicken).

## Shezan

0-50

12:00 - 15:00
18:00 - 24:00

Al Karama — Page 9, D 3

Tel: **378 701**

Shezan offers home delivery (with a choice of over 300 dishes) anywhere in Dubai. The restaurant itself is in the heart of Karama and makes a convenient choice after a day's shopping in the Karama market. It is well maintained, clean and offers a friendly and discreet service.

Lunch time offers special executive lunch packs at cheap prices. Dishes to order include Shezan special chicken, mixed grill, Chicken Malai kebabs, Chicken Phadi kebabs and Chicken Methi.

## Volga Restaurant

0-50

12:00 - 15:00
19:30 - 24:00

Nr. Ramada Hotel
Bur Dubai — Page 7, B 3

Tel: **525 100**

Nine years ago the owners of this establishment ran a contest between Indian ladies in the area for the best food recipes. These recipes now form the basis for this restaurant's menu. There is a vegetarian lunch buffet which costs Dhs.10 and an evening, non-vegetarian buffet consisting of over 20 choices of Indian and Chinese dishes. Upstairs is for large groups and contains a kiddies play area and Karaoke stage for those who want to sing.

## Welcome Restaurant

0-50

12:00 - 15:00
19:00 - 24:00

Opp. Shell Inn,
Khalid Bin Walid Rd , Bur Dubai — Page 6, E 2

Tel: **528 777**

The Welcome Restaurant prides itself on the wide range of its menu. With a large team of qualified chefs, over 400 Indian and Chinese dishes are available, so there should be something for everyone!

Reservations are recommended for Thursday and Friday nights which will allow you to eat from the self-service buffets- very popular with local Indian expatriates. A daily vegetarian lunch buffet is also on offer and will suit the budget conscious at only Dhs.10.

# Pakistani

## Chicken Tikka Inn

0-50

12:00 - 15:00
18:30 - 24:00

**Al Nasr Square**
**Deira**
**Page 7**
**C 3**

Tel: **225 683**

Tucked away in a corner of Al Nasr Square is the original Chicken Tikka Inn, established in Dubai in 1972, and preserving its excellent reputation for the best tikka in town. A capacity of 40 people squeeze onto benches set out dinette style in this friendly restaurant, with an open kitchen displaying charcoal burners and sizzling kebabs.

The parathas are amazingly tasty and if you can manage more that three you'll be doing well! Try a mixed dish of spicy kebabs and boneless tikka, with a cooling bowl of raitha and a refreshing sweet lime juice. They do not serve tea as they encourage a rapid turnover and with another 40 people queuing outside on the street, who can blame them!

## Karachi Darbar

0-50

11:00 - 24:00

**Various Locations**
**Al Karama, Bur Dubai, Deira,...**
**Page 9**
**D 2**

Tel: **224 057**

A chain of eight restaurants in Dubai, offering some of the tastiest and best value food in Dubai. If want to pay for excellent food and service, but not the surrounding decor, then you've come to the best place. There is the regulation standard box of tissues per table.

The restaurant in Karama, offers you the chance to sit outside and experience some street life... well cars anyhow. The little greened terrace outside is extremely pleasant in the cooler months. Service is quick and professional, and prices are incredibly low, with a full meal setting you back no more than Dhs 25, and that's for two people!

Highly recommended is the butter chicken, fish biriyani, Kulfi ice cream and all types of bread. All outlets offer the same high standard.

## Noor Jahan

0-50

11:30 - 15:00
19:00 - 23:30

**Bur Dubai**
**Page 7**
**A 2**

Tel: **530 670**

Noor Jahan is a very busy backstreet Pakistani restaurant in the heart of Bur Dubai. It has a working family atmosphere and makes everybody feel equal.

The decor is basic, but the food is reasonable in terms of quality. Dishes vary from South to North Indian kitchen. Chicken Sukka and Dosas are the restaurant's specialities. They also serve an excellent hot & sour chicken soup.

## Ravi's

0-50

00:00 - 24:00

**Nr. Dubai Plaza Hotel**
**Al Satwa**
**Page 5**
**E 4**

Tel: **315 353**

You won't get Delhi Belly here, as many Jumeirah residents and their guests will testify. Traditional and tasty Pakistani choices are enjoyed by the many Indian bachelors who regularly eat in the clean, bright and utilitarian restaurant throughout the day until midnight.

Dal and chapattis for breakfast is a favourite with both European summer bachelors and sub continent workers alike. A separate large restaurant next door caters to families who prefer carpet on the floor and slightly more upmarket decor. A popular venue due to the low prices and surrounding shops in downtown Satwa.

# Sri Lankan

## Peacock

0-50

11:30 - 15:00
19:00 - 24:00

Al Karama — Page 9 D 3

Tel: 369 999

A basic and rudimentary place to eat. Seated at one of the three small bare wood tables it may seem that you have intruded into someone's private kitchen from, which staple Sri Lankan dishes are dispensed though an open hatch.

These consist of curry, battu (a dry, sour, oval shaped vegetable) or hoppers (flour based dish served plain or with egg) with a variety of different sauces. Clientele are mainly single Sri Lankans, who enjoy the plentiful portions of familiar and inexpensive food.

# Vegetarian

## Bhavna Deluxe Restaurant

0-50

07:00 - 23:30

Bur Dubai — Page 7 A 3

Tel: 524 487

A good place for strict vegetarians, for either a light snack or main meal, as there are no meat or eggs included in any of the cooking. Although on the surface it appears a rather cold and sterile place, it is clean and bright, and the staff are friendly and helpful. The restaurant is open from 07:00 for breakfast. Take-away food and snacks are available throughout the day, and Chapatti Chat is available after 16:00.

The Thali buffet changes every evening and is good value for money at Dhs.8 to eat as much as you like. Don't believe everything you see on the menu as various items i.e. the Chinese and continental sections are now discontinued. For dessert try the Falooda for Dhs.6. A wide variety of fruit juices are available varying from grape and sweet limes, to water melon and orange blossom.

## Chappan Bhog

50-100

12:00 - 14:30
19:30 - 24:00

Trade Centre Rd
Bur Dubai — Page 9 E 1

Tel: 364 176

The ambience and decor provide a particularly homely feeling. Chappan Bhog's efforts to maintain the quality and consistency of their foods very visible.

Chappan means 56. Historically there are 56 main Hindu Gods and Chappan Bhog offers 56 vegetarian dishes as good as those that may be offered to each of their Gods. The varied menu includes dishes such as Navrattan Korma Hari Bhari Tikka, Bhatura Cholley, Sarson Ki Saag, Panner Tikka Nawab and Achar Aloo. Go there and you will discover them.

## Dasaprakash

0-50

08:30 - 15:00
18:00 - 23:15

Nr. Astoria Hotel
Bur Dubai

Page 7
A 3

Tel: **527 429**

A good restaurant for that quick snack if you like Indian vegetarian food. It is a clean and brightly lit place with quick, friendly service and a staff that welcomes children of all ages. Inexpensive snacks are available such as spicy corn on toast (Dhs.8), or various types of Dosa (pancakes) for Dhs.5. If you are feeling hungrier then go for the mini Thali (Dhs.6) or the unlimited Thali (Dhs.8), which consists of vegetarian dips and bread. There are several fruit juices to wash it down, ranging from carrot and grape, to pomegranate or water melon. Finish the meal with an ice cream sundae of your choice.

## India House

0-50

07:00 - 24:00

Nr. Dubai Marine Hotel
Bur Dubai

Page 7
A 3

Tel: **526 006**

Around the corner from the Emirates Petrol Station on the Khalid-bin Walid road, this restaurant makes the most of its two busy floors, serving a comprehensive choice of Indian and Chinese food in a customary groovy and good-natured manner, to the mainly Indian families who visit here.

Try Dosa Masala or Batra for starters, with Green Peas Curry for main course, consisting of a gentle and harmonious mix of vegetables, cheese, nuts, spices and pulses. A full three course meal can be had here for Dhs.15-20, perhaps including something from the many choices of desserts, such as Rasmali or the array of Middle-Eastern sweets on offer.

## Kamat

0-50

10:00 - 15:00
19:00 - 23:30

Trade Centre Rd
Bur Juman

Page 9
E 1

Tel: **372 288**

With a vegetarian menu as varied as the Kamat's, you are bound to hit upon something to your liking from either the Chinese or Indian sections. From the former, dip Crispy Wontons into a savoury garlic sauce or from the latter, choose a Paneer Tikka, - chunks of marinated cheese on a skewer. An extensive selection of superb Indian food, from South Indian, to Punjabi. Unusual Cheese Uttappam, or Onion Rava Masala Dosa are both excellent, or at lunch try the standard Thali for Dhs.14, includes unlimited: three vegetables, chana, dal, rasam, rice, poori, papad, yoghurt and sweet!

Interesting table covers, with twenty or so of the owner's favourite proverbs and sayings - Great reading! Repose with a fizzy Cocum Sherbet and for dessert, the Mango Kulfi is richly superior to a straight ice-cream. Throughout the restaurant there is a crispness of surroundings and service, evidence of a well run, sanitary establishment as recognised by one of the few official certificates proudly displayed at the entrance.

Finally, Kamat offers very reasonable party and outdoor catering.

## Royal Garden

0-50

12:00 - 15:30
18:30 - 24:30

Opp Bur Juman Centre
Bur Juman

Page 9
E 1

Tel: **359 191**

The Royal Garden lies on the edge of Karama notorious for its Asian associations and community. The restaurant is easily visible as you approach, thanks to its large neon name sign above the entrance. As you enter through the smoked glass door you walk into a brightly lit and airy restaurant that has been decorated with soft and pleasing colours. The tables are wrought iron and marble topped.

Let the feast begin with a menu of the largest selection of vegetarian Indian food that you have probably ever seen. Punjabi and South Indian dishes adorn the extremely comprehensive menu and the food is excellent with portions of a sensible size. The restaurant has a family section and 'goes Chinese' once a week, which may be why it's clientele appears varied and cosmopolitan. Meals are reasonably priced and most nights there is a fixed priced buffet.

Try the Malai Kulfi made from cream and saffron - the latter reputed to be more valuable by the ounce than gold. Whoever said that Veggies could never be spoilt for choice?

## Woodland's

0-50

07:00 - 15:00
17:00 - 23:00 Closed Fri

Opp. Old IKEA Bldg
Al Karama

Page 9
D 3

Tel: **370 253**

A basic, no frills, eating house. Offers distinctive and tasty Indian vegetarian cuisine. Great value for money which is reflected in its popularity with the local Indian working-man community. Probably the most well known vegetarian restaurant in Dubai

# European

## Austrian

### Cafe Mozart

50-100

11:00 - 15:00
19:00 - 23:00

Nr. Al-Futtaim Tower
Deira

Page 7
C 4

Tel: **216 565**

Mozart would have been quite content to have supped a hot chocolate and sampled the excellent home-made Apple Strudel here whilst scribbling his Requiem! A fascinating and totally original venue, Cafe Mozart was set up by Austrian-born Suzan nine years ago as a cafe. Now a fully blown restaurant with a menu worthy of a five-star hotel including Lobster soup, Schnitzel and Movenpick ice-cream. Cute and quaint, welcoming, with Mozartania adorning the walls. Suzan will even play any classical cassette you bring along.

## English

### Fryer Tuck - Fish & Chips

0-50

12:00 - 15:00
17:00 - 22:30

Opp. Magrudys, Beach Rd
Al Jumeira

Page 5
C 2

Tel: **444 228**

Good ol' English fish and chips, served with mushy peas and pickled onions. Or how about a steak and kidney pie? Eat in the bright and airy, rather clinical, 50-seater restaurant, or take-away. Standard menu includes sausage in batter, cod, hamour, pies and other easily recognised fare. Deliciously cooked. The Manager, Mr. Mauwli, has been working here since it opened in 1976 and certainly knows how to wrap a mean paper package of chips. Its the real thing!

### See Also:

Bars/Pubs - English

## French

### Le Beaujolais

50-100

12:00 - 15:00
20:00 - 24:00

Novotel
Deira

Page 7
E 4

Tel: **720 000**

Adjacent to the Lobby of the hotel, Le Beaujolais offers a variety of non-standard French food. But don't worry, it also serves everybodys all time favourite of Onion Soup and plenty of it. All portions are hearty and very generous. The wine list is limited and reasonably priced. No need to book to sit in the mini atrium. A great relaxed dinner spot for a crowd after an active Friday, particularly in the cooler months. Make sure you tuck yourself round the corner out of the way of the passing lobby crowd.

## Le Classic

100-150

12:00 - 15:00
19:00 - 24:00 Closed Fri pm

Emirates Golf Club
Al Mina Al Siyahi

Page 2
A 3

Tel: **480 222**

You don't have to be a member to enjoy the fine dining experience of this well loved restaurant. Phone to make a reservation and to check that the place hasn't been booked for a private party. Cordon bleu cooking served in portions large enough to satisfy anyone. Affordable prices for the quality of food and drink that Dubai residents have come to expect.

## Lou Lou`a

100-150

12:30 - 15:00
19:30 - 24:00 Closed Fri am

Sheraton Hotel
Deira

Page 10
C 1

Tel: **207 1717**

Lou Lou'a offers lush, plush, understated class, with cordon bleu choices for those who appreciate good food. Rich sauces, butter and cream additives, delicate herbs and plenty of courses for each meal. In a prime location, be sure to ask for the popular window seats which have excellent views over the Creek. Even the crockery is interesting to look at, with picturesque china used as place settings.

Professional silver service staff provide the top quality service that diners expect, while live entertainment is provided in the form of tinkering tunes on the baby grand piano.

The a la carte menu is descriptive and full of unusual dishes designed to tempt the palate. Seafood lovers should visit on Wednesdays when a decorative buffet of many choices is set out for residents and visitors who book in advance. The Sheraton's Fish Night has been known as the best in town for many years.

## Mushref Rooftop

100-150

19:30 - 24:00
Closed Monday

Jebel Ali Hotel
Jebel Ali

Tel: **835 252**

This is strictly a 'tie and jacket' restaurant so please do dress up for the evening. The welcoming usher will discreetly provide these items of clothing if needs be, or politely ask you to choose another restaurant at the hotel. At night, it's no good asking for a window seat as there is nothing but black night and black sea to see. So enjoy the quietly luxurious ambience.

An extensive a la carte menu, plus a daily gastronomique set menu and a comprehensive beverage list are a pleasure to peruse. Delicious nouvelle cuisine dishes are sublimely presented. Complimented by the melodic and unobtrusive pianist who plays requests.

Clientele are mainly hotel guests of well-to-do Europeans and businessmen entertaining clients. The Mushref Rooftop Restaurant exudes an air of opulence and cultured dining from the moment you enter.

### Palms

100-150

24:00 hrs | JW Marriott Hotel, Deira | Page 11, A 3 | Tel: **607 7773**

During the evening when you visit the new Palms, at the Marriott Hotel, you will appreciate why French cuisine has the best reputation in the world and you certainly will not be disappointed here - the dishes are as authentically French as the waiters' berets!

A full a la carte menu is on offer, with the speciality being fresh fish flown in from Paris. Main courses are cooked in classical French style and served with your choice of delicious creamy or savoury sauce that is guaranteed to melt in your mouth. If you've managed to devour a starter (try the hot goat's cheese in basil salad) and main course and still have room, then try the crepes for dessert, which will be flambeed at your table. The unpretentious informal atmosphere, with the best of haute cuisine is a must for all lovers of fine French food.

During the day the a la carte menu goes beyond the obvious with suggestions such as Almond Chicken Fettucine, Grilled Fresh Salmon and Sauteed Crab Cake. Buffet breakfast, lunch and dinner selections are consistently tempting.

## Greek

### Zorba

100-150

19:00 - 03:00 | Al Khaleej Palace, Deira | Page 10, D 1 | Tel: **231 000**

Zorba's must be the only eating venue in Dubai where you can smash plates and not get arrested, Dhs. 5 per plate. The only Greek restaurant in the city, this is where to find classic dishes such as Tzatziki (yoghurt and cucumber), Spanakopita (spinach pie) and Kalamari (deep fried squid). Choose your night and your time carefully. Arrive before 23:00 on a weekday and you may have a lot of room to move about in, as diners tend to adhere to Mediterranean nocturnal eating times. Traditional murals, vines and Greek/Arabic singer Petro to serenade your meal, all blend to make you feel as if you're on the Aegean islands themselves.

## Irish

### See:

Bars/Pubs - Irish

# Italian

## Capri Italian Grill

50-100

12:00 - 15:00
17:30 - 24:00

Trade Center App - B Block
Sh Zayed Rd/Trade Centre

Page 8
D 2

Tel: **314 673**

The Capri Italian has been serving Italian food since December 1980, and is still going strong! According to the management, the food is always absolutely fresh and is prepared for each individual order with great care. A good place for a quick meal in a cosy, and somewhat romantic restaurant. The service is fast if not a bit rushed, and impersonal, and the menu designed to suit all tastes ie. not only pasta and pizzas, but also chicken, fish, steaks and burgers are available. For the not so hungry, sandwiches and omelettes are also possible. The pizzas are particularly recommended.

The tables are made from wooden cart wheels which add an interesting touch but can be a bit impractical as food has a tendency to disappear between the spokes! Booking is recommended if there are more than four people in the party as only a few larger tables are available. Staff welcome children, so a good place for a family outing.

## Casa Mia

100-150

12:30 - 15:00
20:00 - 24:00

Forte Grand Dubai
Al Garhoud

Page 14
E 3

Tel: **824 040**

Imagine a small Italian village cantina, whitewashed brick walls, polished wood tables, husband cooking in the kitchen and wife welcoming patrons to her pride and joy, her Casa Mia. That is what you get at this restaurant situated near the Forte Grand's tennis courts, behind Jules Bar.

The menu and the list incorporate not just the normal popular Italian exports, but authentically typical and superb Italian dishes, with specially imported Italian vinos hard to find anywhere else in Dubai. This restful place is a classy little restaurant to visit.

## Cucina

100-150

12:30 - 15:30
19:30 - 23:30

JW Marriott Hotel
Deira

Page 11
A 3

Tel: **624 444**

Step through the wrought iron gates into Giullio and Antonella's Cucina, and you're immediately transported to rural Italy. A lively and gutsy atmosphere pervades this charming split-level eatery, where superb Italian specialities are served in portions to satisfy the heartiest appetite. Arguably the best pizzas in town are baked fresh in a traditional open wood-fired oven - even the wood is from Italy - and you can also order to take-away. The fresh pasta is exactly that, with such mouth-watering combinations as "Tortellini stuffed with pumpkin, parmesan and ricotta in a butter-walnut sauce.

You will find it hard to pass on the tantalising selection of antipasti for starters, but make sure you leave room for desert - they're to die for! The house speciality of "Panna Cotta" - a scrumptious Piedmont concoction of milk, eggs and fresh cream, set, and drowned in a rich chocolate sauce and cookie crumbles, vies for first place with Cucina's "Tiramisu", which must rival the best available, inside Italy or out. Booking is essential as this is one of the most popular places in town. Enormous two litre carafes of wine on the table which you pay for by the glass (some how they know!).

## Da Vinci`s

50-100

12:00 - 24:00

Airport Hotel
Al Garhoud

Page 14
D 3

Tel: **823 464**

As far as Da Vinci's is concerned it has undoubtedly discovered the secret of success. Always full, it has just the right mix: a genuinely homely atmosphere, pervading smell of herbs and home-made pasta sauces, friendly staff, very reasonable prices, and an Italian feel...

No music, no live shows, just a lot of happy people talking and chatting in a trattoria type decor. Weekly specials complement the regular imaginative menu, including Small and Full sizes for the pastas.

Try the Duck with Honey and Cognac, and Three-coloured Pasta with Smoked Salmon and Cream. A constant favourite for groups and birthdays (lights out and piped Happy Birthday) as well as for 'dinner-for-two'. An outdoor enclosed patio area allows for additional seating when the eighty person restaurant is full, which happens quite often.

## Don Corleone

100-150

12:30 - 14:30
19:00 - 24:00

Metropolitan Hotel
Sh Zayed Rd/Safa

Page 4
C 4

Tel: **440 000**

A special find among Italian restaurants, Don Corleone is well-loved for its great atmosphere and value for money menu which includes Italian favourites like antipasti, creamy pastas, and veal in an array of special sauces. For the less adventurous, lamb, chicken stew and steaks are also available. The food tends to be quite rich, but simply delicious. Perfect both for groups indoors in the cosy family atmosphere, or an intimate dinner for two on the large terrace overlooking the tree-lined car park. Service is friendly and personal as many patrons are regulars. Reservations are essential.

## Gelato

50-100

12:00 - 24:00

5 Emirates Bld, C-Block
Sh Zayed Rd/Trade Centre

Page 8
A 2

Tel: **443 435**

At last, an Italian restaurant that serves pizza; a surprisingly rare thing for Dubai! Gelato is an easy going restaurant-cum-cafe, specializing in pizza, pasta and piping hot coffee. There are three seating areas, the main downstairs area which is casual and quick, the slightly more formal upstairs area, or at the tables on the terrace outside which are ideal for a quiet coffee. There's a good range of salads and soups for the health conscious. They also serve home made ice creams for the not so health conscious, where flavoured ice cream really is made out of fresh cream. Very popular at lunchtime, especially among Emirates airline crew.

## La Capanna

100-150

19:30 - 23:30

Dubai Marine Beach Resort
Jumeira

Page 5
D 2

Tel: **441 221**

La Capanna's superbly located inside the Beach Club with views of the beach and sea that make you think you are somewhere on the rocks around the Mediterranean. Simple Italian style decoration with lots of greenery and the sound of swishing waves coming through open bay windows add to the ambience.

The restaurant sets a pleasant, friendly, cosy evening with attentive service and good enough food from a la carte menu and weekly menus. Casually elegant, without being tiring, the atmosphere is enhanced by the Italian/Spanish/French style singer in this very popular restaurant.

## La Traviata

100-150

19:00 - 24:00
Closed Sat

Jebel Ali Hotel
Jebel Ali

Tel: **836 000**

With many of the hotel's guests dining in La Traviata, the atmosphere is relaxed and friendly. A singer and guitarist play every night to entertain diners. Menu has a good selection of fish, including swordfish. After dessert try a coffee with amaretti.

## Little Italy

50-100

12:00 - 15:00
19:00 - 24:00

Al Khaleej Palace
Deira

Page 10
D 1

Tel: **231 000**

Little Italy offers various promotions during the summer season. Visit the restaurant four times in one month and get a fifth meal free. And they are worth having, as quality and quantity are hospitable and generous. The restaurant also holds a monthly business card raffle with a prize of dinner for two and a bottle of red vino. A superb restaurant with a warm feel, and its own bar.

## Luciano's

100-150

12:30 - 14:30
19:30 - 23:30

Metropolitan Beach Club
Al Mina Al Siyahi

Page 1
E 2

Tel: **845 000**

A charming setting overlooking the waterfall and swimming pool of the Metropolitan Beach Club, Luciano's has a real ambience of Mediterranean sophistication. Soft light and stone flagged floors give this little Italian restaurant an air of authenticity. A perfect place for a romantic dinner for two with service that is attentive, if a little stilted.

The comprehensive menu features most favourites, which are very tasty, if a little pricey. Portions are generous and well presented. While nothing outstanding hits you about this restaurant, there is nothing bad to say either. If you're looking for good food and a pleasant relaxing atmosphere, where the pace isn't too hectic, this would be an excellent choice.

## Ponte Vecchio

100-150

12:30 - 15:00
19:00 - 24:00

Forte Grand - Jumeira Beach
Al Mina Al Siyahi

Page 1
E 2

Tel: **845 555**

An Italian Chef, an Italian Manager and Italian guests certainly say much about the quality and style of this restaurant. The cast iron structures covering individual gazebos, creeping garden plants, wooden floors and a small stream with waterfall creates a relaxing atmosphere. The a la carte menu features an excellent selection of pasta, meat and fish dishes from Tuscany.

## San Lorenzo

100-150

12:30 - 15:00
19:00 - 24:00

Metropolitan Palace
Deira

Page 10
D 2

Tel: **270 000**

Set in a garden terrazzo atmosphere San Lorenzo offers a wide variety of fine Italian "cucina" at it's best. From home-made pastas to fine dining, to pizzas prepared by a genuine Italian Chef. Raw powerful flavours, subtle use of spices and herbs for that original Italian taste. Relax in the intimate surroundings, enjoy the discreet service, transport yourself back to the Pantheon, the Trevi Fountain and the delights of Trastevre.

## Valentino's

100-150

12:00 - 15:00
19:30 - 24:00 Closed Fri

Met Club, The
Jebel Ali

Tel: **817 100**

If you are in the Jebel Ali area looking for a place to go for an extremely leisurely lunch then Valentino's will almost certainly be on your short list. Food quality is above average and the nouvelle cuisine - style portions certainly won't leave you feeling bloated. There's a tasty selection of main courses, try the recommended Garlic Prawns, unless you have an important meeting after lunch! There's also a selection of salads and soups, with a good vino list if you fancy a snooze in the afternoon.

## Villa Veduta

100-150

20:00 - 23:30

Inter-Continental Hotel
Deira

Page 7
C 4

Tel: **227 171**

Try to get a table in a corner or alcove for a bit more privacy in this relaxing restaurant with a hushed elegance. Outdoors is for the younger more casual crowd who prefer to watch their pizza freshly baked in the brick oven. They arrive via a staircase which leads directly from the street to the hotel's pool/terrace area.

When ordering starters remember that one portion is big enough for two. The Italian Chef will make a mixed platter of three types of pasta, each with a different sauce, on request. To finish, try the rich and chocolaty Tiramisu. You can eat here quite reasonably and it's a bit cheaper on the Terrace, about half the price - although you are more limited to pizza or pasta. The house vino is excellent but expensive as are the rest of the drinks.

# Mediterranean

## Cafe Insignia

100-150

12:00 - 15:00
19:00 - 01:00

Ramada Hotel
Bur Dubai

Page 6
E 3

Tel: **506 1180**

A rare find in Dubai, Cafe Insignia has the feel of a typical European wine bar. Casually chic with a relaxing spacious ambience, it offers a tempting combination of bistro-style food, decent vino and speciality beers. Brown paper place-mats and a pot of coloured crayons on each table set the tone as diners either become over-whelmed by their own creativity, or studiously try and work out the company annual accounts over breakfast, lunch or dinner.

Lunch buffets are varied and excellent value for money, while the full a la carte menu includes exotic salads, award-wining sandwiches such as char-grilled chicken with tomatoes, onion, coriander and tahini; entrée's; and the ever-popular "low fat corner"' is available form 11:30. Particular recommendations are the warm lamb salad with goat's cheese and capsicum cake, and the fillet of chicken breast stuffed with puree of spinach and sun-dried tomatoes, coated with creamed paprika and mushroom sauce. A regular selection of monthly, country-lead promotions is supported by the award winning chef's own weekly specials, which are promoted on strategically placed blackboards. All in all, for a casual meal with a touch of style and panache, Café Insignia is hard to beat.

## Focaccia

100-150

12:30 - 15:30
19:30 - 24:00

Hyatt Regency Hotel
Deira

Page 7
D 2

Tel: **706 4811**

If you like Mediterranean food, you will fall in love with this restaurant, with its gourmet olive oil, pasta and skillet-pan foods. Barbecued choices come suspended on a wrought iron skewer holder, quite an eyecatching sight.

The decor has been carefully planned to give the impression of entering a large villa, with each room in the house giving diners a different aspect of conversation. Browse around before deciding whether to sit in the conservatory, the informal dining room or orangery, the library with books over 200 years old, or even in the kitchen - where fresh Italian foccacia bread is baked. The food is usually excellent, but can be variable. A private dining room is available for groups of up to 20.

## Fontana

100-150

12:30 - 15:30
19:30 - 24:00

**Al Bustan Rotana Hotel**
**Al Garhoud**

**Page 14**
**E 3**

Tel: **820 000**

Italian lighting, colourful mosaic tiles, big windows and a spectacular fountain located in the centre of this spacious open-plan restaurant give it a true Mediterranean feel. Global dining is the theme here and the food is excellent. You can choose between an impressive buffet of International cuisine offering Asian, Arabic and European dishes as well as mouth-watering fresh seafood for breakfast, lunch or dinner. The a la carte menu also includes an all day breakfast - sure to be a hit.

Lot's of light, friendly staff and the sound of running water give a fantastic ambience to the room. All of this, combined with well-spaced tables make this the perfect venue for either a business lunch or a meal with friends at any time of the day. Theme nights are planned for special festivals and celebrations.

## Il Paradiso

100-150

12:30 - 15:00
19:30 - 24:00

**Sheraton Deira**
**Deira**

**Page 11**
**A 3**

Tel: **688 888**

Il Paradiso offers an a la carte Mediterranean menu for lovers of modern cuisine, choises include a wide range of freshly made pizza and pasta from Italy, paella from Spain, light fresh oysters and bouillabaisse from France, mezzeh from Lebanon and much more. Live entertainment is provided by Italian duo, Primiano and Paula.

With its walls murals, shuttered windows, tiled floors and Italian style furniture, Il Paradiso captures the rustic simplicity, romance and magic of the Mediterranean.

Located on the 5th floor with far reaching views, the tables are carefully placed giving one a feeling of space and privacy. The service is excellent and unobtrusive. The ultimate sin in this paradise has to be tasted "Il Paradiso" dessert plate is a calorie filled cocktail of tastes which can only be described as heaven!

## La Provence

100-150

12:30 - 15:00
20:00 - 24:00

**Forte Grand Dubai**
**Al Garhoud**

**Page 14**
**E 3**

Tel: **824 040**

Due to open by November 1997, this new restaurant will be serving regional cuisine from the South of France in a relaxed and convivial atmosphere.

Styled in the form of a Provencal villa, the restaurant will be divided into three areas, each with its own feel and decoration - a warm, wooden village chalet, a traditional French dining room, and a bright winter garden, reminiscent of a French vinyard. The exhibition kitchen adds to the overall French villa style - ensuring prospective diners can keep an eye on the preparation of their food.

## Seabreeze

100-150

12:00 - 24:00 | Forte Grand - Jumeira Beach, Al Mina Al Siyahi | Page 1, E 2 | Tel: **845 555**

A light and airy watering hole for those who are looking for relaxed surroundings and excellent brasserie style food. Set apart from the main hotel in the Royal Club Tower, this restaurant is tastefully decorated and simply furnished in a fresh Mediterranean style. With a sea view terrace overlooking the gardens, diners can chose a table inside or out, or you may prefer a perch at the bar.

The food is excellent with generous portions, the warm goat's cheese salad comes highly recommended. Theme nights kick off after the summer with pasta nights, mussels, paella and fondues, accompanied by live music and cooler weather! Although a trek from the city centre this tasteful brasserie is well worth a visit.

# Russian

## Russian Crown

50-100

20:00 - 00:30 | Palm Beach Hotel, Bur Dubai | Page 6, E 2 | Tel: **512 914**

The first Russian restaurant in Dubai which offers a touch of pre-revolutionary Russia in it's decor. Cream coloured walls, gold line detail and a fine table promises fine dining, Russian style. A dance floor and contemporary band add to the relaxing atmosphere. 90% of the staff are Russian and dishes include black/brown caviar, bread flown in especially from Russia, Mors (Berry) drink and Sturgeon. The bar offers many special cocktails with names such as Alexander Nevsky, Gypsy Road, Gorky Park and more.

## Russian Forest

12:00 - 01:00 | Nr. Hyatt Regency Hotel, Deira | Page 11, A 2 | Tel: **726 688**

50-100

The Russian Forest restaurant combines a mixture of Russian and Uzbekistan flavours, with Russia's Number #1 TV station in the background for authenticity. The atmosphere is pleasant, with clean surrounds and very efficient service, albeit in Russian (not all staff speak English).

The restaurant is run by an Uzbekistani couple, Alex and his wife, from Samarkand - the capital. Authentic dishes from the region are clearly displayed in photo format in the menu (English and Russian language) for those whose Russian is a little rusty ,or who are not sure what to order. Try the traditional caviar and salmon, or the Borsht beetroot and meat soup, Chicken Kiev, or the spicy Manty meat dumplings which are excellent.

Not for the vegetarians or those watching their cholesterol. Sundays are popular with homesick Russians, as it's their holy day. Well worth a visit to try good, value for money Russian food.

# Scottish

**See:**

Bars/Pubs - Scottish

# Swedish

## IKEA Cafeteria

10:00 - 22:00
Closed Fri am | Deira City Centre Mall, Deira | Page 14, D 1 | Tel: **243 434**

50-100

Ideal for a quick snack or light lunch, this restaurant is a favourite with business people and shoppers alike, thanks to its favourable prices and the fact that it is a lot quieter than the food court in Magic Planet. Very Scandic in atmosphere and attitude, the self-service food bar has a choice of over 60 dishes that are rotated on a regular basis. Each new day sees a hot "daily special", "vegetarian special" and "soup of the day", while favourites such as the prawn and mayonnaise open sandwich and Swedish platter are always available, as are a selection of salads.

A good range of freshly baked croissants and pastries are a tasty accompaniment to the surprisingly good cappuccino. Tea, coffee, hot chocolate and fruit juices are also on offer. Open 12 hours a day, seven days a week (Friday 7 1/2 hours), this lively, bustling restaurant provides a pleasant stop off.

# Swiss

## Grotto Ticino

100-150

19:00 - 24:00 | Radisson SAS Jumeira Beach, Al Mina Al Siyahi | Page 1 D 2 | Tel: **845 533**

If you're familiar with Swiss cuisine you may be a little disappointed by the lack of "fondue" or "raclette" on the menu of this Alpine kitchen restaurant. However, don't lose heart as superb home-style cooking is available in abundant portions, with strong influences from both northern Italy and Switzerland.

Choose from a choice of excellent risotto or gnocchi (potato dumpling) dishes, along with the likes of braised beef in Merlot and polenta - another north Italian favourite. The wine list is impressive, and reasonably priced, including two superb house selections which the friendly and efficient waiting staff, rather strangely, encourage you to drink out of a pottery "milk jug"!

The knowledge that the chef is actually Swiss, helps with the authenticity... and they really are trying to create atmosphere with the copper kitchen implements adorning the dining room walls, which were collected by the previous General Manager on his frequent visits to the Alps. If fondue really is your desire, keep your eyes open for the special promotions which the management promise will feature this perennial favourite.

## Links Steakhouse, The

100-150

12:00 - 15:00<br>20:00 - 23:30 Closed Fri | Dubai Golf & Racing Club, Nadd Al Shiba | Page 12 A 3 | Tel: **363 666**

The Links Steak House is becoming increasingly popular as more people discover its great value-for-money fare.

Primarily known for its steaks, this extremely relaxed dinning environment is one of the only places to have Fondues, from cheese, meat and even the die for, chocolate fruit fondue. Get your woolly hats, and ski on down!

Music for dancing on the small dance floor is provided by an excellent band, and of course there's added excitement on race nights. Extremely comfortable dining chairs. Make this place a great change from the other restaurants in town, offering a relaxed, but refined environment.

# Far Eastern

## Filipino

### Fiesta Filipino

0-50

09:00 - 24:00
Closed Fri am

Al Karama — Page 9 C 3

Tel: 344 121

Walk past the cut-price stores and cheap tee shirt shops of deepest Karama, and step through the Fiesta's undistinguished doorway. Inside, the bright Swiss chalet interior of wooden furnishings, strawberry patterned place-mats and cheery checkered table-cloths, cannot fail to make you feel at home. This is the place to go if you are not very familiar with Filipino food and want to give it a try. As a main dish Ginataang Hipon, shrimp in a chilli ginger and coconut milk sauce is recommended. Also tasty is Tapsilog which are strips of sweet, crispy beef served with fried rice and egg. Even simple chicken Adobo has a rich strong gravy worthy as a soup on it's own. Family-run, this restaurant stands out amongst the many competing Indian, Chinese and Filipino establishments as a place to seek out.

### Manilla Garden

0-50

20:00 - 23:00

Novotel Deira — Page 7 E 4

Tel: 235 000

It's easy to miss the entrance to Manilla Garden as it is outside the Novotel. This small restaurant / pub has a night-time appeal with a mainly male clientele. Try the Sizzling Manok (chicken) or spicy Gambas (prawns), good value for money at around Dhs.25. Flickering night sky ceiling decor and friendly waiter service.

### Sampaguita

0-50

20:00 - 03:00

Claridge Hotel Deira — Page 7 E 4

Tel: 716 666

Not a restaurant to visit for its food - nothing is ethnic and it is often cold by the time it eventually arrives on the table. The main point of a visit is to listen to a wide range of Filipino bands and eat snacks. Open for 10 years, it is obviously popular with a regular clientele, mainly men. Very loud music makes conversing impossible. Food is European and mostly served with chips. A place to visit very late in the evening.

### Tagpuan

0-50

10:00 - 24:00

Shop 137, Block L Al Karama — Page 9 D 2

Tel: 373 959

It's name means 'meeting place' in Tagalog and it certainly lives up to this by attracting a regular clientele of Filipino residents and visiting US sailors. Excellent value for money, offering a wide choice of both international and Filipino dishes. Have a complimentary bowl of soup with each main course ordered. Dhs.10 will buy a main course, one vegetable and one rice dish. A working man's diner with formica tables, television and free karaoke mike to sing your heart away. Entertainment is provided by fellow diners and yourself. Tagpuan has an unpretentious and happy atmosphere with a genuine welcome to visitors.

# Japanese

## Benihana

100-150

12:00 - 15:00
19:00 - 24:00 | Al Bustan Rotana Hotel, Al Garhoud | Page 14, E 3 | Tel: **820 000**

The world famouse Japenese-American Teppanyaki and Sushi restaurant. A first in the Middle East. Great entertainment by skilled Chefs whose spectacular cooking methods are a real attraction. The Sushi bar seats 30, and nine Teppanyaki tables each seat eight people. This restaurant should be placed on the MUST list for lovers of, and those not sure about, Japanese cuisine. If you have been to the US, you will already know about this restaurant's reputation for excellent quality at great value for money. There are over 30 restaurants worldwide and the staff have all been trained in the Benihana style.

Along with trademarked Hibachi specials, special soups, tempuras and teppanyaki meals, you can sample the delights of sushi at the sushi bar, normal tables or at the teppanyaki tables which seat 72 people. The teppanyaki show is one of the best in Dubai and you will find it difficult to choose from the selection of cocktails and mocktails, which tempt all tastes. The nonalcoholic ones are a nutritional meal in themselves. Trust me - you won't be disappointed. Share a Hibachi special for the main course unless you have a bear of an appetite. Nouvelle cuisine here is a nasty word. Thoroughly recommended for even those who do not like the traditional raw fish type meal. Excellent. Would go back again, again and again. Great value for money.

## Creekside

100-150

12:30 - 14:45
19:30 - 23:00 Closed Fri am | Sheraton Hotel, Deira | Page 10, C 1 | Tel: **281 111**

Sit in the middle U-shaped table so you can watch the sushi chef in action. Excellent Japanese food in an informal, modern restaurant. The menu is extensive and reasonably priced. Try the smoked eel, also the green-tea ice-cream. Lots of seaweed and steaming makes meals a healthy experience. The cuisine combines the traditional Japanese style of cooking with some unusual combinations. The feather-light tempura and dipping sauce will keep you coming back. Amazing crockery, with every serving carefully presented on a different dish - the shapes, size and colour continuously change throughout the evening.

For all you sushi fans who thought Japanese food was expensive, read on! Every Sunday night, for Dhs.65++ eat as much sushi as you like, from 19:30 this restaurant is transformed into a veritable Sushi haven. No showmanship, but plenty, and we mean plenty of delicious food. Superb value, comes highly recommended. If you fancy yourself as a budding chef or feel the urge to create your own dishes without doing the washing up, then Neptune's Wok Night on Tuesdays is the place for you. The atmosphere is relaxed and unhurried and the service friendly without being overpowering.

## Minato

100-150

13:00 - 15:00
19:00 - 23:00 Closed Sat | Inter-Continental Hotel, Deira | Page 7, C 4 | Tel: **227 171**

Located above the shopping Plaza this is a large restaurant, 77 seats, with smaller areas for private functions in Tatami rooms and Teppanyaki tables. A Japanese consultant was involved with the development of Minato (meaning harbour) from its inception, ensuring that everything from the recruitment of chefs, to the printing of the menu is a true reflection of Japanese culture. You need a bit of help when leafing through the book, sorry, the menu,

as the items are not explained very well. On the other hand, you may enjoy the variety / mystery / enticement as it is interesting to discover new out-of-the ordinary Japanese dishes. Excellent Tempura, assorted Sushi, a Japanese style fondue called Shabu Shabu and red bean ice cream with an interesting flavour are some of the dishes on offer. The service is well timed and very attentive, as it ought to be for these prices.

## Miyako

100-150

12:30 - 15:00
19:00 - 23:00

Hyatt Regency Hotel
Deira

Page 7
D 2

Tel: **706 4818**

Hold onto your eardrums when cross the tiny wooden bridge and enter Miyako as each individual is announced by a gong on the drum, as kimono clad waitresses flow serenly the restaurant floor to greet you.

Japanese people choose to eat here, when they are not eating at home, and the chefs have convinced many non-Japanese that there are other things on the extensive menu worth trying in addition to Teppanyaki. Seating is varied to suit the occasion: Sushi bar, Teppanyaki bar, tables with very Japanese straight backed chairs and a Tatami room. Take away available.

## Sakura

100-150

12:00 - 15:00
19:00 - 23:00

Holiday Inn Crowne Plaza
Sh Zayed Rd/Trade Centre

Page 8
D 2

Tel: **311 111**

Chef Ujihara doesn't speak much English, but he makes up for it with the most glorious Japanese food you'll ever taste outside Japan. Generous helpings of everything you order, plus a few complimentary tasters for you to try. Watch the live cookery display at the Teppanyaki griddle, or have a set menu meal in the dining area for couples and those on their own. The large choice of raw fish delicacie at the sushi bar are tempting enough to make you want to experiment. Japanese families eat here, so they must know a thing or two about it. There is even a long gas barbecue for meats etc., which are served with sauces and oriental vegetables.

A fine Japanese restaurant with an authentic feel. The service is impeccable and the food exquisitely displayed. They prepare all styles of Japanese cuisine and have many superb set menu options for the novice. The Suimono (clear soup) is very flavourful and the Agemono (tempura) delicious. The availability of seating in one of three connecting rooms offers the freedom of choice between a quiet corner, or front row seats to the spectacular preparation of your food.

## Shogun

50-100

12:00 - 15:00
19:00 - 24:00

Al Ghurair Centre, Deira — Page 10, D 1

Tel: **285 568**

The Shogun promises a touch of the Orient in Dubai. This restaurant is superbly furnished, offering private dining rooms, live cooking, and a sit down area for a true Japanese style dinner.

Mr. Jung the owner has personally gone to the Far East to search for the chef, choosing them from many applicants. Three chefs are present for the creation of each of your favourite delights: Japanese, Thai and Korean.

## Teppanyaki House

100-150

12:30 - 15:00
19:30 - 24:00 Closed Fri

Ramada Hotel, Bur Dubai — Page 6, E 3

Tel: **521 010**

If you're a little cautious about trying Japanese cuisine, this is an excellent place to start. Battered vegetables, thinly sliced smoked salmon and bite sized meats to dip in soy and other sauces, are a good introduction .

Unlike many larger restaurants which can often be intimidating the small Teppanyaki House provides a relaxed atmosphere with its four tables and one hot plate bar where the antics of the chef delight many. Check out the quaint wooden framed menus and crockery which has been transported direct from Japan. There is also a dinky Sushi bar, which will undoubtedly change your opinion of raw fish from YUK to YUM!

## See Also:

Korean
Polynesean
Seafood

# Korean

## Hana

50-100

12:00 - 15:00
19:00 - 23:30

Riviera Hotel
Deira

Page 7
C 3

Tel: **222 131**

Hana is really three restaurants in one with a choice of: Korean, Japanese and Thai cuisine. A formidable array of Korean specialties including the traditional Bibimbab (rice with egg and vegetables) and Kimchi is offered, as are the Japanese favourites of sushi, tempura and teppanyaki. Also on the menu is the traditional Thai fish market option, where you choose from an array of fresh fish and ask the resident Thai chef to deep fry it with chilli and lemon grass, bake it in lemon and butter, or simply steam it! Considerably cheaper than its 5-star hotel equivalents, especially as alcohol is not served, Hana is frequented largely by Koreans and Japanese businessmen.

## Lee Hwa

100-150

12:00 - 15:30
18:30 - 23:00

Opp. Al Ghurair Centre
Al Riqqa Rd, Deira

Page 10
D 1

Tel: **280 938**

It's a refreshing change to see such a high class restaurant which is not located in a hotel. Being one of the few restaurants which caters to the Korean market, Lee Hwa certainly has its fair share of this clientele.

Nicely decorated in a cool oriental style, with black floors, tables, chairs and partitions. The restaurant includes two teppanyaki tables for seven people, and two private dining rooms upstairs one large enough for 70 people, and the other for 10 people.

There are two menus: one for Korean food (which is a blend of Japanese, Thai and chinese cooking) and the other for Japanese. Both menus are extensive, with plenty of pictures of the dishes, very useful if you don't know where to start. Waitresses are extremely patient in explaining their dishes. Recommended is the Bul-Kat-Bi (short rib BBQ) for Dhs.50, accompanied by an assortment of cold dishes. The Japanese food is beautifully presented, and tastes great. Quick and efficient service. Relatively expensive considering it is not in a hotel.

## See Also:

Chinese

Japanese

# INTRODUCING HANA...

Overlooking the lively creek in the heart of Dubai is the latest seafood sensation - HANA- the virtual treasure house of Japanese, Korean and Seafood specialities.

Tatami rooms, Tepanyaki stations and a Sushi bar depict the Japanese culinary tradition... Thai chefs visibly indulging in open flame cooking and a mixed menu offering exquisite Korean dishes all reflect our variety of the East.

Visit HANA at the Riviera Hotel...

*The 'in' place for an out of this world experience.*

For reservations please call 222775

HANA

فندق ريفيرا
RIVIERA HOTEL

# Polynesian

## Marco Polo

100-150

12:00 - 15:00
19:00 - 24:00

Dubai Marine Hotel
Bur Dubai

Page 7
A 3

Tel: **520 900**

In the 13th Century, Marco Polo sampled the unique experience of India, China and S.E. Asia. Today, if you care to journey to the 5th floor of the Dubai Marine Hotel you can sample some of the exotic cuisines. Greeted by the Maitre D' you can chose to dine in the bamboo ceilinged restaurant, or outside amongst the leafy greenery of the terrace garden. Or you may decide to relax in the spacious bar area and work your way through the amazing cocktail list!

Thoroughly recommended for starters are Dim Sum and Satay Chicken, whilst chilli addicts may prefer the spicy Tom Yam soup! Those interested in culinary skills can watch their dinner being cooked in the open kitchen. If you can make it to the dessert trolley you are doing well! If you don't have room, the Irish coffee is an excellent alternative, elaborately prepared at your table, lending a perfect ending to the evening. Unfortunately the prices have increased quite considerably from last year. Lively and flamboyant entertainment is provided by Los Maricos Tropicales, a Paraguayan trio and two skilful harpists full of catchy Latino rhythms.

## Spice Island

100-150

12:00 - 15:00
19:00 - 24:30

Royal Abjar
Deira

Page 11
A 3

Tel: **625 555**

A superb concept in mixed cuisine dining, this alluringly named restaurant offers diners the exotic choice of Thai, Chinese, Japanese, Polynesian and Mexican menu's all in one restaurant. A choice of decor and ambience is also available, reflecting the cultures of the different cuisine's, with two cleverly screened areas for private parties.

Make sure you get to see all the options as the Chinese and Mexican menus are separate - and you do need to ask for them.

A great place for big parties as all tastes can be catered for and the "fiesta platter" gives sample of each, although the quality definitely suffers from having so much variety. Exceptionally low lighting does help to create an intimate atmosphere, but makes the rather confusing menu rather difficult to decipher! Both food and drinks are reasonably priced, and the sushi is excellent, but expect a few strange flavours in the Thai and Polynesian dishes.

## Tahiti

100-150

12:30 - 15:00
19:00 - 01:00

Metropolitan Palace
Deira

Page 10
D 2

Tel: **270 000**

This Polynesian theme bar and restaurant provides island cuisine with a twist. The twist lies in the Teppanyaki table which presents a Japanese flavour and an eye-catching show by the chefs as they theatrically prepare the fresh food for cooking. A classy, but casual atmosphere provides the setting for the best of the South Pacific Polynesian Islands. Live sounds from a Calypso band and a tropical cocktail prepared by a most imaginative barman.

## Trader Vic`s

100-150

12:30 - 15:00
19:30 - 24:00

Holiday Inn Crowne Plaza
Trade Centre / SH Zayed Rd

Page 8
D 2

Tel: **311 111**

This American chain of restaurants is well known worldwide for its unique presentation of decor, cocktails and food.

Reserve order - which consists of bamboo lined walls, long ships, parrots and native looking items of all sorts. Choose from the extensive, and expensive, cocktail menu at the bar, while enjoying the cane chairs which are so comfortable. Try a selection of satays and meats which you cook over a blue flame and dip into a variety of sauces before popping into your mouth. A band will rumba and salsa you through the evening!

Offering two distinct areas, the restaurant is set down and therefore distanced from the cocktail bar. There is an extensive menu with some of the delights cooked in a Chinese traditional clay wood fuelled oven, where the food is suspended in the bowl and slowly cooked to perfection. Watch the show of other guests being served flambe meals, or even better, order your own. The Island Brule is mouth watering.

This restaurant is great for parties. You can request long tables or use one of the two private dining rooms which seat a maximum of eight and 16 people. The Trader Vic's exotic experience does not come cheaply, but is always memorable and definitely enjoyable.

# Thai

## Bangkok Thai Cellar, The

50-100

19:00 - 01:00 | Lodge, The, Al Nasa | Page 9, E 4 | Tel: **379 470**

When telephoning for reservations ask what time the cabaret act starts on the small dance floor. It is usually Slovakian dancers at approx. 22:00. This a perfect place to dine before moving onto the Highland Lodge disco next door. The spacious restaurant has an intimate atmosphere, with dim lighting and comfortable cane chairs. It offers a variety of cocktails and a choice of well known Thai and Chinese favourites A sumptuous buffet is available every Thursday night for Dhs.75 per head.

## Blue Elephant

100-150

12:00 - 15:00, 19:00 - 24:00 | Al Bustan Rotana Hotel, Al Garhoud | Page 14, E 3 | Tel: **820 000**

The indisputable King of Royal Thai Cuisine in Dubai, the Blue Elephant is certainly an experience you won't forget in a hurry. Total authenticity is the name of the game, from Thai staff, to décor reminiscent of a Thai village - complete with traditional huts, a waterfall, flowing steams and lush vegetation - Thai table settings, and specially imported Thai flowers. A traditional Thai welcome greets you as you enter the "Land of Smiles" and impeccable and friendly service ensures you an enjoyable meal.

When it comes to the food, it would be very hard to find fault. Fresh produce such as fruits, vegetables and spices are flown in weekly and prepared to perfection by the team of Thai chefs, who like the waiting staff, are all trained in the Blue Elephant's flagship property in London. Unlike many oriental restaurants, the use of monosodium glutamate is forbidden, and so healthy eating is no problem, with every dish as light, fragrant and fresh as the next. Centuries old recipes are re-created in traditional manner and presented beautifully on the Blue Elephant's own personalised dinner service, with everything tastefully monogrammed from the glasses, to napkins, table-cloths to the wonderful cobalt blue serving dishes. You certainly won't forget the name of this restaurant!

It would be hard to pick out recommendations because all the dishes are exquisite, just ensure your appetite is keen before going because you will find it hard to restrict your eating once you start! Reservations, especially at weekends are essential.

## Sanuk

50-100

19:00 - 24:00 | Forte Grand - Jumeira Beach, Al Mina Al Siyahi | Page 1, E 2 | Tel: **845 555**

This is one of the best Thai restaurants near Dubai, as it is actually a short journey out of town. The curved shape of the restaurant is a delightful visual discovery, while the menu offers a wide choice of dishes which are exquisitely prepared by a team of Thai chefs, using the freshest ingredients and traditional spices. This, combined with the oriental surroundings and discrete charming service, creates a very enjoyable and authentic experience. If you end up with a runny nose and watery eyes when you eat spicy food, you will appreciate the chilli index on the menu which indicates how hot each dish is.

## Thai Bistro

100-150

**19:30 - 23:30** **Dubai Marine Beach Resort Jumeira** **Page 5 D 2** Tel: **441 221**

Perfect for both romantic soirees and business dinners, this restaurant excels in its lovely setting and quality of traditional cuisine. Approached by a little wooden bridge, diners have a choice of a pool-side table overlooking the beach, or a table inside the warmly lit, tastefully decorated restaurant which has Thai music gently playing in the background.

Why not start the meal with one of the cocktails from the extensive cocktail list? Follow it with the spicy prawn and lemon grass Tom Yam Goong soup, and one of the many main course dishes on offer, all of which are accompanied by carefully carved animal shapes made from raw vegetables. Round it all off with a delicate Jasmine tea. Once tasted and seen, this is a restaurant you will want to visit time and time again.

## Thai House

100-150

**12:30 - 15:00**
**19:30 - 23:30 Closed Mon** **Sheraton Deira Deira** **Page 11 A 3** Tel: **688 888**

Excellence and authenticity abound in this haven of Thai culture and cuisine. From traditional dress and bowed greeting, to carved wood-panelled walls and traditional music. Take time to savour the surroundings, generously proportioned tables and the exquisite presentation, before treating your palate to the delights of arguably the best Thai food in town.

The extensive menu encompasses favourites such as the spicy Tom Yang Goong (prawn soup) and Som Tum Thai (baby papaya salad) with a few variations on a theme such as the Gaen Pah Kai Nuea Goong (or spicy jungle curry of chicken). The flavours of lemon grass, fresh ginger and a million oriental spices burst from every dish, but be sure to tell your waiter if you don't like hot, spicy food, as chillies are also a common ingredient.

All the staff have been recruited directly from one of Bangkok's top hotels, including the chef, and are more than happy to explain the dishes and help your selection. A must for all lovers of oriental food.

## Thai Room, The

50-100

12:00 - 15:00
19:00 - 23:30

Princeton Hotel
Al Garhoud

Page 14
D 2

Tel: **827 777**

If good Thai food is your overriding goal then the Thai Room is certainly worth consideration. What at first glance appears to be a rather limited menu, is more than compensated for by the quality and authenticity of the food; a credit to the restaurant's Thai chef. The usual favourites are available, but a definite recommendation has to be the 'Yam Thalay' salad to start. A wonderful combination of seafood and vegetables in what is described as the chef's 'special sauce'... It certainly is! Another 'must try' is the 'Tub Tim Grub' for desert - diced water chestnuts in coconut milk.

Slightly lacking in atmosphere due to the overly bright lighting. Undoubtedly more of an eating, rather than dining, experience.

## Thai Terrace

50-100

12:00 - 14:30
19:00 - 23:30

World Trade Centre Rd
Al Karama

Page 9
E 1

Tel: **367 356**

An excellent eatery, the Thai Terrace offers a great selection of dishes from this part of the world. The food is a mix of Chinese and Indian recipes blended to produce a unique taste. The fish with chilli, fried rice with shrimps, Thai style noodles, and many other dishes are well worth trying. The soup is excellent! If you want something different, don't hesitate to chose live fish from the fish tanks, which are cooked to your exact specifications.

The Thai Terrace offers good food at a reasonable price. The service is prompt, food well presented, and the interior is functional. Leave the choice of food to the staff and you will not be disappointed.

## See Also:

Chinese
Japanese
Polynesian
Seafood

# Vietnamese

## Golden Triangle

100-150

12:30 - 15:00
20:00 - 03:00

Forte Grand Dubai
Al Garhoud

Page 14
E 3

Tel: **820 973**

The jungles of Vietnam have come to Dubai at the Forte Grand, near the Airport. Enter the cool, dark environment of bamboo and palms, thatched huts and wooden floors. Pathways between dining huts remind you of cabins on hillsides, treetop rope bridges and holidays in the Far East. Each hut is comfortably furnished, with padded bench seating and chairs. Lunchtime guests eat with filtered light peeping through the decor. Evening is when the fibre optic stars come out in the dark ceiling sky in twinkling fascination. When the dining stops, the nightclub begins, with an in-house DJ who changes the background style of music to more lively tempo music for those who want to use the hi-tec dance floor.

Vietnamese dishes appeal to international taste buds as they are oriental, but not chilli hot. Choose from Tempura vegetables, potato and onion patties, steamed fish stuffed with chopped vegetables and barbecued meats with satay, soy or ginger sauces. Even dessert is tasty, with a Filipino influenced roulade of meringue and custard.

# Global Cuisine

# International

## Aeroplane Restaurant

50-100

12:00 - 16:30
19:00 - 23:30

Deira

Page 7
E 3

Tel: **722 999**

Totally unique in Dubai, this restaurant has been fitted out to look and feel like the inside of an aircraft! A stewardess greets you and allows you to choose your aircraft: Falcon; Airbus or a Rowdha 747. Tables for four have comfortable aircraft style chairs, large overhead screens at each end of the main restaurant showing videos, and window seats to look out at an artist's impression of blue sky and clouds! Once aboard, the whole effect is surprisingly pleasant. The menu has no exceptional dishes, but does have reasonable variety including a decent buffet (Arabic, European, Oriental & Chinese) in the evening and some lunch times. Ladies/family gatherings on Wednesdays and Thursday is seafood night. There's a special separate buffet for children, with smaller tables so they can serve themselves! A separate men-only dining room is also available.

## Al Dana

100-150

12:00 - 15:30
19:00 - 23:00

Holiday Inn Crowne Plaza
Sh Zayed Rd

Page 8
D 2

Tel: **311 111**

You can eat here around the clock, but you may not want to. The buffet has a huge selection of salads, over 65 dishes. Stick with these as the main courses are short on choice and flavour. Desserts look great and taste good too. If you are a vegetarian the buffet will not cater for your needs, but the chef will be happy to make whatever your heart desires. The wine list is extensive and expensive.

## Al Dana

100-150

12:00 - 15:00
19:00 - 23:00

Riviera Hotel
Deira

Page 7
C 3

Tel: **222 131**

If you're in the area, it's worth visiting just to try the hot lunch buffet for Dhs.35++. Dishes from all around the world are produced by the Lebanese chef, who also makes that after lunch cappuccino a little different by putting a few drops of rose-water in it, very refreshing! Menu is changed on a daily basis. The evening a la carte menu has a varied selection of salads, pasta dishes, and fresh seafood dishes.

## Al Dawaar

100-150

12:30 - 15:30
19:30 - 23:30 Closed Friday am

Hyatt Regency
Hotel Deira

Page 7
D 2

Tel: **706 4810**

Dubai's only revolving restaurant, on the 25th floor, and one complete rotation varies between one to two hours, depending on the sun! Split level seating ensures that everyone has a good view of Port Rashid, Dubai town and the coastal area.

A wide selection of delicious international buffet items including Continental, Arabic and Asian cusines. Extensive salad items include Middle Eastern mezzeh favourites, Smoked Salmon, Prawns, Cold Meats and Japanese sushi. Hot dishes include lobster bisque, Hammour Wellington and Veal in White Grape Juice sauce. Carvery stations. Home made chocolates and tiny cakes are on the dessert tables along with fresh fruit, Arabic Umm Ali and other mouthwatering sweets. The buffet priced at Dhs.120++. A 20% discount is offered if you dine between 19:00-21:00.

## Al Fahidi

100-150

12:00 - 15:00
19:00 - 23:30 Closed Fri

Hilton Hotel
Sh Zayed Rd

Page 9
A 2

Tel: **314 000**

When you walk into the Al Fahidi you enter a different world: an elegant world of space and harmony. A live duo playing unobtrusively enhances the ambience. A cocktail of the week is offered before menus are presented and special dishes recommended, some of which have won awards at the annual Dubai Salon Culinaire. Dishes can pop up between courses and you could be forgiven for thinking that you have received someone else's starter, until your waiter explains that it is an in-between taster, with the compliments of the chef. Dress is smart, but a tie is not compulsory. Go early because time flies when you are having fun.

## Amby`s

50-100

12:00 - 15:00
19:00 - 24:00

Ambassador Hotel
Bur Dubai

Page 7
A 2

Tel: **531 000**

Although the Ambassador hotel is well known in Dubai, Amby's is less so, with its interior boasting an unusual frieze and a tiled waterfall, plus an open grill area to watch your food being prepared. It's not often that snails are offered as a starter, especially at a low price of Dhs.20 for six. This large, quiet dining room has a truly international menu at usual prices. Used mainly by hotel guests, it is nonetheless a place that mainly businessmen know about for working lunches. Fish and Chips, Pepper Steaks, Mexican Potato Skins and many other favourites are offered, while Indian specialities include fish curry, biriyani and vegetarian dishes.

A decor of stained glass windows and sectioned off areas, gives a private feel to the large carpeted room. Comfortable and cosy atmosphere.

## Bay Watch

50-100

12:00 - 16:00
19:00 - 03:00

Radisson SAS Jumeira
Al Mina Al Siyahi

Page 1
D 2

Tel: **845 533**

With an inspiring view of the hotel's gardens and beach, Bay Watch offers one of the most extensive menus in Dubai. Choose from over 40 dishes covering appetisers; salads and sandwiches; soups and casseroles; main courses and grills; Gulf and Asian favourites; pasta, pizzas or vegetarian meals; side dishes; spreads and dips and desserts. The famed Radisson SAS Super Breakfast buffet, scandanavian style is also served. There are lunch and dinner buffets and an Arabic corner during Ramadan.

## Blues and Cues

50-100

12:00 - 16:00
19:00 - 03:00

Cyclone
Al Nasa

Page 9
D 4

Tel: **369 991**

Located upstairs at the Cyclone Nightclub, Blues and Cues is an interesting mixture of a bar and pool hall, with the addition of a small restaurant section in one corner. The overall atmosphere is lively as this popular bar is always busy, and the pool tables in constant play.

Additional pinball and games machine add to the smoky games room environment for a clientele of mainly 20 - 35 year-old, European males.

## Boardwalk - Down Under

50-100

12:00 - 01:00 | Dubai Creek Golf & Yacht Club, Al Garhoud | Page 14, C 2 | Tel: **825 777**

Situated on a large wooden deck, built over the sloping creekside lawn near the marina, the Boardwalk allows you to enjoy cool evening breezes, while sipping sundowners and watching dhows and boats sailing up and down Dubai's Creek.

A luxurious and pleasant way to start the evening before moving on to dinner at the Club's haute cuisine restaurant, or even in this restaurant, which serves simple but good food. Come early if you want a seat outside, as unfortunately, no reservations are taken!

As an added bonus, no government tax (5%) is added to prices.

## Brasserie

50-100

12:00 - 15:30
19:00 - 23:00 | Forte Grand - Jumeira Beach, Al Mina Al Siyahi | Page 1, E 2 | Tel: **845 555**

Have a nice cup of tea and a slice of cake while sitting outside on the terrace enjoying the balmy weather, or inside in the air conditioned cool. Either way, the Brasserie provides a far more attractive venue to eat in than most other hotel "lobby" restaurants in town.

Lunch is served buffet-style, with plenty of light and healthy choices. Dinner is also buffet-style with different speciality themes. Try the "Spice Route" on a Thursday night when you can choose from Thai, Malaysian, Chinese or Indian. Watch the expert chefs create the meal of your choice before your very eyes using fresh meats, fish and exotic spices. Under 12's eat at half price, under 5's eat free.

Although this coffee shop is mainly for hotel guests, there are quite a few discerning outsiders who have discovered that big portions and low prices can indeed be obtained at top quality hotels. Try the lunchtime salad bar for Dhs.30 which includes cold meats and breads. Main course buffet meals are regular five-star prices with copious choices of well cooked tastes.

## Cafe Boulevard

50-100

24:00 hrs | Inter-Continental Hotel, Deira | Page 7, C 4 | Tel: **227 171**

Wooden surroundings, an indoor garden terrace and tempting buffet displays make it hard to walk past this upmarket, yet casual, restaurant cafe.

Located in the heart of Dubai, Cafe Boulevard is a bustling outlet set in the exclusive shopping arcade of the Intercontinental Hotel .

Buffet meals are available from early morning to late evening, with an a la carte menu for a 'quick bite'. It features a variety of theme nights every week and is also the focal point for numerous international food festivals which are held regularly in the hotel.

## Cafe de Paris

50-100

00:00 - 24:00

Al Diyafah Rd
Al Satwa

Page 5
E 3

Tel: **451 418**

Cafe de Paris purple and white awnings are highly visible on Satwa's High Street, but start looking for a parking spot further up the road! The balcony is full of cappuccino connoisseurs catching the cool breeze - particularly in the evenings. A popular meeting place for everyone.

Escape inside to a quieter atmosphere and enjoy something from the reasonably priced menu, which offers a variety of good sturdy meals from salads, to steak and chips. The portions are generous. Birthday cakes can be made to order.

## Cafe Renoir

50-100

09:30 - 24:00
Closed Fri am

Wafi Shopping Mall
Wafi Creekside Park

Page 13
D 2

Tel: **366 407**

Depending on which entrance you use, there are two completely different feels to Cafe Renoir. Outside, the patio is remarkably peaceful considering it overlooks the Wafi car park; shady and pleasant, surrounded by a rockery garden, it has wrought iron tables and chairs, and is big enough to comfortably fit 17 tables. Food is excellent, either as a restaurant, or as a coffee shop.

Step inside from the shopping mall and you enter a bright and interesting French cafeteria / diner, with wooden floors, big pillars and varying artifacts scattered around. Healthy and generous salads are offered and main courses at reasonable prices. Or how about a snack meal of savoury pancakes, omelette or onion soup and sandwiches at Dhs 25 each? All meals come with a basket of freshly baked French bread.

## Caravan

50-100

12:00 - 15:30
19:00 - 00:30

Clock Tower R/A
Deira

Page 10
D 3

Tel: **238 805**

Offering Indian, Chinese and Thai buffet this is a classy, value for money restaurant, popular with residents and business folk for both lunches and dinner. It is always busy.

Frequented by Indian families later in the evening, after 22:00, while Europeans usually prefer earlier meals. Simple and filling fare at popular prices.

## Caravan Cafe

50-100

00:00 - 24:00 | Hyatt Regency Hotel, Deira | Page 7, D 2 | Tel: **706 4816**

You never knew when a caravan of camels would arrive at an oasis, day or night, anytime. That is why this Caravan is open 24 hours a day, every day, ready to welcome early birds, lunchers and night owls alike. The restaurant offers a complete international menu and an attractive buffet.

Enjoy afternoon tea in the adjoining lobby lounge with a genteel pot of tea, freshly made cakes and sandwiches, or settle down on the floor cushions within the open fronted tent, or majlis, in the main lobby. A great photo opportunity. Try the tasty breakfast between 06:00 - 11:00.

## Fairway's

100-150

12:30 - 15:00<br>19:30 - 24:00 closed Fri | Dubai Creek Golf & Yacht Club, Al Garhoud | Page 14, C 2 | Tel: **821 000**

That quiet touch of elegance is found in this tapered restaurant built on two levels, with a cosy upstairs area for quiet chats and twosomes. Nouvelle cuisine that is tasty and filling is the order of the day. A special place for special occasions, or business dinners to discuss and impress. Plenty of time between courses to savour the peace and get ready for the next cordon bleu dish.

## Fountain Cafe

50-100

24:00 hrs | Nr. City Tower 1, Sh Zayed Rd | Page 8, C 2 | Tel: **311 502**

A business-like approach to breakfast or lunch is what appeals to the many office workers frequenting the smart Fountain Cafe. Flexible sandwich combinations cater for the most picky professionals, who often prefer these tastes over the more substantial daily special dishes. For something sweet there are many cakes and pastries, though they may not be as delicious as they promise from their shiny glass cabinet.

Bright and clean, the Fountain Cafe is best suited for a quick break from the office rat-race. It is a pleasant place to cram down a crisp wholesome sandwich and criticise your boss, but take care not to be overheard!

## Garden Cafe

100-150

12:00 - 15:00<br>19:00 - 24:00 | Hilton Hotel, Sh Zayed Rd | Page 9, A 2 | Tel: **314 000**

An aptly named hotel coffee shop/restaurant, where a 24-hour meal service can be enjoyed in pleasant and relaxed surroundings. The dominance of lush garden ferns and hanging plants dropping from wooden terracing, the play of natural sunlight as it streams through the high windows and the background bubbling of a fountain, produces the semblance of being in a garden. Choose from a comprehensive, international a la carte menu or opt for a delightful buffet which includes a national cuisine that changes daily.

## Gondole

12:00 - 15:00
19:00 - 22:00

Lords Hotel
Deira

Page 10
D 2

Tel: **289 977**

50-100

A combined restaurant and coffee shop in a new hotel, the decor of Gondole consists of red carpet, yellow seats, a wooden bar and an atmosphere of fine dining. Lighting is bright with no dim corners in this place. A mainly East European clientele. This is a four-star hotel that feels that it can offer five-star quality. A Dh.60 buffet and an average of Dhs.90 for the a la carte menu promises a quality meal. The shrimp cocktail is recommended.

## Khyber

12:00 - 15:00
19:00 - 01:00

Opp. Ambassador Hotel
Bur Dubai

Page 7
A 2

Tel: **534 833**

50-100

With a menu focus on Indian cuisine, but nonetheless offering a good choice of Chinese and international dishes, the Khyber offers a very reasonably priced, swiftly served meal in a friendly family atmosphere. Established in 1977, it's not the food which is remarkable, nor the portions - which dish by dish are a little on the small side, but rather the excellent children's playroom leading off one side of the restaurant. Equipped with an IKEA-style ball room, wendy house, toys and a TV, the reasonably sound proof and windowed door is the only route in and out leaving parents free to enjoy their meal.

## Manhattan

12:00 - 15:30
20:00 - 23:30

Novotel
Deira

Page 7
E 4

Tel: **720 000**

50-100

The Novotel offers an unusual situation here with an ancient bar and warm decorations which were kept when renovations changed this nightclub into a restaurant. Dining in front of a large video screen showing quietly-played music videos, helps to give a homely feel to the place. Well cooked, pleasant buffet for Dhs.24 brings in a variety of customers including Arabic and hotel guests.

## Oasis, The

08:00 - 03:00
Closed Fri pm

Dubai Country Club
Nr Counrty Club RA

Page 12
B 3

Tel: **331 155**

50-100

DCC's wine bar-restaurant is a serious must for food freaks. It's warm Mediterranean bistro atmosphere and brightly coloured decor and cheery crockery, make for a hedonistic evening. A minor point on the down side is the 'sparseness', which somehow makes for a slightly cooler feeling.

The menu leans towards nouvelle cuisine served in large portions, and if you like creamy sauces and filo pastry you won't be disappointed. Presentation of food is excellent, as are the choices. The menu changes once a fortnight and the accompanying vintages are terrific value.

Located in the Country Club, but open to all. Non-members must book in advance, and pay a refundable Dhs.10 entrance fee at the gate.

## Pirates

50-100

12:00 - 16:00
19:00 - 24:00

**Harbour Inn Club, The**
**Jebel Ali**

Tel: **815 415**

If you are looking for lost treasure in Jebel Ali, then look no further than the Pirates Restaurant and Bar. It is a popular dining spot serving hot and cold buffet meals, as well as a range of menu options including Pizza, Shish Tawook, Sandwiches and Burgers. It is a good place to visit with friends, especially if you fancy a drink with your meal. There is usually some form of entertainment in the evenings, including Karaoke nights. A delivery service is also available through Chef Express.

## Taverna

100-150

19:30 - 23:00

**Dubai Marine Beach Resort**
**Jumeira**

Page 5
D 2

Tel: **441 221**

Morning until early evening is for members only but after 18:00 is when those who have booked can also enjoy a good balance of Indian and continental food with enough varieties to satisfy any taste. Happy hour between of 18:30 - 20:30 is popular, as this is when reduced priced drinks are served. A nice way to meet and greet friends before choosing whether to sit in the air conditioned interior, or on the terrace overlooking the beach and lapping sea to eat your meal.

With a good selection of starters, soups and salads, the menu is well balanced between grills such as Australian lamb chops, calamari, Mexican tortillas, and Indian specialties. Generous portions. A very pleasant evening venue mainly due to its position and outdoor warm summer evening's ambiance. Lots of 30-something guests including tourists and residents.

## Tower Restaurant, The

50-100

12:30 - 15:00
19:30 - 23:30

**Aviation Club, The**
**Al Garhoud**

Page 14
C 3

Tel: **824 122**

There are no hidden prices on the menu here, as what you see is what you pay, with no governement taxes charged. A top quality restaurant which serves cordon bleu cuisine to those who like their food with sauces and flavourings. A romantic and cosy restaurant which somehow retains an approachable atmosphere. Great for a quiet evening out with the one you love, or with a small group of friends. Impressive wine list. A connoisseur's choice of venue.

Jazz band and dancing on Thursday and Arabic entertainment until late on Fridays. Booking recommended. Open to non-members.

## Wind Tower, The

50-100

12:00 - 15:00
19:30 - 24:00

**Dubai Country Club**
**Counrty Club RA**

Page 12
B 3

Tel: **331 155**

A dimly lit room, a baby grand piano, delicious food and excellent service make this the ideal venue for either a dinner for two, or a quiet evening meal with friends. Open to members and non-members provided a booking has been made.

Guests can choose from a reasonably priced table d'hote menu wich gives a choice of three starters, main courses and several desserts, or the rather exotic main menu where starters range from Hommous and Tabouleh to fresh Oysters and Mussels; and main courses range from Roast Breast of Pigeon to Medallions of Lobster and Steaks, again all very reasonably priced. All food is expertly prepared and elegantly presented. Be prepared for an evening of formal dining, quiet music and if yours is good company, you will definitely enjoy your night out here.

# Pizzeria

## Pizza Corner

50-100

10:00 - 24:00 | Creek Rd, Deira | Page 7 C 3 | Tel: **222 671**

Pizza Corner in Deira is a cosy little place with a Manager who has been working there since 1976, and knows just how to make you feel at home. Fish tanks and low coloured lighting above each of the tables in the upstairs dining area give a dark and romantic feel to the place. The terrace section allows you to relax and eat in a pavement cafe atmosphere. There is a large car park opposite with free parking after 21:00. A nice range of salads from which you can make up your own combinations. Pizzas too, can be customized to your particular tastes. Good value for money.

## Pizza Corner

50-100

10:30 - 24:00 | Nr. Dubai Marine Hotel, Bur Dubai | Page 6 E 2 | Tel: **528 163**

For a family outing or a quick home-made pizza for the bachelor, go to Pizza Corner, the first pizza restaurant in Dubai. A relaxed atmosphere welcomes you and the unpretentious and comprehensive menu offers the standard international fast food selections as well as a choice of 21 different pizzas, generously spread with your favourite toppings.

## Pizza Hut

50-100

11:00 - 01:00 | Al Dhiyafah Rd, Al Satwa | Page 4 C 2 | Tel: **451 225**

Lots of relaxing green decor for those who want to eat in the diner. Thin or thick crust bases with the standard choice of toppings generously spread on. Try the lunch buffet for Dhs.18 which includes as much as you can eat from the help-yourself salad bar. Deliveries and take-away orders available. A popular choice with teenagers, Pizza Hut also organises children's parties with games, entertainment and food. Try their cheese crust. Yummy!

The chosen one

## Pizza Inn

50-100

12:00 - 01:00

Al Dhiyafah Rd
Al Satwa

Page 6
A 3

Tel: **365 256**

As well as the standard pizza with a choice of toppings, this place provides spaghetti bolognese, parmesan coated chicken and dessert pizzas of both round and oval shapes. Choose from a New York Style dough of chewy soft-crust, or Thin Crust which is the light, crisp base that has made Pizza Inn famous for over 30 years.

## Pizza Pomodoro

50-100

12:30 - 15:00
19:00 - 03:00

Royal Abjar Hotel
Deira

Page 11
A 3

Tel: **625 555**

The latest craze to hit Dubai's restaurant scene. Pizza Pomodoro is a compact, trendy Italian restaurant with a nightclub ambience, combined with a Hollywood theme, based on the international concept of Ciro's Pizza Pomodoro. Almost made up-market by the young yuppyish "in" clientele, who are well dressed and out to impress.

More of Manhattan style pizzeria than your traditional Italian place. Loads of star personality themes around the room. Choose from a wide range of film stars' favourite pizzas, pasta or, the Chef's Special posted on the black board. Over 20 pizzas on the menu with unusual toppings such as artichoke hearts, Brie, asparagus and mozzarella. Well priced, and pizza crust and bread is freshly baked daily on the premisess. European waiters and waitresses add to the different experience.

The bands are rotated every six months. The restaurant also has a separate terrace area, and the Club Havana where Cuban cigars and vintage beverages are available. The cigar room around the corner allows you to talk comfortably, as this place gets very loud. A great place to dance and dine, with daily happy hour from 18:00 to 20:00.

## Pizza Roma

50-100

11:00 - 23:00
Closed Fri am

Bur Juman Centre
Bur Dubai

Page 10
A 1

Tel: **527 200**

Located in the food court, but a 'proper' restaurant as opposed to a food court counter. Maroon tables and crisp uniforms endeavour to smarten up this family orientated restaurant. Tasty Italian food - pizzas like mama used to make.

## Puccini's

50-100

12:30 - 14:30
19:00 - 24:00

Regent Palace Hotel
Al Karama

Page 10
A 1

Tel: **353 888**

Watch out Da Vincis! Once the new Mediterranean crockery has arrived, this place will be set to take the lead.

Puccini's is a fresh new Italian Restaurant in Bur Dubai. Great for the family or an intimate dinner for two. Ask one of the very helpful staff to recommend a speciality or two... or three. You're spoilt for choice, with over 80 different dishes to choose from, and good value to go with it. The handmade pasta is prepared by a female Italian chef, and the food is extremely fresh. Half portions are available so that you have room to try the delicious desserts. The decor is bright, cheerful and warm, with famous movie advertisements with an Italian touch. Try the truly jumbo prawns - Sublima! Great value for money.

## Round Table Pizza

50-100

11:00 - 01:00

Al Dhiyafah Rd, Al Satwa

Page 6
A 3

Tel: **456 684**

Primarily known for its excellent take away pizzas, Round Table Pizza also has a restaurant attached. Located at the end of Al Diyafah St, and their latest near the Dubai Tennis Stadium, Al Garhoud. It is a nice, bright, clean and sterile environment. With its large selections of pizzas most with wacky names such as King Arthur's Supreme, Zesty Santa Fe Chicken and Shrimp Pesto, the top favourites, recommended as musts are the Garlic Parmesan Twist and the thin-pan Gourmet Veggie which is excellent! The list of possible additional toppings is 34 items long, so you can create the wildest pizzas possible.

## Trattoria Pizzeria

50-100

07:00 - 24:00

Al Khaleej Hotel
Deira

Page 7
C 3

Tel: **598 777**

A free and easy atmosphere is reflected in the casual dress of most of the diners here. An evening venue for those who are out and about town. Unobtrusive service allows you to have a good natter with your companion. Allow Dhs.25-Dhs.40 for your meal.

## See Also:

Caesar's Palace - Italian
Capri Italian Grill - Italian
Casa Mia - Italian
Da Vinci`s - Italian
Don Corleone - Italian
Gelato - Italian
La Traviata - Italian
Little Italy - Italian
Villa Veduta - Italia

# Seafood

## Al Boom Dhow Restaurant

100-150

20:30 - 22:30 | Al Boom Tourist Village, Nr. Al Garhoud Bridge | Page 14, A 3 | Tel: **341 000**

Fixed price for a fixed Arabic grill menu consisting of Lebanese mezzeh salads, fish soup, barbecued lamb, chicken, fish and seafood, followed by dessert and tea. The obvious attraction here is a seafood meal aboard an Arabic dhow as it cruises the picturesque water way of a lively city.

## Al Shera'a Fisheries Centre

50-100

10:00 - 16:00, 19:00 - 01:00 | Nr. Royal Abjar, Deira | Page 10, E 1 | Tel: **271 803**

Not to be confused with other similar sounding outlets in Dubai. An ideal place for the fish lover who does not want the expense, or has not got the time for a more lavish meal. Choose your fish, have it cooked in your desired manner, and it is served with chips and side salad. Take away, or eat in amongst the fishing nets decor. A unique chance to try a fish shwarma, cooked by charcoal rather than the more usual gas method.

## Aquarium

100-150

12:30 - 15:00, 19:30 - 24:00 | Dubai Creek Golf & Yacht Club, Al Garhoud | Page 14, C 2 | Tel: **825 777**

You'd think that watching a huge tank of tropical fish swimming amongst artificial reefs in the centre of a two storey bar would put you off ordering hammour steaks, but this is not so. This restaurant is actually well known for both features.

Both fish and meat steaks grace the top class menu, along with king prawns and Dover sole. Traditionally cooked fish in beautiful sauces, served on French tableware. A touch of class in all respects, from the moment one drives through the club's portals.

## Fish Bazaar, The

100-150

12:30 - 14:30, 19:00 - 24:00 | Metropolitan Hotel, Sh Zayed Rd/Safa | Page 4, C 4 | Tel: **440 000**

Cross the little bridge and enter a classy Thai fish restaurant complete with thatched dining areas and lots of colourful umbrellas. Choose your own fish from the many laid out, supermarket style, on a bed of crushed ice and ask the chef to cook it for you in one of a variety of named ways, as indicated on the board on the wall. Or, try the recommended Shrimps with a Mild Chilli Sauce, which are heated at your table in fish-shaped dishes.

Enjoy a complimentary bowl of hot and spicy Tom Yam soup while waiting for the main course to be cooked in your selected style. Hot towels to wipe your hands, are a welcome treat at the end of the meal.

## Sheraton Fish Night

100-150

19:30 - 23:00 | Sheraton Hotel Deira | Page 10 C 1 | Tel: **281 111**

The Sheraton's Fish Night has long been the talk of the town. It's the best! Held every Wednesday, with a choice of many kinds of fish and crustaceans, cooked in cordon bleu styles to gratify the most jaded palate. Cooked and uncooked Oysters, Cigali, Five-finger Jack, Red Snapper and other seasonal offerings, are displayed buffet style in Lou Lou'a restaurant for connoisseurs to enjoy.

## Fishmarket, The

100-150

13:00 - 15:15
20:00 - 23:30 | Inter-Continental Hotel Deira | Page 7 C 4 | Tel: **227 171**

Enjoy the hustle and activity of a "real" Fishmarket as you select your favourites from the extensive range of shellfish and over 30 varieties of fish enticingly laid out on chopped ice, supermarket style- all superbly fresh and sold by the kilo.

The enjoyable shopping experience is continued as a waitress guides you to the vegetable counter where you choose again for accompaniments. Then comes the tricky part as you are asked, "How would you like it cooked?" Thoroughly recommended is the Thai style fish curry, particularly good with Hammour fillets... and the lemon butter sauce over the colourful Omani lobster is exquisite. A good place for those watching their calories as simple grilling or steaming is always an option.

A light and airy Far Eastern setting provides a relaxed mood and this, in conjunction with the breathtaking views over Dubai's Creek and dhow wharfage, makes this restaurant one of Dubai's perennial favourites. Booking is a must.

A wonderful eating experience, but on the pricey side. Be wary of "big eyes, small stomach" syndrome ... remember you pay by the weight, so any leftovers could be costly!

## Gulf Seafood, The

150-200

12:00 - 15:00
19:00 - 24:00 | Forte Grand - Jumeira Beach Al Mina Al Siyahi | Page 1 E 2 | Tel: **845 555**

Ingenious new twists have been added to the favourite Dubai concept of a market place from which to select your food. While perusing the menu, which is printed on your plate, you are presented with a delicious selection of appetisers to arouse your tastebuds.

When it is time to order, your own "market lady" will escort you to the stalls where an ocean of supremely fresh seafood is displayed with names and prices per kg. An impressive range of shellfish such as scallops and three kinds of lobster, jostle for space with 'fishy fish'

such as pomfret and parrot. With so many choices of ingredients, four different cooking methods (saute, steam, deep fried or char-grilled) and ten sauces, including coconut and lemongrass, lemon-butter, oyster, and black bean; assistance is much appreciated in coming up with a perfect meal - which also includes your selection of vegetables, rice and noodles.

Recommendations have to include the Tiger Prawns with Peppered lime and Garlic Sauce, or the steamed Allawayaa with Ginger, Garlic and Spring Onion - absolutely delicious! All in all, the combination of a beautiful setting and wonderful food makes this a perfect place for those really special occasions.

## Neptune's Kingdom

100-150

12:30 - 15:00
19:30 - 23:00 Closed Fri am

Sheraton Hotel Deira

Page 10 C 1

Tel: **281 111**

Sails, small dhows, fishing nets, starfish and fish-shaped statues carved out of ice, decorate this large restaurant, giving it a warm, welcoming interior design. An unpretentious informal eating place, the "Creative Cuisine" of Executive Chef, Lap, encompasses a selection of dishes and styles of cooking predominantly Far Eastern, and featuring dishes from Thailand, China and Indonesia. Also a number of European dishes. A connoisseurs delight! Watch the Chinese wok and Thai wok cooking on Tuesdays, or order what you want and it will be delivered to your table while you continue to make the rest of your selections from the buffet tables. Tempura prawns, and satay style fish in peanut sauce. Delicious!

## Sanobaar

50-100

12:30 - 16:00
18:30 - 23:30

On Rd between Expo Centre & Coast in Sharjah

Tel: **06 281 111**

Located in Sharjah (exit at the first flyover), in-between the Exposition Centre and the coast, this little gem of a restaurant is unique in this part of the world, in that it is a family run establishment, very much as you might find in a Mediterranean village. Husband and wife look after cooking and service respectively, while members of their family help with the tables.

Unpretentious seafood that is both consistently good and modestly priced. The cost of a main course includes Lebanese salads (Hommus etc), dessert and mint tea.

## Sea food Special

100-150

19:30 - 23:30

Forte Grand Dubai
Al Garhoud

Page 14
E 3

Tel: **824 040**

An outstanding evening for seafood fans is Tuesday night at the Forte Grand Brasserie, when maritime decor comes out on display, right down to a fisherman's net. An impressive array of food is spread out on the poolside patio, with different nation's seafood specialities being freshly cooked in the fresh air - Chinese, Japanese, European... and just Dhs.110!

An excellent selection of appetizers is displayed indoors, on the long and winding buffet bar inside the Coffee Shop. Seating is both inside and outside on the terrace, where a live band is also sited. The only real down thing might be if you're a dessert fan, as you're unlikely to have much room left for them!

## Seafood Market

100-150

12:30 - 15:00
19:30 - 24:00

Forte Grand Dubai
Al Garhoud

Page 14
E 3

Tel: **824 040**

Walk over the glass floor tiles and watch golden KoiCarp swim beneath your feet. Step into the huge seafood restaurant built in the style of those found in the Far East and decide which type of seating you want for the evening. Will you and your guests want to eat Japanese style at the two teppenyaki bars, or dine at the well spaced tables where you can spread out your choices and have your own mini buffet?

A large cold counter with freshly caught fish is displayed supermarket style, or choose live lobster, etc from those in the tanks. A selection of vegetables, noodles and rice is also included. Discuss methods of cooking with any of the staff for advice. An active dining experience, in a refined environment.

## See Also:

Arabic
Thai
Korean
Dinner Cruises - Tours

# Middle Eastern

## Arabic

### 1001 Nights

100-150

19:00 - 23:30

Forte Grand Dubai
Al Garhoud

Page 14
E 3

Tel: **824 040**

Perfect for tourists and residents alike, Sunday evenings allow patrons to get a taste of real Arabia. One price gives you access to the Brasserie coffee shop and extensive patio area which is regularly transformed into an Arabian village with Bedouin tents, carpets, hubble bubble pipes, palm trees and a small souk area selling arts and craft items. There is even a camel on the lawn waiting to give rides to those who dare!

An extensive buffet is well spread with dishes from across the Arab world, Middle East and North Africa. Tasty oriental and international choices are also available those looking for something more familiar. Lydia the belly dancer is well known throughout Dubai, and dances on stage and amongst the tables in a very skilled and entertaining manner. Always an enjoyable evening out.

### Al Areesh

50-100

12:30 - 15:30
19:00 - 24:00

Al Boom Tourist Village
Nr. Al Garhoud Bridge

Page 14
A 3

Tel: **341 000**

Probably the most authentically styled Arabic restaurant in Dubai. Al Areesh - named after the traditional Arab bamboo hut - boasts a perfect setting on the shores of Dubai's Creek. Designed to encapsulate local traditions and flavours, with swaying palms, antique wooden doors as tables, family rooms and more, this restaurant offers superb value local delicacies at both lunch and dinner.

A vast selection of Arabic salads and mezzeh adorn the central buffet, while main courses, with a choice of either meat or seafood, are grilled in the open air. The all inclusive buffet prices mean just that, with water, fruit juices, starter, main and dessert all included. Especially good is the 'home-made' lentil soup, and their marinated chicken kebabs just melt in your mouth.

After the meal, is the complimentary Creek Cruise on one of Al Boom's six traditional dhows, which is available every evening and Friday afternoons. Very popular with nationals, this place is a must for all wishing to sample real UAE cuisine and hospitality.

## Al Basha Restaurant & Terrace

50-100

12:00 - 15:00
19:30 - 01:00

Metropolitan Beach Club
Al Mina Al Siyahi

Page 1
E 2

Tel: **845 000**

Owing to recent refurbishments at the Metropolitan Resort Beach Club, Al Basha offers two separate areas for dining - upstairs on the terrace, or downstairs in the restaurant. The terrace is ideal when the weather is cooler as it overlooks the beach and has a relaxed and casual atmosphere. The restaurant downstairs is slightly more formal with traditional Lebanese touches - crisp white tablecloths and a band playing in the background. The Lebanese chef ensures authentic food.

## Al Koufa

50-100

19:00 - 01:00

In between Lodge / Cyclone
Al Nasa Leisureland

Page 9
D 4

Tel: **351 511**

If you want to smoke your shisha pipe, sit outside and eat good Arabic food then make sure you try eating out in the Al Koufa garden restaurant. Enclosed by barasti walls and wind towers made from palms leaves. The large courtyard is filled with plastic chairs and tables, although you'll probably have to fight to get what you need, such is the popularity of this place - eyes like hawks are recommended. Always busy at weekends with entire families frequenting the place - watch out for small children running about. Listen to the sounds of domino players, the Lebanese band, or just sit back and watch everyone else, watching everyone else. A great place for visitors. Service is haywire, but genuine. Tucked away in the corner is a portacabin serving ice-cream - a great way to finish the meal. Covered during the summer months to allow air conditioning.

## Automatic Restaurant

50-100

12:00 - 24:00

Beach Centre, The
Jumeira

Page 5
B 2

Tel: **494 888**

You are practically guaranteed not to leave this restaurant hungry! The menu offers an extensive selection, and the waiters tempt you with 'plat du jour' offerings. A good place to introduce relatives and friends to Arabic food. Excellent fish, standard selection of mezzeh and the mixed grill comes as enormous platters of different types of meats. In addition each table has a vegetable garden placed in the middle. Remember to leave some room for dessert! A large restaurant with a cafeteria ambience. Prepare yourself for a reasonably priced feast and you will not be disappointed. Open until late with loads of parking.

If you like the food in the restaurant, try the Automatic Cafeteria in the Beach Centre which is tiny, cosier and with more atmosphere. Also at the Al Khaleej Centre.

## Awafi

100-150

21:00 - 02:00

JW Marriott Hotel
Deira

Page 11
A 3

Tel: **624 444**

Tables and chairs are situated around the courtyard, as are carpets and coushions in true Arabic style. Climb the stairs to the rooftop viewing gallery overlooking the airport, but mind your head when you stand because the planes fly low in this area! Of course, you could just sit around the rooftop swimming pool, enjoying the starlit skies and peaceful ambience. Or, take your shoes off, relax on the cushions and smoke a hubble bubble pipe.

The simple menu belies the excellent tastes and large portions you will enjoy. Dhs.30 will buy a tandoor cooked chicken, kofta, or shish kebab accompanied by tabouleh, homous, moutabal and baskets of superb, hot and soft tandoori bread. Arabic culinary delights with speciality teas and coffees are served in the warmly-lit ambiance by the pool. Be warned, the alcohol is expensive. However, Awafi is a must for both residents and visitors alike.

## Palmito

100-150

11:00 - 18:00
19:00 - 23:00

Jebel Ali Hotel
Jebel Ali

Tel: **836 000**

The cuisine may be unexceptional but the setting makes up for it. Swaying palms and the sea gently breaking on the beach make the atmosphere at this 'al fresco' outlet truly idyllic. If you are looking for something a little racier, try Monday nights when a live band and belly dancer provide Eastern entertainment to accompany the Arabic cuisine. Menu changes daily with most main course dishes being prepared on the barbecue in the restaurant.

# Arabic Night-Clubs

## Abaya Night Club

150-200

10:30 - 03:00

Dubai Park Hotel
Al Mina Al Siyahi

Page 2
A 3

Tel: **487 111**

A stageside table is the most popular, but be prepared for one of the six Arab dancers to thrust a tightly bound bottom in your salad! Enthusiastic singers make for a very interesting, if noisy, evening. Beware the shooting corks from bottles of sparkling bubbly as a sign of the spellbound audience's appreciation. The dancing may not be what a non-Arab expects, with a few shakes and thrusts broken up by long periods of wandering around the stage and chatting to the other dancers. The entrance fee of Dhs.180 includes dinner.

Maybe not to everyone's taste, but as an experience, it's a must !

## Al Jawhara

100-150

23:00 - 03:00
Closed Sat

Howard Johnson
Deira

Page 10
D 1

Tel: **221 111**

Located in one of the newest hotels in Dubai, this club has a certain uniqueness not found in other Arabic night clubs per se. The decor is created to replicate a traditional Arab fort, with hand painted landscapes that provide the background. The 'Bedouin Tent' theme is incorporated into this entire scenario in order to suggest that a weary traveller can seek respite from a long and arduous journey on the way to his final destination.

Live entertainment provided by Arabic bands and dancers complement authentic Arabic cuisine. This includes a wide array of mezzeh, main courses and desserts, all combined with relatively efficient service. The entrance fee of Dhs.210 includes dinner.

## Al Mushref

100-150

22:00 - 03:00
Closed Sat

St George Hotel
Deira

Page 7
B 2

Tel: **251 122**

There's a nice sleazy feel about going to a nightclub in downtown Deira, but do take precautions by parking your car in the hotel's car park. Sidle past those visiting the Filipino bar on the ground floor, smile at the doormen guarding the corridor and enter a bar on the left, or the nightclub on the right.

After that it's hunky dory. Low lights, spacious room, a pretty young Lebanese singer and an energetic belly dancer are amongst the live entertainment provided. Waiter service is courteous and calculated to allow you plenty of time to enjoy the show. Excess of choices in the mini buffets. The entrance fee of Dhs.180 includes dinner.

## Escoba

100-150

22:30 - 02:00
Closed Fri

Al Khaleej Palace
Deira

Page 10
D 1

Tel: **231 000**

Enter the kingdom of 1001 delights. Fine Lebanese cuisine, distinguished atmosphere and live entertainment. The belly dancer sets the place on fire. Take a camera along.
An elegant taste of Arabia. The entrance fee of Dhs.240 includes dinner.

## Layalina

100-150

23:00 - 03:00
Closed Fri

Metropolitan Hotel
Sh Zayed Rd/Safa

Page 4
C 4

Tel: **440 000**

Go through the innocent doorway, the heavy curtains, and into the low-lit interior of Layalina which exudes a steamy exclusivity when full. Once seated and served, hold a candle close to your plate and you will make out the regulation mixed grill of kebabs, chips and salad, while on stage, the lead singer and band interpret well-known Arabic songs using traditional and the latest Japanese instruments. As the evening develops the band's pace picks up from stroll to trot when the belly dancer jiggles into the arena for the main event. Plush seating in alcoves at the back of the nightclub, or tables around the dance floor offer a choice of location.

If you can stay up very late, this entertainment continues well into the small hours by which time, on a weekend, the place will be full, so book in advance if you want to undertake the whole experience and don't have to get up too early the next day!

The entrance fee of Dhs.222 includes dinner.

# Lebanese

## Al Bahar

50-100

07:00 -00:30 | Chamber of Commerce Building Ground Floor, Deira | Page 10 C 2 | Tel: **278 984**

The view alone is magnificent! If you combine the atmosphere, ambiance, quality of food and service, you know that you are on to a winner. This predominantly Lebanese food restaurant is on the ground floor of the Chamber of Commerce. It is open from 07:00 for breakfast - until very late. Fresh croissants and pastries, a range of coffees, teas and fruit juices are available. The choice of mezzeh, salads and grills is extensive and there is a tempting 'plat du jour'. Al Bahar also does outside catering, take-aways and will soon be carrying out lunch time deliveries. The chairs and tables are wooden, contrasting with the rest of the restaurant's matt silver finish. Ample parking makes this a convenient lunch-time destination. The terrace outside is ideal for coffees in the morning, lazy lunches, or dinner under the stars taking in the atmosphere of the Creek. The view is fantastic - and so is the restaurant.

## Al Diwan

100-150

12:30 - 15:00
20:00 - 02:30 | Metropolitan Palace Deira | Page 10 D 2 | Tel: **270 000**

Traditional Lebanese cuisine in an original setting. Listen to the marvelous songs of Arabia, be enchanted by the rhythmic motions of the belly dancer and a whole evening's entertainment can be found in Al Diwan.

The menu includes traditional Lebanese cuisine with assorted mezzeh and grills. In addition full ouzis, caviar, and other specialities feature on the menu. Of course, all these dishes are accompanied by freshly baked Arabic breads. At night the restaurant offers live entertainment with a band, singers and belly dancer.

## Al Mandaloun

50-100

12:00 - 15:00
19:00 - 24:00 | Al Khaleej Palace Deira | Page 10 D 1 | Tel: **231 000**

If you go down to the souk you might meet your chef for the night, as Al Mandaloun's own butcher carefully selects fresh meat and fish daily, and the chef can be spotted at the vegetable souk, buying the freshest fruit and vegetables of the day.

Reservations are recommended, especially on Wednesday and Thursday evenings which are very busy in this replica of an old Lebanese home. The ingredients for a delightful evening are time and appetite. With 82 dishes in the mezzeh, you really have to pace yourself. Two of the mouth watering delights are hot spinach fatayer and steak tartar, consisting of minced meat and buck wheat eaten with virgin olive oil. Provided adequate warning is given, the whole restaurant may be booked - ideal for a big birthday party!

## Al Qasr

12:00 - 15:00
19:30 - 01:00

Dubai Marine Beach Resort
Jumeira

Page 5
D 2

Tel: **441 221**

A very spacious, airy restaurant ideal for a party booking or equally suitable for a quiet dinner for two. You can start the evening by relaxing in the Arabic style lounge sipping a drink while watching the fountain play. Then go through to the restaurant where an extensive menu awaits you. What better way to wash it all down than with a glass of traditional Arak. This aniseed flavoured beverage comes highly recommended.

## Al Sarab

19:00 - 01:00
Closed Sat

Forte Grand - Jumeira Beach
Al Mina Al Siyahi

Page 1
E 2

Tel: **845 555**

Walk into Al Sarab, which means The Mirage, and be greeted by a clap of hands - you have just been announced! Meet your dinner companions in the bar decorated with local artifacts including antique doors converted into large coffee tables. Stroll through the curtains of an opulent tent into a large Arabic nightclub with huge curved windows overlooking the sea.

It is preferable to reserve a table near the stage if you want a good view of the cabaret acts... and the fluid movements of the new, good looking typically dressed lebanese, belly dancer is something not to be missed. Al Sarab very definitely caters more to the tastes of the affluent local population, rather than the ogling tourist, though they are also welcome. The band, Al Shorooq, is well known and Rifaat Sanam, the resident singer, is popular and highly rated. Extensive wine list and good food with substantial starters and main course.

## Al Tannour

20:00 - 03:00
Closed Fri

Holiday Inn Crowne Plaza
Sh Zayed Rd

Page 8
D 2

Tel: **311 111**

At the Al Tannour hospitality is more than just the welcoming smile or attentive service, it's the authentic Lebanese cuisine, live entertainment and belly dancer. It's in the splendid traditional decor, and, most importantly, it comes from the desire to make the experience very special every time you visit. Late evening start, don't even think of going until well after 23:00 or you might have to watch the cleaners vacuuming the carpet!

## Ayam Zaman

100-150

19:30 - 03:00 | Dubai Marine Hotel, Bur Dubai | Page 7, A 3 | Tel: **520 900**

Walk down the stone clad tunnel leading to Ayam Zaman and you arrive in the heart of Lebanon in "the good old days", which is its literal translation. Waiters wearing traditional Cherwal dress and Tarbouche hats lead you to a table already crammed with food. There are

carpets on the walls, lights straight from 1001 Nights and the smell of freshly chopped tabouleh hangs in the air.

There is no need to know the meaning of Falafel or Kebbeh, nor to spend a lot of time choosing what to order, because this restaurant has a set meal of 24 items starting with a cold mezzeh, a warm mezzeh, a mixed grill and a variety of sweets which are followed by Arabic coffee. Each course stays on the table till it's all gone (impossible) or you nod at the waiter to indicate that you've eaten your fill and wish to embark on the next course. This is not the place for a quick meal, most people start arriving at about 21:30 and stay for three hours or more. For an additional Dhs.25 you can get an apple or strawberry flavoured nargile (water pipe) to puff at. The clientele is predominantly Lebanese, who all seem to know the words sung by the live band and joyously join in.

## Istanbouli

50-100

12:00 - 15:30<br>18:00 - 24:00 | Al Diyafah Rd, Al Satwa | Page 6, A 4 | Tel: **450 123**

There is a typical Mediterranean taverna in Satwa, it has been there since 1979 and is still being discovered by new generations of expatriate residents and tourists alike. The Istanbouli is a whitewashed stucco restaurant with simple furnishings and decor, giving a nice clean feeling. Freshly cooked food is provided by the Metropolitan Hotel's outside catering division as this is an Al Habtoor property.

Complimentary starters, dessert and coffee mean that you pay only for the main course of barbecued meats/fish of your choice. Many enjoy lunching or dining on the outside verandah.

## Mawal

100-150

13:00 - 16:00<br>19:00 - 01:00 | Al Bustan Rotana Hotel, Al Garhoud | Page 14, E 3 | Tel: **820 000**

If you are looking for authentic, fresh, home-cooked Lebanese food, this is the place to go. Offering what must be the best Lebanese food in Dubai, you will certainly not leave on an empty stomach. Ask any of the welcoming staff for their house specialties and recommendations. Try the small sausages, goat labneh, or marinated orange peel for something a little different. Both traditional and the more exotic and interesting Lebanese dishes are served. The restaurant is very handy for Sharjah residents and residents in the Deira area and the new interchanges make it easy to get to/from Bur Dubai and Jumeira.

## See Also:

**Dinner Cruises - Tours**

# Persian

## Alborz

50-100

12:30 - 16:00
19:00 - 24:00

Nr. City Tower
Sh Zayed Rd

Page 8
D 2

Tel: **318 777**

A beautiful restaurant with stone walls and tiles, a small fountain, Persian music in the background, small intricate paintings of Persian nobles from a long ago era, and beautiful carved tables. Little alcoves provide privacy and a romantic touch with a view of the Abu Dhabi highway. This is a classy place and definely worth a visit.

Try "Mumtaz Alborz" the Iranian kebab which is 60cm long and very tasty. If you're feeling adventurous, try the Iranian caviar and Iranian ice-cream. Friday lunch offers a Persian buffet at Dhs.55 per head (Dhs.25/child) and live classical Persian music.

## Iranian Club

50-100

22:00 - 03:00

St George Hotel
Deira

Page 7
B 2

Tel: **251 122**

The Iranian Club is one of Dubai's best kept secrets with regard to nightlife. Seven musicians perform in English, Arabic and Farsi to a packed audience (250 on Thursdays) which is very mixed - Turkish, Locals, Armenians, Iranian and Lebanese to mention but a few. The cover charge on a Thursday - Dhs.100 nett includes a buffet dinner. It is advisable to come before 24:00 to get a table.

## Pars Iranian Kitchen

50-100

12:00 - 15:30
18:00 - 24:00

Nr. Dubai Plaza Hotel
Al Satwa

Page 6
A 4

Tel: **452 222**

A great restaurant for that intimate meal for two in a cosy Arabic/Asian environment, and also for groups. Dhs.450 will get you a full Quzi (whole lamb) cooked for your party at home. The menu offers a wide variety of typical Iranian dishes which are very good value for money. Starters vary from soups and salads, to Iranian caviar, and main courses from steaks, seafood and kebabs, to Iranian BBQ and stews. But if all this choice seems too much, the Pars Iranian Special for two or four people comes highly recommended as it offers a combination of kebab, chicken, shrimps and potato, with different types of steamed, flavoured rice.

## Persian Garden

100-150

12:30 - 15:00
19:30 - 24:00

Sheraton Hotel
Deira

Page 10
C 1

Tel: **207 1731**

Authentic Iranian decor including lots of blue mosaic tiles and filigree metalwork. A live band every night and a belly dancer on Sundays, Wednesdays and Thursdays offer lively entertainment. It is advisable to book to ensure a comfortable seat at the middle tables.

Persian haute cuisine, with helpful advice from staff about content. Generous servings. Try the caviar, kebabs and stews. Easy access from the car park means no traipsing through a hotel lobby and guests. Friday brunch available.

## Shabestan

100-150

13:00 - 15:15
20:00 - 23:15

**Inter-Continental Hotel Deira** | **Page 7 C 4** | Tel: **227 171**

Step through the entrance and follow the beautiful tiled corridor, where a tantalising smell of spices entices you into the restaurant. A complimentary platter of fresh vegetables,

warm sesame bread and a delightful yoghurt dip, are immediately placed on your table. The menu has a great range of hearty soups, salads, fish, kebabs, stews and desserts.

The Shabestan and Daily specials are highly recommended as they carefully blend the fruits and meats to offer a delightful generous Persian experience. Reservations necessary, ask for a table by the window if you wish to see Dubai's night lights. Three function rooms, seating up to 10 people, are also available.

## Shahrzad

100-150

20:00 - 24:00

**Hyatt Regency Hotel Deira** | **Page 7 D 2** | Tel: **706 4812**

Stroll into the luxuriously elegant atmosphere of this Iranian restaurant to experience the 'olde worlde' charm of Persia. Colourfully costumed staff show you to one of several different types of seating, at tables on the balcony overlooking the main hotel foyer, in peek-a-boo screened alcoves, or at party sized tables.

Authentic musicians serenade you as you dine. Try the stew where the cooler top layer is eaten separately from the meat, and potatoes which are mashed at the table with a pestle and mortar. There is a supplementary menu that changes on a weekly basis - guaranteeing freshness and variety. Helpings are perfectly balanced, allowing the hearty eater to partake in a three course meal. The wine list is extensive, as is the price.

# Friday Brunch

## Alamo, The

50-100

11:00 - 16:00 | Dubai Marine Beach Resort, Jumeira | Page 5, D 2 | Tel: 441 221

Recently voted as the top Friday Brunch by *What's On,* and probably the most popular. Options - include a generous buffet of fresh fruit, waffles, croissants and the complete range of cooked breakfasts. Especially popular are the omelettes, where you choose your fillings and watch it being made. If all this is not enough for Dhs.55 (Dhs.35 for kids), then you had better move on to the Mexican favourites, including enchiladas, fajitas, spare ribs and other Tex-Mex titbits. The pace is unhurried and service is leisurely, inducing you into relaxation mode. Happy faces are seen all around with laughter the predominant sound. Reservations are a must.

## Biggles

0-50

11:00 - 15:00 | Airport Hotel, Al Garhoud | Page 14, D 3 | Tel: 823 464

Walk into this English pub, with its World War II Royal Air Force memorabilia, and you either remember the fictitious character of your childhood reading, or the comical copycat sketch by Russ Abbott. It also displays collected items from the more recent Gulf War. Informal, great pub food, light entertainment and a favourite meeting place for expat residents. Carvery night every Tuesday. Children are welcome to the Friday brunch. Brunch consists of a breakfast buffet and barbecued food. (Dhs.35, Dhs.15 for kids)

## Cafe Insignia

50-100

11:30 - 15:00 | Ramada Hotel, Bur Dubai | Page 6, E 3 | Tel: 506 1180

Cafe Insignia is tastefully decorated to give a European-style atmosphere, with Italian plastered walls hung with garlic, onions and pots of olive oil. Wrought iron furniture, potted plants and brightly coloured hanging prints add to the feel.

The Mediterranean style buffet is more of a lunch than a breakfast and is somewhat smaller in choice than other brunches, particularly given the set price of Dhs.65 nett. However, tasty alternatives are offered from continental salads, hot fish and meat dishes, chicken coconut curry, and beef bacon, to tempting gateaux, fresh fruit and cheese. Blackboard menus, as well as a la carte, are also available. The staff are very friendly, helpful and prompt but unobtrusive, which also adds to the tranquil atmosphere. It's easy to relax in this unhurried atmosphere, enjoy the buffet and loose track of time.

## Cheers

11:00 - 15:30 | Lodge, The, Al Nasa | Page 9, E 4 | Tel: **379 470**

0-50

If you thought that the Lodge was for the young, free and single, or you thought that Friday brunches were from around 11:00 to 14:00, you couldn't be more wrong! Number one, this is a real family affair, and number two, its for the whole day! Fun for the kids includes magic shows, kids disco, videos, cartoons and even soft toys. The lodge is thoroughly cleaned from the night before, and large tables are filled with a continental and Thai style buffet. All for Dhs.40 (Dhs.20 for children). Breakfast is served from 11:00 - 12:30, and then lunch from 12:30 - 15:30.

In the early evening, yet more food, but this time for their retro show, and "a feast of specialities from the British Isles", including sea-food and all you can eat for Dhs.20. At 17:00 the karaoke starts! Once again reservations for a table are a 'must'.

## Dubliners

12:00 - 15:00 | Forte Grand Dubai, Al Garhoud | Page 14, E 3 | Tel: **702 2508**

0-50

The first of Dubai's Irish pubs, Dubliners has rustic wooden furniture, bits and pieces from old Ireland and a fun-loving clientele. An atmospheric courtyard almost doubles the capacity.

A hearty breakfast for Dhs.35 is offered on Fridays, consisting of streaky bacon, eggs, sausage, beans, grilled tomatoes, mushrooms, black pudding, home-made chips and a drink. Other meals from the menu are also available. A 'must' is the fresh home-made bread which is really superb, and can also be bought by the loaf to take-away.

Dubliner's Breakfast Club meets every other Friday with activities ranging from scuba diving to clay-pigeon shooting. Membership for the day includes breakfast, BBQ, 3 drinks and the activity of the day - very popular with deserted husbands in the summer, and an excellent way to meet new friends.

## Harvesters Pub

12:00 - 16:00 | Holiday Inn Crowne Plaza, Sh Zayed Rd | Page 8, D 2 | Tel: **311 111**

0-50

A great place to relax and enjoy an extensive and good quality selection of either traditional English breakfast, Sunday lunch dishes (Roast lamb, potatoes and gravy) or to sample more exotic specials such as the local seafood. A la carte dishes also available, as are excellent desserts and fresh fruit. Outside, the breezy and shady terrace provides a perfect environment in which to relax.

Friday brunch here attracts local residents leisurely scanning newspapers, families, and tourists staying in the hotel. Available from noon through to 16:00 it is good value at Dhs.40 (Dhs.20 for a child) plus tax.

## Inter-Con. Fun Food Festival

100-150

13:00 -16:00 | Inter-Continental Hotel, Deira | Page 7, C 4 | Tel: **227 171**

One set price per adult (Dhs.99++) gives a choice of selections from many of the hotel's popular outlets. The idea is that brunchers stroll around the balcony that connects restaurant to restaurant and choose specialities from each of them. Japanese sushi or tempura prawns/vegetables; Persian mezzeh, herb rice and meat kebabs; Italian pasta; fish from the Fish Market; and, of course, traditional English breakfast from Pub, are all available. Children's selections such as burgers and flat breads are available too. Oh, by the way, children pay according to their height so the social meal starts with them seeing which archway they can comfortably walk through.

## Le Classic

50-100

12:00 - 16:00 | Emirates Golf Club, Al Mina Al Siyahi | Page 2, A 3 | Tel: **480 222**

You don't have to be a member to enjoy the fine dining experience of this well loved restaurant. You don't have to book ahead, either, but it helps to get past the security gateman if you phone prior to setting off. Typical British, American and Continental breakfast are on offer items such eggs, kidneys, mushrooms, tomatoes, waffles, croissants and danish pastries. But leave room for the lunch part of brunch as the steaks, pies, salmon wellington and other delicacies are cooked to perfection and very yummy. Light and bright dining room overlooking the quiet and more wooded part of the golf course. Dhs.60 per person (Dhs.30 for children).

## Marco Polo

50-100

11:00 - 15:30 | Dubai Marine Hotel, Bur Dubai | Page 7, A 3 | Tel: **520 900**

" I definitely know one of the reasons that drive Marco Polo's passion to travel between China, India and Thailand for 17 years". Covering the entire 5th floor of the Dubai Marine Hotel, the Marco Polo experience entails a spacious lounge, dining area with a large aquarium of exotic fish and spacious terrace garden. A sumptuous brunch buffet is set out to entice even the most difficult of palates as you are serenaded by the resident Paraguayan band. A team of chefs have prepared a breakfast selection, including fruit juices, Danish pastries, Croissants, breakfast station - eggs cooked to your liking, omelettes with mushrooms, tomatoes etc, pancake station - fruit and sweet pancakes made to order, pasta station, salad counter (hot & Cold), Carvery - special of the day, selection of cheeses and desserts. For Dhs.55 (plus tax) per person you can eat as much as you like plus free welcome drink on arrival and unlimited tea and coffee. Excellent value for money.

## Spice Island

50-100

12:00 - 15:00 | Royal Abjar, Deira | Page 11, A 3 | Tel: **625 555**

Forget about Adventure or Treasure Island - there is a new island you will wish to get marooned on: The Spice Island at the Royal Abjar Hotel. Step through the beckoning entrance and enter another world.

The surroundings are very relaxing with a waterfall fountain so that you can truly imagine that you have been cast upon a Polynesian island.

Picture yourself in a food souk with a great variety of fresh dishes from China, Polynesia, Thailand, Korea, Japan, Malaysia, India and Mexico - and all for a set price. It is not possible to savour all of the 300 delights on your first visit and once tempted you won't want to go to any other Dubai Friday Brunch. Except for the traditional English breakfast goodies, dessert buffet and a salad bar, all other items are cooked a la minute which means they are fresh, fresh and fresh!

Children - young and old are looked after with continuous videos, a magician and a children's buffet to make them feel even more special. (Those under 12 are free).

# Friday Brunch / BBQ

## Metropolitan Beach Resort

100-150

10:00 - 15:30 | Metropolitan Beach Club, Al Mina Al Siyahi | Page 1 E 2 | Tel: **845 000**

A great way to spend a lazy Friday. The barbecue is situated beneath the palm trees, on a grassy area next to the beach and an excellent musical duo adds to the very relaxed, pleasant atmosphere. The menu for the day is chalked up on a board and ranges from chicken kebabs, to gorgeous steaks and seafood. After you have made your choice, the food is expertly barbecued to your requirements - the barbecued lobster is something not to be missed! The entrance fee is Dhs.150, two thirds of which entitles you to use the beach, swimming pool and all the facilities while Dhs.50 goes towards your food and beverages.

## Forte Grand Jumeira Beach

100-150

12:00 - 15:00 | Forte Grand - Jumeira Beach, Al Mina Al Siyahi | Page 1 E 2 | Tel: **845 555**

Forget your worries and enjoy the holiday ambience of swaying palm trees, South American band, shady patio umbrellas and comfy sunloungers around the pool. Tantalising smells of barbecued meats and seafood, without a sausage in sight, can be slowly enjoyed at this up-market buffet lunch. High quality international cuisine includes Arabic, Italian, Thai and Indian. Don't rush, take your time and enjoy the afternoon. Swim up to the pool bar for a welcome beverage, or ask the waiter to get one for you. Dhs.110 per person for lunch only, Dhs.150 pp with pool and beach access. Half price for under 12's.

## Hyatt Regency Poolside BBQ

50-100

19:00 - 23:30
Mondays only

Hyatt Regency Hotel
Deira

Page 7
D 2

Tel: **706 4839**

Whether you wish a romantic dinner or an evening with friends, this first floor poolside barbecue is definitely something to try, especially when the surroundings are Arabian skies, twinkling stars and hopefully, a pleasant breeze.

Let temptation overwhelm you when viewing the extensive array of international dishes. Help yourselves once, twice, or more, but do remember to save a little room for desserts of chocolate brownies, cheesecake or small Arabic cakes and sweets. The buffet barbecue takes place from 19.00 onwards and is priced at Dhs.75++. Available as long as weather permits. Call to avoid disappointment.

Cook your steak, lamb medallion, chicken, hammour, shrimps or salmon exactly the way you like it on your own personal sizzling hot stone, carefully brought to the table. If the cooking goes wrong blame it on the chef- i.e. you!

## Jebel Ali Hotel

100-150

11:30 - 16:00

Jebel Ali Hotel
Jebel Ali

Tel: **836 000**

With the Arabian Sea on one side and extensive gardens on the other, this barbecue has a luxurious feel about it. Hawaiian shirt clad waiters and gentle Caribbean music combine to create a sunny, carefree, holiday atmosphere. Excellent food with plenty of salads, grilled dishes and seafood comprise an extravagant feast with varied types of cooking. Mixed clientele of hotel guests and families of Dubai residents.

Stroll through the lush gardens to see the hotel's peacocks, grouse and stables with horses, deer, camels and llama. Try out the gymnasium and table tennis at Club Joumana, view the private boats in the marina or just snooze under the palms. Dhs.150 per person includes use of hotel facilities including Club Joumana. Dhs.95 for children.

# Cafes

## Academy

07:00 - 23:00 | Dubai Creek Golf Club, Al Garhoud | Page 14, C 2 | Tel: **822 789**

Found within the clubhouse building which houses a golf shop and the main booking desk for the Par Three Course, this small cafe area has half a dozen well spaced tables which are casually served from midday onwards. Sandwiches and coffee mainly for those who have just played, or are waiting to start their golf lessons. Terrace overlooking the putting and driving range.

## Admiral Tea Lounge

10:30 - 21:00 | Admiral Plaza, The, Deira | Page 6, E 2 | Tel: **521 111**

The Admiral Tea Lounge is located on the mezzanine floor overlooking the Lobby and offers a variety of choices in both Tea and Coffee. Special High Tea menu for early/late afternoon.

## Cafe Des Pyramides

09:30 - 13:00
16:40 - 21:30 Closed Fri am | Wafi Shopping Mall, Al Nasa | Page 13, D 2 | Tel: **346 866**

Located on the first floor of the Wafi shopping centre Cafe Des Pyramides conveying the upmarket style of a Parisian street cafe, complete with window flower boxes and authentic French prices. Situated under one of the Wafi's pyramids it provides a convenient and airy retiring place for the weary shopper. Tempting selection of gateaux, snacks and light meals prepared freshly each day in continental style.

## Cafe Wien

08:00 - 24:00
Closed Fri am | Beach Centre, The, Jumeira | Page 5, B 2 | Tel: **448 001**

Among the palm fronds and fig trees lies an Austrian patisserie which also serves meals and snacks. Relax and listen to the tinkling sounds of a baby grand piano being expertly played each evening, or chat and watch shoppers walking around the large shopping mall. Evening gowns and toys, carpets and leather bags, rosewood furniture and glass ornaments vie for your attention in the shops. Let them wait while you sit and sup in peace.

Excellent variety of choice and prices for items as diverse as cappuccino, weiner schnitzel and Austrian tortes and cakes. Selected menu of the day for Dhs.25. Part of a chain with similar outlets in Vienna, Brazil and France.

## Earls

09:00 - 22:00 | Hamarain Centre, Deira | Page 11, A 4 | Tel: **661 922**

This is the type of lunch time restaurant you would find in central London, being frequented by businessmen and women during their office break. Conveniently located in the Hamarain Centre's Food Court, part of the J.W. Marriott hotel complex, and there's lots of parking. Earls is aptly named after the Earl of Sandwich but there is more to choose from here than just sandwiches. There are four new salads every day, a hearty soup, baked potatoes with a choice of fillings, fruit juices, various sandwiches and rolls - fresh or toasted plus a variety of freshly made cakes.

Earls will also deliver near and far; companies in Jebel Ali are currently making use of this facility. There are seven small tables with modern wrought iron chairs to sit on and chat the day away. Very popular with the ladies!

## Gelato

**10:00 - 01:00** | **Dune Centre, Al Satwa** | **Page 5, E 3** | Tel: **451 685**

Gelato can be found in the pink/bronzed glass Dune Centre mall. Tastefully decorated with comfortable wrought iron chairs and glass walls that allow you to relax and watch the world go by. There are several tables outside on a terrace - great in the cooler months. Boasts 48 flavours of exotic and traditional Italian ice creams, all home made by the company, and also available in local supermarkets. Upstairs is a speciality restaurant that offers scrumptious Italian salads, delightful sandwiches, fresh Italian pastas and delicious pizzas - not forgetting espresso, cappuccino, fresh juices and traditional Italian desserts. The 'piece de resistance' is the Tiramisu that you can take home for your next dinner party!

## Gerard

**08:30 - 22:00** | **Magrudy Shopping Mall, Jumeira** | **Page 5, C 2** | Tel: **443 327**

Gerard's Cafe was one of the first European-style coffee shops to be established in Dubai. It is a typical French Coffee shop where people of all nationalities meet. In general, a very pleasant atmosphere, especially the one located in the Magrudy centre, with its ever popular shaded terrace.

A wonderful place to enjoy reading the papers, together with coffee and freshly baked croissants in the traditional French manner. Also on offer are various freshly made cakes and sandwiches. Very popular Friday morning.

Gerard's in the Al Ghurair Centre offers pretty much the same, however the clientele is slightly different, orientated more towards Nationals. Both coffee shops have the added attraction of being well placed, and thus allowing the casual coffee drinker the pleasure of watching the world go by. A place to see and be seen!

## Internet Cafe

**09:00 - 01:00, Closed Fri am** | **Dune Centre, Al Satwa** | **Page 5, E 3** | Tel: **453 390**

Without a doubt this is probably the coolest cafe to arrive in Dubai... reaches parts that others can not. Apart from being the only coffee shop in Dubai to access the Internet, it's also the only place to have such a good mix of ages and nationalities. Nice contrast between the tastefully decorated traditional Arabic style, with wooden beam, palm leaves and brass lanterns. A peaceful environment combining the gurgling of the cappuccino machine and clicks of the keyboard and mouse.

Access to the Internet from one of the 35 terminals costs Dhs.12.50 per hour (cheap).

Each terminal has its own custom built table with well angled monitor, and if you want to download information onto a floppy, or print, even in colour?... Hey, everything is possible! Membership scheme allows people to have their own e.mail address. Technicians on hand all day to offer guidance and assistance. Courses during the day in a separate room upstairs.

Opening at 09:00, everything has been thought of, with a choice of American / Continental / Arabic breakfasts at Dhs.12, or sandwiches, burgers and even a buffet for lunch. If this is too much, try the variety of teas, coffees, fruit juices, cocktails or assortment of cakes. Amusing service... Remember though that once you're surfing time flies.

## La Brioche

**07:30 - 23:00** | **Jumeirah Plaza, Jumeira** | **Page 5, C 2** | Tel: **490 588**

Savoury filled croissants, hefty salads and pasta dishes for Dhs.10-30. Wash it all down with an espresso or cup of hot chocolate - Delicious! A pleasant place to sit gossiping with a friend or the children during a shopping trip. Quiet lunchtimes makes these preferred meeting places for business ladies and gents.

## La Gaufrette

**08:00 - 22:30** | **Bur Juman Centre, Bur Dubai** | **Page 10, A 1** | Tel: **518 688**

Four different locations for this quiet coffee shop which has a range of in-house baked pastries and cakes, ice creams, Belgian chocolates, and a great menu for meals. The house speciality is waffles, and salads that are very fresh and healthy. Cappuccinos have lots of froth and you could allow a morning to float by if you were keen to sit around catching up with friends. Congenial atmosphere. Local delivery service, perfect for all the offices close to one of the four locations. Very reasonable prices.

## Lobby Lounge

**24:00 hrs** | **Hyatt Regency Hotel, Deira** | **Page 7, D 2** | Tel: **706 4816**

A traditional open fronted Arabic tent awaits your arrival in the Hyatt's lobby. Sit down on the cushions, tuck your feet into the carpets and drink a cup of cardamon coffee with your host. If he is not there, sit down anyway and enjoy a moment or two of traditional welcome. Lovely photo opportunity. Located right next to the 24-hr Caravan Cafe. If you are lucky, the sound of a piano will accompany you, as well as a strolling band of three musicians. Afternoon tea is enjoyed 15:00 - 17:30 when tiny freshly baked cakes, pastries and sandwiches tempt you to indulge, with a pot of tea. Open seven days a week with a 24hrs buffet.

## Tower Bridge Cafe

**10:00 - 22:00** | **Lamcy Plaza, Al Karama** | **Page 9, D 4** | Tel: **345 050**

Fancy tea on top of Tower Bridge? Stop for refreshment on London's Tower Bridge overlooking the expanse of Dubais biggest department store. A light airy cafe offering light meals, pastries and a range of fruit juices and other beverages.

## Trocadero

19:30 - 03:00 | Jumeira Plaza, Jumeira | Page 5, C 2 | Tel: **497 777**

Where else can you enjoy the sun in an air conditioned atmosphere? The pink shopping plaza, of course. The central, glass domed atrium lets in plenty of natural light while decorative fountains, marble floors and cool air conditioning make this a quietly pleasant place to meet for a pot of hot chocolate, cup of espresso, or a nice cup of tea. Early morning breakfast is served from 07:00 onwards and singles can often be seen downing a coffee and hot croissant for Dhs.6.

## West One

07:00 - 19:00 | Safa Tower, Sh Zayed Rd | Page 8, C 2 | Tel: **316 900**

You have to be doing something right to sell over 500 sandwiches a day! One located in Safa tower, with a balcony converted into a colourful terrace, and mainly known for its take-away and delivery service of sandwiches. New location on the first floor in the Al Markaz Centre in Jumeira. Sharon, the founder, tries to ensure that her customers receive superior service with personal attention. Also provides catering from cold and hot buffets to barbecues with tailor made menus and prices. These can vary from Dhs.30 - 75 per person depending on chosen menu and numbers. From boardrooms to back gardens, all the necessary items are supplied. The colourfully designed sandwich menu also includes a wide variety of salads, jacket potatoes and ice cream. Recommended is the W1 Club sandwich at Dhs.16, which comes with potato salad, coleslaw and crisps.

# Ice-Cream Parlours

## Baskin Robbins

10:00 - 22:00 | Various Locations | Tel: **366 636**

There are many Baskin Robbins' around town, usually not very far from a shopping area or fast food outlet. The outlet in Al Diyafa Street, Satwa has customers at all times of the day, right up to late evening when teenagers like to finish their burger meal with a crunchy cone and two flavours of ice cream, please. Malls such as Markaz Al Jumeira and Park N Shop, however, attract families and single people who just like the choice of American flavours such as Banana Nut, Cookies And Cream, Fudge Brownies or Chocolate Chip Mint. Speciality cakes available, made totally from ice cream, ask to seek the photo album of designer cakes.

## Gelato

10:00 - 01:00 | Dune Centre, Al Satwa | Page 5, E 3 | Tel: **451 685**

You get a little more flavour for a little more money at Gelato where home made Italian ice cream is the order of the day. Choose from a comprehensive list of sundaes, toppings, concoctions and plain old fashioned ices. Plenty of flavourful ideas displayed on the pictures on the menu. Gelato also serves Italian meals of pasta in full and half size portions. Choose your own shaped pasta and mix it with one of the many well loved sauces. Everything is freshly made to order.

## Lazzerin

15:00 - 24:00 | Forte Grand Dubai, Al Garhoud | Page 14, E 3 | Tel: **824 040**

Real Italian ice-cream prepared for you by the chef, Mauricio Lazzarin, third generation of a family of ice-cream / makers from northern Italy. Served in creations rich in shapes and flavours, as well as in straight scoops. Twelve flavours are prepared daily. Enjoy your choice of ice-cream with coffee and drinks sitting inside Lazzerin, or on the terrace. Very favourable prices, or take-away your ice-cream in boxes of 1/2, 1 or 2 kilos.

## Le Glacier Moderne

08:00 - 22:00, Closed Fri am | Bur Juman Centre, Bur Dubai | Page 10, A 1 | Tel: **517 027**

Two enormous counters with over 36 flavours on display. The premises is fitted with six black art deco tables and chairs. Either buy the standard cones at Dhs.5 a scoop, or the special take out, well heat insulated family boxes (One litre Dhs.35, one and half litre at Dhs.45). Ice cream for all types, from yogurt, nougat, Kulfi, coconut, bubble gum to fruit flavours; lemon, strawberry, mango, banana and pineapple. For chocolate fans, there is white chocolate, dark chocolate, hazelnut, chocolate nuts, with almonds, black chocolate, chocolate chip, mint chocolate, etc. For something unusual, order one of their ice-cream cakes.

# Bars / Pubs

## Beach / Water Front Bars

### Barasti Bar

09:00 - 23:00 | **Dubai International Marine Club**, **Al Mina Al Siyahi** | **Page 2**, **A 2** | Tel: **846 111**

Located in the Dubai International Marine Club, there's no taped music here, just the occasional mellow band and the lapping of waves on the beach to provide the perfect background for an intimate starlight rendezvous. Go there during the day and you can amble past the sunbathers and children to enjoy a drink under thatched palm fronds. Reminiscent of secluded Far Eastern beach bars, this type of place is a novelty in Dubai. Enjoy a cocktail and savour the peacefulness.

A boardwalk runs from the beach up to a two-level terraced bar, come early to enjoy that holiday feeling overlooking the sea, in natural surroundings. Sandwiches available for the peckish. Probably the coolest, down to earth outside bar in town!

### Poolside Bar

10:00 - 23:00 | **Hyatt Regency Hotel**, **Deira** | **Page 7**, **D 2** | Tel: **706 4839**

You'll never guess where this snack bar is located! One of the coolest places to have a drink, literally, due to its incredible location besides the pool overlooking the sea. This first floor bar is set amongst Roman style columns, a beautiful pool and tennis courts. A relatively quiet place serving food prepared on the spot. Phone to find out about the speciality nights that are held here as they are good fun and of a high standard. Winter months can bring a chilly breeze so remember to take a jacket, open to non-members after 18:00.

### Spike Bar

06:00 - 24:00 | **Dubai Creek Golf & Yacht Club**, **Al Garhoud** | **Page 14**, **C 2** | Tel: **821 000**

A place to wear your best casuals. Members and non members use the lounge style dining area for lunch as it is a lovely spot to meet business friends. Look through the picture windows and see a haven of green calmness in the hustle and bustle of a busy desert city. Inexpensive menu of large salads, well known pasta dishes and plain choices.

Large bar area for those who want to sip while they try out the complimentary hot nibbles during early evening, i.e. between 18:00 and 19:00. Get there before they run out. Special golf rates apply for early evenings until dusk, and this Bar is usually well used until then.

### See Also:

Restaurants - **Boardwalk**

**Breakwater** - Dubai Marine Beach Club (~Nov 97)

# English Pubs

## Biggles

12:30 - 24:00 | Airport Hotel, Al Garhoud | Page 14, D 3 | Tel: **823 464**

Walk into this English pub with its World War II Royal Air Force memorabilia and you either remember the fictious character of your boyhood reading, or the comical copycat sketch by Russ Abbott. It has also collected items from the more recent Gulf War. Informal, great pub food, light entertainment and a favourite meeting place of expat residents. Carvery night every Tuesday.

## Carpenter's Bar

12:00 - 15:00, 18:00 - 02:00 | Hyatt Regency Hotel, Deira | Page 7, D 2 | Tel: **706 4815**

"Meet you at Carpenter's before we go on to... " is an often repeated phrase. A convivial place to meet the gang before moving onto one of the many shows/restaurants/theme nights organised by the hotel. Located at the far end of the hotel lobby this is a popular bar with residents, hotel guests and Hyatt Galleria apartment tenants.

The bar, bathed in the soft glow of polished woodwork and mirrors, creates a cosy atmosphere which is warm and welcoming. A full range of drinks are available (fairly expensive) including both alcoholic and non alcoholic cocktails, plus draft beverages. The atmosphere becomes very alive in the evenings with a Filipino band who dance, sing and play all kinds of tunes. Food is only available in the evenings.

## Cheers

11:00 - 15:30 | Lodge, The, Al Nasa | Page 9, E 4 | Tel: **379 470**

If you want a really quiet place to eat, and I mean quiet, have a casual meal at Cheers in the early evenings before the revellers for next door arrive. Located inside the Highland Lodge nightclub, this is a great place to "meet and eat" before the dancing starts. It is well known for theme and promotion nights, so it may be useful to check what's on. Traditional hearty British dishes, as well as Italian, Indian or vegetarian from The Lodge's other nearby outlets. At lunchtime, Cheer's transforms into a bright and airy restaurant with a special buffet lunch at Dhs.45 per person.

## Chelsea Arms

12:00 - 16:00, 18:00 - 01:00 | Sheraton Hotel, Deira | Page 10, C 1 | Tel: **207 1721**

Begorrah, begosh. A real English pub run by an English Manageress. A long, dark panelled room with stained glass windows: no flashing lights, disco beat or excessive loud noise, except on special nights. Clientele is "older" and jazz and blues is played a lot. High quality familiar pub food such as pies, is available at reasonable prices. Relaxed, friendly and very mixed clientele. Talented Filipino band plays on Mondays and Wednesday. Daily traditional English buffet costs Dhs.36.

## Cyclone Pub

12:00 - 15:00
19:00 - 24:00

Cyclone, Al Nasa — Page 9, D 4

Tel: **369 991**

This is definitely not a lively place in the early evenings, which makes it ideal for those who want to talk over old times while enjoying a pint. Wait until after 21:00 for the pace to hot up and the punters to arrive from other venues. Many use it as a warming up place for the Cyclone's nightclub next door, especially on a Thursday night. A live band performs throughout the week.

Friday night is 'gig night' with local bands playing live, encouraging members of the young audience to jam or join along with them. Whether you play drums, saxaphone or sing, an audience awaits you. Become a Cyclone member for free, get there around 21:00, grab a table and have a drink. Then tuck into the rough and ready buffet (pub food fare recommended over the menu dishes, not least because it's also free). Now you are ready to enjoy the music which starts after ten. The smokey live-gig environment is soon throbbing, with members interested in a bite, a pint and music with soul.

## English Pub, The

18:00 - 01:00

Carlton Tower, The, Deira — Page 7, C 4

Tel: **227 111**

Entering the smokey, dark, low-ceilinged room is like stepping into an English working mens club - without the Englishmen. Seating is either in booths or at round tables throughout the room. From these vantage points men of various Arab nationalities stare at any new people entering the pub, which can be very disconcerting. Not a place for women to go alone.

## Fox & Hounds

12:00 - 16:00
18:00 - 02:00

Novotel, Deira — Page 7, C 4

Tel: **235 000**

Bright, light and plenty of seats. Perfect for a sociable chat amongst friends, with a live band singing catchy tunes for those awkward pause moments. Enjoy a quiet early evening drink as the atmosphere doesn't start to warm up until after 21:00. Excellent mainly English dishes, but also some international choices. Go for the "Ocean Pie" at Dhs.30 or the traditional English breakfast at Dhs.24. You won't be disappointed !

## George & Dragon

12:00 - 16:00
18:00 - 01:00 Closed Fri am

Ambassador Hotel, Bur Dubai — Page 7, A 2

Tel: **531 000**

The G&D is very much a reminder of local pubs back home for the many expat English regulars. Lunch time and evening menu provides reasonably priced pub food favourites such as Guinness pie or a Chicken Tikka Masala that is friendly on the English palate. Check out the lunchtime specials.

Evening entertainment ranges from pub quiz, music from a band, or DJ, to live sports broadcast on a big screen such as English football or boxing. If your ideal English pub includes hearty food, sports on TV, a cheery crowd to watch it with you, and a bit of a knees-up as the night gets going, then this the place for you.

## Harvesters Pub

12:00 - 16:00
18:00 - 24:00

Holiday Inn Crowne Plaza
Sh Zayed Rd

Page 8
D 2

Tel: **311 111**

With the manager keeping a strict and disapproving eye out for scantily dressed clientele or those who have had a bit too much to drink, it is wise to dress smart/casual when visiting this clean cut and friendly steakhouse bar room. Not just any pub, but a place to take the family, enjoy a good meal and play bar billiards too.

From all the favourite bitters and appetizers, through to Soup Kettle delights, Hot and Cold Sandwiches and Berkeley's Meals. Harvesters has plenty going on every day of the week. Be warned though, drinks are relatively expensive!

## Humphrey's Tavern

12:00 - 16:00
18:00 - 12:00

Hilton Hotel Trade Centre
SH Zayed Rd

Page 9
A 2

Tel: **314 000**

Of all the bars in all the world, you walked into... Humphrey's! As Bogart would have said! A good place to grab generous portions of lunchtime pub grub as it boasts an excellent range of food, from the more traditional cholesterol inducing egg and chips, pies and authentic Cumberland sausage, to healthier smoked salmon sandwiches, baked potatoes and traditional British ploughman's fayre. Even veggie favourites are finding a niche in the menu. E.T.A. from placing your order to table delivery is less than ten minutes! However the time is rather reflected in the microwaved dishes, not quite home cooking, but tasty none-the-less. A lively duo persevere over the lunchtime chatter, but the quieter evening clientele may prefer a lower volume! Lunchtime locals spill out from the Trade Centre and Exhibition Halls, so reservations are recommended.

## Hunter's

12:00 - 15:00
18:00 - 23:30

Imperial Suites Hotel, The
Bur Dubai

Page 6
E 3

Tel: **515 100**

Reminescent of a typical country pub environment with high stools, bar and cosy alcoves, right down to the faded upholstery and hunting pictures. A lunchtime venue or a stop-gap after a long day at the office, Hunter's has a traditional menu offering good portions of Bangers and Mash at Dhs.17, as well as Steak and Guinness pie, Fish and Chips, etc. Good value for money, especially if you sample the monthly special promotions.

## Lords Tavern

12:00 - 15:00
19:00 - 01:00

Lords Hotel
Deira

Page 10
D 2

Tel: **289 977**

Drinks are very cheap indeed and the Kilkenny is perfect. Bar food available. Good for a quiet drink away from the maddening crowd.

## Nelson's

12:30 - 15:30
18:00 - 03:00

Maredias Hotel, Deira — Page 10, E 1

Tel: **289 393**

Named after Admiral Horatio Nelson, this is a bar with a decidedly nautical air. Decorated throughout with dark green wood and old-fashioned lamps, Nelson's has all the atmosphere of a traditional seafarers pub from days gone by, complete with antique telescopes and navigation equipment. Lunch and dinner is available from the galley, otherwise known as a kitchen to landlubbers, with a variety of dishes to satisfy the heartiest of appetites - from traditional pub grub such as Fish and Chips, Shepherd's Pie and Lasagna, to snacks of cocktail Sheekh Kebabs, Spring Rolls and Chilli Cheese Toast. Daily specials are on offer including both vegetarian and meat dishes.

## Old Vic, The

12:00 - 16:00
19:00 - 24:00

Ramada Hotel, Bur Dubai — Page 6, E 3

Tel: **521 010**

If you fancy a relaxed drink after work, why not prop up the bar at the Old Vic? Horseshoe in shape, the pub is split quite definitely into eating and drinking areas. Subtly lit and sectioned with dark wooden panelling, the place really grows on you. Patroned by an older crowd of mixed clientele with a lot of regulars, both hotel guest and nearby residents.

The food is traditional pub fayre with favourites such as Bangers and Mash, Steak and Kidney Pie and Shepherd's Pie. Service is efficient and the generous portions arrive at your table piping hot from the microwave. The live band takes a holiday in the summer, but there's plenty of entertainment to keep the regulars going. Saturday is cocktail night; Sunday is Ladies night; Monday hosts a quiz night; while Tuesday is for pool competitions. Wednesday is the day to eat pasta and the Thursday Night Fever Buffet rounds off a busy week's activities!

## Pub, The

12:00 - 14:30
18:00 - 24:00

Inter-Continental Hotel, Deira — Page 7, C 4

Tel: **227 171**

Landlady Sally knows how to transport the best of British tastes and atmosphere to this traditional English venue. Open from noon to midnight, enjoy authentic British cuisine and beverages in high wainscoted alcoves in the dining room area, or while balancing on a high stool at the round pub tables.

What you expect is what you get! The name describes it. This is the place to sip, chat and perhaps eat when hungry. Mostly European clientele, lots of businessmen and quiet tourists. Decorative wooden panelling creates a snug Lounge Bar atmosphere that compliments the good quality, down to earth, superior, English pub food. Study the chalk board for daily specials which should not be overlooked. The Pub also features a popular Monday quiz night and a mid monthly murder mystery dinner.

Tired of repeat reads of your favourite books? Every Saturday from 19:30 - 22:30 there is a Book Swapping Service available to anyone - but in order to receive a book you must bring a book. (English language preferred and nothing too saucy!)

## Red Lion

12:00 - 16:00
18:00 - 01:00

Metropolitan Hotel
Sh Zayed Rd/Safa
Page 4
C 4

Tel: **440 000**

Classic, English, urban, pub - fake wooden beams and all. Traditional pub grub on Mondays which is also Darts Night. Live band - with occasional jamming sessions with members of the crowd joining in. The biig screen television is turned on for special occasions such as football and rugby Cup Finals. A Complimentary buffet is served on these occasions. Lunchtime and early evening food includes Steak and Kidney Pie, Ploughmans lunch, etc.

## Slug & Lettuce

11:00 - 16:00
06:00 - 03:00

Gulf Inn Hotel
Deira
Page 10
D 2

Tel: **243 433**

Here we have a small Bar/Pub with very little atmosphere, trying hard to be an "English Pub", but not really succeeding. The name has come from the famous "Slug & Lettuce" Chain based in the UK, but beware, they are in no way related.

Reasonably priced menu offering typical English food such as Steak & Kidney Pie. Good value for money for a quick bite and a quiet drink after work. Tends to attract mainly hotel guests and people from the local area.

## Swan, The

12:00 - 16:00
18:00 - 24:00

JW Marriott Hotel
Deira
Page 11
A 3

Tel: **624 444**

The Swan is more a bistro than pub. Dark, carved wood prevails, complemented by brass trimmings. Super-soft sofas and armchairs enhance the casual yet chic atmosphere. Thanks to a fine selection of drafts and premium spirits and a relaxing atmosphere, the Swan Bar is the ideal place for intimate drinks and informal conversation.

The service is friendly and efficient. Located next to JW's Steakhouse on the lower lobby level.

## Thatchers

12:00 - 16:00
18:00 - 24:00

Dubai Marine Hotel
Bur Dubai
Page 7
A 3

Tel: **520 900**

Such is the popularity of this hustle and bustle place that you must phone ahead and book a table if you want to eat at this traditional pub during the week. As many European residents do. Or stroll in and join the revellers at the bar.

A typical British pub, with wooden panelled decor, dimly lit gas lamp -style lighting and no music! As such, it attracts a slightly older than average crowd, who enjoy drinking and talking in pubs. The popular restaurant area spills over into the rest of the pub, forcing drinkers to sit up at the bar. Most of the clientele come here to eat. The menu offers the usual pub fare - Steak Pie, Fish and Chips - with the additional option of a good selection of Thai specialties. The quality of the food here is far better than the standard pub grub - it is well presented, perfectly prepared and quite delicious.

During the week there are the usual pub/restaurant theme nights, e.g. accumulator nights for members, ladies night, curry night etc. - but the Wednesday quiz night is particularly popular.

## Victory Pub, The

11:00 - 15:30
18:00 - 20:00

Admiral Plaza, The
Deira

Page 6
E 2

Tel: **521 111**

Due to open by October 1997, The Victory Pub aims to be a sophisticated English Pub named after the Historical English warship HMS Victory. An English Duo will play the right kind of music and create an ambiance that has been missing in the city. Theme nights during weekdays and lots of activities on offer. Watch this place!

# General Bars

## *Baron's Table*

12:00 - 16:00
18:00 - 03:00

Penninsula Hotel
Bur Dubai

Page 7
A 2

Tel: **533 000**

A small, friendly bar offering reasonably priced bar snacks both at lunch time and evening. Suitable for visiting on your own or with a friend. Happy hours are 12:00 - 14:00 and 18:00 - 20:00 when drinks are reduced by 20%.

## Bodega

21:00 - 03:00

Ramee International Hotel
Deira

Page 7
C 3

Tel: **240 222**

Imagine a romantic beach scene somewhere in the Philippines. No, don't imagine it, just visit Bodega and see it for yourself. A Filipino band provides entertainment for an international clientele every night, although no dancing. Situated on the first floor of this relatively new hotel off Al Nasr Square.

## Constellation Lounge

11:00 - 15:00
19:00 - 01:30

Aviation Club, The
Al Garhoud

Page 14
C 3

Tel: **824 122**

It's got its own car park with lots of free spaces, which is a very big plus towards making this a desirable watering hole. Inside is darkish, stylish and cosy-ish. Dominated by a splendid circular bar, this is a smart and elegant place to drink. It is also good value as everything is priced net of tax & service. Order a Dhs.20-25 one course meal from a comprehensive snack menu, or choose a three course meal from the a la carte restaurant menu which will cost an average of Dhs.85. Good live music every night. Tuesday is Member's Night when a quiz, accumulator draw and raffle prize provide extra fun!

## Equator Bar

18:00 - 03:00 | Lodge, The, Al Nasa | Page 9, E 4 | Tel: **379 470**

Just next door to the Lodge's established congregation of disco-seekers, the Equator Bar provides a regular haunt for those not joining in the dancing. Unselfconscious and boisterous, with it's own crowd who enjoy themselves in a less fashionable setting than their nightclubbing neighbours. Entertainments include pool, darts and electronic games, with satellite TV providing a non-stop audio-visual backdrop to the shady red-lit interior. A handy menu with unpretentious pub food caters for the hungry, a plate of Fish and Chips or a Madras curry will fit the bill nicely, thank you. And since it is opened until 03:00 you have plenty of time to eat, drink and get merry.

## Gallery Bar

16:00 - 01:00 | Forte Grand - Jumeira Beach, Al Mina Al Siyahi | Page 1, E 2 | Tel: **845 555**

Comfortable lounge suites and arm chairs make this a relaxing, comfortable and upmarket spot for a drink before or after dinner at any of the hotel's restaurants. A pianist and singer play background contemporary music Tuesday to Saturday. Situated on the first floor overlooking the foyer.

## Lindbergh's

15:00 - 01:00 | Sheraton Deira, Deira | Page 11, A 3 | Tel: **688 888**

Overlooking the exciting airport view, a cosy place to enjoy a drink while awaiting that long flight schedule. The bar is designed as a typical runway with bright neon lights and a matching world map displayed on the ceiling.

Named after the famous aviator, this lounge/bar is situated between the Mediterranean and Indian Restaurants at the Four Point Sheraton Hotel. Enter this rather open planned lounge and you are surrounded by black and white prints of various old flying machines, yet the rest of the decor is extremely modern with aluminium nuts and bolts studding the seams of the walls, to give an overall effect of a mid-flight experience, be it ancient or modern. To top it off, a huge map of the world with glowing capital cities sprawls over the ceiling of the octagonal bar area, creating a rather nostalgic atmosphere.

Drinks are reasonably priced. A good venue to gather before dinner, or simply to enjoy a quiet drink with friends before moving onto the lively nightclub downstairs.

## South Indian Bar

18:00 - 03:00 | Ramee International Hotel, Deira | Page 7, C 3 | Tel: **240 222**

Catering almost entirely for a South Indian male clientele this small bar has a crowded, busy and dimly lit atmosphere. It offers a self-service buffet of typical Keralite dishes and is a casual meeting place, a home away from home, for the Indian residents of Dubai. Large video screen and television playing Indian TV programmes. Waitresses wear traditional saris.

## Spike Bar

07:00 - 24:00 | Dubai Golf & Racing Club, Nadd Al Shiba | Page 12, A 3 | Tel: **363 666**

Big, comfortable, leather, Chesterfield sofas; sports on the overhead television screens; low priced snack menu and a welcome cold drink at club rates, make this golfer's bar a pleasant place to meet. Well-used by the pay-as-you-play crowd of golfers and their friends as well as club members. The floodlit golf course is open until midnight and this bar is usually busy until then.

It's a good idea to order your first round of drinks at the bar before deciding whether to sit in a sofa alcove or at the small dining tables, as service is not as quick as it could be. Dhs.35 or less will buy you a three-course meal, although everything can be ordered individually, and often is. Soup and rolls, Sausage and Mash with Gravy, and apple Crumble and Custard are all on offer.

# Irish Bars

## Dubliners

12:00 - 15:00, 19:30 - 22:30 | Forte Grand Dubai, Al Garhoud | Page 14, E 3 | Tel: **702 2508**

Stepping into Dubliners is like stepping into an old Hollywood movie set of an Irish pub. The set up includes the genuine Irish lilt of the bar staff and unmistakable sound of Irish Folk music. The warm and vibrant atmosphere makes it hard to believe that this is not Dublin's fair city.

Guinness, known as black gold, is expertly pulled from the pumps, food is wholesome and fresh, and the Irish Coddle is highly recommended. Dubliners ambience is such that one should make this outlet the last on a pub crawl, but the dilemma will be that by then, you may not have enough money to pay the bill. A nice little secluded courtyard outside, with a replica of a 1950s delivery van completes the scene. On Thursday evenings, many join in by dancing in traditional Gaelic fashion.

## Fibber Magges

11:00 - 03:00 | Nr. Holiday Inn Crown Plaza, Sh Zayed Rd /Trade Centre | Page 8, D 2 | Tel: **328 098**

'Fibbers' has quickly become an institution amongst the expatriate population, always busy and lively, this is the place to meet and drink. 'Fibbers' has the almost unique double distinction (along with the Irish Village) of not being attached to a hotel and having windows, which gives it an authentic pub atmosphere not matched by hotel bars. Open seven days a week from noon to 03.00, Fibbers attracts the lunchtime and late afternoon office crowd, early evening diners and then from around 21:00 onwards, it fills with the nightime social drinking set.

An excellent and very reasonably priced menu provides substantial and high quality pub grub. The Fish n' Chips at Dhs.25 is unbeatable! The only drawback, which the establishment are trying to resolve, is the ventilation - the pub can become a little too smoky at times. Direct access to the Venue nightclub which is located upstairs.

## Finnegans

12:00 - 01:00 | Dubai Park Hotel, Sh Zayed Rd | Page 2, A 3 | Tel: **487 111**

Although this three-star hotel is half an hour's drive from, town some residents do frequent it, mainly at weekends, and the place is packed on Irish occasions. Guinness and beef stew can be ordered at the bar. Large dance floor for those who want to do an impromptu act or join the Irish singer in his ballads and songs.

## Irish Village

11:00 - 23:00 | Next to Dubai Tennis Stadium, Al Garhoud | Page 14, C 3 | Tel: **824 750**

In Ireland they say that the centre of village life is the pub, and here we have a pub set in its own mock-up village. A traditional street scene fronts the pub and tea shop, opening onto an authentically paved courtyard with an old pony trap, telephone box and fire hydrant - all originals from the Emerald Isle. Perfect for lunch, you could be in Ireland as you gaze across the tidy lawns, complete with village pond and ducks!

If you prefer to dine inside, you can chose from the ambience of the 'Saddlery', 'Winner's Enclosure' or 'Poet's Corner' - adorned with verse from greats such as George Bernard Shaw, Joyce and Wilde.

From the wholesome traditional fayre we recommend Grilled Salmon, Fish and Chips or the Baked Potato, which is good value for money (but not as good as it used to be). With excellent house wine at Dhs.35 a bottle you can hardly go wrong. Packed outside at the weekends and on cooler winter evenings.

# Scottish Bar

## Tartan Bar

12:00 - 15:30
19:00 - 03:00

Lodge, The
Al Nasa

Page 9
E 4

Tel: **379 470**

This is the place to come for a pint, some good traditional cooking and congenial company. The Tartan Bar will not present you with any surprises but that is exactly its attraction. A normal, quiet, home-town pub with standard items on the menu for both lunch and evening meals. All prices shown are inclusive of taxes and service charges. Part of the Al Nasr entertainment area of restaurants, pubs and nightclubs.

# Jazz Bars

## Jules Bar

12:00 - 15:00
19:00 - 02:00

Forte Grand Dubai
Al Garhoud

Page 14
E 3

Tel: **824 040**

Cajun and Creole cooking with a splash of New Orleans, the perfect combination for a jazz club/restaurant. Apart from the 'Louisiana Cooking' menu, guests can choose from Hot and Cold sandwiches, as well as the famous "Jules Globetrotters" menu which offers dishes from Mexico, USA, India, Sri Lanka, China, Turkey, Greece, France and of course the UAE. All cooked to perfection and served with a smile.

Entertainment is provided by a very talented Filipino band turning out tunes from Ella Fitzgerald to Neil Diamond, and the Carpenters. The brightly coloured walls (all different), the odd saxophone or trumpet hanging on the wall, combined with dim lighting and kerosene candles on the elegantly laid out tables, give an all around cosy authentic jazz club feeling to a rather large area.

Reservations are essential, especially on Tuesday, Thursday and Fridays. Also opened daily for lunch. Sunday is Ladies Night when, along with a free drink, ladies of

SPY

quiet confidence

AS WORN
BY
DAVID,
AL AND NEIL

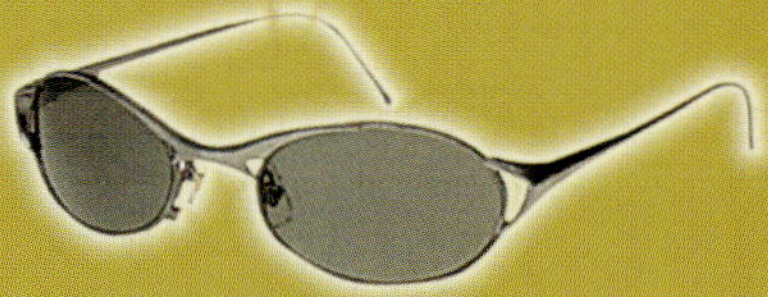

SPY

WINDOWS FOR YOUR HEAD™

receive a single red rose... very sweet. Superb daily buffet lunch for Dhs.35. Jules also boasts Dubai's longest happy hours, from 10:00 - 18:00.

## Key West - Entertainment Centre

12:00 - 01:00 | Al Bustan Rotana Hotel, Al Garhoud | Page 14, E 3 | Tel: **820 000**

The new hang out for Jazz aficionados, Key West claims to be Dubai's only authentic Jazz Club. Enjoy the smooth sounds of accomplished international bands in an Art Deco setting. The adjacent Floridian Bistro has a casual South Florida ambience and an extensive Southern State's menu.

Open for lunch, dinner and late night night snacks, this is a great place to meet friends, complete, with games room for added attraction.

## Up On The 10th

18:30 - 03:00 | Inter-Continental Hotel, Deira | Page 7, C 4 | Tel: **227 171**

A classy place to take your girlfriend, and perhaps her parents too! The mood is mellow here and the setting elegant. The clientle is distinguished, and one is immediately struck by the low tones and suaveness with which everyone conducts themselves. Not a place to go for a wild night out, but it gets top marks for a quiet, pleasant, romantic evening.

The drinks list is relatively expensive, although entertainment by an extremely talented jazz duo makes it all worthwhile. This is Dubai's best loved live jazz venue, renowned for it's authentic bar atmosphere and fine musical talent. Featuring a variety of international jazz artists. Transport yourself to the clubs of Chicago or New Orleans. Late night Cajun snack bar menu certainly adds to the sultry ambience.

## See Also:

Restaurants: The Americas - **Bourbon Street**

# Karaoke Bars

## Hibiki Music Lounge

Check | Hyatt Regency Hotel, Deira | Page 7, D 2 | Tel: **732 1234**

The hotel claims that it is one of the "first truly authentic karaoke lounge in the UAE, offering guests the chance to sing in front of an audience, or in the privacy of one of the three intimate private rooms". Everyone joins in, including the waiters and waitresses.

There's the main hall and private rooms which are equipped with their own private Karaoke systems. The three private rooms are called the Japanese Room, Singapore Room and Thai Room and the decor also reflects the different Asian regions.

The system installed has an access to some 5,000 songs, to be expanded to 10,000 selected form the latest selection of Japanese, English, Chinese, Korean, Indonesian and Malay titles. The music lounge will operate on a club-style membership at Dhs.500 per person

## Misty Karaoke Lounge

Check | Mayfair Hotel, Deira | Page 10, D 2 | Tel: **284 444**

Opening shortly in the new Mayfair Hotel in Deira, this bar is filled with the latest, no-expense-spared, hi-tech Karaoke gadgets and more. One microchip holds all the video images and lyrcs. In addition to the one cosy karaoke bar area, there are two private cubicles, for your private singing pleasure.

Run by the enterprenurial Korian, Gene Char, this is bound to attract the serious karaoke clientel. This is will be the most modern and high-tech dedicated Karaoke bar in Dubai.

## Oye Karaoke

18:00 - 03:00 | Maredias Hotel, Deira | Page 10, E 1 | Tel: **289 393**

If you like the sound of your own voice, look no further than this bar located in Deira's Maredias Hotel, Dubai's first full time Karaoke bar. Regulars sing so well that you could could even mistake them for the real thing. Limited bar snacks, including Fish & Chips, and alcoholic drinks. A hint to groups of singing fans: put your requests in early as regulars are often favoured and unfortunately there is only one microphone to go round.

A large screen located on stage displays the lyrics which are accompanied by films that appear to have no reference to the songs themselves. In fact passion is the theme with exotic women wooing the hearts of young men.

Clientele range from Filipinos, western expatriates to local Arabs, this is an ideal place to go if you're in a group or celebrating a hen, stag or birthday party. So if you fancy yourself as the future Tom Jones or Barbara Streisand, here is your chance.

### See Also:

Bar/Pubs, English - **Cyclone Pub**

Restaurants, Friday Brunch - **Lodge, The**

# Wine Bars

## La Cave

**19:00 - 01:00**
**Closed Fri**

**Inter-Continental Hotel**
**Deira**

**Page 7**
**C 4**

Tel: **227 171**

Located on the second floor of the hotel, this cosy and intimate wine cellar seating around 20, offers a large selection of fine vintages for connoisseurs. More than 70 varieties on offer starting at Dhs.100 per bottle and also served by the glass. Cheeses available to compliment your drink.

## Shutters

**12:30 - 15:00**
**19:00 - 24:00**

**Sheraton Deira**
**Deira**

**Page 11**
**A 3**

Tel: **688 888**

A sophisticated cocktail lounge located on the 1st floor opposite the Thai restaurant, Shutters is decorated colonial style with wooden chests, simulated animal skin covered chairs and artwork evocative of a bygone age. Warm and relaxing in atmosphere, this is a small and relatively quiet lounge, frequented mostly by couples and business people - the majority of whom are dining within the hotel. House specialities include a range of delicious wine cocktails which are reasonably priced, and well worth a try for something a little different. Popular concoctions include the 'Ice Berg' - sparking white wine, white wine and orange fruit and "Cardinal" - sparking white wine, white wine and strawberry. Appetisers from the Thai Room are also served. Perhaps a little lacking in atmosphere for a regular drink but definitely worth a visit for a pre or post meal drink, if dining nearby.

### See Also:

Restaurants, Mediterranean - **Cafe Insignia**

# Cocktail Lounges

## Diwan Lounge

18:00 - 01:30 | Sheraton Hotel, Deira | Page 10, C 1 | Tel: 281 111

Up the escalator, across the lobby and into The Diwan Lounge for a quick night cap! The lounge has comfortable deep sofas that a group of friends can sink into and enjoy their own private space, alternatively, there is seating at the long bar if you prefer to be in a more central and lit position. Live Filipino group. Phone to find out which night is Karaoke Night and join in with the singing. A popular place, used mainly by locals and hotel guests.

## Falcon Bar

19:30 - 01:00 | Hilton Hotel, Trade Centre/ Sh Zayed Rd | Page 9, A 2 | Tel: 314 000

Arabian decor sets the scene for an intimate gathering of friends. An ideal place to meet before visiting the Al Fahidi Restaurant next door. A live duo entertain most evenings and are more than happy to play any special requests. Try the many cocktails on offer. Open till late, the bar is also an ideal place for a nightcap after one of the many functions that occur within the hotel, or at the nearby conference centre.

## Lobby Bar

18:00 - 24:00 | Royal Abjar, Deira | Page 11, A 3 | Tel: 625 555

If you want a pleasant place to meet your friends before moving on elsewhere, try this genteel hotel lobby bar offering low comfortable chairs and sofas as well as a relatively relaxed atmosphere. The menu incorporates various cocktails and snacks, including Crispy Fried Chicken Fillets, to Spring Rolls and Scottish Smoked Salmon. As far as cocktails go, proportions are generous and prices standard. Try the Planters Punch, or the non-alcoholic version, called Royal Abjar, which includes orange juice, pineapple juice, raspberries, strawberries and bananas.

## Office, The

12:00 - 03:00 | Metropolitan Palace, Deira | Page 10, D 2 | Tel: 270 000

A clever name for this new cocktail lounge which will be opening in the new Metropolitan Palace Hotel on Sheikh Maktoum Road in October 1997 enabling punters to say. "I'm at the Office". Located on the mezzanie floor, The Office is an ideal rendezvous for businessmen. Fine cocktails and light snacks available all day, with a spectacular view over the Dubai Creek.

## Pearls Bar

10:00 - 01:00 | Forte Grand Dubai, Al Garhoud | Page 14, E 3 | Tel: 824 040

Located in the central lobby, the Pearl Bar offers a relaxing and convivial atmosphere where guests can order from the vast selection of teas, or, in the evening, sample the exotic beverages from the tempting cocktail menu. Also in the evening, pleasant melodies from the Evergreen Jazz band will soothe away the troubles of a busy day.

## Sirocco

11:00 - 01:00 | Radisson SAS Jumeira, Al Mina Al Siyahi | Page 1, D 2 | Tel: **845 533**

With very much a Polynesian resort getaway theme in mind, the atmosphere of Sirocco cocktail lounge is relaxed and benevolent. Listen to the pianist while enjoying happy hour prices from 17:30 to 19:30 after a long day, and you will feel rejuvenated and ready for the evening ahead. This bar is more casual than city ones and a small selection of snacks is available from 11:00 to 01:00 every day.

## Trader Vic's

19:30 - 01:00 | Holiday Inn Crowne Plaza, Trade Centre / SH Zayed Rd | Page 8, D 2 | Tel: **311 111**

Take the lift to the third floor and step out into a Polynesian den of delight. There is a spacious indoor verandah-type bar area complete with wooden floor, barrel tables, cane chairs and plenty of artifacts to gaze at.

Cocktails are a speciality, with an extensive menu to choose from. Served in shrunken heads, or adorned with feathered parrots, these potent concoctions are the same as those found in Trader Vic's worldwide. Not cheap, but worth every dirham. Try the bar menu for oriental snack delights such as satay, prawns with a selection of dipping sauces, crispy wontons and native pacific finger food.

# Night Clubs

## Amy's Key Club

21:00 - 03:00 | Airport Hotel, Al Garhoud | Page 14, D 3 | Tel: **823 427**

Amy's is a members only, exclusive, intimate night-club offering dancing into the small hours. It is surprisingly small inside, creating the intimacy of a club rather than a nightclub, and wall to wall with mirrors, black high stools and tables. Saturday to Wednesday various promotions and entertainments are provided, attracting a cosmopolitan clientele (i.e. Saturday night is Advertising executives night).

On Thursday and Friday the club draws a large number of regular Arabic members who enjoy the live Arabic entertainment. Non-members are welcome, but a cover charge of Dhs.60 per male is required. Reservations are recommended well in advance especially at weekends. Meals are available with a set menu option on Tuesdays, Thursdays and Fridays. There is a resident DJ nightly and Arabic live entertainment at the week ends. This place is also known as The Key Club as regular and approved customers receive their own key to the door. Dress is smart casual, open till late.

## California Discotheque

**20:00 - 03:00** | **Swiss Plaza Hotel, Bur Dubai** | **Page 6, E 2** | Tel: **533 737**

Not one, but two DJ's take turns in playing Arabic and European music, both with a heavy beat. Reminiscent of a bad 1970's film, this is a seedy venue in downtown Bur Dubai. The clientele is mainly Local or Asian. Europeans may find that they do not feel particularly welcome. Closed atmosphere.

## Chequers

**22:00 - 02:00**
**Closed Sat** | **Inter-Continental Hotel, Deira** | **Page 7, C 4** | Tel: **227 171**

For those who like to party until the early hours of the morning Chequers is a sophisticated night-club with it's own resident, international DJ. If you prefer the intimacy and personalised service of a private club, this is the perfect venue for you. Monthly theme parties, Karaoke, crew and ladies nights should definitely not be missed. Located on the second floor of the Inter Continental Plaza Hotel.

## Cyclone

**20:00 - 03:00** | **Cyclone, Al Nasa** | **Page 9, D 4** | Tel: **369 991**

Apply for free membership and enjoy the late night atmosphere of a lively disco which is packed at weekends. There's a long oval bar to circulate around, with some seating downstairs and more upstairs on the balcony where a strict dress code is enforced: gentlemen must wear jacket and tie. A large dance area with flashing lights, smoke machine and other disco accompaniments throbs to trendy music all night long.

The Cyclone often has pop singers and groups performing live on stage - usually preceded by complimentary finger food and happy hour prices at the bar.

## Garage Club

**21:00 - 03:00** | **Ramee International Hotel, Deira** | **Page 7, C 3** | Tel: **240 661**

An unpretentious nightclub. As the name suggests, the garage actually contains cars - six altogether - plus a bus which you can sit in. Don't miss the Morgan sports car when you arrive, it's parked in the entrance. And this is the only place in Dubai where you can drink a 'Carburetor'. It is rare to find a nightclub where one can talk without breaking your vocal cords, but at the same time this is a place where the dancing is lively and uninhibited.

The place for men to visit if they are interested in meeting unattached single women; but probably not the place for single women to frequent unless interested in meeting such men. This means that the establishment attracts a truly international clientele! Entrance is free to Airline staff, couples and females. Dhs.50 may be charged to others at the Management's discretion. Annual membership is Dhs.500. Drinks cost Dhs.15 per pint,

Dhs.10 per can/bottle and Dhs.15 for a cocktail. Complimentary veggie sticks, peanuts and popcorn are served to every table. Special nights: Sun and Tues - Ladies night (2 free drinks), Mon - Buy 3 drinks and get one free, Thurs & Fri. - Club night, Sat - Hotel staff - 20% discount.

## Lodge, The

**16:00 - 03:00** | **Lodge, The, Al Nasa** | **Page 9, E 4** | Tel: **379 470**

Popular haunt of the young set, and the young-at-heart set. Early evening is for eating at the sectioned off dining area - inexpensive menu choices for a hearty meal. With a long bar and central pub, tables fill up quickly with those who want to see and be seen coming after 22:00. At midnight the dividing doors are pushed back from the adjoining nightclub and the whole place throbs with music, dancers and friendships. Over five different bar areas, and weather permitting, on Thursday nights, the action continues outside on a canopied dance floor erected out back. One of the few places which just seem to keep going. Great breakfasts. Entry restricted to over 21's and on managment approval. Members only. Application forms available at reception (Dhs.25 + 2 photographs) Need we say more!

## Options

**22:00 - 03:00, Closed Sat** | **Metropolitan Hotel, Sh Zayed Rd/Safa** | **Page 4, C 4** | Tel: **440 000**

This small nightclub caters to a specific clientele who are willing to party hard in a classy sort of way. On the busy nights of Tuesdays and Thursdays, people are packed from wall to wall listening to trendy music from all over the world, with a slight leaning toward Arabic, and generally partying until the wee hours of the morning.

On quieter nights, service is a little more personal and the loud music is tailored to it's audience. This is when the bar staff display some of their talents not dissimilar to those of Tom Cruise in the movie "Cocktail" - very entertaining indeed! The light show is spectacular, with the entire room transforming in a matter of minutes as the DJ builds up the effects until every wall and table vibrates in the time with the thumping music. Open every night except Saturday. Drinks are reasonably priced.

## Premiere, The

**22:00 - 03:00** | **Hyatt Regency Hotel, Deira** | **Page 7, D 2** | Tel: **706 4819**

The Premiere of a movie in the 1940's and 50's was often heralded with photos in the newspapers of movie stars and directors on the set. This nightclub has a film set theme complete with scaffolding rigs, light cans and stages of that era. Dramatic black and red colours are used boldly throughout. The place attracts a mixed and international clientele and has a unique feature in the Directors Box, an exclusive glass room overlooking the discotheque, offering a quiet corner for those who enjoy nightlife but wish to be slightly apart from the rest. A strict dress code of smart-casual and entry is restricted to those over 21. A popular late night spot for all types and ages, with the occasional VIP hotel guest mingling with revellers and boppers. Juliana, a London based company provides latest dance hits and top chart releases, allowing this particular disco to be ahead of the competition.

## Raqs

19:00 - 03:00 | Gulf Inn Hotel, Deira | Page 10, D 2 | Tel: **243 433**

The nine member band that belts out popular tunes at Raqs has five energetic Filipino girls who seem to have a different dance routine for every song they sing. Their act is obviously enrapturing as most guests spend their time staring unashamedly at the hot-pant clad singers.

Like most nightclubs the place is dark, loud and has a small dancing area in front of the band. The kitchen is open until 02:00 and serves a choice of Indonesian, Vietnamese, Filipino, Korean and Thai food. Airline crew and Hoteliers are welcome to a 20% discount on their Food and Beverage bill.

## Rumours

21:30 - 03:00 | Ramada Hotel, Bur Dubai | Page 6, E 3 | Tel: **521 010**

Rumours has undergone some small aesthetic changes to make the atmosphere even more comfortable and cosy than before. New TV monitors, lighting, and a new young Scottish DJ - Jason, complement the existing warm environment and staff who treat you as part of the Ramada family, rather than customers. The head barman Rosario, has been a part of Rumours for 15 years !

Try the discounted prices during happy hour between 21:30 - 23:00, or the many special evenings - Thursdays is 'Weekend Party', Wednesdays is 'Hoteliers Night', Fridays is 'Techno Night', Tuesdays is 'Ladies Night' and to top it off, Sundays is 'Surprise Prize Night' when you can win spot prizes and beverage vouchers. Mixed nationalities, mainly Arab expats and Asians. Management have tightened up on the dress code and who they allow in, to improve their image.

## Stars Studio

18:00 - 02:00 | Sheraton Deira, Deira | Page 11, A 3 | Tel: **688 888**

An Afro/American theme fun restaurant, where guests can enjoy the best music of the 90's with a live band. A wild menu with crocodile, ostrich served with honey bees, buffalo and fried banana chips. Tasty salads, juicy marinated hamburgers, cool margaritas and a first class disco.

Star's Studio is one of Dubai's newest nightspots and its decor and ambience must rate it as one of the top

clubs here. The theme is 'African', from the furnishings right down to the food on the menu. From the entrance of the club, a wooden bridge leads the way to the main bar area overlooking the dance floor and the band. The regular dance band 'Exotique' are superb entertainers, playing all the favourite soul dance hits spanning five decades - Gladys Knight, Donna Summer, The Temptations, to name a few. Exotique convincingly won the battle of the bands competition which took place recently. It consisted of the top ten Dubai bands, and they won! The atmosphere is casual with alcoved seating areas positioned around the dance floor. The 'Nairobi Times' newspaper-cum-menu offers tropical cocktails and some tasty traditional African snacks and food - try the Smoked Ostrich fillet with paw paw salad!

## Trax

**20:00 - 03:00**
**Closed Sat**

**Forte Grand - Jumeira Beach**
**Al Mina Al Siyahi**

**Page 1**
**E 2**

Tel: **845 555**

A little nightclub far from the hustle and bustle of Dubai. Steve McKinley, the amiable manager, who doubles as DJ through the evening, has a feel for the mood of the crowd and does a good job of keeping the party going by deft changes in music. Clubbers are a pleasant mixture of nationalities which contributes to the Trax's rather unique atmosphere. Anything goes in this place and you are likely to hear a recent Indian hit, or a popular Arab song that has been specifically requested, or brought along by one of the enthusiastic dancers for Steve to play, in addition to the regular remixes of current Billboard charters. Most importantly the drinks are reasonably priced - with a pint costing Dhs.14, spirits Dhs.12 and cocktails Dhs.18.

## Tropicana

**21:30 - 03:00**

**Dubai Marine Beach Resort**
**Jumeira**

**Page 5**
**D 2**

Tel: **441 221**

A late night dining and dancing venue, Tropicana is a sedate and intimate cocktail bar-cum-restaurant between 21:00 and midnight. By 01:00 it has transformed into a stylish, but bustling, night club attracting an interesting variety of Middle Eastern and Western clientele who dance through to 03:00.

Best to reserve a table in advance to enjoy an excellent a la carte menu. Management discretion is strictly applied at the door to restrict entrance to smartly dressed couples and mixed groups. A stylish place for those who have something to celebrate, or simply enjoy good dining and dancing.

Membership at Dhs.500 (free to members of the beach club) ensures 'no hassle' entry, priority for reservation of tables and invitations to special promotion nights.

## Valentinos

12:00 - 15:30
18:00 - 03:00

Penninsula Hotel
Bur Dubai

Page 7
A 2

Tel: **533 000**

One big happy party with plenty of regulars who obviously know their Eric Clapton and Eagles classics off by heart. Just watch them strum an imaginary guitar, or hold their lighters up in respect. After a few pints you will probably be keeping them company. There is no pretention here whatsoever and you may proceed with the drinking while drooling over the Ukrainian dancers who entertain on stage. The extra bit charged for drinks goes towards their maintenance. The food is surprisingly good, with a choice of Indian, Chinese, Continental, Italian or Filipino.

## Venue, The

20:00 - 03:00

Above Fibber Maggee
Sh Zayed Rd

Page 8
D 2

Tel: **314 809**

The latest nightclub to hit Dubai, the Venue buzzes with good solid dance music and people having an unpretentious, good time. Upstairs there is a more refined lounge area and two cocktail bars; on a third level an intimate and secluded lounge looking down onto the main dance floor. It draws on the popularity of Fibber Maggees pub located below, attracting those looking for a less boisterous and clamorous night than experienced at the Lodge. All three places are owned by the same proprietor.

Less well known is that the Venue "trebles up" as a functional business lunchtime place and a genteel dining-cum-cocktail bar experience in the evening, to be enjoyed prior to serious "boogying" which starts at midnight. Restaurant prices are competitive, offering a set menu or a la carte dining.

Whilst a strict membership policy is enforced (currently 2,500), occasionally membership (including taking of photograph) can be processed immediately whilst you wait. 25% reduction on drinks during 17:00 - 21:00 "Sundowner time". Special Events - Monthly "change of zodiac sign" party (zodiac sign theme runs throughout the Venue.)

# Night Club Summary

| Night Club Name | Tel No. | Membership (Dhs.) | Entrance Fee Male Week/Weeken | Female | Clientele | Note |
|---|---|---|---|---|---|---|
| Amy's Key Club | 823 427 | - | - | - | Ar | - |
| California Discotheque | 533 737 | - | - | - | As | - |
| Chequers | 227 171 | 250 | -/50 | - | Ar/We | - |
| Cyclone | 369 991 | 1,000 | 35/50 | 35/50 | Ar/As/We | Members & Guest Only |
| Garage Club, The | 240 661 | 500 | 50/50 | - | Af/Ar/As | - |
| Lodge, The | 379 470 | 25 | 50/50 | - | We | Members & Guest Only |
| Options | 440 000 | - | - | - | Ar/We | - |
| Premiere, The | 706 4819 | 800 | 50/70 | 30/70 | Ar/We | Members & Guest Only |
| Raqs | 243 433 | - | - | - | As/Fi | - |
| Rumours | 521 010 | - | 35/35 | - | Ar/We | - |
| Stars Studio | 688 888 | 100 | 50/50 | - | Af/Ar/We | Members receive a Dhs.125 voucher |
| Trax | 845 555 | - | - | - | Ar/As/We | - |
| Tropicana | 441 221 | 500 | - | - | Ar | No membership required if dinning |
| Valentinos | 533 000 | - | | | As/ | - |
| Venue, The | 314 809 | 25 | 50/50 | - | We | Members Only |

**Key:**

African (Af), Arabic (Ar), Asian (As), Filipino (Fi), Western (We)

**Clientele:**

Specified in order of nationality which tends to frequent the particular nightclub

# Liquor Stores

Permanent residents who are non-Muslims are eligible to apply for an alcoholic drinks permit. To obtain a permit they must hold a valid residence visa. Application forms are available from the Dubai Police Headquarters, near the Galadari Roundabout on the Dubai Sharjah Road, and must be completed both in English and Arabic. The application forms must be signed by your employer, validated with a company stamp and submitted along with your passport, copy of your labour agreement and two passport photographs. The fee is Dhs.105 and processing your application will take around 10 days.

Outlets licensed to sell alcoholic supplies, for private consumption, are listed below:

## African & Eastern N.E. (A&E)

| | | | |
|---|---|---|---|
| 10:00 - 21:00<br>Closed Friday | Next to Spinneys<br>Jumeira | Page 5<br>C2 | Tel: 440 327 |
| 10:00 - 21:00<br>Closed Friday | Bur Dubai | Page 7<br>A3 | Tel: 524 521 |
| 10:00 - 21:00<br>Closed Friday | Al Karama | Page 9<br>C3 | Tel: 348 056 |
| 10:00 - 21:00<br>Closed Friday | Deira | Page 10<br>D2 | Tel: 222 666 |

## Maritime & Mercantile International (MMI)

| | | | |
|---|---|---|---|
| 10:00 - 21:00<br>Closed Friday | Al Karama | Page 9<br>C2 | Tel: 351 722 |
| 10:00 - 21:00<br>Closed Friday | Sheikh Maktoum Road<br>Deira | Page 10<br>D2 | Tel: 222 342 |
| 10:00 - 21:00<br>Closed Friday | Nr. Spinneys<br>Ramada | Page 6<br>E4 | Tel: 516 282 |
| 10:00 - 21:00<br>Closed Friday | Nr. Spinneys<br>Al Jumeira | Page 5<br>C2 | Tel: 440 223 |
| 10:00 - 21:00<br>Closed Friday | Nr. Spinneys<br>Umm Sequim | Page 4<br>A3 | Tel: NA |
| 10:00 - 21:00<br>Closed Friday | Opp Dubai Marine Hotel<br>Bur Dubai | Page 7<br>A 3 | Tel: 511 586 |

# Party Service

Everything you need to get your party going. Glasses (wine & pint), ice buckets, waiter's trays, bar towels, coasters Maritime & Mercantile International (MMI) offers this service free of charge. Leave a Dhs.500, fully refundable deposit, and then receive all the items detailed below, which are to be returned within 5 days.

24 - 1 Pint Beer Glasses, 24 - Wine Glasses, 2 - Ice Buckets, 2 - Waiter trays, 3 - Bar Towels, 24 - Coasters. Minimal breakages charge (Dhs.5/glass) will be deducted from your deposit and the full balance refunded.

# In-House Catering

The following companies offer in-house catering. They will take care of everything from table and chairs, waiters, cutlery and crockery, napkins and table cloths, and even the food and drink! Costs vary according to the number of people, dishes ordered, etc. Each company will normally ask you how many people are expected, nationalities, menu preferences, etc. and will then determine a per person cost.

For more information on each of the outlets listed below, where applicable, please refer to the appropriate reviews, and the restaurant quick view index.

## General Catering

| | |
|---|---|
| Abela & Co. LLG | Tel: 225 251 |
| Cafe de Paris | Tel: 451 418 |
| Dubai Marine Hotel | Tel: 520 900 |
| Dubai World Trade Centre | Tel: 321 000 |
| Delicious Prospects | Tel: 555 760 |
| Fountain Cafe | Tel: 311 502 |
| Jebel Ali Hotel | Tel: 836 000 |
| West One | Tel: 316 900 |

## Arabic / Lebanese

| | |
|---|---|
| Al Barhar | Tel: 278 984 |
| Al Mandaloun | Tel: 231 000 |
| Al Qasr | Tel: 441 221 |
| Automatic | Tel: 277 824 |

## Austrian

| | |
|---|---|
| Cafe Mozart | Tel: 216 565 |

## Chinese

| | |
|---|---|
| Cascade | Tel: 522 020 |
| China Garden | Tel: 440 253 |
| China Times | Tel: 442 930 |
| Chinese Diwan | Tel: 229 886 |
| Chinese Kitchen | Tel: 381 864 |
| Chinese Palace | Tel: 281 043 |
| Chinese Pavillon | Tel: 444 432 |
| Golden Dragon | Tel: 366 122 |
| Mr Chow | Tel: 510 099 |
| Pumpy's | Tel: 528 484 |
| Shanghai Kitchen | Tel: 456 131 |
| Taipan | Tel: 348 835 |

## Indian

| | |
|---|---|
| 10 The Restaurant | Tel: 364 547 |
| Al Tandoor | Tel: 526 098 |
| Caesar`s | Tel: 527 300 |
| Down Town Restaurant | Tel: 525 219 |
| Dubai Mughal | Tel: 518 833 |
| Gulzar | Tel: 289 393 |
| Kitchen | Tel: 453 043 |
| Midnight Cafeteria | Tel: 368 899 |
| Mughal Mahal | Tel: 347 600 |
| Shezan | Tel: 378 701 |
| Volga Restaurant | Tel: 525 100 |
| Welcome Restaurant | Tel: 528 777 |

## Japanese

| | |
|---|---|
| Shogun | Tel: 285 568 |
| Teppanyaki House | Tel: 521 010 |

## Pakistani

| | |
|---|---|
| Chicken Tikka Inn | Tel: 225 683 |
| Noor Jahan | Tel: 530 670 |

## Persian

| | |
|---|---|
| Alborz | Tel: 318 777 |
| Pars Iranian Kitchen | Tel: 452 222 |

## Vegetarian

| | |
|---|---|
| Chappan Bhog | Tel: 364 176 |
| Dasaprakash | Tel: 527 429 |
| Kamat | Tel: 372 288 |
| Royal Garden | Tel: 359 191 |

# Eating Out - Privilege Cards

The following is a list of some of the more popular eating out 'privilege', or discount cards currently in use around Dubai. The cards are listed in alphabetical order, either by the hotel which operates the card, or if not affiliated to one hotel, then by the card name.

## Dining Club

Tel: **697 080**

Not to be confused with the Diners Club card! Annual membership of Dhs.150 (Dhs.250 for two years) will entitle you to privileged unlimited dining at various restaurants around Dubai (over 70), and in other 300 restaurants in the GCC countries. Dining Club is an independent organisation managing this discount card, with varying discounts ranging from 10% - 20% on food and beverage.

## Hyatt Regency Hotel - Club at the Hyatt

Tel: **706 4858**

Annual membership of Dhs.610 (Dhs.585 renewal member, or Dhs.295 supplementry membership for spouse or direct family member) will entitle you to privileged unlimited dining at five main restaurants at the Dubai Hyatt Regency, provided you are accompanied by at least one other person. For two people, you will be entitled to a 50% deduction from your food bill, if there are three people, 33%, four people, 25%. If you dine on your own, or with six people or more, 15% will be deducted from the food bill. For all groups there is a 15% discount on beverages during lunch. Discounts are also available for Club Olympus memberships and drinks for you and two guests in The Premiere nightclub.

## Inter-Continental Hotel - Gold Card

Tel: **227 171**

Annual membership of Dhs.500 entitles you to a discount of up to 50% on food at all the Dubai Inter-Continental Hotel restaurants, and entitles you to a booklet with 15 discount coupons. This card does not entitle you to unlimited dining, but is restricted to 15 times usage in one year. The coupons offer various discounts from, a 25% discount to join their gym, to 10% discount on your next banqueting function at the hotel. In addition to the above, there are special offers every month for all members, at one of the restaurants.

## Metropolitan Hotel - Privilege Card

Tel: **440 000**

Annual membership of Dhs.450 will entitle you to privileged unlimited dining at all the Dubai Metropolitan Hotel restaurants. Your card entitles you to a complimentary meal for one person, provided at least two persons are dining. For groups of six or more, a 20% discount is offered. Offer is valid on beverages and taxes for lunch only. A gift voucher of Dhs.200 is also given to be used at select outlets. Also entitles you to reductions from the full room tariffs.

Completely independent of the Privilege card, and open to all, is the Metropolitan's Rolls Royce service. When celebrating a special day, and when eating at any of the Metropolitan restaurants, you can book a complimentary Rolls Royce to travel to and from the hotel. Book in advance. For celebrating a Birthday - a Rolls Royce Limousine Service, a free birthday cake and glass of Champagne for you and all guests at the table.

A bottle of House Wine with your lunch or dinner for every new Privilege member introduced by you.

## Radisson SAS Privilege Card

Tel: **845 533**

Annual membership of Dhs.685 entitles you to a discount of up to 50% on food at all of their restaurants. Each time you and a guest go for breakfast, lunch or dinner, the waiter will discretely deduct 50% off the total food bill. Accompanied by two other people 33% will be deducted and so on. Each time you dine alone, 15% discount will be deducted from your total food bill. It also entitles you to special room rates in the Radisson SAS hotels in Dubai and Abu Dhabi.

Together with your Card you will also receive: Two fully-transferable vouchers for a complimentary night in a double room, including breakfast, and valid every day of the week at the Radisson SAS Hotel Dubai; One fully-transferable voucher for a one night complimentary stay in a junior suite, excluding breakfast, and valid every day of the week at the Radisson SAS Residence Abu Dhabi; six fully-transferable vouchers allowing free access to the Jumeira Health and Beach Club of the Dubai Radisson SAS Hotel, valid daily except Friday and public holidays; and three fully-transferable vouchers valid for a one day complimentary banquet or conference room (paid catered function needs to be taken.)

## Ramada Hotel - Advantage Card

Tel: **521 010**

Annual membership of Dhs.350 will entitle you to privileged unlimited dining at all the Dubai Ramada Hotel outlets. Your card may be used for a 25% discount on food and beverage for bills under Dhs.500, and a 30% discount for bills over Dhs.500. A maximum of eight people can be entertained on the card at any one time. In addition, a 15% discount is given on food and beverage from the Dubai Royal Abjar outlets. Discount for beverages when consumed with food on the same bill.

## Royal Abjar Hotel - Platinum Choice Card

Tel: **625 555**

The Royal Platinum Card is valid immediately, up until 30th April 1998 and costs Dhs.600. As a Card holder you receive your own personalised membership card which entitles you to dine in the hotel as often as you wish throughout the coming year, and receive a special discount from your food bill!

For those dining in a party of between two to five people, one person will eat completely free of charge. Enjoy a complimentary starter and dessert, but this only applies if you have ordered a main course as well. Only one card per table. (Discount does not include beverages or service charge).

The package also includes: a complimentary night's stay for two people at The Royal Abjar Hotel, and one complimentary meeting room for up to 20 delegates - bookable in advance.

## SAM Privilege Card

Tel: **211 555**

Annual membership of Dhs.300 will entitle you to discounts ranging from 20% to 50% at various selected four and five star hotels. Discounts at restaurants and night clubs vary from 15% to 20% on food and beverage. In addition, various discounts in beauty salons and health clubs. An independent organisation manages this card, which currently has around 4,000 members within the UAE. A quarterly newsletter, with updates, is also circulated.

## Sheraton Deira - Platinium Card

Tel: **688 888**

The Platinum Privilege Membership of Dhs.525 (valid until 31 May 1998) allows you to enjoy numerous hotel privileges and can be used at 37 participating Sheraton Hotels in the Middle East and Asia Pacific, including the Sheraton Deira Hotel.

Enjoy one complimentary meal for every visit at a restaurant when accompanied by at least one or more paying guest(s). When 2 people dine 50% of the total food bill is deducted, when 3 people dine 33% is deducted, when 4 people dine 25% etc. This complimentary meal is valid for fifteen visits, either for breakfast, lunch or dinner.

Accommodation Benefits; One free night accommodation inclusive of free breakfast at the Four Points Sheraton Dubai only. Five 50% room accommodation certificates at any participating ITT Sheraton Hotels in the Middle East and the Asia Pacific Region. The dining card and room certificates are fully transferable (25% discount on beverages during lunch, free birthday cake and a complimentary drink).

## Sheraton Plus Club — Tel: 281 111

Annual membership of Dhs.550 will entitle you to privileged unlimited dining (breakfast, lunch and dinner) at all the Dubai Sheraton outlets. For two people, you will be entitled to a 50% deduction from your food bill, 33% if there are three people, 25% four people and 20% discount will be deducted for 5-10 diners. Also entitles you to reductions from the full room tariffs, and reciprocal accommodation and dining benefits are available in over 20 Sheratons in the Middle East. Check closely for more details.

# Other - Privilege Cards

## MMI - VIP Card Member — Tel: 516 282

Spend your full license with MMI in any three out of four months and you can become a VIP Card Member. This entitles you to various discounts from bookstores (10%), jewellers, a couple of restaurants (15%), and even a hotel (30%).

## Spinneys Card — Tel: 555 250

The Spinneys card, jointly launched with BBME, combines convenience and financial flexibility, offering a variety of benefits and services. The card is free of cost, with no joining or membership fee. This allows the user to extend up to 60 days interest free credit and can be used in any of the Spinneys stores in the UAE. It is also a privilege card as it entitles a cardholder to discounts at a growing number of restaurants, boutiques, health clubs, etc.

## Allied Advantage Card — Tel: 283 793

This is a customer loyalty program introduced by Allied Enterprises in 1996. The program offers two different cards to choose from:

1. The Allied Advantage Classic Card - without a credit facility - Annual Membership Dhs.100.
2. The Allied Advantage Master Card - a full featured credit card - Annual Membership Dhs.200.

Membership to the program brings entitlement to Cost Reduction Levels on purchases at the Allied Stores varying from 5% - 25%, depending on your level of spending over a fixed period. Purchases also earn Advantage Points which can be redeemed for goods. Special privileges and benefits include invitations to sale previews, launches and exclusive offers on the Allied Advantage Collection. Membership also entitles cardholders to benefit from promotional offers with certain other companies. This card is valid in their UAE stores.

# Shopping

# Shopping Malls / Centres

## Al Bustan Centre

**10:00 - 22:00**
**Closed Fri am**

**Al Qusais** **Page Z**

Tel: **630 000**

They don't call it the new heart of Dubai for nothing. The Al Bustan Centre, one of the newest shopping-cum-residential complexes is located in one of the fastest growing areas of Dubai.

It incorporates a large residential complex of 640 beautifully appointed five-star suites with every service on call. It's ground-level mall has over 100 varied retail outlets, an international multi-cuisine food court with seating for 500, and a children's amusement arcade called Fantasy Kingdom.

## Al Ghurair Centre

**10:00 - 22:00**
**Closed Fri am**

**Deira** **Page 10**
**D 1**

Tel: **232 333**

This was the first purpose-built shopping mall in Dubai, a huge complex with the less expensive goods, clothes and provisions on the ground floor, and prices rising as you go upwards in the building. Reasonable prices compared with other speciality and designer clothes stores in other malls.

Step into the large Fashionway outlet for cotton goods ranging from a few dirhams to Dhs.200. Visit the textile area at one end of the mall for a variety of inexpensive bolts of cloth for sale by the yard. If you buy clothes you will no doubt need accessories, so stop and gaze at the jewellery barrows in the central foyer. Shoes are just a step away down the marble lane. Watches available from Rivoli.

Wedding finery for the bride and all her guests can be found on the first floor. Either buy the fashionable frills ready-made, or step into the quiet haven of a tailors' consulting room to discuss your requirements. There's an entertainment centre called Sindbad's on this floor, consisting of arcade games and rides. A fun 'pick n mix' sweet shop with over 100 varieties of novelty sweets from Europe. Plenty of fast food outlets for shoppers.

## Al Hanna Centre

**10:00 - 14:00**
**16:00 - 23:00 Closed Fri am**

**Al Satwa** **Page 6**
**A 4**

Tel: **455 661**

A quite mall situated near Plaza Hotel. Offers some of the more unusual specialist shops in Dubai. There is a small food court upstairs. A good mall for gift buying.

## Al Khaleej Centre

**10:00 - 13:00**
**16:00 - 22:00 Closed Fri am**

**Opp. Ramada Hotel**
**Bur Dubai** **Page 6**
**E 3**

Tel: **558 627**

What a refined mall this is, both in shops and customers. Vaguely divided into men's interest on the top floor and ladies items on the first, this mall nevertheless knows shoppers well and has mixed the stores so that families can visit each floor. Plenty of jeans stores, from high priced designer jeans to fashionable youth attire, sold in wooden floored outlets.

A two storey Macdonalds serves well loved fare which pleases the smaller children who also love to play in the Fun Corner room full of thousands of rubber balls.

## Al Mulla Plaza

10:00 - 13:00
17:00 - 22:00 Closed Fri am | Al Qusais | Page 11 C 4 | Tel: **665 885**

For discerning Middle Eastern families who want to cut a dash fashionwise or pick up a bargain for the home. Some Dhs.10 stores where all items are for sale at one price, as well as toy shops. Eid and other holiday times bring a variety of special bargains throughout the Plaza, as well as children's entertainments to amuse the little ones in the central area: clowns, bouncy castle, puppets, etc.

Exclusive ladies tailoring and embroidery centre on the first floor. Private, luxurious and exclusively for women.

## Beach Centre, The

08:30 - 13:30
16:00 - 20:00 | Al Jumeira Rd Jumeira | Page 5 B 2 | Tel: **449 045**

Known as the blue glassed Centre to distinguish it from the Pink Plaza and Markaz malls further up the road. The Beach Centre is a large, airy place to visit with spacious restaurants on the Beach Road frontage specialising in Lebanese, Chinese food, burgers, pizzas and Italian pasta. A good place to meet friends, do some shopping and then sit and chat for a time. There is a sociable atmosphere with the central coffee shop area having a pianist to soothe the cares of the day away.

There is a bank, jewellery shop, clothes and knick-knack outlets. Good selections of rosewood furniture, carpets and souvenir-type antiques. The corner alcoves upstairs cater mainly for women, while the music/instrument shop downstairs attracts teenagers and budding musicians.

## Bur Juman Centre

10:00 - 22:00
Closed Fri lunch | Bur Dubai | Page 10 A 1 | Tel: **520 222**

Plenty of underground parking as well as a spare plot of land next door for 4WD cars. Stores on the first and second floors include British Home Stores, Rivoli Watches, J.C. Penney and Fashionway amongst other well known European and American names. Classy outfits for all the family from babies to grandparents. Some sports stores, music centres, shoe shops, a specialist greeting card outlet and an innovative gift shop. A young person's delight. Watch out for the decorative fountains on the first floor which periodically spray a jet of water into the opposing fountain three metres away. It amazes unwary shoppers , especially if they are walking between the two pools at the time!

The top floor is for eating, at one of the dozen fast food outlets serving Thai, chicken, Italian, French and other well liked specialities. Top floor is also where the popular arcade games are situated.

## Centre, The

10:00 - 22:00
Closed Fri am | Nr. JW Mariott Hotel Deira | Page 11 A 3 | Tel: **665 756**

With a large Spinneys supermarket at one end and Jashanmals department store at the other, this mall can't really go very wrong. Quality specialist shops fill in the in-between gaps with plenty of variety for the browser to remember and come back for.

## Deira City Centre Mall

10:00 - 22:00
Closed Fri am

Deira | Page 14 D 1

Tel: **232 344**

Frequented by residents and visitors alike who need lots of time to discover the vast amount of goods on offer. Browse through IKEA for furniture and those little home knick-knacks that you didn't know you needed, as well as Woolworths from South Africa, Next, Rivoli Watches and Sun and Sand, the largests sports store in the Gulf. Music Master has a coffee bar area within the store for you to relax while listening to your choice of CD's. Continent supermarket sells both food and non-food items, supposedly the cheapest place in town, including special buys of fishing equipment, towels, clothing, toys, electrical goods etc.

Sections leading off the main indoor mall are full to brimming with antiques, decorative items from other Gulf countries, gold jewellery and carpets. Take your time looking up and down the shelves and walls so as not to miss the wonderful array. Large recreation hall area with places for the children to play while you rest your weary feet and have a quick bite to eat. The recently opened second floor has a vast array of classy boutiques and specialist shops.

## Dune Centre

10:00 - 13:00
16:30 - 21:30 Closed Fri am

Al Dhiyafah Rd
Al Satwa | Page 5 E 3

Tel: **455 042**

A very quite and select mall offering little other than it's food outlets... Gelato, Burger King, Internet Cafe and Popeye's.

## Hamarain Centre

09:00 - 13:00
17:00 - 23:00

Next to JW Mariott Hotel
Deira | Page 11 A 4

Tel: **621110**

Next door to the J.W. Marriott hotel this French-styled mall has a selection of goods not usually seen in Dubai. Perfect for those who want something different for the home or personal attire.

This shopping centre gives you the choice between a lot of high quality items, but you will also be able to find medium prices. Big popular food court, with various other food outlets scattered around the centre.

## Jumeira Plaza

09:00 - 13:00
16:30 - 21:30 Closed Fri am

Al Jumeira Rd
Jumeira | Page 5 C 2

Tel: **497 111**

This is the pink stoned, pink glassed building on the Beach Road. Very easy to spot and a delight to enter and browse around. Full of ornaments and items for the home, arty implements for craft and needlework, small silver items such as charms, chains, gifts and presents. There are often raffles or competitions taking place here and sometimes an art or book exhibition too.

## Lamcy Plaza

10:00 - 22:00

Al Karama | Page 9 D 4

Tel: **345 050**

You've heard of theme parks, well this is a theme mall, with it's topic being the Tower of London. Step into the large central foyer and take time to gaze around at the four grey towers stretching upwards to the extremely high ceiling. Or walk through their archways into

Room for togetherness.
IKEA offers a wide range of dining furniture and tableware, perfect for every occasion from quiet family meals to elaborate dinner parties.
Opening hours:
Saturday to Thursday 10 am - 10 pm
Friday 2 pm - 10 pm
Location: Deira City Centre
More for less
IKEA
Al-Futtaim trading
IKEA, P.O. Box 50618, Dubai. Tel: 04 243434, Fax: 226162
© Inter IKEA Systems B.V. 1997
GMASCO 106808/97

open plan shops merging from one to the other, with a multitude of fashions, designs, colours and items to attract every type of shopper. Expensive items sit check by jowl with saucy fashionwear and clumpy shoes. The Al Ansari Exchange booth allows visitors to change their currencies. Watches available at Rivoli. Don't be in a rush to dash in, buy what you want and dash out, it's not that simple. Take time to enjoy the sight of the many things which are there to catch your eye and tempt.

In the depths of the dungeons there is a soothing Food Court with tree trunks, wrought iron tables and chairs, fast food and eastern plates of delights sufficient to fill a lunchtime tum. There's also a television showing MTV with the music quietly filtering through the speaker system. Children love it.

## Magrudy Shopping Mall

**08:30 - 13:30**
**16:00 - 20:00 Closed Fri am**
**Al Jumeira Rd**
**Jumeira**
**Page 5**
**C 2**
Tel: **444 192**

An open-air courtyard area outside Magrudy's card, toy, swimwear and knitting shop. A classy area that most people walk through on their way to the nearby Markaz Al Jumeira. Gerrard's is the place to sit in the dappled sunshine while sipping a cappucino, munching a freshly baked croissant and watching the world walk by. Friends meet here, greet and move on. A top notch ladies couturier, Damas jeweller, pharmacist and other shops constitute the ground floor while upstairs are the hairdressers and veterinary clinic.

## Markaz Al Jumeira

**08:30 - 13:30**
**16:00 - 20:00 Closed Fri am**
**Al Jumeira Rd**
**Jumeira**
**Page 5**
**C 2**
Tel: **499 702**

Prices in the shops are not the cheapest, but not overly expensive either. Exclusive ladieswear boutiques are side by side with the Body Shop and a Baskin Robbins ice cream parlour, which is why this mall is so popular with Jumeira residents. Well-stocked stationers and toy shops keep youngsters occupied, while men can see the latest watch design at Rivoli or choose Persian rugs and unusual art items for their homes. La Brioche is a great stop-off for a quiet hot chocolate and tasty baguette.

## Warba Centre

**09:00 - 22:30**
**Closed Fri am**
**Nr. JW Mariott Hotel**
**Deira**
**Page 11**
**A 3**
Tel: **666 376**

A smart new mall located next to the JW Mariott Hotel in Deira. The usual mix of boutiques and outlets - including Dubai's first Dunkin Donuts. Plenty of parking.

## Wafi Shopping Mall

**09:30 - 13:00**
**16:30 - 21:30 Closed Fri am**
**Wafi**
**Creekside Park**
**Page 13**
**D 2**
Tel: **367 125**

Look for the three glass pyramids atop a large building complex on the road near Al Garhoud Bridge, Bur Dubai side. This is the distinctive feature of the Wafi Shopping Mall. The large central area inside the mall often houses speciality displays and entertainments, especially at Ramadan, Eid and Christmas.

Quality shops with unusual items. '60's type hippie clothing, classic black dresses, Arabic designs, are all here under one roof. The mall's own shop Sharper Edge has many unusual gift items for the person who has everything. Large supermarket with low priced food and goods. Watches at Rivoli. Artificial flower store has many craft decoration ideas, a boon at Christmas and for special presents and thank you gifts.

# Places and Streets to Shop

## Al Diyafah Street

**09:00 - 14:00**
**16:00 - 21:30 Closed Fri am**
**Al Diyafah St** **Al Satwa** **Page 5** **E 3**
Tel: **NA**

Fondly known as 'Uptown Satwa' to residents, as opposed to the cheaper shopping area around the corner called 'Downtown Satwa'. This is the place to buy designer evening wear, matching 'casual' ensembles, fondue sets and perfumeries. For those who have a special event to go to, tuxedos and ball gowns can be hired at Elegance, Elegance for Men and Formal wear.

Evenings are a good time to visit this busy little street for social eating in the form of fast food outlets such as Hardees, Pizza Hut, Kentucky Fried Chicken and Baskin Robbins. Or sip a sundowner expresso on the pavement tables of Cafe Royale. There's also a classy Lebanese diner, Chinese restaurant and a shwarma stand to choose from, amongst others. A place to see and be seen.

## Al Faheidi Street

**08:00 - 13:30**
**16:00 - 21:30 Closed Fri am**
**Al Faheidi St** **Bur Dubai** **Page 7** **A 2**
Tel: **NA**

This is a busy place to visit so don't get annoyed with the jostling. Thomas Cook Al Rostamani is where to go to change your currency or travellers cheques at a favourable rate. Then visit the multitude of electrical shops offering brand names such as Sharp, Phillips, Grundig, GEC, etc. at negotiable prices. The Thomsun shop has a large range of original cassettes at below European prices. Approx. Dhs.15 per tape and Dhs.60 per CD.

## Karama

**08:30 - 14:00**
**16:00 - 22:00 Closed Fri am**
**Al Karama** **Page 9** **D 2**
Tel: **NA**

Not really a Centre, more of a long street with veranda covered shops on both sides enticing you to buy, buy, buy cheap and cheerful goods at below average prices. Plenty of mix n' match ideas direct from the Far East, sports apparel, T-Shirts, shorts, sunglasses, shoes, gifts and souvenirs. Make sure you ask for 'best price'!

Wander around the fish market to buy locally caught hammour, prawns, crabs, etc., or bargain at the fruit and vegetable shops for bananas, mangoes and a variety of different vegetables from the subcontinent, including gourds and mouli.

# Maps & Indexes

# Dubai Map Overview

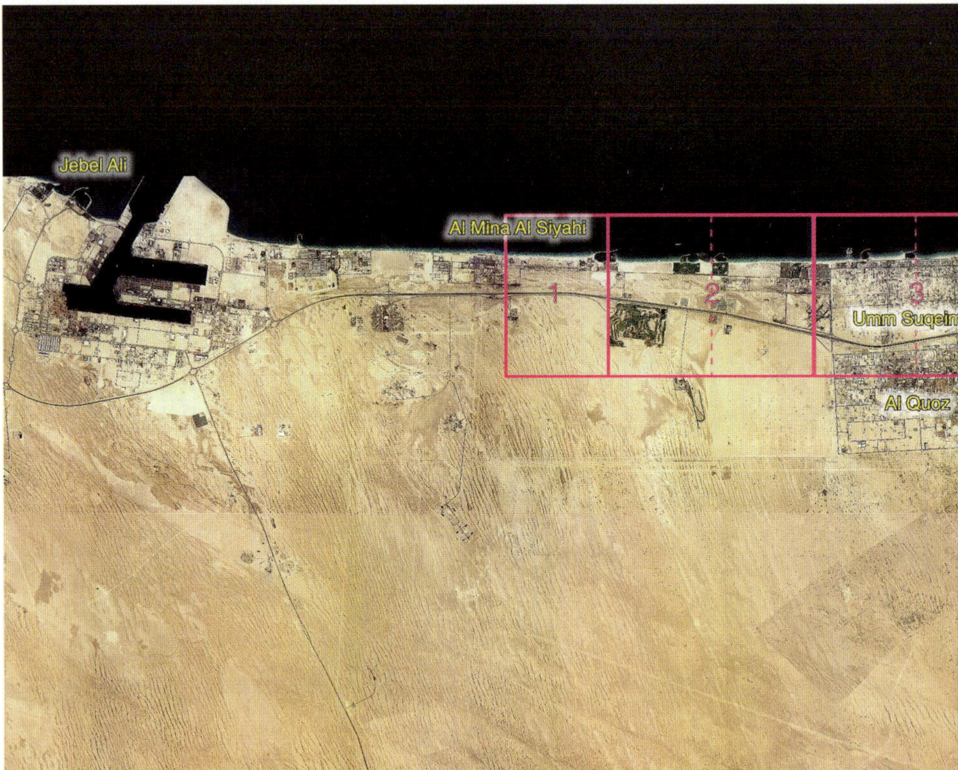


## Overview

The maps are based on colour aerial photography (Jan 1997) which have been fully digitally rectified to produce these orthoimages. For the purpose of easy reference, the maps are oriented parallel to Dubai's coastline. These images have been split into 26 pages.

- This overview page is at a scale of 1:200,000 (1cm = 2Km)
- Pages 1-4 and 12 are at a scale of 1:24,000 (1cm = 240m)
- Pages 5-12 are at a scale of 1:12,000 (1cm = 120m)
- Page 11 is at a scale of 1:36,000 (1cm = 360m)

The images have been superimposed with additional information such as roads (including new roads), significant sites & landmarks, and roundabouts. Once again due to Dubai's incredibly rapid development, many new roads and buildings have been added since these photographs were taken, and where possible, we have attempted to indicate these developments.

# Orthoimage Sheet Index

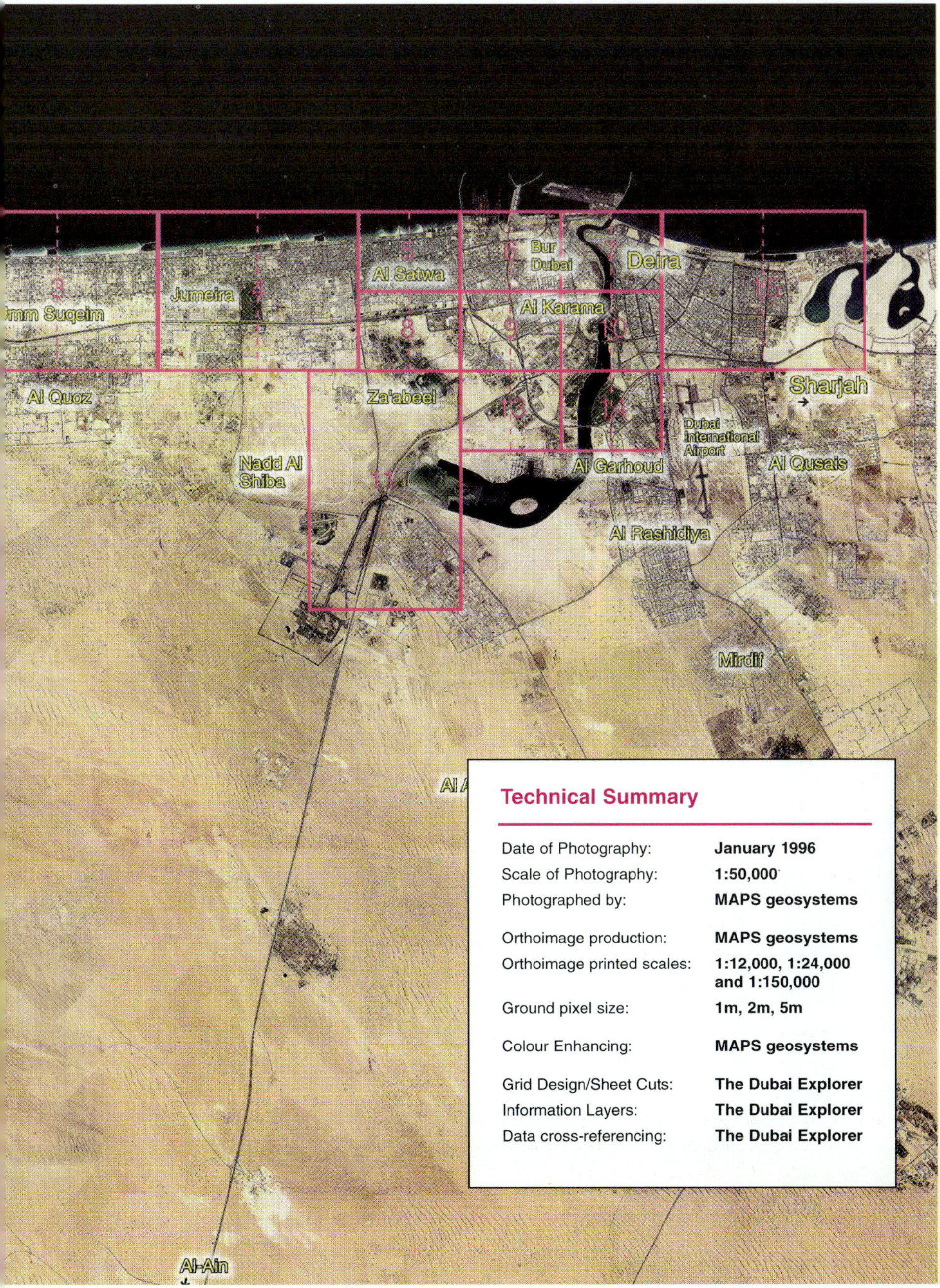


## Technical Summary

| | |
|---|---|
| Date of Photography: | **January 1996** |
| Scale of Photography: | **1:50,000** |
| Photographed by: | **MAPS geosystems** |
| Orthoimage production: | **MAPS geosystems** |
| Orthoimage printed scales: | **1:12,000, 1:24,000 and 1:150,000** |
| Ground pixel size: | **1m, 2m, 5m** |
| Colour Enhancing: | **MAPS geosystems** |
| Grid Design/Sheet Cuts: | **The Dubai Explorer** |
| Information Layers: | **The Dubai Explorer** |
| Data cross-referencing: | **The Dubai Explorer** |

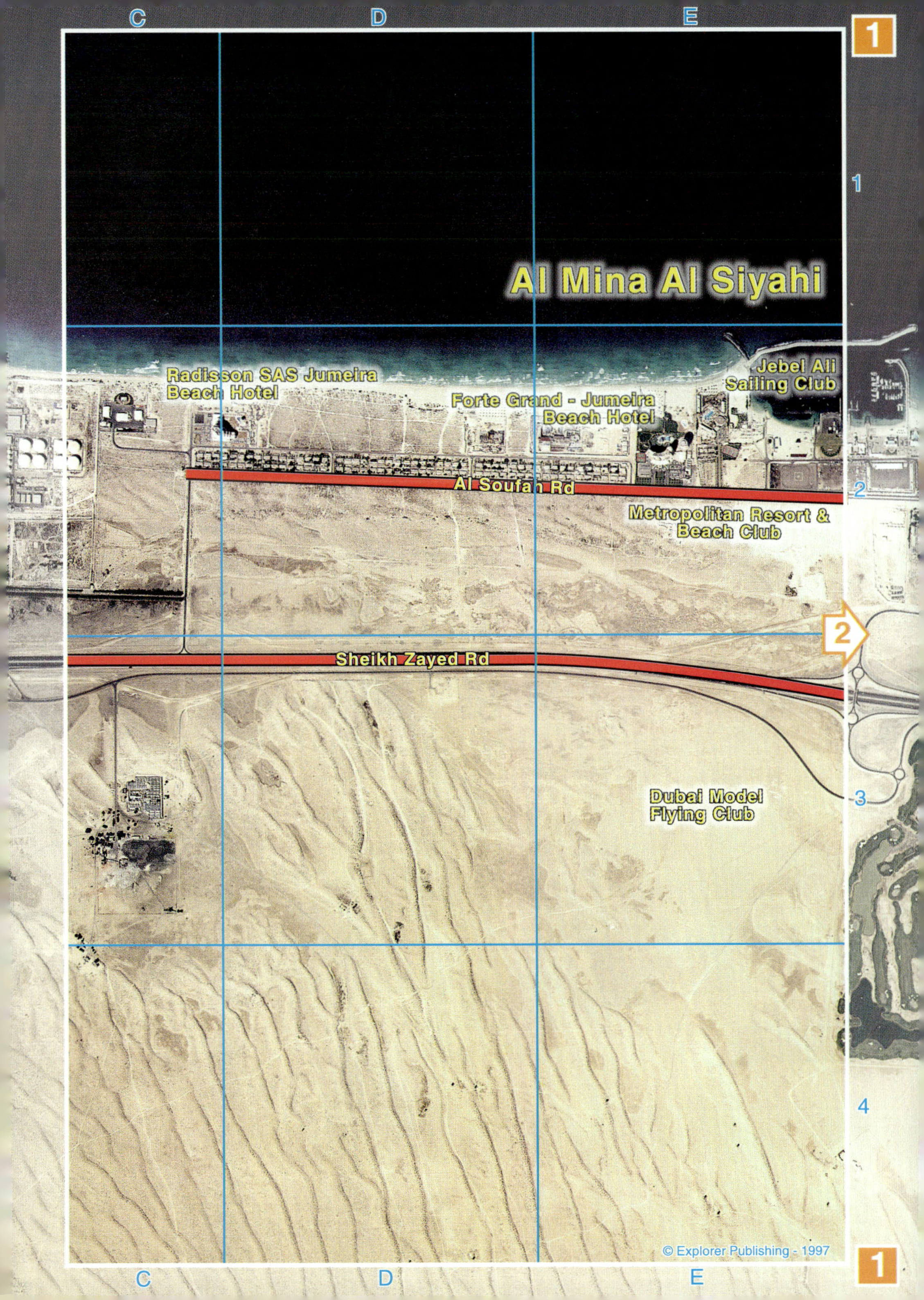
C
D
E
1
Al Mina Al Siyahi
Radisson SAS Jumeira Beach Hotel
Jebel Ali Sailing Club
Forte Grand - Jumeira Beach Hotel
Al Soufah Rd
2
Metropolitan Resort & Beach Club
2
Sheikh Zayed Rd
3
Dubai Model Flying Club
4
© Explorer Publishing - 1997
C
D
E
1

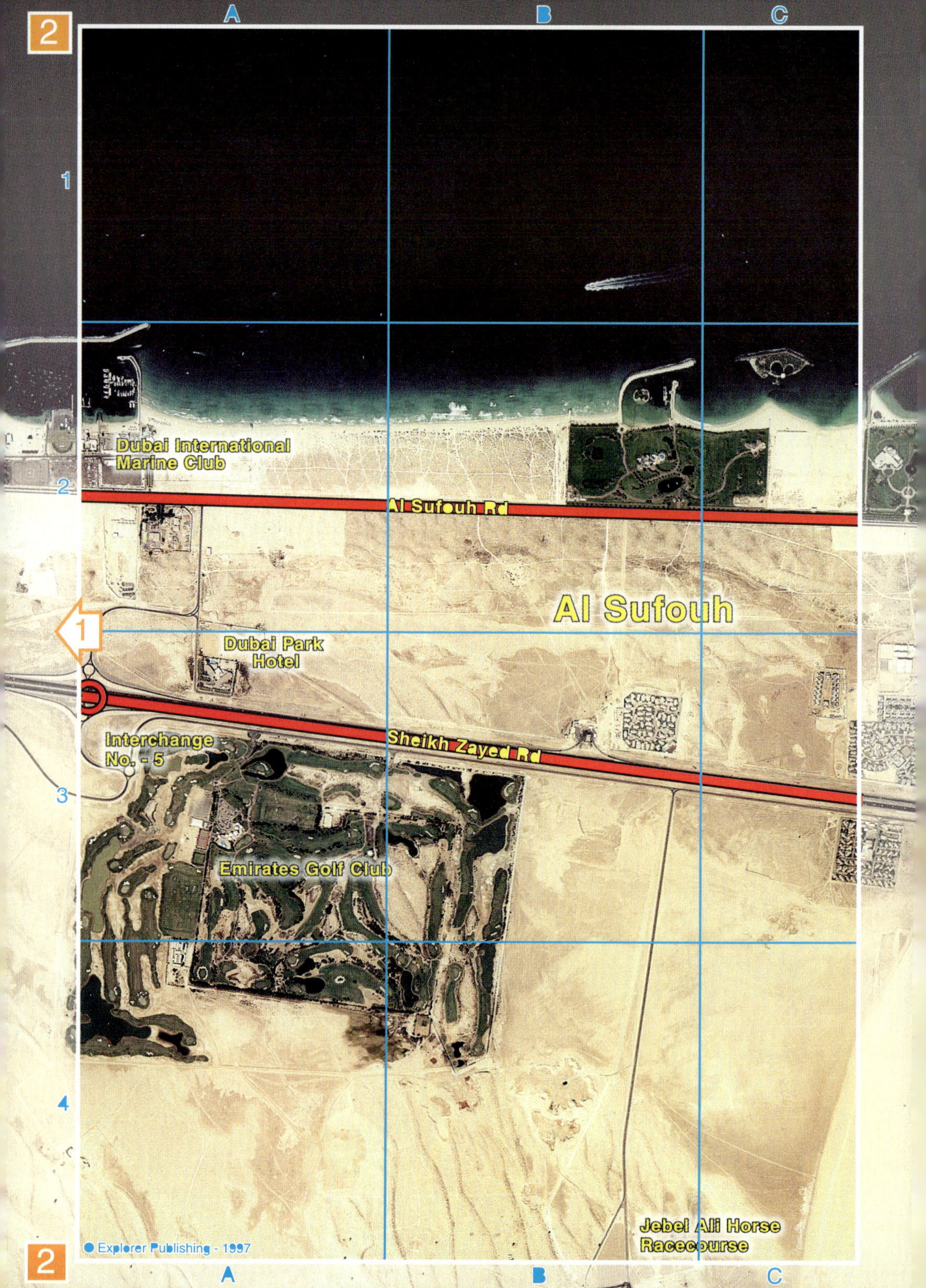
A
B
C
1
2
3
4
Dubai International Marine Club
Al Sufouh Rd
Al Sufouh
1
Dubai Park Hotel
Interchange No. - 5
Sheikh Zayed Rd
Emirates Golf Club
Jebel Ali Horse Racecourse
A
B
C

C
D
E
1
2
3
4
Al Sufouh Rd
Dubai College
3
Al Sufouh
Desert Spring Village
Sheikh Zayed Rd
© Explorer Publishing - 1997
C
D
E

A
B
C
1
2
3
4
Chicago Beach Hotel & Tower
Chicago Beach Village
Al Jumeira Rd
Umm Suqeim
2
Al Sufouh Rd
Police Training College
Al Wasl Rd
ETISALAT Tower
Dubai Television Relay Station
Emirates International School
Interchange No - 4
Sheikh Zayed Rd
Al Quoz Industrial Area
A
B
C

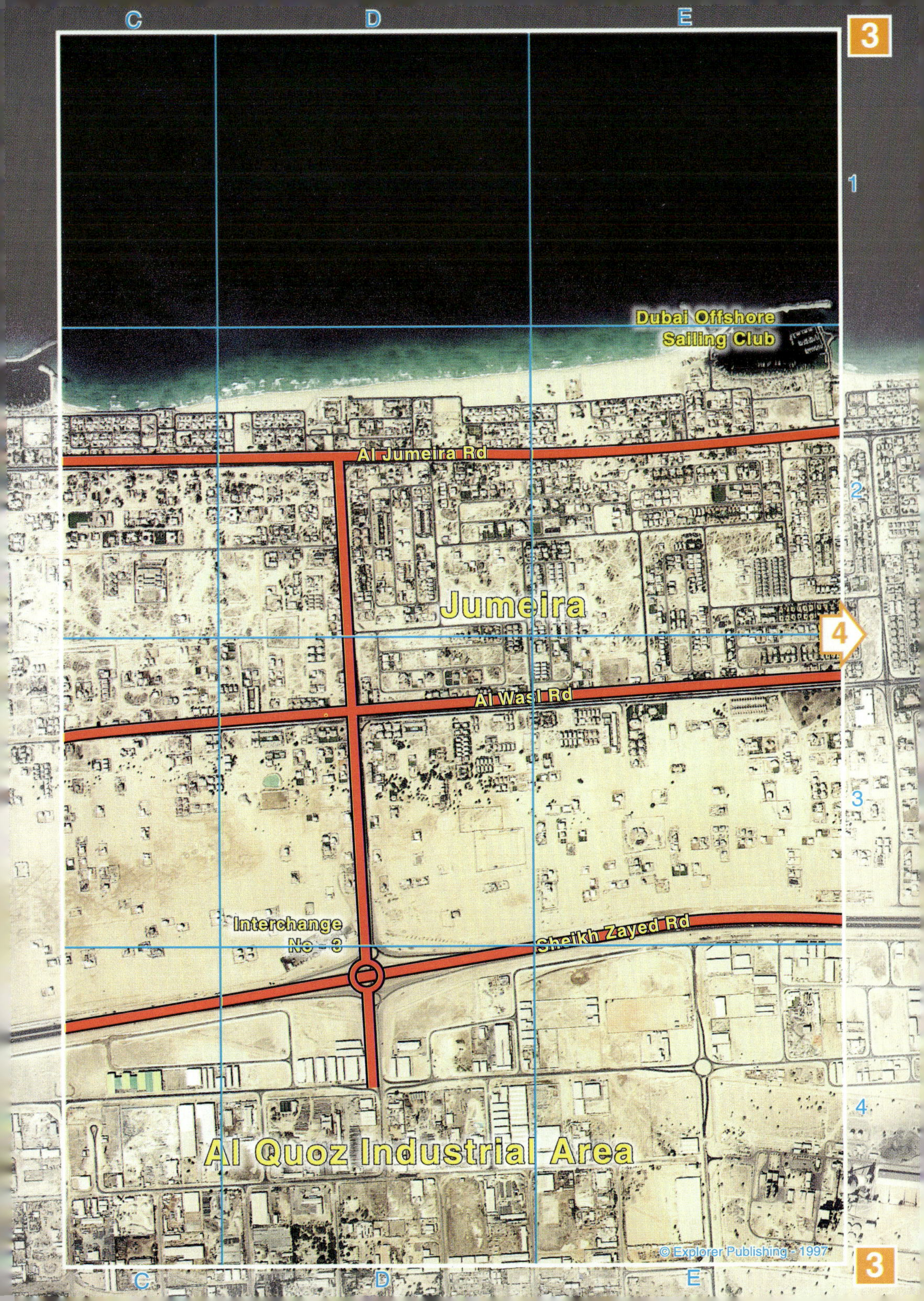
C
D
E
1
2
3
4
Dubai Offshore
Sailing Club
Al Jumeira Rd
Jumeira
Al Wasl Rd
Interchange
No - 3
Sheikh Zayed Rd
Al Quoz Industrial Area
© Explorer Publishing - 1997

A
B
C
1
2
3
4
Al Jumeira Rd
Jumeira
Al Wasl Rd
Park N Shop
Al Hadiqa St.
Safa Park
Jumeira English Speaking School
Sheikh Zayed Rd
Interchange No - 2
Metroplex
Al Quoz
© Explorer Publishing - 1997

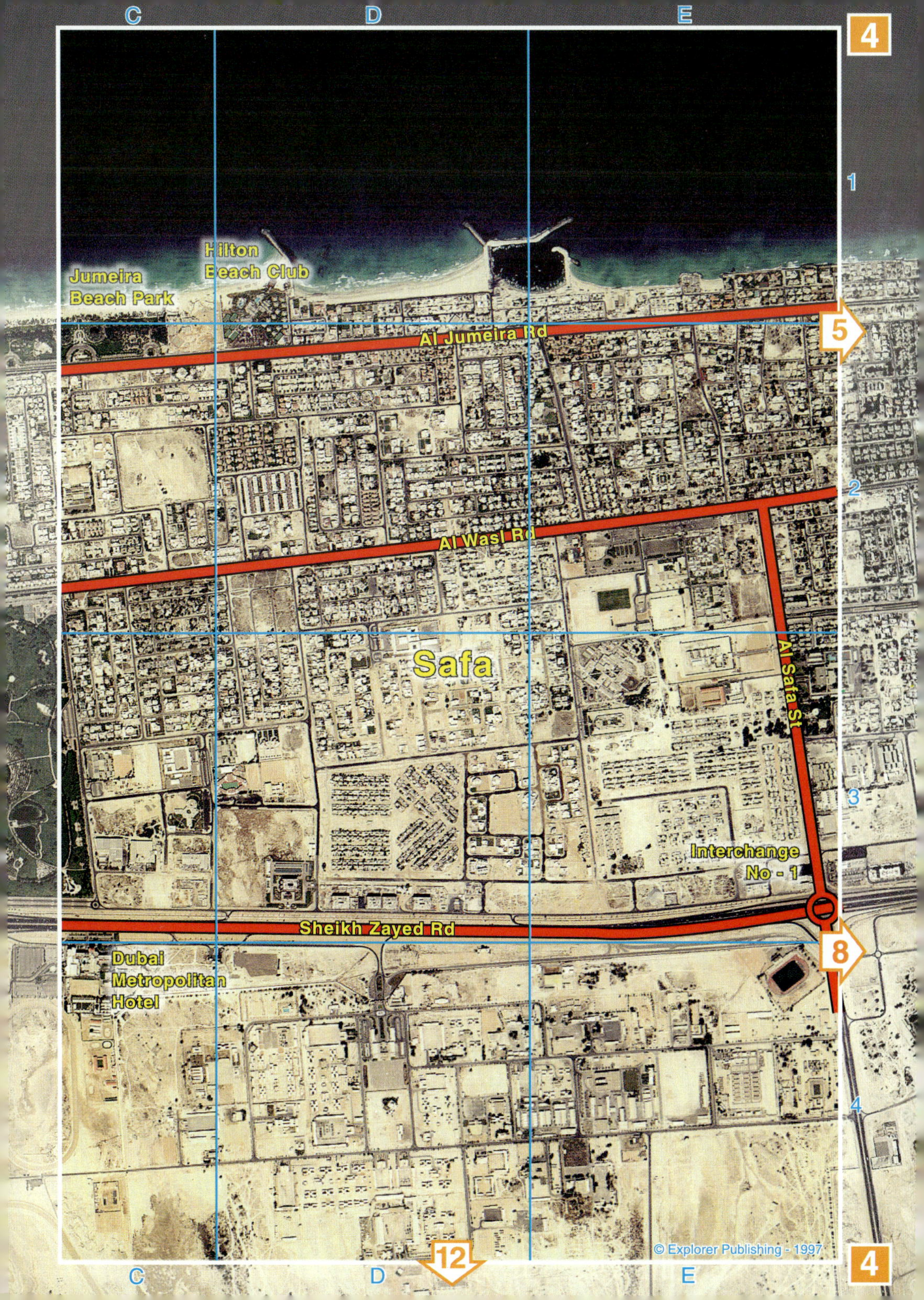
C
D
E
1
2
3
4
Jumeira Beach Park
Hilton Beach Club
Al Jumeira Rd
5
Al Wasl Rd
Safa
Al Safa St
Interchange No - 1
Sheikh Zayed Rd
8
Dubai Metropolitan Hotel
12

5
A
B
C
1
2
3
4
Beach Centre
Jumeira Plaza Mall
Dubai Zoo
Jumeira
Jumeira American School
Al Wasl
© Explorer Publishing - 1997
8

C
D
E
5
1
2
3
4
6
8
H.H. The Ruler's Guesthouse
Dubai International Art Centre
Dubai Marine Beach Resort
Al Jumeira Road
Al Dhiyafah Roundabout
Jumeira Mosque
Spinneys
Magrudy's & Markaz Al Jumeira
Al Wasl Road
Iranian Hospital
Dune Centre
Al Satwa
Al Satwa Rd
© Explorer Publishing - 1997

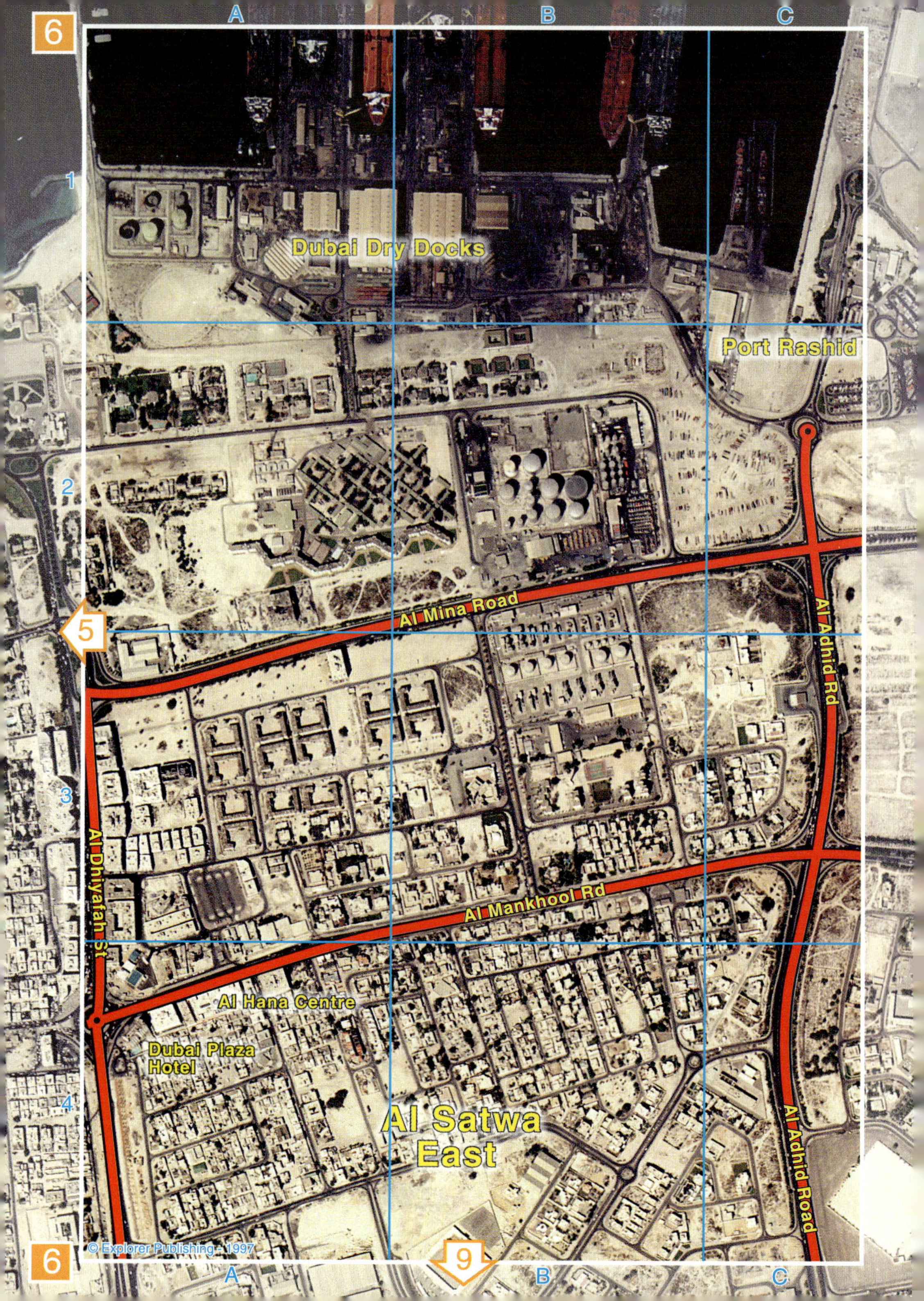

6
A
B
C
1
2
3
4
Dubai Dry Docks
Port Rashid
Al Mina Road
5
Al Adhid Rd
Al Dhiyafah St
Al Mankhool Rd
Al Hana Centre
Dubai Plaza
Hotel
Al Satwa
East
Al Adhid Road
© Explorer Publishing - 1997
9
6
A
B
C

C
D
E
6
1
2
3
4
Port Rashid
Al Saqr (Falcon) RA
Al Shindagha Market
Arif Castle Hotel
Palm Beach Hotel
Sea Shell Inn Hotel
Khalid Ibn Al Waleed Rd
Admiral Plaza
Al Mina Road
7
Dubai Marine Hotel
Bur Dubai
Imperial Suites Hotel
Al Khaleej Centre
Al Mankhool Road
Ramada Hotel
Spinneys
Golden Sands Area
© Explorer Publishing - 1997
9
C
D
E
6

A
B
C
1
2
3
4
Port Rashid
Al Khaleej Road
Heritage & Diving Village
Sheikh Saeed Al Maktoum House
Al Shindagha Tunnel
Dubai Creek
Plaza Cinema
Ambassador Hotel
St George Hotel
Gold Souk
Astoria Hotel
Deira Old Souk
Souk / Textiles
Dubai Marine Hotel
6
Al Fahedi St
Deira Covered Souk
Beniyas Road
Bur Dubai
Dubai Museum
Bastakia
Khaleej Hotel
Al Mussalla Road
Khalid Ibn Al Waleed road
Dubai Creek
British Embassy
10

C
D
E
1
2
3
4
Arabian Gulf
Deira Fish, Meat & Vegetable Market
Gold Souk
Hyatt Regency Hotel
Hyatt Golf Park
Deira
Al Khaleej Road
11
Deira Covered Souk
Naif RA
Naif Park
Al Naif Road
Riviera Hotel
Carlton Tower Hotel
Al Maktoum Hospital
Inter-Continental Hotel
Novotel
Claridge Hotel
10
© Explorer Publishing - 1997

5
A
B
C
1
2
3
4
Al Salam Tower
Al Rostamani Tower
Sara Tower
Moosa Tower 2
Moosa Tower 1
Sheikh Zayed Rd
Interchange No - 1
Al Kawakeb
4
12
© Explorer Publishing - 1997

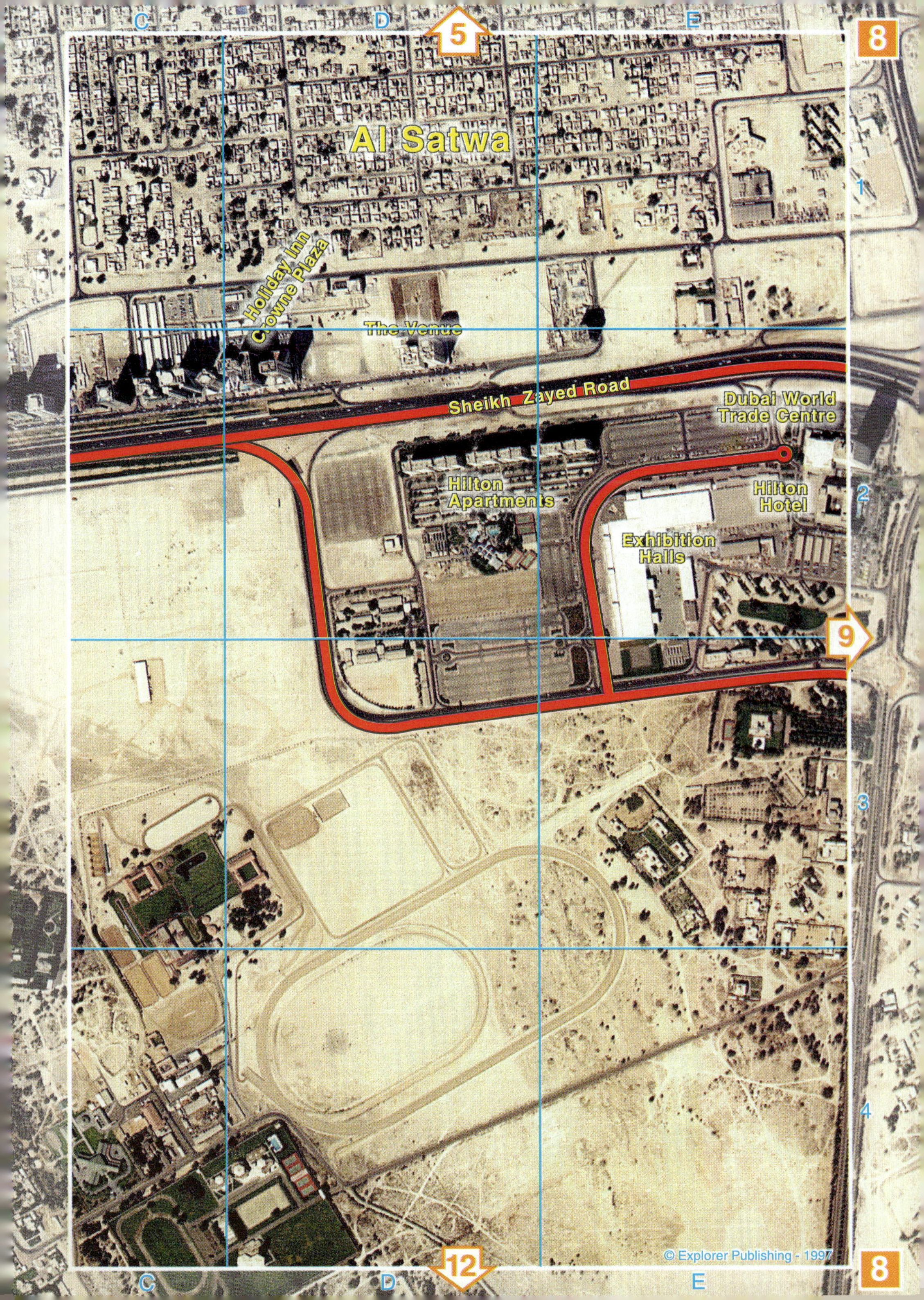

8
5
C
D
E
Al Satwa
Holiday Inn
Crowne Plaza
The Venue
Sheikh Zayed Road
Dubai World
Trade Centre
Hilton
Apartments
Hilton
Hotel
Exhibition
Halls
9
1
2
3
4
12
© Explorer Publishing - 1997

9
A
6
B
C
Al Satwa East
Al Dhiyafah Road
1
Department of Health & Medical Services
Passport & Immigration Office
Dubai Regional Police Headquarters
Underpas
Trade Centre Road
Dubai World Trade Centre
2
Hilton Hotel
8
3
Za'abeel
4
© Explorer Publishing - 1997
9
A
13
B
C

C
D
E
6
9
Bur Dubai
1
Trade Centre Road
President Hotel
Al Karama
2
Al Qutaeiyat Road
Al Karama Shopping Centre
Za'abeel Road
10
Umm Hureir Road
3
Al Nasr Cinema
Lamcy Plaza
Lodge
Al Nasr Leisureland
Cyclone
4
American Hospital
EPPCO HQ
© Explorer Publishing - 1997
13
C
D
E
9

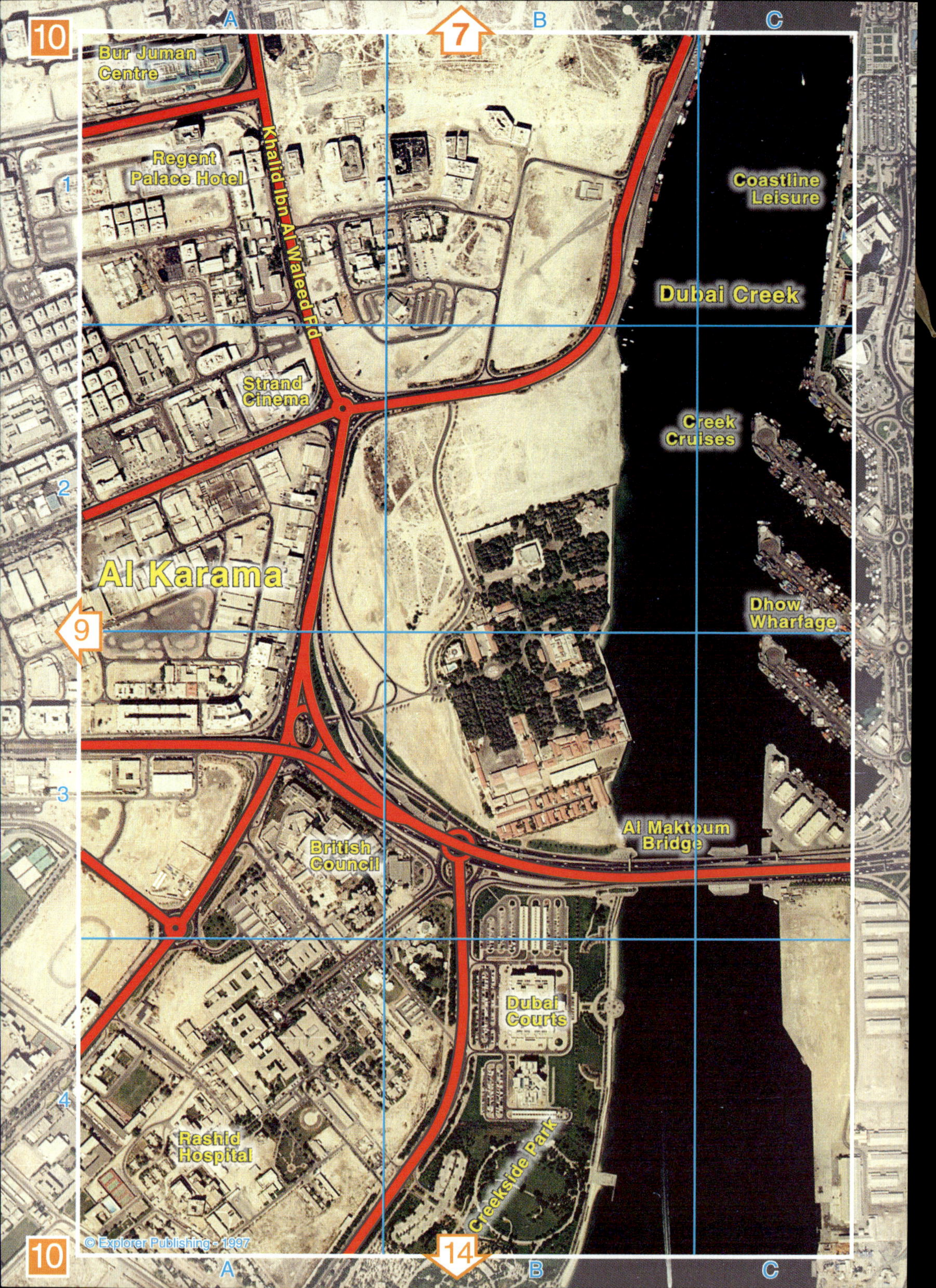

10
A
7
B
C
Bur Juman Centre
Regent Palace Hotel
Khalid Ibn Al Waleed Rd
Coastline Leisure
1
Dubai Creek
Strand Cinema
Creek Cruises
2
Al Karama
9
Dhow Wharfage
3
Al Maktoum Bridge
British Council
Dubai Courts
4
Rashid Hospital
Creekside Park
© Explorer Publishing - 1997
10
A
14
B
C

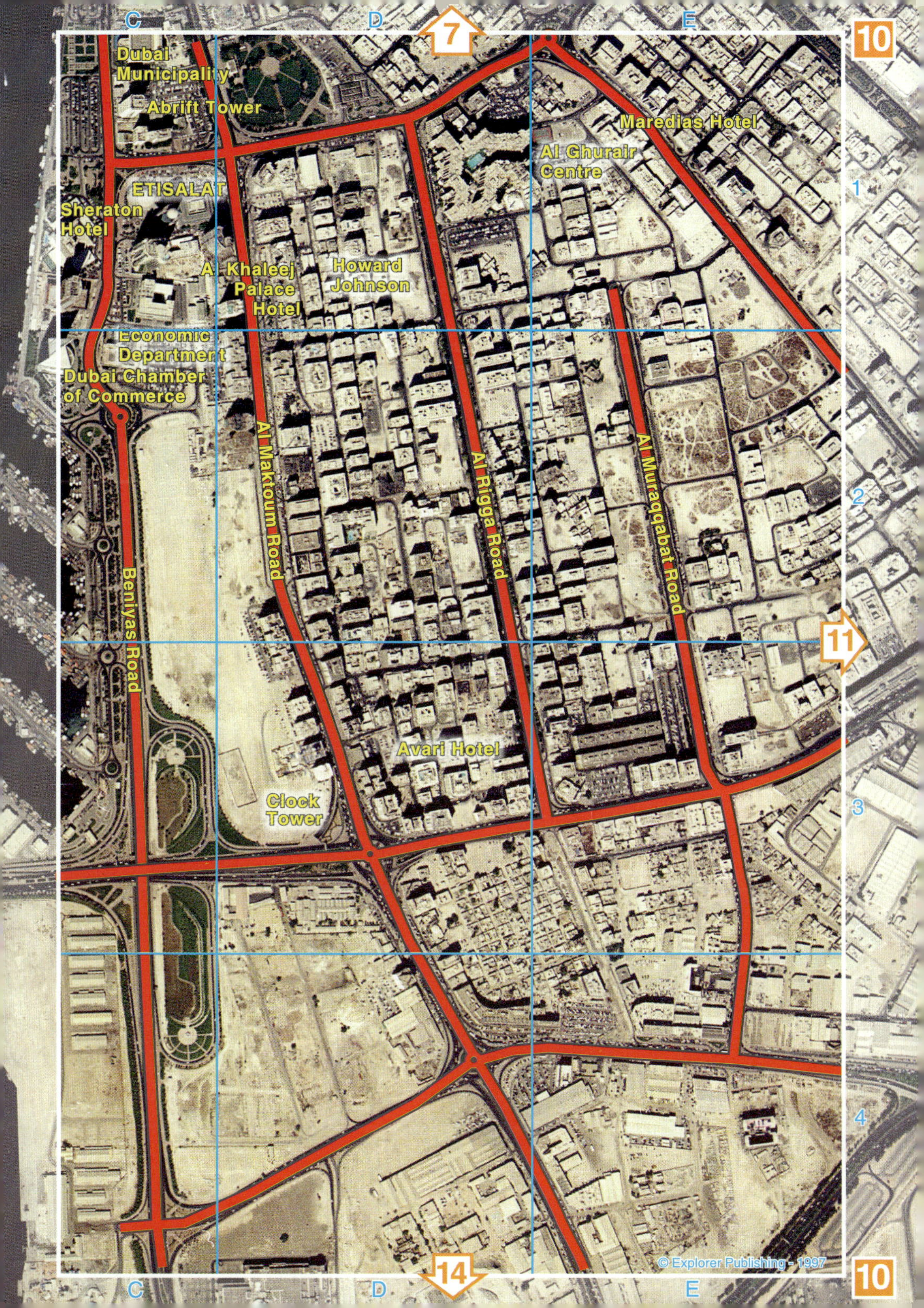
C
D
E
7
Dubai Municipality
Abrift Tower
Maredias Hotel
Al Ghurair Centre
ETISALAT
Sheraton Hotel
Al Khaleej Palace Hotel
Howard Johnson
Economic Department
Dubai Chamber of Commerce
Al Maktoum Road
Al Rigga Road
Al Muraqqabat Road
Beniyas Road
Avari Hotel
Clock Tower
11
1
2
3
4
14
© Explorer Publishing - 1997

A
B
C
1
2
3
4
7
10
Arabian Gulf
Wholesale Fruit & Vegetable Market
Kuwait Hospital
Al Khaleej Rd
New Dubai Hospital
Al Hamriya
Al Mateena Street
Sheraton Deira
Royal Abjar Hotel
Al Rasheed Road
The Center
Hor Al Anz
Al Hamriya Shopping Centre
JW Marriott Hotel
Dubai Cinema
Hamarain Centre
Abu Hail Rd
Salah Al Din Road
Al Ittihad Rd
Police HQ
A
B
C

C
D
E
1
2
3
4
Al Hamriya Port
Al Mamzar
Al Mamzar Beach Park
Khor Al Mamzar
Sharjah
© Explorer Publishing - 1997

A
B
C
8
1
2
3
4
2nd Za'abeel Rd
Oud Metha Rd
Nadd Al Shiba
Camel Racetrack
Dubai Wildlife &
Waterbird Sanctuary
Bu Kidra/Country Club
Roundabout
Dubai
Creek
Dubai Exiles
Rugby Club
Dubai Polo
Club
Dubai Golf &
Racing Club
Dubai Country
Club
Ras Al Khor Rd
Nadd Al Shiba
Dubai - Al Ain Rd
Al Awir
Industrial Area
A
B
C

A
B
C
9
Za'abeel
1
2
Al Wasl
Hospital
12
Oud Metha Road
Al Wasl
Club
3
4
A
B
C

C
D
9
E
1
Wafi Shopping Mall
Wafi Residence
2
Dubai Electricity and Water Authority
14
Al Quta'eyat Rd
Dubai Police Club
3
Dubai Municipality Nursery
4
Jaddaf
C
D
E

A
B
C
10
1
2
3
4
13
Creekside Park
Dubai Creek Marina
Dubai Creek
Dubai Creek Golf & Yacht Club
Wonderland
Al Boom Tourist Village
Al Garhoud Bridge
Jet Ski Area
Dhow Building Yard
A
B
C

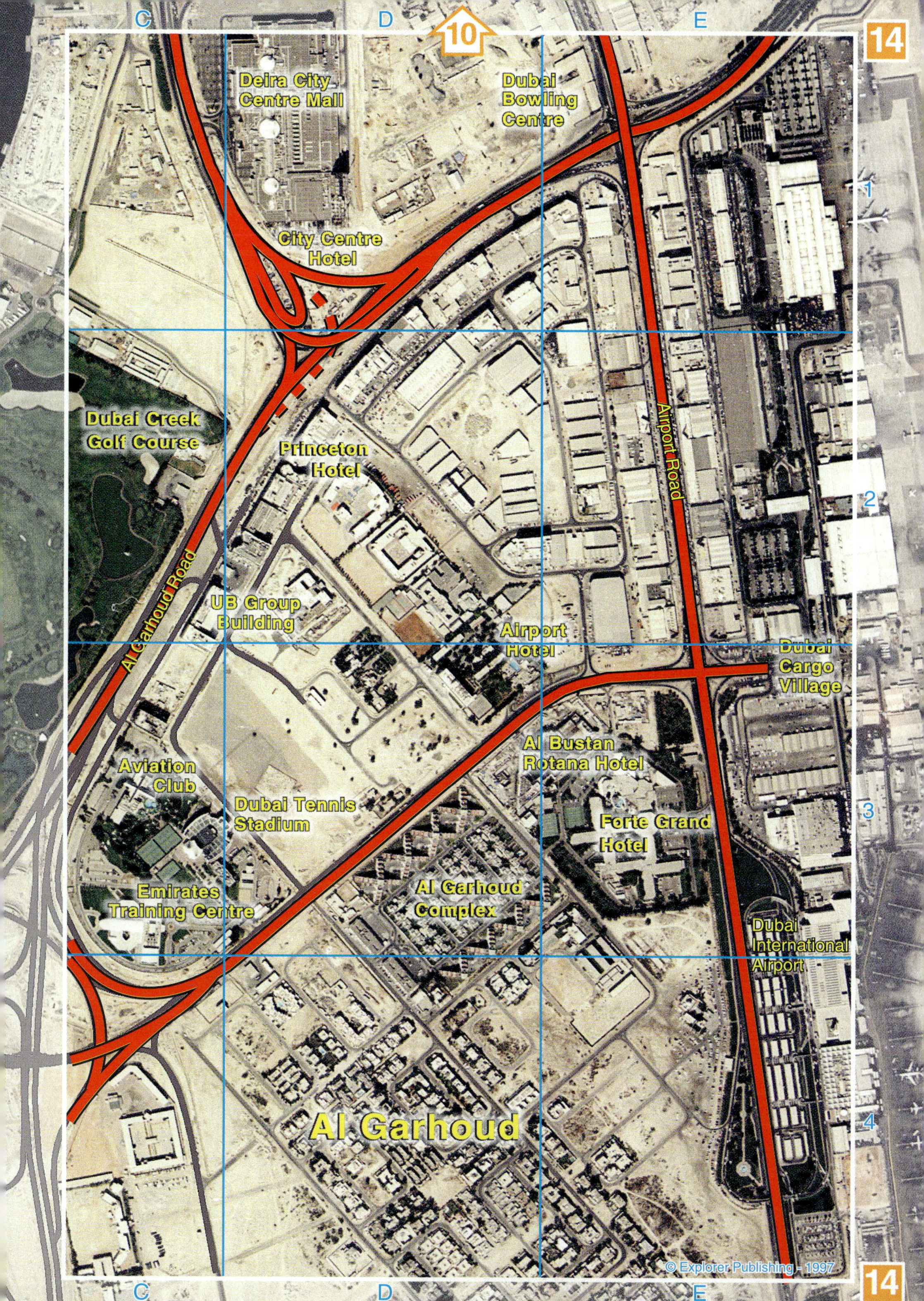
C
D
10
E
Deira City Centre Mall
Dubai Bowling Centre
City Centre Hotel
1
Dubai Creek Golf Course
Princeton Hotel
Airport Road
2
Al Garhoud Road
UB Group Building
Airport Hotel
Dubai Cargo Village
Al Bustan Rotana Hotel
Aviation Club
Dubai Tennis Stadium
Forte Grand Hotel
3
Emirates Training Centre
Al Garhoud Complex
Dubai International Airport
Al Garhoud
4
© Explorer Publishing - 1997
C
D
E

# A-Z Index

## a

## b



MAPS & INDEXES

## C

## d

## e

## h



## i

## j



## k



## l

MAPS & INDEXES

## q



## r

## S

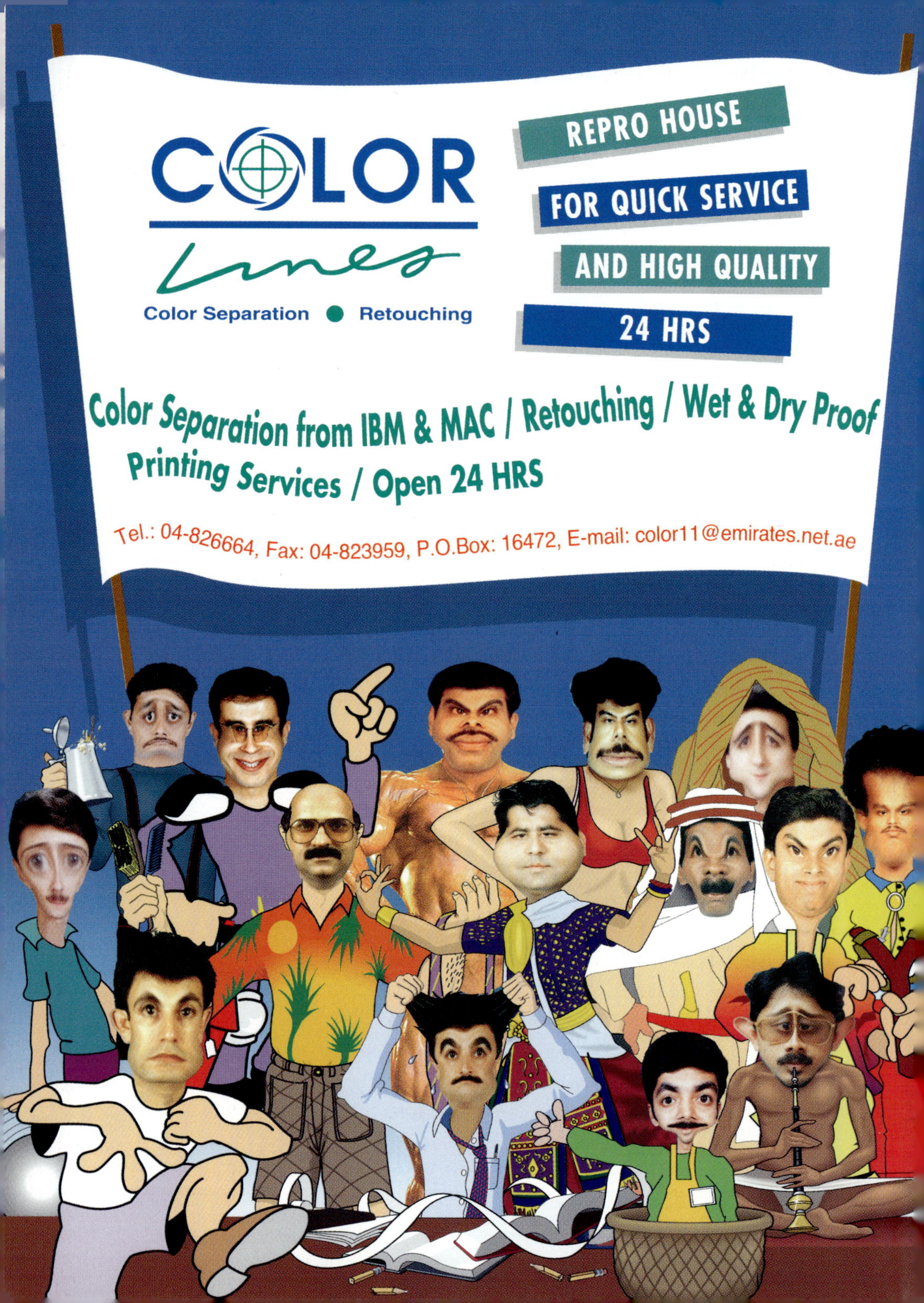
COLOR
Lines
Color Separation • Retouching
REPRO HOUSE
FOR QUICK SERVICE
AND HIGH QUALITY
24 HRS
Color Separation from IBM & MAC / Retouching / Wet & Dry Proof
Printing Services / Open 24 HRS
Tel.: 04-826664, Fax: 04-823959, P.O.Box: 16472, E-mail: color11@emirates.net.ae

# Reader Profile Survey

**Fax Response Form** To: **Explorer Publishing** Fax: **+971-4 822 710**

Page **1 of** __

**We would love to know more about you!** Please take five minutes of your time to complete and return this questionnaire, enabling us to better understand you, and hopefully what you are looking for. Any other comments you have, please feel free to write them and send them along with this questionnaire. Fax, post or email your competed questionnaire to Explorer Publishing, P.O. Box.53041, Fax: 822 710, Email: Info@The-Explorer.com.

**Please circle the relevant answer.**

**1 - What is your Country of residence?**
**a)** UAE - Emirate__________________
**b)** GCC **c)** CIS
**d)** Other _________________________

**2 - What are you here for?**
**a)** Tourism **b)** Business
**c)** Residence
**e)** Other (please specify) ________________

**3 - How long have you been in Dubai?**
**a)** Less than 1 month **b)** 1 - 6 months
**c)** 7- 12 months, or **d)** _____ years

**4 - What is your nationality?**
**a)** UAE National **b)** Expate Arab
**c)** Asian **d)** European
**e)** American/Canadian/Australian/NZ/SA
**f)** Other (please specify) _______________

**5 - Are you?**
**a)** Male **b)** Female

**6 - What is your total household monthly income?**
**a)** Under Dhs.5,000 **b)** Dhs.5,001-9,000
**c)** Dhs.9,001-13,000 **d)** Dhs.13,001-17,000
**e)** Over Dhs.17,000

**7 - What is your age?**
**a)** Under 15 **b)** 16 - 25
**c)** 26 - 35 **d)** 36 -45
**e)** 46 - 55 **f)** Over 56

**8 - How many of your household members would refer to this guide?**
**a)** One (1) **b)** Two (2)
**c)** Three (3) **d)** Other__________

**9 - What is your present occupation?**
**a)** Owner/Self-Employed/Partner
**b)** General Manager **c)** Manager
**d)** Professional (Doctor/Lawyer/Engineer,...)
**e)** Office Worker
**f)** Government/Police/Military
**g)** Unemployed **h)** Student
**e)** Other (please specify) ________________

**10 - How often do you eat out/order food home per week (Breakfast/Lunch/Dinner)?**
**a)** Every Day **b)** 2 to 3 times a week
**c)** 4 to 5 times a week **d)** weekly
**e)** Other (please specify) _____________

**11 - How much would your household typically spend on one average restaurant meal? (excluding beverages)**
**a)** Less than Dhs.50 **b)** Dhs.50 - Dhs.100
**c)** Dhs.100 - Dhs.200 **d)** Over Dhs.200

**12 - Do you undertake one or more sporting activities regularly? If so how often?**
**a)** Every Day **b)** 2 to 3 times a week
**c)** Weekly **d)** Monthly
**e)** None

**13 - Which are these leisure activities do you undertake regularly (At least once a week)?**
Cinema Watching TV
Restaurants Bars/Pubs
Night-clubs Shopping Malls
Theatre Museums
Art Classes Visiting Parks
Spectator Sports Sports
Desert/Wadi Driving Camping

**14 - What attracted you to buy this book?**
a) Needed a guide b) Front cover
c) Display stand d) Price
e) Was recommended by friend
f) Saw advertisement, if so where_________
g) Saw promotion, if so where___________
h) Read leaflet, if so where_____________
i) Other (please specify)_______________

**15 - Most useful section(s) to you was/is:**
**a)** General Info. **b)** Leisure section
**c)** Sporting section **d)** Food & Drink section
**e)** Shopping section **f)** Map section

**16 - May we know your name and details?**
Name: ______________________________
Address: ____________________________
____________________________________
Country:_____________________________
Tel:______________ Fax: _______________

**Many Thanks!**

THINK POSITIVE
THINK COLORFUL
THINK OF ....
RAINBOW
COLOR SEPARATION SERVICES
For excellent quality,
reasonable prices,
prompt & reliable
service.
THE COLORS OF IMAGINATION
P.O. Box : 27862 - Dubai - U.A.E
Tel: 04-686851 - Fax: 04-627602

FILA
FILA
FILA
FILA
HEAD
RUSSELL ATHLETIC
CONVERSE
Chuck Taylor
ALL STAR
DIADORA
FILA